50% OFF Online SHRM-CP Prep Course!

Dear Customer,

We consider it an honor and a privilege that you chose our SHRM-CP Study Guide. As a way of showing our appreciation and to help us better serve you, we have partnered with Mometrix Test Preparation to offer you **50% off their online SHRM-CP Prep Course**. Many SHRM-CP courses are needlessly expensive and don't deliver enough value. With their course, you get access to the best SHRM prep material, and you only pay half price.

Mometrix has structured their online course to perfectly complement your printed study guide. The SHRM-CP Prep Course contains **in-depth lessons** that cover all the most important topics, over **900 practice questions** to ensure you feel prepared, and **more than 450 digital flashcards**, so you can study while you're on the go.

Online SHRM-CP Prep Course

Topics Covered:

- Behavioral Competencies
    - *Leadership*
    - *Interpersonal*
    - *Business*
- Technical Knowledge
    - *People*
    - *Organization*
    - *Workplace*
    - *Strategy*

Course Features:

- SHRM-CP Study Guide
    - Get content that complements our best-selling study guide.
- 6 Full-Length Practice Tests
    - With over 900 practice questions, you can test yourself again and again.
- Mobile Friendly
    - If you need to study on the go, the course is easily accessible from your mobile device.
- SHRM-CP Flashcards
    - Their course includes a flashcard mode consisting of over 450 content cards to help you study.

To receive this discount, visit their website: mometrix.com/university/shrm/ or simply scan this QR code with your smartphone. At the checkout page, enter the discount code: **TPBSHRM50**

If you have any questions or concerns, please don't hesitate to contact them at universityhelp@mometrix.com.

SCAN HERE

FREE Test Taking Tips Video/DVD Offer

To better serve you, we created videos covering test taking tips that we want to give you for FREE. **These videos cover world-class tips that will help you succeed on your test.**

We just ask that you send us feedback about this product. Please let us know what you thought about it—whether good, bad, or indifferent.

To get your **FREE videos**, you can use the QR code below or email freevideos@studyguideteam.com with "Free Videos" in the subject line and the following information in the body of the email:

   a. The title of your product

   b. Your product rating on a scale of 1-5, with 5 being the highest

   c. Your feedback about the product

If you have any questions or concerns, please don't hesitate to contact us at info@studyguideteam.com.

Thank you!

SHRM CP Exam Prep 2022-2023
SHRM Certification Study Guide
Book with 3 Practice Tests
[3rd Edition]

Joshua Rueda

Interested in buying more than 10 copies of our product? Contact us about bulk discounts: bulkorders@studyguideteam.com

ISBN 13: 9781637758823
ISBN 10: 1637758820

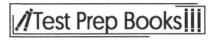

Table of Contents

//Test Prep Books!!!

Quick Overview

As you draw closer to taking your exam, effective preparation becomes more and more important. Thankfully, you have this study guide to help you get ready. Use this guide to help keep your studying on track and refer to it often.

This study guide contains several key sections that will help you be successful on your exam. The guide contains tips for what you should do the night before and the day of the test. Also included are test-taking tips. Knowing the right information is not always enough. Many well-prepared test takers struggle with exams. These tips will help equip you to accurately read, assess, and answer test questions.

A large part of the guide is devoted to showing you what content to expect on the exam and to helping you better understand that content. In this guide are practice test questions so that you can see how well you have grasped the content. Then, answer explanations are provided so that you can understand why you missed certain questions.

Don't try to cram the night before you take your exam. This is not a wise strategy for a few reasons. First, your retention of the information will be low. Your time would be better used by reviewing information you already know rather than trying to learn a lot of new information. Second, you will likely become stressed as you try to gain a large amount of knowledge in a short amount of time. Third, you will be depriving yourself of sleep. So be sure to go to bed at a reasonable time the night before. Being well-rested helps you focus and remain calm.

Be sure to eat a substantial breakfast the morning of the exam. If you are taking the exam in the afternoon, be sure to have a good lunch as well. Being hungry is distracting and can make it difficult to focus. You have hopefully spent lots of time preparing for the exam. Don't let an empty stomach get in the way of success!

When travelling to the testing center, leave earlier than needed. That way, you have a buffer in case you experience any delays. This will help you remain calm and will keep you from missing your appointment time at the testing center.

Be sure to pace yourself during the exam. Don't try to rush through the exam. There is no need to risk performing poorly on the exam just so you can leave the testing center early. Allow yourself to use all of the allotted time if needed.

Remain positive while taking the exam even if you feel like you are performing poorly. Thinking about the content you should have mastered will not help you perform better on the exam.

Once the exam is complete, take some time to relax. Even if you feel that you need to take the exam again, you will be well served by some down time before you begin studying again. It's often easier to convince yourself to study if you know that it will come with a reward!

Test-Taking Strategies

1. Predicting the Answer

When you feel confident in your preparation for a multiple-choice test, try predicting the answer before reading the answer choices. This is especially useful on questions that test objective factual knowledge. By predicting the answer before reading the available choices, you eliminate the possibility that you will be distracted or led astray by an incorrect answer choice. You will feel more confident in your selection if you read the question, predict the answer, and then find your prediction among the answer choices. After using this strategy, be sure to still read all of the answer choices carefully and completely. If you feel unprepared, you should not attempt to predict the answers. This would be a waste of time and an opportunity for your mind to wander in the wrong direction.

2. Reading the Whole Question

Too often, test takers scan a multiple-choice question, recognize a few familiar words, and immediately jump to the answer choices. Test authors are aware of this common impatience, and they will sometimes prey upon it. For instance, a test author might subtly turn the question into a negative, or he or she might redirect the focus of the question right at the end. The only way to avoid falling into these traps is to read the entirety of the question carefully before reading the answer choices.

3. Looking for Wrong Answers

Long and complicated multiple-choice questions can be intimidating. One way to simplify a difficult multiple-choice question is to eliminate all of the answer choices that are clearly wrong. In most sets of answers, there will be at least one selection that can be dismissed right away. If the test is administered on paper, the test taker could draw a line through it to indicate that it may be ignored; otherwise, the test taker will have to perform this operation mentally or on scratch paper. In either case, once the obviously incorrect answers have been eliminated, the remaining choices may be considered. Sometimes identifying the clearly wrong answers will give the test taker some information about the correct answer. For instance, if one of the remaining answer choices is a direct opposite of one of the eliminated answer choices, it may well be the correct answer. The opposite of obviously wrong is obviously right! Of course, this is not always the case. Some answers are obviously incorrect simply because they are irrelevant to the question being asked. Still, identifying and eliminating some incorrect answer choices is a good way to simplify a multiple-choice question.

4. Don't Overanalyze

Anxious test takers often overanalyze questions. When you are nervous, your brain will often run wild, causing you to make associations and discover clues that don't actually exist. If you feel that this may be a problem for you, do whatever you can to slow down during the test. Try taking a deep breath or counting to ten. As you read and consider the question, restrict yourself to the particular words used by the author. Avoid thought tangents about what the author *really* meant, or what he or she was *trying* to say. The only things that matter on a multiple-choice test are the words that are actually in the question. You must avoid reading too much into a multiple-choice question, or supposing that the writer meant something other than what he or she wrote.

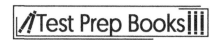

5. No Need for Panic

It is wise to learn as many strategies as possible before taking a multiple-choice test, but it is likely that you will come across a few questions for which you simply don't know the answer. In this situation, avoid panicking. Because most multiple-choice tests include dozens of questions, the relative value of a single wrong answer is small. As much as possible, you should compartmentalize each question on a multiple-choice test. In other words, you should not allow your feelings about one question to affect your success on the others. When you find a question that you either don't understand or don't know how to answer, just take a deep breath and do your best. Read the entire question slowly and carefully. Try rephrasing the question a couple of different ways. Then, read all of the answer choices carefully. After eliminating obviously wrong answers, make a selection and move on to the next question.

6. Confusing Answer Choices

When working on a difficult multiple-choice question, there may be a tendency to focus on the answer choices that are the easiest to understand. Many people, whether consciously or not, gravitate to the answer choices that require the least concentration, knowledge, and memory. This is a mistake. When you come across an answer choice that is confusing, you should give it extra attention. A question might be confusing because you do not know the subject matter to which it refers. If this is the case, don't eliminate the answer before you have affirmatively settled on another. When you come across an answer choice of this type, set it aside as you look at the remaining choices. If you can confidently assert that one of the other choices is correct, you can leave the confusing answer aside. Otherwise, you will need to take a moment to try to better understand the confusing answer choice. Rephrasing is one way to tease out the sense of a confusing answer choice.

7. Your First Instinct

Many people struggle with multiple-choice tests because they overthink the questions. If you have studied sufficiently for the test, you should be prepared to trust your first instinct once you have carefully and completely read the question and all of the answer choices. There is a great deal of research suggesting that the mind can come to the correct conclusion very quickly once it has obtained all of the relevant information. At times, it may seem to you as if your intuition is working faster even than your reasoning mind. This may in fact be true. The knowledge you obtain while studying may be retrieved from your subconscious before you have a chance to work out the associations that support it. Verify your instinct by working out the reasons that it should be trusted.

8. Key Words

Many test takers struggle with multiple-choice questions because they have poor reading comprehension skills. Quickly reading and understanding a multiple-choice question requires a mixture of skill and experience. To help with this, try jotting down a few key words and phrases on a piece of scrap paper. Doing this concentrates the process of reading and forces the mind to weigh the relative importance of the question's parts. In selecting words and phrases to write down, the test taker thinks about the question more deeply and carefully. This is especially true for multiple-choice questions that are preceded by a long prompt.

9. Subtle Negatives

One of the oldest tricks in the multiple-choice test writer's book is to subtly reverse the meaning of a question with a word like *not* or *except*. If you are not paying attention to each word in the question, you can easily be led astray by this trick. For instance, a common question format is, "Which of the following is...?" Obviously, if the question instead is, "Which of the following is not...?," then the answer will be quite different. Even worse, the test makers are aware of the potential for this mistake and will include one answer choice that would be correct if the question were not negated or reversed. A test taker who misses the reversal will find what he or she believes to be a correct answer and will be so confident that he or she will fail to reread the question and discover the original error. The only way to avoid this is to practice a wide variety of multiple-choice questions and to pay close attention to each and every word.

10. Reading Every Answer Choice

It may seem obvious, but you should always read every one of the answer choices! Too many test takers fall into the habit of scanning the question and assuming that they understand the question because they recognize a few key words. From there, they pick the first answer choice that answers the question they believe they have read. Test takers who read all of the answer choices might discover that one of the latter answer choices is actually *more* correct. Moreover, reading all of the answer choices can remind you of facts related to the question that can help you arrive at the correct answer. Sometimes, a misstatement or incorrect detail in one of the latter answer choices will trigger your memory of the subject and will enable you to find the right answer. Failing to read all of the answer choices is like not reading all of the items on a restaurant menu: you might miss out on the perfect choice.

11. Spot the Hedges

One of the keys to success on multiple-choice tests is paying close attention to every word. This is never truer than with words like almost, most, some, and sometimes. These words are called "hedges" because they indicate that a statement is not totally true or not true in every place and time. An absolute statement will contain no hedges, but in many subjects, the answers are not always straightforward or absolute. There are always exceptions to the rules in these subjects. For this reason, you should favor those multiple-choice questions that contain hedging language. The presence of qualifying words indicates that the author is taking special care with their words, which is certainly important when composing the right answer. After all, there are many ways to be wrong, but there is only one way to be right! For this reason, it is wise to avoid answers that are absolute when taking a multiple-choice test. An absolute answer is one that says things are either all one way or all another. They often include words like *every*, *always*, *best*, and *never*. If you are taking a multiple-choice test in a subject that doesn't lend itself to absolute answers, be on your guard if you see any of these words.

12. Long Answers

In many subject areas, the answers are not simple. As already mentioned, the right answer often requires hedges. Another common feature of the answers to a complex or subjective question are qualifying clauses, which are groups of words that subtly modify the meaning of the sentence. If the question or answer choice describes a rule to which there are exceptions or the subject matter is complicated, ambiguous, or confusing, the correct answer will require many words in order to be expressed clearly and accurately. In essence, you should not be deterred by answer choices that seem excessively long. Oftentimes, the author of the text will not be able to write the correct answer without offering some qualifications and modifications. Your job is to read the answer choices thoroughly and completely and to select the one that most accurately and precisely answers the question.

13. Restating to Understand

Sometimes, a question on a multiple-choice test is difficult not because of what it asks but because of how it is written. If this is the case, restate the question or answer choice in different words. This process serves a couple of important purposes. First, it forces you to concentrate on the core of the question. In order to rephrase the question accurately, you have to understand it well. Rephrasing the question will concentrate your mind on the key words and ideas. Second, it will present the information to your mind in a fresh way. This process may trigger your memory and render some useful scrap of information picked up while studying.

14. True Statements

Sometimes an answer choice will be true in itself, but it does not answer the question. This is one of the main reasons why it is essential to read the question carefully and completely before proceeding to the answer choices. Too often, test takers skip ahead to the answer choices and look for true statements. Having found one of these, they are content to select it without reference to the question above. Obviously, this provides an easy way for test makers to play tricks. The savvy test taker will always read the entire question before turning to the answer choices. Then, having settled on a correct answer choice, he or she will refer to the original question and ensure that the selected answer is relevant. The mistake of choosing a correct-but-irrelevant answer choice is especially common on questions related to specific pieces of objective knowledge. A prepared test taker will have a wealth of factual knowledge at their disposal, and should not be careless in its application.

15. No Patterns

One of the more dangerous ideas that circulates about multiple-choice tests is that the correct answers tend to fall into patterns. These erroneous ideas range from a belief that B and C are the most common right answers, to the idea that an unprepared test-taker should answer "A-B-A-C-A-D-A-B-A." It cannot be emphasized enough that pattern-seeking of this type is exactly the WRONG way to approach a multiple-choice test. To begin with, it is highly unlikely that the test maker will plot the correct answers according to some predetermined pattern. The questions are scrambled and delivered in a random order. Furthermore, even if the test maker was following a pattern in the assignation of correct answers, there is no reason why the test taker would know which pattern he or she was using. Any attempt to discern a pattern in the answer choices is a waste of time and a distraction from the real work of taking the test. A test taker would be much better served by extra preparation before the test than by reliance on a pattern in the answers.

FREE Videos/DVD OFFER

Doing well on your exam requires both knowing the test content and understanding how to use that knowledge to do well on the test. We offer completely FREE test taking tip videos. **These videos cover world-class tips that you can use to succeed on your test.**

To get your **FREE videos**, you can use the QR code below or email freevideos@studyguideteam.com with "Free Videos" in the subject line and the following information in the body of the email:

   a. The title of your product

   b. Your product rating on a scale of 1-5, with 5 being the highest

   c. Your feedback about the product

If you have any questions or concerns, please don't hesitate to contact us at info@studyguideteam.com.

Thanks again!

Introduction to the SHRM-CP

Function of the Test

The Society for Human Resource Management designed the SHRM-CP for Human Resource (HR) professionals to earn credentials that make them a recognized committed leader and expert in the field of human resources. The exam serves as a gateway for this professional distinction that once earned, gives the employee a competitive advantage in today's economy by asserting that a certain level of HR knowledge and skills have been obtained.

The SHRM-CP exam is for those who:

- Implement strategies
- Act as point of contact for staff and stakeholders
- Deliver HR services
- Perform operational HR functions

SHRM-CP eligibility includes both education and experience, but the years required of experience differs with the degree.

It should be noted that the job title for the work experience does not necessarily need to be explicitly in human resources. The crucial factor in satisfying the eligibility requirement is the HR-related work functions, not the title itself. One "year" of experience is achieved when at least 1,000 hours have been devoted to HR-related work functions. These hours can be accrued in part-time or full-time roles. However, individuals whose positions involve a variety of functions, such as administrative or office management tasks, can only count time that is spent on direct HR functions, and supervising other employees does not qualify.

The SHRM Body of Applied Skills and Knowledge (SHRMBASK™), which is the basis for SHRM credentialing, identifies 15 functional areas of HR skills and knowledge. Job functions that fall under one of the 15 areas qualify towards the work experience time requirements. These areas are divided among three domains as outlined below:

1. People: HR Strategic Planning, Talent Acquisition, Employee Engagement and Retention, Learning and Development, and Total Rewards

2. Organization: Structure of HR Functions, Organizational Effectiveness and Development, Workforce Management, Employee and Labor Relations, and Technology Management

3. Workplace: HR in the Global Context, Diversity and Inclusion, Risk Management, Corporate Social Responsibility, and U.S. Employment Laws and Regulations

More information about these competencies and exam eligibility can be found at the SHRM website at www.shrm.org.

Test Administration

Although individuals do not need to be SHRM members to sit for the SHRM-CP exam, membership does come with a variety of benefits including a significant exam registration fee discount. Either way, interested test takers must apply to take the exam and pay the fee by the deadline for the applicable testing window: winter or spring. The application deadlines and the window of dates that the exam is offered are available on the SHRM website. The application form includes fields where the candidate must enter information proving their exam eligibility, including education and job details.

The exam is administered via computer at more than 8,000 Prometric testing centers in 160 countries worldwide. Candidates in the United States can register for the exam at their preferred center and date either online at prometric.com/shrm or via phone at (888) 736-0134. Candidates must wait to register until they have received their Authorization to Test (ATT) letter because this letter will contain their eligibility ID, which is necessary for registration.

Test takers in the United States needing accommodations for disabilities must submit a Testing Accommodations Request form and the required supporting documentation with their exam application. This form, along with information about documentation, is available in Appendix A of the SHRM Certification Handbook available on the SHRM website.

After a short tutorial to familiarize test takers with the testing platform, the exam lasts four hours. There are 160 multiple-choice questions, 95 of which are knowledge-based and 65 scenario-based situational judgement questions. The knowledge-based questions assess the candidate's understanding of factual information pertinent to HR. There are two categories: HR-specific knowledge Items (KIs) and foundational knowledge items (FKIs). KIs cover key concepts addressed in the 15 HR functional areas, while FKIs cover key concepts that the SHRMBoCK™ considers foundational to the eight behavioral competencies in three categories:

- Leadership: Leadership and Navigation, and Ethical Practice, Diversity, Equity, and Inclusion
- Business: Business Acumen, Consultation, and Critical Evaluation
- Interpersonal: Relationship Management, Communication, and Global and Cultural Effectiveness

The situational judgment items (SJIs) evaluate the test taker's judgment and decision-making skills. These questions present a realistic work-related scenario and four possible solutions to address the issue in the scenario. Although there may be multiple viable strategies to resolve a given scenario, test takers must select the single best choice or most effective option to receive credit for the question. A panel composed to experienced HR professionals determines the correct response for each work-related scenario.

The exam also contains 30 unscored field-test items that are only used to gather data on their effectiveness before potentially including them as scored questions on future exams. These questions are randomly interspersed with and indistinguishable from scored questions on the exam.

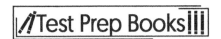

The distribution of questions by content and type relative to the entire exam is shown in the table below:

Behavioral Competencies	Question Type
Leadership (13%)	Situational Judgement (40%)
Business (18.5%)	Foundational Knowledge (10%)
Interpersonal (18.5%)	
HR Knowledge Categories	**Question Type**
People (16%)	HR-Specific Knowledge (50%)
Organization (17%)	
Workplace (17%)	

Scoring

Test takers receive credit for choosing the single best possible answer for each multiple-choice question. Incorrect answers are not penalized.

Test takers' performance on SHRM-CP and SHRM-SCP is not measured relative to other test takers; instead, it is measured against a predetermined standard. This standard is the level of knowledge and competency expected of early- to mid-career HR professionals. Test takers either meet the predetermined standard (minimum score) and pass the exam or do not pass. Upon completion of the exam, a provision passing status is available for test takers before they leave the testing center. Official results are available on the test taker's online portal approximately four weeks after the testing window has ended. A Candidate Feedback Report, which reports the test taker's official score along with a diagnostic graph showing the performance in each behavioral competency and each knowledge domain, is also provided. Individuals who successfully pass the exam will be mailed an official letter of congratulations, a lapel pin, and their SHRM-CP or SHRM-SCP credential certificate.

For May–August 2020, the pass rate for the SHRM-CP exam was 67% and the pass rate for the SHRM-SCP exam was 54%.

Study Prep Plan for the SHRM-CP

1 **Schedule** - Use one of our study schedules below or come up with one of your own.

2 **Relax** - Test anxiety can hurt even the best students. There are many ways to reduce stress. Find the one that works best for you.

3 **Execute** - Once you have a good plan in place, be sure to stick to it.

One Week Study Schedule

Day 1	SHRM Behavioral Competencies
Day 2	Business
Day 3	SHRM Technical Knowledge
Day 4	Organization
Day 5	SHRM Practice Test #1 & #2
Day 6	SHRM Practice Test #3
Day 7	Take Your Exam!

Two Week Study Schedule

Day 1	SHRM Behavioral Competencies	Day 8	SHRM Practice Test #1
Day 2	Interpersonal	Day 9	Answer Explanations for Practice Test #1
Day 3	Business	Day 10	SHRM Practice Test #2
Day 4	SHRM Technical Knowledge	Day 11	Answer Explanations for Practice Test #2
Day 5	Total Rewards	Day 12	SHRM Practice Test #3
Day 6	Organization	Day 13	Answer Explanations for Practice Test #3
Day 7	Workplace	Day 14	Take Your Exam!

One Month Study Schedule						
Day 1	SHRM Behavioral Competencies	Day 11	Consultation	Day 21	Workplace
Day 2	Managing HR Initiatives	Day 12	Change Management	Day 22	Risk Management
Day 3	Professional Integrity	Day 13	Critical Evaluation	Day 23	Corporate Social Responsibility
Day 4	Interpersonal	Day 14	Evidence-Based Decision-Making	Day 24	SHRM Practice Test #1
Day 5	Teamwork	Day 15	SHRM Technical Knowledge	Day 25	Answer Explanations for Practice Test #1
Day 6	Negotiation	Day 16	Employee Engagement and Retention	Day 26	SHRM Practice Test #2
Day 7	Communication	Day 17	Total Rewards	Day 27	Answer Explanations for Practice Test #2
Day 8	Listening	Day 18	Organization	Day 28	SHRM Practice Test #3
Day 9	Global and Cultural Effectiveness	Day 19	Employee and Labor Relations	Day 29	Answer Explanations for Practice Test #3
Day 10	Business	Day 20	Technology Management	Day 30	Take Your Exam!

SHRM Behavioral Competencies

Leadership

Leadership and Navigation

Quality leadership skills are essential to any organization, and thus leadership training is typically provided to mid and upper management professionals. Effective leadership skills include strategic thinking, solving problems as they come, and managing time in the most financially responsible manner. While these skills are essential, there are also more human characteristics that must be mentioned. A successful leader must have the ability to build confidence within their organization, obtain the trust of others, inspire others, and engender a sense of pride and purpose within their company.

Navigating the Organization
Work Roles, Leader Goals, and Relationships
Competent human resources (HR) personnel are able to do the following:

- Develop job postings that clearly and concisely explain the responsibilities required by the job.
- Have the educational qualifications and knowledge skillsets that will support managing those responsibilities.
- Acquire the soft skills that will ensure potential candidates will be a good fit for the role.

Not only must hired candidates be able to carry out the requirements of the job, their personal interests factor into their productivity and happiness over the long-term. HR professionals may utilize a number of personality assessment tools to determine good fits between candidates and roles. Jobs within an organization are developed based on goals and objectives established by leadership to ensure that qualified employees perform duties that contribute to the overall interests of the organization. Finally, HR personnel work with those in leadership roles to influence a company culture that sets the tone for how employees behave during work hours and how they interact with subordinates, lateral colleagues, and superiors.

Communication and Involvement
Encouraging communication and involvement is often a step in the right direction toward changing company culture. And much like climate and culture, communication and involvement are closely related, but not necessarily identical. For example, if John's boss gives him increased responsibility over an aspect of his work, then John has become more involved. However, if John still has no input from his boss on the decision process, or has no formal way to share his ideas with management, then the boss has not encouraged communication. Conversely, if John's boss starts sending regular memos detailing company activities and the strategies behind them, communication increases. However, if John and other employees have no way to act or contribute to this knowledge, then the boss has not encouraged involvement. To make meaningful changes to company culture, both communication and involvement should be addressed.

Organizational Policies and Political Environment
An organization's policies and political environment will vary depending on the overall goals and function of an organization, but most HR initiatives focus on several key categories that intend to most

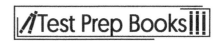

effectively utilize the personnel within the organization. These include, but are not limited to, the following:

- Finding, hiring, and retaining qualified candidates

- Employee compensation and benefits (such as hourly pay, salary, health insurance, paid leave, disability benefits, pension, and other perks based on employee interests)

- Organizational and employee development activities (such as professional trainings)

- Termination and retirement tasks

- Risk management, such as drug screening employees and providing safety courses relevant to job functions

The details and successful implementation of these initiatives are largely subjective, beginning with understanding an organization's mission. This is often defined by an established mission statement or company vision. All HR initiatives should contribute to the advancement of the organization's mission.

Attitudes and Relationships
How employees think and feel about a company is critical to an employer. If members of an organization have negative associations with it, it can be difficult to motivate them. The overall "mood" of an organization is known as its climate, and organizational climate cannot be directly controlled. However, climate is closely affected by work environment, company standards, interactions, and a general sense of "how things are done around here." All these factors add up to what is called organizational culture. So, if an employer wants to improve the company's climate, they need to make changes to the company culture. The organization's political environment can also have an effect on employees. This refers to the hierarchy and behavior of the management of a company.

Vision
Envisioning Organizational Culture
For any organization to be successful, it must have a clear idea of what it's doing and where it's going. Mission and vision statements are two ways for an organization to verbalize its objectives. A mission statement focuses on the work of the organization on a day-to-day basis and answers the following questions:

- What do we do now?
- Why are we doing it?
- What makes us different from other companies?

A vision statement focuses on the organization's future goals and answers the following questions:

- What do we want to accomplish?
- Where do we aim to be in the future?

An organization should also have a clear idea of what the corporate culture looks like. The corporate culture is the general attitude of employees and management toward regular workday activities and how employees interact with one another. Policies and values should align with this culture to promote cohesion.

Developing Actionable Goals

A successful mission statement should be clear and direct. In short, it states *why* the organization exists, and in turn guides its values, standards, and other organizing principles. For example, an organic restaurant might have the following mission statement: "To serve customers healthy meals made from the freshest, locally sourced organic ingredients." With this mission statement, the restaurant could decide to focus its efforts on building relationships with local farmers or staying up-to-date on health food trends.

Leaders translate vision and strategic direction into goals and objectives. Systems for performance accountability can clarify what is expected of people. Only then can consequences or rewards be aligned with actual performance. The best organizations develop simple processes that are internally efficient while being locally responsive.

Strategic Vision and Direction

A strategic vision statement focuses on specific future goals, and in turn guides the steps that the organization will take to achieve them. The same restaurant might decide on the following vision statement: "To become a top-rated restaurant in the city." The restaurant can then design a plan accordingly, perhaps by focusing on marketing campaigns or inviting influential reviewers to dine at the restaurant.

Managing HR Initiatives

Project Requirements

Senior leadership plays a role in dictating project timelines and end goals for an organization, and HR initiatives can support the processes that bring forth outcomes through high-level project management. In the planning stage of projects, HR professionals will need to take into account the skills that are needed in order for projects to be completed. Additionally, they will need to consider factors like timeline development, establishing mini-goals and deliverables, the resources needed and associated costs (such as labor, time required, materials needed, and so on), risks that may need to be mitigated, and analyses that determine returns on investment (ROI) of resources. These are often intrapersonal activities that may require the input and cooperation of stakeholders from various departments across the organization. Therefore, to move project processes forward in the most productive manner, HR professionals should anticipate selecting the appropriate stakeholders and fostering positive communication between them.

Project Goals and Milestones

Project goals are stepping stones toward organizational goals, and projects are comprised of milestones that indicate outcome success. Milestones are progressive in nature and influence the general timeline of the project. In order to be useful, both goals and milestones should exhibit SMART qualities. SMART is a commonly used acronym in goal and milestone setting that states an effective end point should be Specific, Measurable, Achievable, Relevant, and Timely. This ensures the goal or milestone is detailed, can produce data to show evidence of its effectiveness, can feasibly be attained, is relevant to the organizational goal at hand, and occurs at appropriate and useful intervals that benefit the project. When developing project goals, HR personnel should be able to address each of the five SMART aspects. Often, these values are documented before the project begins.

Project Budgets and Resources

A project can require a wide array of resources depending on its scope. Beyond the number of personnel needed and their individual compensation packages, resource costs also include time spent, materials, potential trainings needed, long-term sustaining actions, and so on. Costs can be categorized into direct costs, which impact one project specifically (such as labor and materials), and indirect costs, which may affect specific projects but also serve the organization as a whole (such as leadership salary and permanent office furniture). These costs can be fixed, or they can vary over time. Developing a budget includes reviewing a project proposal fully and anticipating all projected costs over the completion of the project. These may be divided into chronological milestones (such as monthly, quarterly, or annually) or by outcome benchmarks (such as when a department is fully staffed or when a component of a product is developed). Budgets and resources should remain flexible and be updated as needed.

Overcoming and Removing Obstacles

No project is likely to be without obstacles. Anticipating potential obstacles and preparing for them can help the project remain on track for completion. Start-up plans should be reviewed and revised throughout the course of the project to account for any unexpected changes. Most importantly, these revisions must be communicated to project members. Most often, obstacles arise when team members do not have the skillset or resources to contribute to their role, when the content and timeline of deliverables are not clear or documented, and when communication from relevant leadership and between colleagues is lacking. Beginning the project with SMART attributes and allowing for communication with project staff and key stakeholders can reduce any obstacles that should arise. While some obstacles may be out of the organization's control (such as a sudden loss of external funding), internal obstacles can often be mitigated with appropriate contingency planning.

Necessary Resources

Once a project outcome has been identified, finding the resources needed to see the project to fruition is key. Allocating resources is a balancing act. Utilizing too many resources will lead to waste, but utilizing too few resources can result in delays, errors, or other obstacles. Skilled HR personnel will know how to produce the best value from the least resources—a concept based on the Lean approach, which was once used primarily in manufacturing. HR personnel can examine internal data from similar projects to anticipate what resources other initiatives might need. Tools from the Six Sigma approach, such as process mapping and value stream mapping, can also help objectively determine the resources needed at each step of the project and the actual value-add associated with them.

Resource Allocation

Milestones can serve as an indicator of when resources are inconsistent with project needs. If deliverables are not fulfilled by an established milestone, HR personnel may choose to examine the role of the resources that are in use. A gap analysis, a root cause analysis, or a cause-and-effect diagram, which pinpoint why an expected outcome was not met, can review discrepancies between expected and actual performances. Often, these indicate that there is a constraint in one or more resources, such as lack of material, lack of qualified employees, or lack of time. Once the resource in question has been addressed, implementing a test of change may show if shifting resources allows established milestones to be met. If not, this may indicate that components of the timeline for the project are not reasonable. Milestones, outcomes, or the construction of the timeline itself may require revision.

Agility and Adaptability

Project requirements, goals, and constraints are developed and anticipated during the planning stage. They are, however, subject to changes that may or may not be in the team's control. Changes in funding, personnel, and regulation are examples of items that often cannot be fully accounted for during the project planning stage. HR project managers may benefit from managing their own expectations during the project planning stage, and by accepting that all baseline plans are fluid. Project plans should be continuously reviewed, and they should be revised when unexpected changes arise. Developing contingency processes during the project planning stage, cross-training team members, and developing the ability to critically and creatively think about new solutions are ways to mitigate unanticipated changes. Becoming aware of the professional strengths and weaknesses of team members and drawing on this knowledge during times of change can also help to fill gaps. These techniques allow the entire team to cohesively demonstrate agility and adaptability when needed.

Influence
Building Credibility

There are numerous ways to build credibility as an HR expert, like having a formal educational background in industrial organization and related fields, such as psychology, project management, business, and communication. Continuing education after formal schooling, such as through earning certifications through nationally recognized credentialing bodies, is another way to further develop one's theoretical skillset. Staying abreast of literature pertaining to topics relevant to human resources is yet another avenue to illustrate professional expertise. From a practical standpoint, using one's knowledge to offer solutions to personnel issues within the organization is a way to showcase credibility. Sharing success stories with colleagues in the field can build professional credibility outside of one's organization.

Promoting Buy-In

The most effective way to promote buy-in among organizational stakeholders for HR initiatives is to show the added value of an initiative to the stakeholders, employees, and organization as a whole. Added value will need to be large enough that it is worth the associated costs of implementing the initiative. To this end, HR personnel who are proposing initiatives have the responsibility of understanding what outcomes each of their stakeholders perceives as valuable. An initiative that the HR team finds valuable may not have meaning for stakeholders. Often, stakeholders consist of leadership personnel whose buy-in is necessary for the initiative to be approved. Leadership buy-in is also crucial in order to successfully implement change (known as top-down change), otherwise gaining subordinate approval proves extremely challenging. Finally, determining what is of value may vary across departments. Therefore, finding umbrella goals or interest overlaps can be useful.

Motivating HR Staff and Stakeholders

An effective leader understands that team motivation is influenced by a number of factors, and that some fall outside the leader's locus of influence. The first step in motivating HR staff is ensuring that candidates who are passionate about the field, the organization, and the organization's interests are hired as staff. Candidates who are not a good professional or cultural fit for the team may be difficult to motivate, may be unhappy on the job, and may not find success within the organization. Ensuring that qualified employees remain motivated may include providing opportunities for professional growth, recognizing and rewarding professional excellence, promoting work-life satisfaction, and creating an open, encouraging, and positive work environment. Motivating other stakeholders to support HR's visions and goals is most likely to include continuous highlights of the value that the department provides to both the stakeholder as an individual, and to the organization as a whole. This may be expressed in program evaluations, reports, presentations, graphs, anecdotal evidence, or employee testimonials.

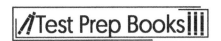

Advocating for Employees

HR personnel are responsible for managing the productivity and welfare of an organization's employees, but also for ensuring that employees are able to safely perform their jobs in a way that advances the organization's interests. It can be a balancing act to manage employee needs with business needs, especially during times when one side needs more than the other (such as if an essential employee has to take an extended medical leave, or if a valued business customer needs a complex product on short notice). It is also important that employees do not take advantage of the organization, and vice versa. HR personnel are often in charge of developing guidelines that help to regulate these dual needs; these are often documented in a company handbook that is accessible to all employees. Guidelines may be established for instances such as leaves of absence, overtime, meal breaks, harassment, and other contexts specific to the industry.

Ethical Practice

Sound business ethics are essential to establishing an organization's trustworthy reputation. If an organization is ethical, its conduct is fair, moral, and socially acceptable. Of course, some unethical practices are expressly prohibited by law. However, in other cases, the difference between ethical and unethical behaviors must be enforced by the organization itself. If the organization has a strong sense of right and wrong, it will be able to maintain positive relationships with customers and vendors. If the organization has questionable ethical practices, it may face legal charges, loss of business, or damage to its reputation.

Personal Integrity
Consistency in Values

Other HR policies to consider with respect to ethics include the process of reporting unethical behavior. How will the organization protect employees who report unethical business practices within the organization? Are employees able to make anonymous or confidential reports about unethical behavior? HR professionals should implement training programs to educate managers and other employees about expected standards of ethical behavior. When it comes to controversial business practices, employees may not be sure what behaviors are acceptable or unacceptable. When an organization's code of conduct changes or when new legal regulations are introduced, it's important to provide appropriate training and education for employees. Finally, HR professionals must have organized review systems in order to evaluate how well the organization is adhering to ethical practices and reporting all business practices appropriately.

Mistakes and Accountability

HR professionals must be willing to admit to any mistakes made and take responsibility for their actions. This inspires other employees to hold themselves accountable for their mistakes. Ultimately, executive leadership must put the framework in place to implement ethical standards that support accountability. Organization leaders can set the tone and encourage transparency and ethical behavior. Instilling a culture of accountability that spreads through the organization helps every staff member understand why meeting ethical standards is important.

Biases of Self and Others

Employees come from all backgrounds. It is important that HR professionals do not make any prior negative judgments regarding the personality or attributes of any employees. Each individual has worth. It is essential for HR to be mindful of any personal prejudices or biases they may have and employ empathy and sensitivity when working with employees. As HR professionals become aware of their own personal biases, they should gain skills and awareness of differing cultural needs and ethical standpoints to ensure they are providing appropriate communication and programs to all employees.

Serving as a Role Model
In any work environment, there are certain standards of professionalism that must be met. The HR professional's conduct, way of dress, and even conduct outside of work is subject to these high standards. HR professionals should behave in an ethical manner to be a role model of personal integrity within their organization.

Professional Integrity
Withstanding Adverse Actions
An adverse action occurs when an employee feels that treatment from their employers puts them at a disadvantage in their workplace. HR professionals must ensure that their biases, whether conscious or unconscious, do not result in adverse actions to employees.

There are two types of discrimination: disparate treatment and disparate or adverse impact. **Disparate treatment** occurs when an employer treats protected classes differently than other employees. Examples of disparate treatment include holding genders to different standards, sexual harassment, and blatantly rejecting a member of a protected class due to stereotypes.

A famous disparate treatment case was McDonnell Douglas Corporation vs. Green. Green was a black employee who was laid off during a regular reduction in force. He protested at the company (as part of a group), chained and locked company doors, and blocked an entrance to company property. His activities did not please the company. When the company began hiring again, they advertised, and Green reapplied. He was denied, and the company continued looking for candidates. Green claimed the rejection was due to his race and his involvement in civil rights activities. This was a precedent-setting EEO case that established criteria for disparate treatment and ruled that a *prima facie* (at first glance) case can be shown if an employee:

- Belongs to a protected class
- Applied for a job when the employer sought applicants
- Was qualified and yet rejected
- Was rejected but the employer kept looking

In disparate treatment cases, an individual must prove:

- They are a member of a protected class
- They applied for a job for which they were qualified and for which the employer was seeking applicants
- They were not hired even though they were qualified
- After they did not get the job, the position remained open and the employer continued to receive applications

Adverse impact refers to a form of discrimination where an employer's policy seems neutral but in fact has an adverse impact on a certain group or a certain characteristic such as race, sex, or disability. This was identified by the Supreme Court in 1971 in the case of Griggs v. Duke Power Co., where it was proven that the requirement of a high school diploma for higher-paid positions was unfairly affecting African-American employees in lower-paid labor positions who had a history of receiving inferior education.

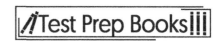

As another example, if an employer requires a potential employee for a position to be at least 5'10", it may exclude an entire group, such as women. Because statistically, men are taller, this requirement is based solely on biological reasons rather than if the candidate can adequately perform the required role.

An employer discriminating based on certain physical elements, however, can be justified if it is in correlation with job requirements. For example, it is necessary for a fire department to discriminate based on height, facial hair, or grooming to ensure the safety of its employees.

Maintaining Privacy

In order to have an effective and active reporting system, HR professionals must establish a supportive environment for reporting that protects the privacy of employees who report occurrences of unethical behavior. Employees should feel safe from negative consequences of reporting unethical behavior. The Whistleblower Protection Act, passed in 1989, is one law that regulates the protection of employees who report a violation of any law, rule, regulation, or other ethical standard. HR professionals should be aware of this law and other regulations that affect the duty to report unethical behavior.

Communicating Sensitive Information

The Health Insurance Portability and Accountability Act (HIPAA) is an amendment (ERISA). It was passed to improve the continuity and portability of healthcare coverage. This act addresses pre-existing medical conditions or those for which an employee or a member of their immediate family received medical advice or treatment during the six-month period prior to their enrollment date into the employer's healthcare plan, such as a serious illness, injury, or pregnancy.

If an employee had creditable healthcare coverage—a group health plan, Medicare, or a military-sponsored healthcare plan—for a period of twelve months, with no lapse in coverage of sixty-three days or more, then an employer cannot refuse them coverage in a new group health plan due to a pre-existing medical condition and cannot charge them a higher rate for coverage. However, if an employee did not previously have creditable healthcare coverage, then an employer can exclude coverage for the treatment of a preexisting medical condition for a period of twelve months—with the exception of pregnancy—or for a period of up to eighteen months for late enrollees in the plan.

Additionally, this act only permits covered entities to use or disclose protected health information for treatment, payment, and healthcare operations. If protected health information is to be released for any other reason, written authorization is required from the patient.

Medical records related to the request for work-related accommodations under the Americans with Disabilities Act (ADA) and leaves of absences under the Family Medical Leave Act (FMLA) are not covered under this law. Employers must have a designated privacy officer who will oversee the organization's privacy policy, along with conducting all necessary training for employees. Employers who fail to comply with this act may face both civil and criminal penalties. Some criminal penalties can cost companies as much as $250,000 and up to ten years in prison.

Ethics Laws, Standards, Legislation and Emerging Trends

One of the major roles of the HR team is to maintain awareness of all statutory and regulatory requirements that affect organizational HR practices and to ensure that the organization meets all of their goals. Emerging trends in the HR field should also be monitored so that the HR team can utilize best practices in their workplace.

Leading HR Investigations

Reports of unethical behavior and violation of standards should be investigated in a timely manner by HR professionals. Investigations should be both thorough and impartial. HR professionals should have policies and procedures regarding investigations in place including when to alert company leaders or law enforcement. Investigations should fulfill any legal requirements, workers' compensation processing needs, and applicable internal policies and procedures.

Managing Political and Social Pressures

Organizational politics is best described as leaders' relative influence, power, authoritative influence, and negotiation skills compared to other colleagues seeking to achieve their own goals and objectives. Politics are often competing forces within an organization and can hinder or enhance the progress of the HR professional and the ability to implement HR programs, practices, and policies. Careful analysis of how the project fits within the organization's people, structure, and culture will lead to better leadership. Social factors within the workplace can also place pressure on HR professionals and their ability to implement and enforce HR programs.

Providing Feedback

HR professionals can help organizations have clear and enforceable ethical standards. Three ways to do so are by establishing a values statement, establishing a code of conduct, and conducting HR audits. A code of conduct also guides employee behavior, but with greater detail. The code of conduct lays out all policies governing employees' actions, defining acceptable and unacceptable behaviors. HR professionals also must carry out HR audits to ensure that all employees are following organization policies. HR managers can also develop and distribute an Employee Handbook that outlines the company's code of conduct and employee expectations.

Ethical Agent

Empowering Employees to Report

An organization's culture dictates what behaviors employees view as unethical or conflicts of interests and how likely employees are to report them. HR personnel play a key role in defining this culture and creating communication lines in which employees feel comfortable participating. Defining what is ethical and moral professional behavior may be expressed during the hiring process, in a company manual, or during new hire onboarding. Beyond simply documenting what constitutes as acceptable or unacceptable behavior, HR personnel should serve as leaders in demonstrating an ethical work culture and encouraging others to do the same. These guidelines should be continuously reviewed and updated, and should be shared at regular intervals with the rest of the organization. Even if the organization's ethical culture is clearly defined and regularly reviewed, employees may struggle with reporting questionable instances, especially if it involves a friend or a superior. HR personnel can help mitigate reporting fears by providing confidential or anonymous methods of communication designed specifically for these events.

Mitigating Bias in Business Decisions

Bias can present itself in both obvious and unconscious ways. It inadvertently favors some employees while putting others at a disadvantage. Mitigating the influence of bias within the organization and in making business decisions is an important responsibility of HR professionals. HR personnel should continuously examine factors that are scientifically associated with bias, such as gender and race, and how they are associated with reward variables such as pay and performance reviews. Standardizing reward variables, such as awarding the same pay to all employees with a particular title, is a way to mitigate bias. Removing identifying factors from resumes that do not have to do with talent can also

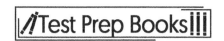

reduce the effect of subconscious bias. Additionally, HR professionals should continuously self-reflect. By bringing awareness to their own personal attitudes and belief systems, they may notice that they hold biases that they wish to release.

Transparency

The number of employees that place a high value in transparent workplaces is rapidly increasing. Transparency allows employees to feel connected to their work environment and their colleagues. It also allows them to feel secure and validated in their role within the organization. Finally, a transparent work environment fosters brainstorming and innovation, which promotes organizational growth. Without transparency, employees often report feeling undervalued, disrespected, and blindsided by organizational changes. This leads to decreased morale over time and high turnover rates. HR personnel can promote a transparent work environment by encouraging that general information, the intention behind decision-making and company goals, and other employee-centric news is shared freely. Communication remains direct in times of achievement as well as during times of struggle. While not all company data is relevant to each specific employee's role, employees should at least feel comfortable in believing that they have accurate information about programs, practices, and policies as it relates to their job.

Organizational Risks and Conflicts of Interest

HR personnel have a responsibility to continuously review standard operating procedures, internal organizational dynamics, and external relationships with other organizations to ensure no individual employee or group is marginalized and that all business transactions are moral and legal. Continual review is important, as some ethical risks or conflicts of interest can be subtle, socially engrained, and easily overlooked. Additionally, as social, cultural, political, or organizational climates shift, ideas that are considered ethically risky or as posing a conflict are likely to shift as well. All reported ethical risks and conflicts of interest should be taken seriously without the influence of any subjective bias. Potential or actual risks should be immediately taken to leadership who have the ability to eliminate them. HR personnel have a responsibility to advocate on behalf of an organization's employees for an ethical and conflict-free workplace.

Access to Ethical Standards and Policies

The initial introduction to an organization's ethical standards and policies should be in its job postings. This indicates the company's culture and values and ideally attracts candidates with similar beliefs. Interviewing the candidate can further explore this fit. This can take place by sharing the nature of the organization's ethical environment and gauging the candidate's response. Investigative interview questions exploring the candidate's personal ethics can also benefit the hiring process. Finally, tools such as background tests can indicate personal values, although it may be useful to openly discuss red flags further with the candidate to understand the context and impact on the job role. This practice also sets the foundation for a transparent workplace. An organization's ethical standards and policies should be documented in an easily accessible location that can be updated in real-time, such as in an employee handbook on the company Intranet. HR personnel should always notify employees of any updates to the standards.

Diversity, Equity, and Inclusion

Diversity, Equity, and Inclusion (DE&I) focuses on the significance of creating a workplace environment concerned with treating all employees fairly and respectfully. DE&I also focuses on ensuring that all employees have equal opportunities and access to resources at their work. This might look like making sure all qualified personnel are considered for a new position rather than the boss's favorite; or all qualifying employees get a break throughout the day. DE&I not only organizes what the company can do for the employee, but it also helps to make sure the employee is able to use their own personal knowledge and experience to contribute and take part in the company's success. Allowing employees to integrate the components of their lives that make them unique individuals helps to foster a sense of community and belonging within the organization/workplace.

Creating a Diverse and Inclusive Culture

Investing in creating a diverse and inclusive workplace culture is one of the most important things an organization can do. In this type of workplace environment, everyone feels valued, needed, respected, and supported. These characteristics increase employees' senses of belonging and even willingness to continue working for the organization. The HR professional plays an integral role in not only educating heads of organizations on the importance and value of a diverse and inclusive work culture, but they also play a significant role in enforcing that expectation.

The HR professional enforcing the cultivation of a diverse and inclusive work environment by advocating for diverse representation across the kinds of employees that are hired. This look like pushing for the company to hire qualified candidates regardless of race, gender, sexual orientation, religious beliefs, education, abilities, country of origin, and ethnicity. In an ideal diverse and inclusive workplace, people from all different walks of life would be represented; the company would hire with a stronger focus on whatever technical qualifications are needed for the job rather than the aforementioned qualities.

As previously mentioned, cultivating and helping to build the diverse and inclusive work environment is only half of the HR professional's responsibility. Additionally, they must first communicate the benefits of this type of DE&I to the organization's supervisors and current employees. This can sometimes be difficult as many people are not very fond of change. However, by presenting the benefits of such an environment, the HR professional can show the business leaders how the company can grow. The HR professional will need to be able to communicate a few other things as well. They will need to be able to explain the benefits of interpersonal risk taking, having and showing mutual respect and trust, and advocating for the voices of the employees within an organization.

Ensuring Equity Effectiveness

Equity effectiveness is all about making fair treatment in accessibility, opportunities and advancement within a workplace available to all members of that workforce. When thinking about equity effectiveness, the HR professional should be researching and seeking out ways to elevate the equity policies of an organization. This might look like coordinating benefits packages and programs that appeal to and promote a diverse workplace population. The HR professional is also responsible for essentially tracking the effectiveness of an organization's equity practices and reporting back to the supervisors any problems or issues surrounding performance of DE&I differences.

Connecting DE&I to Organizational Performance

DE&I practices are not only meant to benefit the employees, but they also help organizations to achieve their goals and objectives. By diversifying one's workforce, the organization opens itself up to a wider pool of knowledge to incorporate into projects and problem solving. The HR professional is responsible for showcasing and communicating a company's DE&I efforts to the organization's stakeholders, both internal and external. They also play an important role in helping to determine what are the company's goals and then creating strategies and initiatives to help achieve said goals through the lens of DE&I. The HR professional keeps track of the organization's efforts, progress, and effectiveness in integrating the

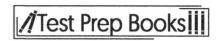

specifically curated DE&I strategies and initiatives. They are responsible for relaying this information to the organization's stakeholders and superiors to help ensure that the company is meeting the expectations for what a diverse and inclusive work environment should look like for them.

Interpersonal

Relationship Management

Networking
Maintaining Network of Professional Contacts
Professional networking benefits employees within the organization, as well as the organization as a whole. This can take place through individual conversations, group meetings, social events, workplace events, or other interactive activities. Networking is a means of building valuable relationships, understanding the strengths that colleagues bring to a specific industry or goal, and supporting others with similar visions. To this end, when HR professionals regularly network with colleagues within their department, across other departments, and through the organization, they can better understand the pulse of the organization and what topics are important to its employees. In turn, this knowledge allows HR professionals to tailor their initiatives so that they are met with acceptance and support rather than a lukewarm response or resistance. These qualities also showcase the HR professional as a team player with passion and enthusiasm, which can help to advance their own career.

Maintaining a Network of External Partners
Some of the reasons that companies may elect to outsource their payroll function include the following:

- To free up staff time to allow resources to be more strategic in nature
- To reduce costs
- To improve compliance
- To possibly avoid fines associated with incorrect/late payments or IRS filings
- To have the ability to offer direct deposit of payroll checks to employees

An employer can choose to outsource its entire payroll function or only one or more areas of its payroll function, such as W-2 form printing services. When outsourcing payroll, an employer should select a vendor with an excellent reputation for paying employees on time and providing a high level of customer service.

In an effort not to create additional work, it is important to determine if the vendor's systems are able to effectively integrate with the employer's systems—e.g., time tracking and self-service technologies used to update employees' personal data and payroll-related information. An employer should ensure that the vendor chosen will be able to provide the level of service that the company requires at an affordable cost.

Due to a lack of staff resources, time, or in-house expertise, companies may choose to outsource their employee rewards program to a trusted recognition vendor. Since a vendor can, ultimately, determine the success or failure of a company's rewards program, there are a number of items that an employer should evaluate when entering into this type of relationship.

An exceptional recognition vendor will take the time to learn about a company's culture, business goals, employee rewards needs, and program budget. The recognition vendor should have an offering of high quality awards and be able to accommodate rush orders and unique awards, if needed.

Additionally, world-class customer service is the key to employees receiving timely reward fulfillment and recognition for their efforts and achievements. An employer should be assured that the company will receive correct invoices and accurate reporting from the vendor. The ultimate goal for both the employer and the recognition vendor is to ensure that employees feel valued and remain loyal.

Maintaining a Network of Professional Colleagues

Networking should expand beyond one's own organization to include colleagues across the HR industry. Learning from others who are in the industry allows for the sharing and implementation of new ideas. Often, an HR initiative that works well at one company can translate to another company. This can benefit an individual organization as well as advance the profession of HR as a whole. Networking with leaders outside of one's organization also allows for professional growth and may lead to opportunities for career advancement. In addition, it may allow HR professionals to meet talent they can recruit. Finally, learning more about different aspects of the field can help HR professionals find the best fit. While many HR professionals begin their careers as generalists, they might discover a niche of HR that is a perfect fit for a long-term career.

Relationship Building

Mutual Trust

Developing mutual trust with colleagues promotes a positive work environment. Since many people spend the majority of their time in the workplace, cultivating a friendly, productive work environment benefits everyone involved. Building trust and respect with colleagues takes time but is a wise investment. It can be done by being open and empathetic, supportive and accepting of others, showing gestures of kindness, maintaining a positive attitude as much as possible, and accepting help from colleagues when it is needed. Some colleagues may become good friends even outside of the workplace. However, this is not necessary in order to simply maintain professional trust and respect within the workplace.

Exchanges of Support, Information, and Resources

A two-way rapport involving support, feedback, and information sharing related to work is a positive way to build relationships. HR professionals can build rapport by inquiring about professional projects and asking detailed questions that show genuine interest rather than a perfunctory inquiry. HR professionals can also build reciprocal exchange by offering assistance to others when needed and welcoming guidance from others. Furthermore, HR professionals can share valuable resources with other coworkers (i.e., a new article about emerging trends in the industry). Finally, HR professional can build rapport with others by sharing other aspects of themselves, such as discussing hobbies and welcoming others to share the same. It is important to note that not everyone in the organization will reciprocate someone's desire to build rapport.

Wellbeing of Colleagues

Showing concern for the well-being of colleagues is one way to show others that they are viewed as a whole person, and not just as the job function they perform at work. This can be a wonderful way to build employee morale, develop positive relationships with colleagues, allow employees to feel cared for, and develop a sense of work-life satisfaction. Demonstrating concern for the well-being of colleagues can be simple as asking someone how their current project is going and listening with attention for the duration of their answer. Or, it could look like noticing when a colleague appears to be in a negative mood and asking if anything can be done to help. If it appears that a colleague is struggling with their work environment, workload, a specific project, or the nature of the job, offering to support them to find resolution can have a tremendously positive impact.

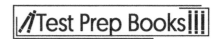

Positive Reputation

Establishing a reputation as an approachable HR professional involves networking, relationship building, and displaying credibility. In addition, HR professionals should advertise to others in the organization that their main organizational goal is to help the personnel effectively carry out their job duties and acknowledge all communication from employees in a friendly and timely manner. HR professionals should always remain open to feedback, questions, and concerns, regardless of whether it is positive or negative in nature. HR staff often have to handle negative situations, such as workplace conflicts or employees who are unhappy about an issue, and maintaining a neutral, composed demeanor in these situations can lend credit to serving as an approachable and objective professional. HR staff should work to respond to situations with logic-driven resolutions and avoid reacting to situations in overly emotional ways or taking complaints personally.

Acknowledging Stakeholder Voices

When developing and implementing HR initiatives, ensuring that all stakeholder voices are heard and acknowledged influences the success of the initiative. If stakeholder opinions are not sought or utilized in the development, implementation, or sustainability of the initiative, the initiative will not integrate into the organization's culture (and can even break stakeholder trust). Before developing an initiative, communication should be made to all stakeholders to show that their voice is of interest and to provide an overview of the initiative topic and goals. This can occur in a focus group, an email, or some other recruitment method. During development and implementation, it is important to directly ask each stakeholder for their opinions on the topic at hand. Stakeholders may be busy or may feel uncomfortable voicing their opinions, so recordkeeping can help HR professionals know that interactions took place. This can involve conducting one-on-one meetings with an email follow-up, noting comments during larger meetings, or compiling email messages or survey responses that show each stakeholder has responded.

Interests of Stakeholders

Most stakeholders will have varied interests. Choosing an initiative that focuses on overlapping interests between stakeholders is a way to provide the most value to the most people for the least resources. Some stakeholders may feel comfortable openly sharing the topics that are valuable to them and the sorts of initiatives they would like to see in the organization. If one or more stakeholders appears less inclined to share their values, it is important to make an effort to objectively understand what may be of value, rather than guessing or assuming. It may help to ask the stakeholder's colleagues, work friends, or superiors what is of value to the stakeholder or their department. Otherwise, assumptions can lead to a biased and unwanted initiative that may face resistance. Stakeholder mapping is a tool that identifies the value an initiative would bring to a stakeholder and the investment and influence a particular stakeholder has in promoting the initiative.

Relationship Management

HR professionals can develop effective and satisfactory working relationships with supervisors and HR leaders by engaging in two-way communication about project expectations, deadlines, needs, and goals. These aspects should be discussed and documented when a work assignment is first received and should take priority during the planning aspect of the project. HR professionals should expect superiors to dedicate time to this planning period. In return, HR professionals should utilize this time to ask questions about the project and bring up any questions so as to best respect the time that leadership is providing. Developing a written project proposal with leadership that outlines the timeline, milestones, resources needed, and concrete dates for deliverables can be a useful method to ensure that both HR staff members and leadership have the same expectations. Once expectations are communicated, HR professionals should make every reasonable effort to deliver results autonomously, without the need for constant leadership follow-up.

<u>Teamwork</u>
Relationships with Team Members
As an HR professional, high levels of human interaction are inherent to the nature of the work. Beyond serving employees within an organization, HR professionals can expect to work in a team within and outside of their department. Team members may be assigned by project rather than personally chosen; therefore, it is important to develop wide-ranging engagement skills that promote positive interactions. HR professionals can build their intrapersonal skills by examining their own strengths and weaknesses through analytical personality tests, and actively working to improve areas of weakness. This can be achieved by utilizing pockets of time to practice intrapersonal skills with colleagues, such as over lunch or during a meeting. Developing emotional intelligence (EI) skills also helps one recognize others' feelings and communication styles, and this information can be used to build better relationships. Maintaining a positive attitude, showing appreciation for support and tasks done well, and avoiding negative talk and behaviors also fosters team cohesiveness.

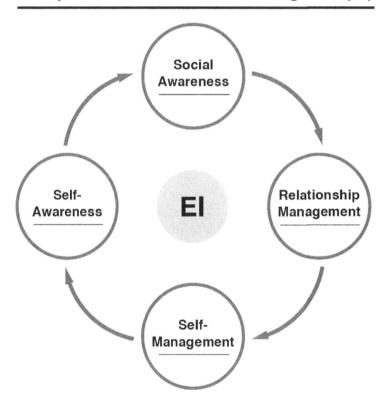

Components of Emotional Intelligence (EI)

Fostering Collaboration
It is also important to create teams that have members with similar professional interests and goals, in order to minimize resistance as the project progresses. However, open communication may be the most crucial component of fostering collaboration among a team. While cultivating open communication lines is a team effort, those who choose to actively model behaviors that lend to open communication are

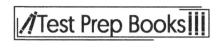

likely to become leaders within the team. Team leaders should promote an encouraging environment that allows all members and stakeholders to voice their opinions and concerns without fearing retribution. This may involve speaking with team members individually, especially if they are quieter or prefer speaking one-on-one. Finally, building relationships outside of the work setting, such as over creative social events, allows team members to get to know one another better. This can allow team members to feel more open and collaborative during the work setting.

Team-Oriented Organizational Culture

A team-oriented organizational culture is one that actively views professional efforts as a group accomplishment. Individualistic terms (such as "I achieved this") are rarely used. Knowing each team member's strengths and leveraging those when establishing project responsibilities promotes effective use of resources. However, implementing cross-training sessions to address weaknesses also helps to establish a strong team unit by allowing members to feel as though they can support one another in times of need. All members should feel accountable for their work in the team. This can be achieved through documenting expectations for each member and discussing how individual objectives integrate to create results. Finally, resources that support team culture (such as physical space in the organization to accommodate groups) should be available.

Developing Teams

An effective HR professional will be able to develop teams that work toward specific goals, as well as develop teams across other departments that can contribute to organizational goals. In addition, HR professionals should be able to contribute as a part of both types of teams. By understanding the goals and interests of other departments in the organization, HR professionals can contribute their strengths in the best way that aligns with company goals. This is strategic behavior that requires cross-departmental communication to cover each area's expertise, budget, and resources available. Often, HR professionals can add value to this practice by providing guidance, resources where needed, and finding areas of similar interest to guide initiatives. Finally, HR professionals can serve as evaluation experts in project teams consisting of HR and non-HR employees to share what practices are working and where opportunities for improvement lie.

Leading a Team

Serving as a team leader can be both professionally and personally rewarding. It allows one to apply theoretical knowledge to practice, serve as a mentor, and build credibility as an HR expert. HR professionals can volunteer to lead projects that interest them. In doing so, HR professionals can expect to learn more about other aspect of business, such as financial operations, process improvement, metric development, and regulatory affairs. HR professionals in a position of leadership should strive to showcase the highest degree of work ethic. Additionally, they should not expect a role of leadership to be an endpoint in their theoretical learning. HR leaders should pursue opportunities to continue their education, stay abreast of emerging trends in the industry, and effectively disseminate new knowledge to their team.

Team Roles

HR professionals are the go-to resource when there are unfulfilled team roles within an organization. If a department is in need of a specific skillset or additional labor resources, they may consult with the HR department to recruit their need. The role may be temporary, contract-based, part-time, full-time, or permanent. Additionally, HR professionals may be able to determine when a department needs to acquire labor resources before the department realizes it. This may occur as a result of poor team performance or from reports of employee dissatisfaction. These needs may be fulfilled immediately. HR professionals should have a pool of potential talent to recruit from. New job postings can take a longer period of time to post, while leveraging talent already available within the organization can be more effective from a time, cost, and training perspective.

Conflict Management
Conflict Resolution
A grievance is a complaint made by an employee that is formally stated in writing. A formal grievance procedure allows management to respond to employee dissatisfaction appropriately through formal communication. Additionally, if a unionized employee is being questioned by management in a situation where a disciplinary action may result, they have the right to union representation during that conversation, which is also known as Weingarten rights (after a famous court case). If that right is violated and the unionized employee is let go, they can be reinstated with back pay.

Every contract will lay out a slightly different process to address potential contract grievances. However, many will follow a similar pattern. The goal is always to remedy the situation before it escalates to the need for arbitration. Typically, employees first discuss the grievance with the union steward and the supervisor. Next, the union steward discusses the grievance with the supervisor's manager and/or the HR manager. The next step is for a committee of union officers to discuss the grievance with the appropriate managers in the company. Then, the national union representative discusses the grievance with designated company executives. If, after this process, the grievance is still not settled, it then goes to arbitration. Grievance arbitration is a process in which a third party is used to settle disputes that arise from conflicting interpretations of a labor contract. Decisions that are reached through this process are enforceable and cannot go to court to be changed.

Underlying Causes of Conflict
HR professionals should be aware of when organizational behavior can lead to interpersonal conflict. Identifying, resolving, and preventing conflict is vital to the HR team, especially one who interacts complex and multi-disciplinary teams. HR professionals should build trust and actively work to prevent and resolve disagreements. The HR professional, together with organizational leadership, can help prevent disruptive conflicts by creating a culture of collaboration, trust, and communication.

Difficult Interactions
HR professionals are often called on to facilitate difficult interactions between employees or senior leaders. The HR professional should be honest when dealing with conflict and relationships and hone their skills at negotiating, persuasion, and diffusion. Honest and open communication lines make conflicts less likely to happen and easier to resolve.

Productive and Task-Related Conflict
Low to moderate levels of conflict among a team is common and supports a healthy level of team performance and decision-making if it is productive and respectful. When conflict resolution becomes necessary, the HR professional must decide the most effective approach to conflict resolution on a case-by-case basis while considering conflict intensity, team relationships, and impact to team motivation.

Five key techniques—differentiated by degrees of active or passive engagement as well as win/lose combination—are commonly used to resolve conflicts.

Approach	Active/Passive	Description
Collaborative	Highly active (win-win)	Assessing the conflict from multiple viewpoints in a shared approach to solve the root cause problem(s).
Forced resolution	Active (win-lose)	The authoritative party (HR or manager) forces the decision upon the team or individuals without feedback.
Compromise	Neutral (neutral)	Both sides of the conflict make concessions to a satisfactory outcome. The root cause of the conflict may not get resolved, and the situation may be win-win or lose-lose.
Accommodation	Passive (lose-win)	By accommodating one party's desires to avoid conflict, the underlying root causes remain for a future day.
Avoid	Very passive (lose-lose)	The conflict resolution is avoided and may increase in severity if ignored further.

Resolving Harmful Conflict

Unfortunately, discrimination exists in some organizations, and sometimes official charges are brought forth. In these cases (and even in cases where the organization is confident that no wrongdoing has taken place), an organization has a decision to make. It can follow the process through the Equal Employment Opportunity Commission (EEOC) and be investigated by a Fair Employment Practices Agency (FEPA) at the local or state level. Or, the organization may choose to settle the charges rather than face an investigation. Employee charges of discrimination must be filed with the EEOC within 180 days of the alleged incident. If probable cause is found, then the EEOC will attempt conciliation, and the employer is required to settle.

The complaint charge is either settled, or the process may move to litigation with either the EEOC or a private court. If the EEOC is not able to determine probable cause, the employee can request a right-to-sue letter after the end of the 180-day period and must file suit in court within ninety days. Finally, if the EEOC does not find probable cause, the employer and employee are both notified. The employee can request a right-to-sue letter, and the EEOC's involvement with the case ends. The employee can then sue the employer in court.

There are a number of factors that can influence a company's decision to settle discrimination charges. One is the financial cost of an investigation. Lawyers and court fees can be a financial strain on a company's finances, not to mention additional obligations if the court rules against the company. There are also the challenges of the investigation itself to consider. If charges are brought to the EEOC or FEPA, a company may be required to devote considerable time and resources to cooperating with the investigation. Thus, an organization may decide that a one-time financial penalty is preferable to an extended period of disruption. A company also faces damage to its reputation.

A long, drawn-out trial and investigation, potentially widely covered on social and traditional media, can do irreparable harm to the company's image. Even in cases where the company is found to be blame-free in the case, the general public may still associate the organization with the charges of discrimination. Therefore, a company may find it is better to accept the financial expense to avoid the potential long-term damage to its reputation. Finally, there are systemic problems to think about. If the company is aware of deeper issues of discrimination among its employees, it may choose to settle charges to avoid having the investigation uncover an ongoing pattern that may be hard to address.

If a company is found guilty of workplace discrimination, it is usually required to allow the individual in question to return to their position within the organization. However, in some instances, the court may rule that the company should require front pay. Front pay is money awarded to an individual in a workplace discrimination case and is generally equal to lost earnings. Front pay is usually required when the position is not available, the employer has not made any effort to address an ongoing issue of discrimination throughout the company, or the employee would be forced to endure a hostile work environment if they were to return to the original position.

Negotiation

Maintaining a Professional Demeanor

Negotiation is a skill used to derive compromises on decisions between two parties. HR professionals are often called upon to fill the negotiator role both internally, between members of the organization, and externally, between a member of the organization and an outside party. One of the most important things to remember during negotiations is to maintain a professional demeanor. The focus should be on the conflict rather than on any personal issues with the parties. A calm, professional demeanor will lead to more effective resolution to discussions.

Negotiating Skills

One of the main areas where HR professionals use their negotiating skills is when negotiating terms of employment with a potential employee. It is important to understand the needs and issues of both parties to reach a satisfactory negotiation.

A company goes through the process of analyzing application forms, prescreening, inviting selected candidates to participate in on-site interviews, and conducting any necessary selection tests and background investigations. Then a contingent job offer is made to the top-rated candidate. This is a conditional job offer and may depend on verification of the individual's identity and right to work (under the Immigration Reform and Control Act) and/or the pending results of a medical exam (if it is proven to be consistent with business necessity and is job related).

The next step in the hiring process is extending an employment offer to the top candidate. This is communicated formally through an offer letter. Because time is of the essence, the offer letter is often sent electronically. A job offer can also be extended over the telephone, which is then followed up with a formal offer letter mailed to the candidate. The following items are typically communicated within the offer letter:

- Basic position information: job title, responsibilities, and reporting structure
- Salary information (including guaranteed or discretionary bonuses and signing bonus, if applicable)
- Information about any deferred compensation (i.e., stock option programs)
- Benefits information (i.e., health insurance, short- and long-term disability insurance, retirement plans, etc.)
- Clauses referencing non-compete agreements
- Acceptance details and deadline

An employment-at-will situation is always presumed if there is no written employment contract.

A candidate will frequently reach out to a prospective employer in an attempt to negotiate some terms of the employment offer, such as salary or vacation time. If the employer does not have room to increase the candidate's base salary, a discussion can take place about other perks that the employer

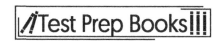

may be willing to offer, such as a set number of work-at-home days per month, additional time off during the Christmas holiday or another typical period of down time, use of a company car, relocation assistance (if applicable), or a signing bonus.

If an employer knows there is room to negotiate a base salary with a candidate, it is important for the employer not to offer the highest possible base salary amount in the offer letter, so there is still room to negotiate. Ultimately, it is imperative that the employer be upfront and honest with a candidate about what is possible in terms of negotiation, to stress the value of the corporate benefits that the candidate would receive, and to openly discuss if there is room for growth in the role itself or in other opportunities within the company over time. These can all be convincing reasons for a candidate who is on the fence to choose to accept the employment offer.

It is also important for an employer to know when it is time to stop negotiations with a candidate. Offering a significantly higher salary than what was initially planned to a candidate risks throwing off the internal pay equity of a team and also reducing morale if the other employees find out.

The offer letter is placed in the candidate's personnel file after they have accepted the position and returned a signed hard copy.

Negotiation- and Bargaining-Related Laws

Collective bargaining is the act of negotiation between an employer and its employees, where a union represents the employees' interests. The NLRA addresses the collective bargaining process and lays out legal definitions for negotiating in good faith, both on the part of the employer and the union. Some examples of negotiating in bad faith include employers making contract proposals directly to employees without working through the union that represents them, employers urging employees to engage in activities that would weaken the union's negotiating power (for example, encouraging employees to decertify the union), and employers making unfavorable changes to workplace terms and conditions (such as pay, hours, and special pay) during the process of collective bargaining. Additional examples of negotiating in bad faith include unions refusing to disclose critical information during the collective bargaining process, unions refusing to reasonably cooperate in the logistics of the negotiation process (for example, time and location), and unions engaging in an unfair labor practice, as defined by the Labor Management Relations Act.

Progression Toward an Agreement

The NLRB helps define and limit the subjects that can be discussed during a collective bargaining negotiation. Illegal subjects cannot be discussed during negotiations and generally involve actions that fall outside the realm of contract negotiations. Examples include hot cargo agreements, security clauses, or any illegal activity on the part of the employer or union. Mandatory subjects must be discussed during negotiations. Mandatory subjects typically involve the basics of employees' working conditions and terms, covering areas such as hours, benefits, pay, and worker safety concerns. Voluntary subjects are topics that parties are permitted to discuss but may choose not to. Voluntary subjects include all issues not covered under the categories of illegal or mandatory subjects.

The goal of collective bargaining is to develop a mutually agreed-upon collective bargaining agreement (CBA). The CBA should address basic terms and conditions including the following:

- Hours, benefits, pay, and workplace safety

- The contract grievance process, which is a clear statement of the procedures to be followed in case of a dispute as well as the actions the organization can take if employees do not follow the terms of the contract

- A zipper clause stating that the CBA has been agreed to and is final. The zipper clause also dictates that any issues not covered in the current contract cannot be discussed until it expires.

Communication

There are also numerous communication strategies that companies can implement. For instance, a brown bag lunch program is an informal meeting including employees and management that is used to discuss company problems. The company-provided meal can help create a relaxed setting for exchanging ideas. Additionally, department meetings allow everyone involved to share solutions to company challenges.

Town hall meetings are formal gatherings for the entire company that are commonly referred to as "all-hands meetings." They tend to focus on sharing information "from the top down" concerning the overall organization. Thus, town hall meetings are not usually designed to allow feedback from employees about smaller detail issues. An *open-door policy* is used to establish a relationship where employees feel comfortable speaking directly with management about problems and suggestions. In essence, an open-door policy enables a supervisor to be a "human suggestion box." There are several potential roadblocks to a successful open-door policy. In certain situations, it can be difficult to create an environment where employees feel comfortable discussing problems in person. In addition, depending on the problem reported, it may not be possible to maintain confidentiality. However, in the right situation, an open-door policy can help companies identify problems quickly without having to wait for a formal meeting.

Management by Walking Around (MBWA), as the name suggests, involves having managers and supervisors physically get out of their offices and interact with employees in person. MBWA allows management to check on employee progress, inquire about potential issues, and gain other feedback without relying on employees to "make the first move" through an open-door policy or online suggestion form. This strategy prevents management from becoming isolated behind a desk and disinterested in employees problems.

Delivering Messages

Necessary Information

The first step of any business interaction is communication. No matter how carefully an idea is researched and planned, it could all fall apart if it isn't properly communicated to those who must carry it out. For this reason, all HR policies must be clearly communicated to employees, particularly when new policies are enacted or when the same HR issues occur often. Communication can occur in a variety of ways, such as through e-mail, individual interviews, or department meetings. In large organizations where executives cannot be directly involved in every detail of every department, it's important to have a clear process for communicating the most crucial management information to executives so they can continue to make informed decisions. The HR team should be careful to present only needed information to executives and other stakeholders.

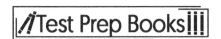

Communication with Audience

There are multiple means that a company can use to communicate with its employees. Each method has its own potential advantages and drawbacks. *Email* makes it easy to get information to a lot of people very quickly. However, this communication method can result in employees suffering from "information overload" from too many emails, making it more likely that important information is overlooked. Also, there is a danger that confidential information may be accidentally communicated to the wrong people.

The *intranet* (internal website and computer network) has the benefit of no risk of important information being accessed by someone outside the organization. Intranets can be very effective at communicating important ongoing information about the company, such as policies and procedures. In addition, companies often store necessary workplace documentation, such as HR-related forms, on an intranet, allowing employees to access that information when they need it. However, if outside parties need information on the intranet, they cannot access it. In addition, intranet communication is often "top-down" and does not allow for feedback from employees. It is also important to note that some intranet systems are not user-friendly, and employees can be discouraged from using them.

Newsletters can provide a variety of information, and have the potential to do so in an engaging, welcoming manner. However, newsletters can be labor-intensive. Since they are relatively infrequent (compared to the ease of sending an email), newsletters are not always useful for communicating urgent or immediate information. In addition, newsletters do not allow for formal two-way communication from employees (although this can be remedied by involving employees in the creation of the newsletter).

Finally, *word-of-mouth* communication can quickly spread information throughout a group of people. However, as in the children's game "Telephone," information can become muddled, misinterpreted, and downright unrecognizable as it is passed from person to person. A manager or supervisor has no control over misinterpretations and misunderstandings that can result from word-of-mouth communication.

Clarity of Message

Strategic communication must be consistent and deliver the message in a way that results in organization-wide understanding. Leadership must be actively involved in daily conversations and be engaged enough to unite people around a common cause. This reduces uncertainty and keeps people focused.

Compelling Arguments

When creating persuasive and compelling arguments, HR professionals strive to sway readers to an opinion or conclusion. To be effective, they must consider the intended audience and use methods of appeal or persuasion to convince that audience. Arguments should be well written and properly researched. They should be presented in a clear, organized, and error-free format so they are easy to understand and follow.

Exchanging Organizational Information

Communicating within the HR Department

Organizational communication must be appropriately delivered by the sender and received by the intended recipient in order to be effective. Communicating within the HR department may be an easier task for the HR professional than communicating with outside departments, as the HR department is likely to house similar values, interests, goals, and methods of communication. The HR department, however, establishes many crucial programs, practices, and policies that affect the operations and culture of the entire organizations. Entities such as employee benefits, ethical handbooks, and company-wide events often originate in the HR department and must be shared across all departments. Effective communication strategies often employ the influence of top leadership, a reliable mode of dissemination that is favored by the majority of recipients, and evaluation practices that focus on utilizing recipient feedback to analyze the overall efficacy of the communication channel. When communicating, HR professionals should also account for informal avenues, such as break room conversation.

Helping Non-HR Managers Communicate HR Issues

Managers are excellent vectors of communication and leveraging the relationships and influence managers have with their team members can be a method of communicating organizational HR issues. In order to effectively utilize this resource, HR professionals should network with managers to build rapport. This also helps HR professionals understand what values are important to the manager. Consequently, HR professionals can illustrate how HR issues impact the manager and their team. Managers may welcome or resist serving as their team's communication channel for HR topics. It is important to make this process easy for the manager to implement, rather than seem like an additional burdensome responsibility. Finally, once this practice is established, HR professionals should remain an open liaison for the manager to return to should any HR-related concerns arise.

Supporting HR and Organizational Initiatives

HR professionals serve as a champion for their department. Their interactions with stakeholders should reflect pride, value, and confidence in the department's work in order to maintain positive engagement from the stakeholders. Stakeholders are more likely to remain resistant if HR personnel display neutral or negative stances about their own department's initiatives. Additionally, previously engaged stakeholders may begin to lose interest or feel a loss of value. If an instance occurs where the HR professional feels they cannot support an initiative in communications with stakeholders, leadership should be notified in order to find a resolution. This may involve changing a component of the initiative, altering the communication process between the department and the stakeholder, or shifting job responsibilities in order to achieve a better fit.

Communicating with Senior HR Leaders

Effective communication with senior HR leaders allows both leadership and subordinate personnel to openly share information related to the organization's HR needs. It allows both groups to communicate in a timely manner. HR personnel should be mindful of leadership's time and commitments. This means limiting unnecessary interaction. Communication should remain concise, professional, and on topic. This can be achieved by specifically addressing why the communication is being made, what is needed from the leader, and if there is a time constraint associated with any of the needs. It can also be beneficial to recognize leadership's preferred method of communication. Finally, HR staff members should take initiative to communicate expected correspondence, such as monthly department reports or deliverables.

Listening

Active Listening

Active listening pushes the listener into an engaged position. Beyond using their sense of hearing, active listeners also use their sense of sight to notice the speaker's body language. Both auditory and visual information are consciously synthesized to perceive what the speaker is trying to communicate. In addition, the listener verbally reflects the information provided by the speaker, and then asks for confirmation that the information was perceived in the way the speaker intended. Only then does the

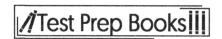

listener formulate a response. Empathetic listening includes placing oneself in the perspective of the speaker and formulating a response based on how the speaker will accept it. HR personnel often face emotionally charged conversations dealing with an employee's job or family. Utilizing active and empathetic listening skills conveys concerns for the employee and helps diffuse tense situations.

Competing Points of View

Competing points of view, when expressed respectfully, are healthy components of communication that often lead to new perspectives, collaboration, innovation, opportunities, and improvements. HR professionals should always remain open to hearing dissenting opinions and actively seek to understand the reasoning behind them. Rather than perceiving dissenting opinions as a personal attack, competing points of view should be welcomed as part of the inherent business process. They should be treated with logic and objective reasoning in order to come to a resolution. While it is impossible to satisfy every employee's opinion, HR initiatives and decisions should be made with trying to achieve the highest percentage of employee satisfaction and the best processes for company productivity in mind.

Clarifying Ambiguity

Ambiguity can cause conflict, affect business processes, and cause distress to employees. Unfortunately, ambiguity is not always preventable due to factors that are often outside of the organization's control. In situations that are within the control of the HR professional, active listening practices are an important component of clear communication. The listener may need to directly state that they are confused and ask specific questions that result in a clear "Yes" or "No" answer. The listener may also need to observe the speaker's body language to determine whether the content is purposely being presented with ambiguity. However, speculation is never a good route to take to determine answers. When possible, directly asking the speaker to clarify is most likely to result in a positive result.

Responding to Stakeholder Communications

Stakeholders are considered as such because they are directly impacted by the actions of the HR department. Therefore, they are highly valuable to the efficacy of HR initiatives. Comments from them should be prioritized. Stakeholder communications can take place in person, in meetings as a group, through email, or through social media. There may not always be time to respond to stakeholder questions, especially if they are unanticipated and come up in person. In these instances, it is important for HR professionals to clearly indicate that they will need to source more information and follow up with the stakeholders. Additionally, it is important to always have the best method of contact information for each stakeholder on hand.

Received Communication

When HR professionals receive communication, they should be able to accurately identify the reason behind it. While motives for a message may not be directly stated, HR professionals can use contextual understanding. However, HR professionals should form this understanding based on objective logic, without making assumptions that are not rooted in fact. When motives for a message cannot be objectively determined, the HR professional should feel confident responding in a way that asks clarifying questions and dispels any ambiguity. Otherwise, assumptions about intention within a message can cause muddled decision-making that can have widespread ramifications.

Soliciting feedback

Soliciting feedback is a crucial component of program evaluation, guiding and sustaining initiatives, and providing valuable customer service. HR professionals serve all units of an organization. Therefore, they should solicit feedback from leadership in all areas, keeping in mind that different leaders may have various needs and values. Learning organizational needs through the lens of each department can increase employee engagement, provide the value that leadership are asking for, and propel operations. HR professionals can solicit feedback from leadership through online evaluation surveys, in-person meetings, and group meetings. They should ask leadership what initiatives are going well and why, and what areas need more support. HR professionals should always leave open communication channels for leadership to propose new projects and ideas. These endeavors highlight the value of a company's HR department.

Global Mindset

Operating in a Diverse Workplace

Culture Differences

A current trend in workforce demographics is increased diversity in terms of gender, race, and ethnicity. In today's world, there are more women in the paid labor force than in the past, and employees that fall within the Asian and "other groups" categories are experiencing birthrates and immigration rates above the national average. This will affect organizations as they work to comply with the immigration laws and associated audits and paper trails. In addition, companies must strive to create cultures that value diversity and promote career development and advancement for women and minorities.

Culture refers to the way a group of people lives, behaves, thinks, and believes. This can include behaviors, traditions, beliefs, opinions, values, religion, spirituality, communication, language, holidays, food, valued possessions, and family dynamics, among other factors. Geography, social status, economic standing, race, ethnicity, and religion can determine culture. Cultural values and differences need to be examined and understood so that HR professionals can work from a place of awareness and respect.

Adapting Behavior

HR professionals must be adept at working with diverse populations. Diversity includes race, culture, gender, ethnicity, sexual orientation, socioeconomic status, religion, and age. As part of the profession, HR will provide services to individuals and families with whom they have no cultural similarity. Thus, it is essential to develop and maintain a level of cultural competence. The first step is to engage in self-awareness and gain an understanding of their own identity, including their belief systems and biases. HR team members should be able to acknowledge differences and communicate to other employees with trust and credibility while demonstrating mutual respect. They should engage in ongoing professional development, both to gain skills and awareness of differing cultural needs, as well as from an ethical standpoint to ensure they are treating everyone fairly and ethically. To navigate different cultural conditions and situations, HR professionals should adapt their behavior to take into consideration cultural variations.

Colleagues from Different Cultures

Organizations are also working to increase the level of employee engagement by connecting colleagues through the formation of employee business resource groups. These also further promote diversity and inclusion efforts. Examples include groups for African-Americans, Asian-Americans, Latino-Americans, individuals with disabilities, LGBT (lesbian, gay, bisexual, and transgender) individuals and allies, former members of the military, multicultural groups, emerging professionals, and women.

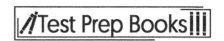

Benefits of a Diverse and Inclusive Workforce
A commitment to diversity and inclusion improves a company's relationship with its employees, customers and clients, and the community. Both a business case and a legal case can be made for engaging in diversity and inclusion initiatives. One common way for companies to improve community outreach and develop a new generation of diverse employees is through an internship program. Having interns can be a win-win for the company and the community. People who are new to their field have a chance to develop their skills and learn more about the business. The company gets to evaluate new talent and build a pool of prospective employees; many companies hire full-time employees from previous interns, and these employees already have a great deal of loyalty to and knowledge about the organization.

Organizations are also working to recruit potential employees via various **diversity groups**, which also help to further promote their inclusion efforts.

Promoting Inclusion
Companies are making more of a conscious effort to value the talents of employees through their career development efforts. To promote a positive organizational culture, it is important to embrace employees' unique qualities. Therefore, it is imperative for management to cultivate a workplace that encourages staff to share their suggestions. Staff must work to identify biases and be aware of how these biases affect their decision-making processes. Employees must make an effort to reach out to team members with whom they have not previously connected, and to find opportunities for diversity and inclusion in their daily work activities.

Cross-Cultural Differences in Customs
Cultural values and beliefs should be researched and acknowledged when working with employees from different cultures. HR professionals can use communication skills to interpret meanings across cultures and understand how cross-cultural differences will affect workplace behavior. Business should be conducted with knowledge of and sensitivity to diversity, including cultural, racial, sexual orientation, economic, and family status. Cultural norms, beliefs, attitudes, and values that are considered to be normal or consistent within a culture, can shape the way culturally diverse employees function in the workplace and should be taken into consideration.

Operating in a Global Environment
Organization's Line of Business
As more organizations begin to operate in the global economy, HR professionals should understand the role of the organization on a macroeconomic level. HR professionals should familiarize themselves with the organization's vision and be able to explain this on a local and global level. They should also be aware of differences within sites located in different regions. These differences may include cultural practices that need to be taken into consideration in the workplace, financial customs, immigration for work laws, demographics and volume of customers, cost and quality of product development, and other process values.

Tailoring HR Initiatives to Local Needs
If an organization has multiple sites, it is likely that each site serves different local needs even if they are located in the same state or country. Sites tend to develop "mini-cultures" of their own that may encompass broad values of the company. For example, a company's new site near a university that mostly hires new graduates may find that their employees value a laid-back work environment more than salary, while an established site with mostly older workers near retirement age may value stable

retirement benefits more than professional development opportunities. HR professionals will need to tailor initiatives based on what certain sites need. This can be accomplished by surveying candidates in order to find out what HR initiatives are considered valuable.

Differences in Regulations

Adhering to an area's regulations and practices is a crucial component of domestic and international organizations. In the United States, for example, organizations must follow federally-mandated industry regulations. However, state-specific environmental, labor, tax, and business laws may affect aspects of the organization's operations. For example, a state that has strict environmental waste regulations may require an organization to spend more resources on high-level waste management, reduction, and recycling initiatives. A site's geographic location can also affect business operations. For example, an organization that has a site near a coastline will need to ensure that HR provides employees with tropical storm or hurricane guidelines. A site that is not near a coastline will not have to dedicate HR initiatives to this type of context.

Global Trends

A wide-reaching HR program can affect employees beyond a specific department or site location. Incorporating evidence-based global trends into HR initiatives increases the likelihood that employees will be positively affected. Current global trends pertaining to HR issues include culture and diversity training, utilizing an international recruitment pool to find top talent, familiarizing organizations with immigration policies that are relevant to international recruitment, supporting workers to embrace and use new technologies, and shifting initiatives to support the work-life values from all backgrounds. Honing in on best practices with a global perspective provides exposure to practices that may not have been noticed otherwise. This offers an opportunity to provide employees with a positive work environment and better benefits while also allowing the organization to progress.

Global and Local Mindset

A global mindset has become a fundamental skill to have in the modern business age. In order to have a global mindset, HR professionals should do the following:

- Cultivate their knowledge of global trends and markets for their organization's industry
- Know the talent pool available by geographical region
- Have the ability to think critically and to think outside of the box
- Understand cultural influences on organizational practices and talent

However, the ability to show respect for individuals from various backgrounds, inquire about the values most important to employees, and understand how the organization influences its environment allows the HR professional to display sensitivity to local issues and needs. While meeting production, service, or financial criteria is often an important end goal for many organizations, assimilation in a new area occurs through showing empathy, establishing trustworthiness, and relationship building. This is crucial for long-term success.

Contradictory Practices

Contradictory and paradoxical practices, policies, and cultural norms are likely to arise when an organization is large. As more people are present in the workplace, more perspectives, backgrounds, opinions, and influences become present. The HR professional can manage this in a few different ways. First, clearly defining organizational expectations in an objective manner that considers a myriad of perspectives can help eliminate some candidates during the hiring process who would not be a good

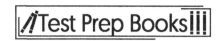

organizational fit. Next, HR professionals should understand that even employees who are an overall excellent company fit may have competing professional values when working with others in a team. In these instances, coaching sessions that focus on how to best compromise on important values to reach a project's end goal can be beneficial. Finally, regularly working with teams to establish aligned values and beliefs by which to operate can be a useful management tool.

Advocating for a Culturally Diverse and Inclusive Workplace

Valuing Diversity and Promoting Inclusion

Inclusive workplaces are hallmarks of progressive organizations that can benefit from the variety of perspective available. Workplaces that are more diverse are associated with better financial gains and higher rates of employee retention, reported satisfaction, and performance. HR professionals can support an organizational culture that values diversity and promotes inclusion by actively recruiting talent with diverse, yet skilled, backgrounds that are otherwise underrepresented in the organization. If this talent pool is not available, HR initiatives can include internship, mentoring, or certification programs for candidates that are interested in careers offered within the organization. Celebrating and sharing the different cultural backgrounds that employees bring can be another way to advocate for a diverse and inclusive workplace. Most importantly, HR professionals should create a culture where employees are able to actively learn about one another as whole individuals. This practice builds relationships, breaks down barriers, and promotes acceptance between employees.

Personal Values of Employees

When informing business decisions and implementing HR programs, practices, and policies, HR professionals should seek to understand their employees' personal lives and family needs. These programs, practices, and policies attract a larger pool of talent, as employees feel their personal values are respected. Finally, based on the demographic makeup of an organization's labor force, HR professionals can focus on offering programs that address cultural sensitivity, such as through focus group trainings, and celebrate diversity within the staff, such as through a shared cultural meal or other community event.

Diversity and Inclusion Programs

Designing and recommending HR programs, practices, and policies that ensure diversity and inclusion is a way to introduce these components into an organization. Auditing them is a way to ensure that the practices are sustainable for the organization. These programs should include auditing all levels of the organization hierarchy for knowledge relating to external and internal inclusivity regulations, in addition to ensuring that the organization's labor force is diverse. If basic diversity and inclusion standards are not met, HR professionals should work with leadership to brainstorm how to recruit diverse talent. HR professionals may also need to note if employees with unique backgrounds enjoy the workplace and feel accepted, or if there is a high turnover rate among groups that are underrepresented. This could indicate that a barrier exists in the work environment.

Equitability of HR Policies

HR professionals should ensure that their department's programs, practices, and policies favor all staff as equally as possible. HR initiatives should not unjustly favor one group over another. One way to manage this is to standardize HR initiatives as much as possible and make them equally accessible to all groups. For example, if an organization offers employee health insurance discounts, they should ensure that all employees have the opportunity to participate and that the program offers something of value for a wide range of interests. Additionally, organizational aspects such as promotions and other merit-based recognition should result from standardized and objective performance reviews. Consistent and respectful HR practices can be implemented by ensuring a diverse group of stakeholders is able to contribute to them as needed. For example, deciding which employee to promote from a team could be handled by a panel of leadership professionals, rather than by a single manager who may carry bias.

Business

Business Acumen

Business and Competitive Awareness

Organization's Inner Workings

HR professionals should be aware of the inner workings of an organization's operations, functions, products, and services. This knowledge influences fundamental aspects of the HR department's purpose, such as talent recruitment and placement, compensation and benefits, and employee conflict resolution. HR professionals can learn about different aspects of the organization in the following ways:

- Reviewing available internal documents and external literature
- Formally meeting with the leaders of different departments
- Informally meeting with colleagues in other departments and discussing their responsibilities
- Seeking feedback from customer service specialists (or even customers themselves)

Finally, HR professionals can research organizations that compete with their own and analyze what processes are performed better. They should especially focus on whether competitors attract top talent for the field, and if so, what opportunities are available that set competitors apart. This can provide information that guide HR-focused process improvement projects.

PESTLE Analysis

A PESTLE analysis is a structured tool that can be used to learn about the political, economic, social, technological, legal, and environmental trends that can influence or impact the goals, processes, or employees of the organization. These trends are often indicators of process improvement needs or some other type of impending change and can help an organization prepare to embrace anticipated opportunities or mitigate potential risks. When planning initiatives, HR departments should examine current aspects of these six categories to guide their work. While organizational resources may include leadership reports, standard operating procedure documents, internal auditing repots, and professional trainings, external resources can be much more varied and a rich source of information about systems that the organization serves. External resources can include entities like newspapers, magazines, conferences, or other avenues that discuss breaking news in the six PESTLE analysis categories. HR professionals should expect to think critically in order to analyze how trends may indirectly impact the organization, as ramifications may not always be obvious.

Organization's Business Operations, Functions, Products, and Services

Internal knowledge of an organization, such as business operations, functions, products, and services, are important drivers of HR solutions and initiatives that impact business decisions. While HR professionals within an organization will often specialize in one area (i.e., compensation and benefits), they should aim to familiarize themselves with all aspects of an organization. HR job responsibilities and initiatives are highly interconnected with other aspects of the organization, and work done in this department has the potential to have a ripple effect through other sections. An HR professional's determination of what talent the organization needs, who is hired to fill these needs, how employees are compensated, how to mitigate personnel liabilities, and so forth should be based off internal

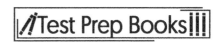

demands of the organization. For example, an HR professional may never directly build on a product that an organization sells; however, they must understand the product well enough to recruit the most qualified engineers for the product.

Industry and PESTLE Trends
Just as internal knowledge of an organization plays a role in developing HR solutions and initiatives, external knowledge from industry news and PESTLE trends also drive HR decision-making. HR professionals should keep abreast of the following:

- Current scholarly literature
- Editorials
- Innovation and trends reporting
- Recommendations of reputable thought leaders in the HR field, as these provide key insights for the future of the industry

Data, information, and trends shared here allow HR professionals to compare internal workings of their organization and determine if it is lagging behind in some way. Additionally, external trends can provide support for internal initiatives. For example, if an HR professional felt that one department's employees were paid below the industry standard, they could use external data to support a proposal for pay raises. Finally, current PESTLE trends can be used to provide information about topics that could indirectly affect the organization.

Business Analysis
Cost-Benefit Analysis
HR professionals should have an understanding of cost-benefit analysis techniques, organizational metrics, and key performance indicators (KPI) in order to illustrate how their department's initiatives provide value. A cost-benefit analysis aims to detail the projected labor, equipment, material, time, and other costs of the initiative in juxtaposition to the expected positive outcome. A cost-benefit analysis that shows that long term benefits will outweigh upfront and sustaining costs is a persuasive tool to use when proposing a new initiative or desiring stakeholder buy-in. HR professionals should understand internal metrics and KPI that are used by the organization to show how proposed objectives and goals are in line with the organization's mission. Typically, cost-benefit analyses should focus on utilizing established internal metrics and KPI when exploring proposed benefits to the organization. This provides a baseline and recognizable measurements of value upon which process improvement projects can operate.

Industries within an Organization
The functions and responsibilities of the HR department affect every other sector of an organization. Therefore, HR professionals should have a basic understanding of the industries that make up an organization. Most organizations have a department dedicated to the following:

- Finances
- Marketing for their products or services
- Sales related to their products and services
- Legal regulations and issues
- Information and technology
- Economic concerns like customer demand
- Sustaining and improving business systems

When developing internal HR programs, practices, and policies, HR professionals have to ensure that they take into account the wide-ranging responsibilities across all of the organization's departments. For example, the technology department may have more access to personal employee information than the sales department; this context is important to note when developing and implementing HR initiatives. While standardizing HR programs is usually the most efficient and objective method, department-specific guidelines can sometimes help provide clarity in unique contexts.

HR Information Systems (HRIS)
Business technology, of which HRIS are a component, manage a great number of operations in organizations today. Business technology can refer to any software, online system, application, or other technological innovation that automates or simplifies jobs within an organization. Based on organization needs, HRIS can perform functions such as the following:

- Creating and managing online employee information systems
- Managing and updating job postings
- Updating candidate profiles over the course of the hiring process
- Managing and storing HR documents and reporting

HRIS can also store data related to the following:

- Employee productivity
- Performance
- Job satisfaction
- Benefit usage
- Historical data

This data can be analyzed through the HRIS to generate reports indicating internal trends, which can pinpoint organizational problems, needs, or successes. Due to the advent of HRIS, it is critical for business professionals to embrace new technologies and continuous learning on the job.

Strategic Alignment
Effective HR and Core Business Functions
Careful planning and goal-setting are essential elements for success in any organization. Strategic planning is an opportunity for an organization to identify the steps and resources needed to get where it wants to go.

First, an organization must start with its objectives, which are often embedded within the mission statement and vision statement. The organization should have a clear idea of its day-to-day operations, as well as what it wants to achieve in the future. An organization may have large-scale, primary goals, as well as various secondary goals that must be accomplished in order to reach the primary goals. Having well-defined objectives gives structure and direction to all of the organization's activities. Measurable goals also help the organization to evaluate its strategic plan's progress and effectiveness. (Did this plan help us to reach our goal? If not, what should we change about our strategic plan?)

Strategic Planning Analysis
The next step of strategic planning is analysis. Internal analysis takes a close look at the organization, its strength and weaknesses, and its assets and liabilities. External environmental analysis takes a wider look at the organization's field or industry in order to identify threats and opportunities. These analyses give strategic planners a better idea of what obstacles they might face when trying to achieve their

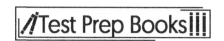

objectives, as well as what factors are on their side. One type of analysis is a *SWOT analysis*, which stands for Strengths, Weaknesses, Opportunities, and Threats. Strengths and weaknesses are internal factors. An organization's strength is anything that gives it an advantage over other organizations, while a weakness is anything that puts it at a disadvantage.

Examples of strengths include highly skilled personnel, state-of-the art technology, or excellent quality control; weaknesses might be poor management structure or lack of manufacturing capabilities. After identifying internal factors, a SWOT analysis next looks at external factors, such as opportunities and threats. In this sense, an opportunity is anything that an organization can use to its advantage, and a threat is anything that might present an obstacle to its objectives. An example of an external opportunity might be a customer need that isn't currently met by any other organizations. An external threat could be a new tariff or trade regulation.

Next, the strategic plan itself finally begins to form. Keeping in mind the strengths and weaknesses of the organization and potential external threats, strategic planners consider the best steps to maximize their strengths, take advantage of industry opportunities, and reach their established objectives. The strategic plan may go through several forms, growing in complexity and nuance before it's ready to be implemented.

Strategic Planning Implementation

Implementing a strategic plan is an especially important step at mid-size or large organizations, where those making the strategic plan may not be the same people carrying it out. It's important that the strategic plan is clearly communicated to and understood by employees at all levels; even the most well-prepared plan can face failure if it's not properly followed by all members of the organization.

Finally, strategic planning isn't simply a one-time activity, but rather an ongoing, recursive process. The final stage of strategic planning is strategy evaluation. Even after the plan has been implemented, it must be routinely monitored to ensure that it's still the best way to achieve the organization's objectives. If the current plan isn't progressing towards goals as expected, the organization must change the strategic plan. Also, as internal and external factors evolve, so must the strategic plan change to address them. Of course, strategic plans are carefully considered and take time to put into place, but they shouldn't be set in stone. Rather, they should be regularly improving to best serve the organization's mission and vision.

If a strategic plan calls for any changes in employee skills and behaviors, it's up to HR management to facilitate these changes by implementing new training and policies. The strategic plan will be executed by employees, so HR professionals ensure that current employees have the necessary skills to carry out the plan. If necessary, HR also recruits new employees as required if the strategic plan calls for a workforce increase.

Consultation

Evaluating Business Challenges

Current and Future HR Challenges

HR professionals should remain aware of current and future HR challenges within their organization. Identifying challenges precedes the development of initiatives and process improvement changes to address them. One indicator that an HR challenge might exist is when certain benchmarks or milestones are not met, such as retaining an established percentage of newly hired employees, or when a high volume of complaints around a certain issue are received. These often serve as flags for further investigation. Additionally, utilizing gap analysis tools to analyze current processes can not only provide insight to where current gaps may exist, but can also help HR professionals note the future impacts that gaps may have. This allows them to address future state issues before they become too problematic. A root cause analysis can also help identify challenges. This tool aims to pinpoint the "why" of an overarching issue, as well as discern which causes are within the organization's capacity for change.

HR-Related Threats and Liabilities

HR-related threats and liabilities refer to events that could produce a negative impact on the organization's ability to recruit, retain, reward, and manage skilled employees who fit with the company's culture and with its professional needs. HR-related threats and liabilities can come internally, such as from high turnover rates, or they can come externally, such as from a lack of qualified applicants in an area. SWOT analyses are comprehensive tools that help to identify both internal and external threats and opportunities. In addition, they can also be used to identify strengths and weaknesses, which can then be utilized to addresses the more challenging aspects of established threats and opportunities. The SWOT matrix is a flexible tool that can be used to analyze small HR-related issues at the individual or departmental level, or larger issues that impact the entire organization.

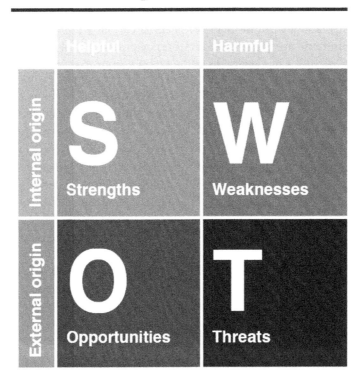

Reviewing HR Programs, Practices, and Policies

HR professionals should be mindful to continuously review HR programs, practices, and policies that are already in place to ensure that these support, rather than impede, business success. It is important to realize that once a program, practice, or policy has been worked on and established, it will still need attention as time passes. Programs, practices, and policies can be affected by employee or leadership response or demand, changes in social or cultural norms, or as the organization's needs change. Over

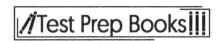

time, they can also become obsolete as technological advances shift the way businesses operate. When reviewing existing HR initiatives, HR professionals should ask themselves if the program, policy, or practice is relevant, accepting of and acceptable to all employees in the organization, is cost-effective, and being performed in the most efficient way. Answers to these questions will determine whether it should be revised or removed.

Designing HR Solutions
Creative Solutions
HR professionals should work in partnership with stakeholders to provide creative, innovative, and effective solutions; stakeholders can provide valuable insight into the type of results they hope to see from a solution, and HR professional can use this information to guide the development of solutions that address business needs. HR professionals can stay current on documented best practices and research by regularly reviewing new studies through search tools like Google Scholar and PubMed (among others), which provide access to peer-reviewed, evidence-based research studies conducted in a variety of fields. A number of full manuscripts are free to access through research search tools, but paid access to an account is a valuable investment. Reputable business publications, such as digital and paper magazines, also publish summaries, thoughtful editorials, and case studies that highlight best practices. HR professionals should have the ability to seek out this information and translate high-level knowledge to serve their specific organization.

Offering Guidance
Non-HR managers are likely to welcome guidance regarding HR practices, compliance, laws, regulation, and ethics, as this information is needed in their role when working with employees but can be a burdensome task to maintain on top of their regular job responsibilities. When HR professionals are able to concisely share this information, how to best apply it to the manager's team, and the value it will ultimately bring to the department, it provides a sense of support. Most non-HR managers will need support with updates to changes that are made within the HR department that affects their team, periodic compliance and ethics trainings for the team, and reminders about laws and regulations that pertain to their team. HR professionals can also provide specialized trainings tailored to the specific needs of a department. HR professionals should remain flexible, open-minded, and ready to provide support when approached by non-HR managers. Additionally, they should be willing to reach out and let non-HR managers know of valuable opportunities available for their teams.

Defining Clear Goals and Outcomes
When setting expectations for a goal, vague, ambiguous, or subjective outcomes should be avoided at all costs. Effective HR solutions deliver an end result that is documented, has clearly defined values for what constitutes as a successful outcome, and is measurable. These parameters allow team members to stay focused on a singular endpoint, establish milestones to track progress, ensure that daily activities are productive rather than a waste of resources, and provides information that can be easily shared should new leadership, customers, or stakeholders become involved. Once a need is defined and a desired outcome that fulfills the need is established, the path between these two points can be designed. Typically, this process involves planning a timeline and budget, determining stakeholders, meeting with stakeholders for insight, and developing new operational processes to implement, study, and sustain (if successful). These activities cannot take place without a clearly defined endpoint in place.

Advising on HR Solutions
HR-Related Solutions
HR-related solutions are often components of larger strategies within non-HR departments of an organization. Therefore, HR professionals have a responsibility to integrate proposed solutions as seamlessly as possible with the processes of the department they are supporting. When working with other departments, HR professionals should ensure that its managers and team members realize the added value of incorporating HR-related solutions into their process, and ensure that the team is not simply following orders from leadership or blindly implementing new procedures. Understanding the value of new solutions is more likely to provide buy-in and acceptance from the team, making implementation an easier task. Then, HR professionals can work with managers to determine what is the best course of guidance for the team. Some managers may prefer that their team receives regular support, such as weekly trainings, while others may prefer something simpler, like a weekly check-in call. This is likely to vary based on the context of the collaboration.

Overcoming Obstacles
Even with diligent planning, unexpected obstacles can arise during the implementation of HR solutions. HR professionals should anticipate the event of unforeseen circumstances, and prepare themselves to view the setback objectively, positively, and with an attitude of resolve. A strong network of business partners within the organization (and even some external mentors) can provide a tremendous support system to rely on for mental brainstorming and guidance, as well as hands-on assistance when an improved process is established. Collaborating with business partners who provide different strengths and experiences can provide innovative solutions to obstacles that the HR professional may not have thought of independently. HR professionals should remember that with creativity and persistence, most obstacles can be overcome. However, once resolution has been reached, reviewing the steps and factors that may have led to the obstacle in the first place can be a vital learning opportunity for future projects.

Providing Follow-Up
Sustainability of a new initiative or solution is a fundamental component of its effectiveness. Solutions that show positive results at first can indicate that it may be a good step in the direction of the desired long-term outcome; however, if positive results cannot be sustained over a lengthy period of time, the solution really has no value, as it is unlikely to lead to long-term results. When implementing a new solution, HR professionals should establish regular milestones at which to review the process with the team that they are supporting. This review can include testing changes between current and baseline (pre-implementation) data, collecting quantitative feedback from stakeholders and employees who are part of the solution, and making revisions where necessary. New solutions are fluid models, and it should be expected that there will be some variance when the solution is applied in a real-world, real-time context.

Defining Goals and Outcomes
Before implementing a new HR solution, the desired goals and outcomes for the solution should be clearly defined using specific, measurable, relevant, and feasible terms. If there are multiple desired goals, each should be broken further into separate entities with these characteristics without overlap that could ultimately cause ambiguity or confusion about the solution's effectiveness. Detailed goals define the strategy by which operational processes are set in place, set expectations for employees regarding their daily job duties, and ensure that the correct skillset is in place to work toward desired results. Therefore, HR professionals should continuously review the standard operating procedures that drive new solutions. This can be achieved through value stream mapping—a tool that deconstructs a

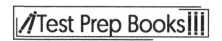

procedure and defines the value each step provides in relation to an established goal. Value stream mapping clearly illustrates when a process step is wasteful or misaligned with goal achievement.

Change Management

Improving HR Programs, Practices, and Policies

In order to remain competitive, adopt industry best practices, and adapt to changing markets, an organization will undergo change at many points. Change might be undertaken to benefit company shareholders and increase the profitability of the company. Change can also occur to reduce costs and increase efficiency. However, especially from an HR perspective, it's important to keep in mind how change affects employees. The truth is that most people don't like change. Also, work force changes in particular (such as outsourcing or downsizing) are certain to be met with employee resistance. Even more minor changes like revised vacation policies may go through an unpopular adjustment period. Change management helps to smooth over these difficulties.

Change is inevitable for any organization, especially in fields affected by global markets and technological innovation. Change management seeks to aid organizations through significant transitions in resource allocation, operations, business processes, or any other large-scale changes. Careful change management helps the organization to function effectively even while undergoing a major evolution.

Promoting Buy-In

How should an organization implement change? The classic 1961 text *The Planning of Change* tackles this question. The book outlines three strategies for managing change: the empirical-rational strategy, the normative-reeducative strategy, and the power-coercive strategy.

The empirical-rational strategy assumes that people are rational and will naturally follow any course that's in their self-interest. Therefore, they are likelier to accept change when they think it will directly benefit them. To implement change in line with this strategy, an organization must either 1) demonstrate the benefit of the change or 2) demonstrate the harm of the status quo (or both). One way of accomplishing this is to incentivize change. For example, a growing company is gaining new employees, but it doesn't want to expand its available parking. The company decides to limit the number of parking spots and encourage public transportation use. Employees are reluctant to give up the freedom to drive, so the company holds an educational seminar about how to save money by using public transportation and also offers monthly reimbursement for employees who use public transportation.

The next approach proposed in *The Planning of Change* is the normative-reeducative strategy. This strategy assumes that people will closely follow social norms and expectations. In order to implement change, it's necessary to first change people's idea of what is socially acceptable. This is the strategy that harnesses the power of advertising. For example, think of anti-tobacco advertising campaigns over the past few decades. Throughout most of the twentieth century, smoking was socially acceptable just about anywhere. However, especially in the 1990s and 2000s, aggressive anti-smoking advertisements attacked the tobacco industry and started anti-smoking education programs for students. The social norm turned *against* smoking in most public places, and now there are more anti-smoking laws than ever before.

Finally, the power-coercive strategy assumes that people are followers who will listen to authority and do as they are told. This approach to change is basically, "My way or the highway!" Where the empirical-rational strategy seeks to demonstrate how change will benefit employees, the power-coercive strategy says that *not* following change will be *harmful* to employees, who might be punished or even fired for failure to comply. For example, a factory undergoes an intense safety inspection and decides to completely renovate its safety standards. Employees now have new dress code requirements. If they don't follow the dress code, they are not allowed to work that day; after the third dress code violation, they will be fired.

Deciding which strategy to employ depends on the overall character of the organization (for example, an otherwise friendly and collegial office might respond negatively to usage of the power-coercive strategy) as well as the importance and sensitivity of the change (the power-coercive strategy would be useful for changes with clear legal or financial liabilities, such as when an organization must follow new government regulations).

Service Excellence
Customer Needs
HR professionals serve a wide range of "customers." These can be leaders within the HR department, non-HR managers in other areas of the organization, specific subsets of employees, stakeholders for specific initiatives, or a single employee in the organization that is experiencing a work issue. Therefore, HR professionals may need to tailor their interactions based on their customer. A leadership team may need a higher level of customer service at a faster pace, whereas a single employee's request may be less detailed or urgent in nature. However, HR professionals must work to show respect and commitment to all customers without directly relaying that another request may be taking higher priority. When working with customers, HR professionals should use active listening skills to identify, define, and clarify the outcome that the customer hopes to achieve. Developing concrete, documented goals that both parties agree on, with a feasible timeline of deliverables, can set appropriate expectations for both parties.

Responding to Customers
In order to show respect and commitment to their customers, HR professionals should be easily accessible for customer needs. Delivering a prompt response to emails and telephone calls, offering established office hours for appointments, and creating a viable around-the-clock contact method (such as an Intranet-based email or departmental hotline number) that is regularly managed are ways to ensure that customers feel their issues will be handled quickly. Timeliness in responding to customer needs is often defined by the organization's internal culture; while a 24 to 48-hour response time is a good guideline for answering general issues, HR professionals should align their practices with the organization's. HR professionals should treat customers with undivided attention, empathy, and support when listening to their request; customers should walk away feeling valued. HR professionals should set expectations when setting a timeline for resolution and adhere strictly to it. When applicable, setbacks should be communicated to the customer as soon as possible.

Risk Management
Risk management is a foundational component of HR practice. Risk management begins with identifying the potential risks in a process. While not all anticipated risks may come to fruition, it is important that HR professionals prepare to mitigate or eliminate all potential setbacks, especially when delivering a solution to a valued customer. In addition to making the process of solution delivery easier, this practice shows commitment to, work ethic for, and care regarding the customer's needs. Risk identification includes mapping the full timeline and processes of customer solutions, then brainstorming with all contributing team members about potential failures, obstacles, or setbacks that could occur at each stage. A potential resolution for each feasible failure, obstacle, or setback should be formulated, taking into consideration all associated time, labor, and resource costs. All team members should clearly

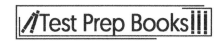

understand their roles and responsibilities in risk management procedures in order to provide cohesive, seamless customer service.

Maintaining Service Quality

Vendors and suppliers contribute largely to the quality of services and products that an organization provides. The relationship between suppliers and organizations that utilize them should be a partnership based on mutual respect, understanding of needs, and clear communication, as each party is a key player in the successes of the other. When HR professionals work with vendors or suppliers, they should establish a reliable communication channel from the very beginning. HR professionals should relay communication focused on the supplier's role, the expectations of the organization, and the desired end result of the partnership. Additionally, HR professionals should solicit information about the supplier's perspective of expectations, ability, and interest to meet the organization's needs, and hopes for meeting goals in collaboration. Maintaining this quality of interaction throughout the relationship can establish an effective and warm business alliance that provide benefits to both while delivering exceptional service quality to the organization's customers.

Analytical Aptitude

Data Advocate
Using Data to Inform Business Decisions

Data that is collected from reliable, relevant, and unbiased sources can provide a tremendous amount of objective information from which evidence-based, logical decisions can be made. Therefore, good data can provide a number of benefits to business and non-profit organizations. Data can provide information about consumer trends, customer preferences, client engagement, and advertising techniques. Internally, data can provide information about employees, including productivity trends and influencers, job satisfaction, the effects of specific performance rewards and benefits, turnover rates, and so forth. This information can then be further explored to develop and implement process changes that affect how business operations take place; how employees are recruited, trained, and rewarded; and how the organization impacts its surrounding environment. A number of data collection, management, and analytical tools that convert raw data into clear trends are available for use. This allows even individuals who have limited background experience using statistical methods to learn how to best leverage information available within the organization.

Evidence

Evidence-based decision-making is a concept that utilizes information grounded in statistically significant data, peer-reviewed scholarly research, the reported values and preferences of stakeholders, and reputable anecdotes of industry experts to drive industrial, organizational, or scientific efforts. When HR professionals make decisions based on evidence, they provide credibility and logical support to their endeavors as they can show that such decisions have had consistent prior success. Published evidence also provides transparency—a vital component of communication that builds trust—as to why certain decisions are made; it can be easily communicated to and shared with employees who are interested. Utilizing established, proven information to drive decisions is also associated with outcomes that are of higher quality and less prone to failures or errors. Finally, evidence-based decision-making allows the process to be a collaboration between leadership personnel, individuals who are affected by the decision, and other stakeholders as necessary. This can be an empowering practice for all parties involved.

Validating HR Programs, Practices, and Policies

Validation as it relates to HR programs, practices, and policies refers to monitoring their step-by-step processes from start to finish to ensure that the same, desired output occurs every time. They should be regularly audited for strict operating parameters, controlled processes, and clearly-defined outcomes within each of these categories. Validation ensures that a program, practice, or policy delivers results in a consistent and predictable manner. Each of these aspects of HR should be reviewed at periodic intervals to ensure that they are still valid, as variable circumstances such as employee changes, regulatory reforms, customer preferences, and environmental factors are inputs which can influence process validity. When process validation is compromised and products or services are not produced in a consistent manner with expected specifications, there is an increased risk to product or service quality. In turn, this can translate to poor customer or stakeholder experiences, failure to meet expected deliverables or metrics, and an overall waste of resources.

Decision Points

Decision points for which large sets of clean, relevant data exist should always draw upon analytics of the data to drive decision-making. Analytics software can analyze large data sets for trends that show how certain decisions have played out historically. Additionally, external studies conducted by universities or other research groups may have published manuscripts that provide relevant evidence to guide a decision. When HR professionals finds themselves at a point where an organizational decision needs to be made, they should first examine if any data or published research exists that could indicate best practices relevant for the decision at hand. If absolutely no data or published research on the topic exists, HR professionals have a responsibility to make an educated hypothesis to drive decision-making, implement a test of change, and gather relevant data along the course of the initiative that can be later analyzed. Outcomes should be shared with colleagues.

Data Gathering

Data Collection

Data collection should procure information that is relevant to the process or outcome of interest. Quality assurance is the process of establishing a relevant, unbiased system of data collection. HR professionals must define data to be collected (i.e., qualitative, quantitative, anecdotal), standardize collection processes and instruments, and train data collectors. Data collection should be free from bias, confounders, unethical practices, and any other influences that skew the reliability and validity of the data. When possible, data collection should be random, objective, and standardized to the greatest extent. HR professionals will need to understand basics of different research design methods (i.e., experimental, observational) in order to select the most appropriate one for the context. Benchmarks and HR metrics should guide the type of research design and data collection utilized. For example, a metric focused on employee satisfaction will collect data differently than a metric focused on employee absenteeism.

Relevant Data

When using data to solve organizational problems and answer questions, HR professionals can expect to come across less than ideal sources. These sources of data may be factually inaccurate, collected with poor research design methods, irrelevant to the interest at hand, biased, or otherwise ineffectual. HR professionals should turn to high quality, reputable sources of data and data synthesis before reviewing it and relevant studies. This can include internal sources, such as a data information or statistics team within the organization whose sole purpose it is to collect and analyze data, or external sources, such as academic journals or industry renowned publications. HR professionals should ensure that data and studies are recent (ideally collected or published within the past three years). Meaningful data should be

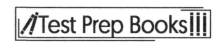

statistically significant, answer questions of interest, and come from a controlled collection mechanism. All sources should be cited and dated to provide complete context.

Data Gathering Methods

Data collection methods will vary based on the type of solution or review process that is needed. Surveys can be used to gather individual feedback from a wide demographic. They can be conducted in person, online, or over the telephone; however, they are subject to interviewer bias, voluntary completion, and low completion rates. Focus groups utilize the services of a skilled facilitator who solicits feedback and opinions about a specific topic from identified stakeholders. Focus groups run the risk of low engagement or facilitator bias. Observational data collection utilizes one data collector to observe a specific context and take notes; however, this is highly subject to bias if the data collector is visible. Other types of data collection can be quantitative, such as records of sales, customer satisfaction scores, number of process failures, or returning clients. If an organization maintains diligent data management practices, these can usually serve as easily accessible sources of information. Permission to use personal information is normally required.

Scanning External Sources

External sources for data relevant to the organization can include reputable news sources, highly regarded digital and paper publications, key note speakers and workshops at industry-specific conferences, discussions at high-level networking events, and data disseminated by successful competitors or colleagues. HR professionals should note any threats or opportunities that may present from competing organizations, demographic changes in the organization's geographic region, new relevant federal or state regulations, consumer trends relevant to their organization's products or services, changes in technology or innovation that could impact the organization's operations and output, potential environmental factors that could affect the organization's productivity, shifts in political climate and social culture, and so on. This type of information can be organized into a PESTLE chart or SWOT analysis to best review the potential impact to the organization. HR professionals should always ensure that external sources are credible and legitimate before utilizing information in any capacity.

Benchmarking HR Initiatives

Benchmarking, or comparing one's initiatives and outcomes against competition, industry established standards, and industry established goals, is one way for HR professionals to determine the efficacy and value of their endeavors. It allows the organization to understand if they are creating, pricing, and delivering products or services appropriately for their targeted consumer base. Benchmarking involves developing internal metrics for key variables that can be translated to provide a comparable review against other top players in the industry. HR professionals should ensure that their benchmarking practices are relevant and comprehensive. For example, if they are trying to compare average compensation for a certain department against a competitor's, they may need to look beyond annual salary to include benefits such as 401(k) matching rates, time off, flexible work culture, and other aspects that employees could view as benefits in order to draw a true comparison between organizations.

Data Analysis
Statistics and Measurement Concepts

While a number of software and online applications exist to make statistical methods and measurement concepts easier to use, HR professionals should maintain a basic working knowledge of these fields in order to create functional research designs and collect clean data that can be interpreted with an end goal in mind. In addition, this knowledge allows HR professionals to understand, accurately communicate, and productively apply trends derived from data sets. HR professionals should feel comfortable inputting data into software and running appropriate analyses to find the information they want. HR professionals should have a basic understanding of concepts such as means, hypothesis testing, regression analysis, and variance analysis in order to compare tests of change from baseline levels. This provides evidence that implemented initiatives are effective and can also provide insight toward certain factors which may be more effective than others.

Misleading Data

Working knowledge of statistics, measurement concepts, and other aspects of data allows the HR professional to understand when data are flawed, misleading, or should otherwise be avoided. When reviewing scholarly literature or articles in which statistics are cited, it is important to read beyond the conclusion drawn by the author. HR professionals should review sampling and methodology text within manuscripts to ensure that the sample of data collected was large enough to be statistically significant, that all influencing bias or confounders were controlled for, and that inappropriate correlations were not drawn from the data. Visual representations of data can also misconstrue the true meaning and should always be examined further. For example, if a bar chart shows a large pay gap between two sets of employees in the same department, it may appear that the organization has an unjust compensation system. However, further investigation could show that one set of employees is entry-level in experience while the other is senior.

Research Practices

HR professionals must be able to apply research of best practices to practical application within their workplace, and test these applications to ensure efficacy. In order to determine which research findings are critical and could make an impact within their organization, HR professionals need to examine the context in which best practices were determined. For example, a case study may correlate the implementation of a worksite wellness program with a reduction in employee health insurance claims. However, if this case study took place in an organization with 100 employees, it may not produce the same correlation in an organization with 1,000 employees. Therefore, HR professionals may need to tailor the methodology for their specific organization if this is an initiative they hope to pursue successfully. Additionally, they will need to establish a basic framework for evaluating new initiatives, including measurements that indicate whether the initiative was implemented successfully produced outcomes in line with established SMART objectives. Finally, HR professionals should be eager to solicit verbal or written anecdotal feedback from key stakeholders.

Maintaining Objectivity

Once data is collected, it can be challenging to maintain objectivity when interpreting it, especially if personal responsibility, time investment, or interest is at stake. Data collection is always subject to confirmation bias by the researcher, which can skew results. Additionally, data analysis does not always reflect trends that an organization hopes to see, and these findings can be indicative of ineffective processes or performance. It can be difficult to maintain an objective, rather than emotional, stance when this occurs. Additionally, negative qualitative data, especially data that come from interviews with personal opinions of stakeholders, can be difficult for interpreters to not view as a personal attack. However, it is vital to treat these contexts as learning opportunities and to reflect upon setbacks that may have occurred to cause such outcomes with nonjudgmental clarity. From there, rational and effective process and performance improvements can take place.

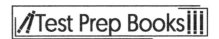

Evidence-Based Decision-Making

Reporting Findings

HR professionals should have clear communication channels with the senior business and HR leaders that they support. Before conducting any type of research into evidence that could support potential initiatives or solutions, HR professionals should have a clear understanding of what desired goals, metrics, objectives, or mission senior leadership hopes to achieve. This knowledge dictates what is considered a "key finding" that should be reported; otherwise, it is possible to communicate irrelevant information that ends up wasting time, energy, labor, and other resources. When relevant key findings need to be communicated, the HR professional should follow the protocol of the established communication channel (i.e., in-person meeting, email report, shared drive update) and relay the finding, the source, and how it impacts the desired outcome in a concise and timely fashion. The HR professional should also include follow-up details or questions for any related next steps.

Different Courses of Action

Even legitimate and reputable research findings will translate slightly differently within different real-world settings. When HR professionals find research or implementation practices that support a proposed initiative, it is likely that aspects of their organization will have an influence on how outcomes are achieved. When possible, HR professionals should map out a course of action that details how new solutions will be implemented, and include all possible derivations of each step based on variables that are unique to the organization. This process may show that certain steps are riskier or more likely to fail within their particular organization; these steps can be eliminated or amended before the new initiative is put into practice. This level of detailed planning may seem labor- and time-intensive, but spending more resources up front often drives down the higher costs that come with risk and failure at later stages in the process.

Data-Driven Knowledge

Data-driven knowledge and evidence-based best practices should drive decision-making, although there may be times where leaders, employees, or other stakeholders may have personal or contextual knowledge that contributes to the final decision. While most organizations will have large quantities of data to access, knowing which data sets to analyze and interpret is a skill in itself. This requires examining individual situations for context, such as the metrics and benchmarks used, the data collection method, and details about the sample pool. Once these questions have been answered for the situation at hand, specific data sets that are relevant to the context can be pulled for analysis. By filtering data for relevance, HR professionals are able to remain focused on information relating to the outcome. However, since as all departments work together to fulfill the overall mission of the organization, HR professionals will likely need to integrate multiple analyses to provide insights that pertain to the organization as a whole.

Best Practices

HR professionals should be mindful to update their departmental programs, practices, and policies to continuously reflect the most current research findings and best practices in order to remain cutting edge and competitive. Otherwise, their organization risks becoming obsolete. As new research emerges or best practices shift, HR professionals should compare evidence-based findings with their organization's current practice to truly assess if any changes would benefit the organization, employees, or other stakeholders. Even small changes made in the organization's best interest, however, can be uncomfortable for those affected. Any changes that are made to programs, practices, and policies should be communicated immediately to employees and other stakeholders; communication should also include that the changes were made in order to reflect the most current research. HR professionals should share with other employees and stakeholders the value and benefits that come from these changes.

Examining Findings in Light of Data

Program evaluation and process evaluation are the primary methods with which to examine HR programs, practices, and policies objectively for effectiveness and sustainability. When developing HR programs, practices, and policies, HR professionals should establish a basic evaluation framework in the planning phase that examines the implementation process. However, this can progress to more detailed investigation if needed or desired by stakeholders (such as a retroactive analysis of certain quality factors or employee satisfaction with specific activities). During evaluation, all relevant data should be reviewed to assess if the processes in question led to the desired outcomes, if SMART values were met, the successful aspects of implementation, the obstacles of implementation, and lessons learned for future endeavors. Necessary changes should be implemented as soon as possible and communicated to stakeholders.

SHRM Technical Knowledge

People

HR Strategic Planning

Systems Thinking
Strategic planning refers to the process of determining where an organization wants to be in the future and the steps it needs to take to get there. There are numerous opportunities for human resources (HR) professionals to take part in strategic planning. Before designing a strategic plan, an organization needs timely and accurate information about its current status, and HR can provide information critical to decision-making. This includes information about the number of employees, office structures, current skill sets and competencies, education and development initiatives, and budget for total rewards plans. Upper management can use these metrics to evaluate what resources the organization currently has and how best to organize them for future success. Because strategic planning tends to be a recursive process rather than a linear one, HR professionals should also engage in ongoing management of this relevant HR data and be able to quickly provide reports on it to management.

Knowledge of Strategy and Goals
In addition to supplying information about the organization's internal status, HR can also help with external evaluation. An important step of strategic planning is conducting a SWOT analysis; as mentioned, SWOT stands for Strengths, Weaknesses, Opportunities, and Threats. While strengths and weaknesses are determined based on internal capabilities, opportunities and threats are determined through environmental scanning—that is, through collecting information about other organizations in the same field or industry. This scanning helps establish where an organization stands in its field and what makes it stand out from other organizations (in other words, its competitive advantage). Environmental scanning also aids in benchmarking, or setting goals, by comparing the organization's performance against others in the industry. By understanding workforce trends, HR professionals can help their organization plan how to attract the necessary talent to achieve its strategic plan and how to use and develop the skills of its current workforce.

Individual Action Plan
Being aware of internal and external conditions helps HR professionals to make appropriate recommendations to organizational leadership throughout the strategic planning process and to align HR's strategy with that of the organization as a whole. For example, if the organization's strategic plan calls for new technology capable of remaining competitive in a rapidly digitizing industry, HR needs to devise an education plan to fill any skill gaps for current employees as well as a recruitment plan to attract employees who have cutting-edge knowledge. In this case, HR might recommend partnering with universities with technology programs that meet the needs of the organization. Such partnerships could involve offering student internships or participating in college job fairs.

Market Position and Competitive Advantage
Because they are often the intermediary between management and employees, HR professionals are uniquely qualified to make recommendations about how business decisions and elements of the strategic plan may affect employees. This means that HR professionals need a strong understanding of the organization's strategy and goals as well as an ongoing awareness of their impact on the workforce. The market position and competitive advantage of the organization must also be considered from a

workforce perspective. The market position of an organization refers to the niche occupied by that organization's brand. The competitive advantage of an organization is what makes them different and stand out among its competitors.

HR professionals have a responsibility to inform leadership personnel of any instances where the strategic plan and workforce considerations could be better balanced. For example, a magazine has recently been bought out by new owners who have a strong business background but little familiarity with journalism. To remain competitive with other publications, management wants to bring in photojournalists who graduated from top universities as permanent staff members rather than using freelance photographers with diverse backgrounds. However, HR may be aware that work experience, rather than classroom experience, is more predictive of a photographer's skills, or that many photographers prefer the freedom and flexibility of fairly-compensated freelance work rather than a restrictive contract with one organization. It is up to HR to first have an objective record of these metrics (for example, to maintain a list of photography awards and recognition, or the results of employee satisfaction surveys) and to then present these findings to leadership during the planning stages.

Opportunities
HR also needs to use the perspective of systems thinking, which means understanding how different units within an organization work together and influence each other. While managers and employees often have a limited view of work in their own areas, HR should maintain a wider understanding of the organization and how its operation depends on input from different areas. This allows HR to make recommendations about how to allocate and organize workforce resources, how to bridge communication and skills gaps, and how to draw from various knowledge and skills bases to achieve strategic goals.

Timely and Accurate Information
HR can also help develop and implement individual action plans that work toward fulfilling the strategic plan. While an organization's strategic plan gives an overall view of its goals for the future and how to achieve them, an individual action plan provides a specifically tailored set of actions for how individual employees can contribute to the goals of the strategic plan. Developing an individual action plan involves understanding the organization's objectives, outlining the steps needed to transition from its current status to its future goals, and breaking down the roles and responsibilities associated with these steps. Because HR professionals have an understanding of the essential functions of each job as well as the available workforce resources, they can provide guidance on how to appropriately distribute tasks throughout the organization. An important aspect of both strategic plans and individual action plans is ongoing evaluation to ensure that progress is being made, so HR can also aid in developing metrics and guidelines for evaluating and revising plans as necessary.

Talent Acquisition

A keystone of HR's value to an organization is talent acquisition. HR professionals assess their organization's needs, design meaningful and relevant job descriptions, and use various recruiting methods and hiring strategies to help build the best team of employees.

Talent Needs of the Organization
To begin with, HR professionals need to know what they are hiring for. This starts with designing job descriptions. A job description provides clear and useful details about the position's responsibilities, duties, and functions, as well as how that work relates to the other positions, departments, and the

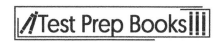

organization as a whole. A well-written job description provides clarity for both employers and employees.

There are several steps to creating a job description. First, a job analysis can be conducted by observing and interviewing employees who are already doing the work, or by collecting data on similar jobs from outside sources. A job analysis will help determine the knowledge, skills, abilities, and experience necessary to perform the job, as well as any physical or environmental factors that might impact job performance. Next, the essential functions of the job, including how frequently they must be performed, should be compiled. An effective job description should also include details regarding the job structure, such as who the worker will be reporting to and whether the job includes any supervisory responsibilities. Other factors to include may be salary or pay grade, level of travel, and required education or other qualifications. HR may decide to expand the scope of an existing job description by adding different tasks (job enlargement) or responsibilities (job enrichment).

Talent Sources and Recruiting Methods

After creating job descriptions, HR personnel must then ensure that advertisements for job openings reach the right candidates. There are several methods for an organization to connect with job seekers. First, the source of hires can be either internal or external, and each has its advantages. Internal sources can be employee referrals, internal moves, and recruiter-sourced hires. Internally-sourced candidates tend to have higher interview-to-hire rates as well as higher retention rates after hiring, thanks in part to the fact that these candidates arrive with a greater familiarity with the organization. This strategy tends to be more cost- and time-effective than externally sourcing candidates, too. For most large organizations, employee referrals are the top source of new hires. External sources include job fairs, campus events, walk-in applicants, and online job boards. One of the strongest advantages of external sourcing is that it aids in building diversity and bringing fresh perspectives to an organization. However, external sources, particularly job sites like Indeed and LinkedIn, can prove costly to HR in subscription fees and in time spent evaluating large numbers of candidates.

Sourcing and Recruiting Employees

These job recruitment websites do indicate, though, that technology plays an increasingly central role in sourcing and recruiting prospective employees. Job posting and recruiting websites generate a huge amount of traffic, helping HR to reach a larger candidate pool. Organizations can also use their own sites and social media channels to drive recruitment. A well-designed careers area of an organization's site can help prospective employees easily find job openings and navigate the application process. This includes making mobile-friendly job applications. Social media can also be used as a branding opportunity to present the company's image as a workplace. For example, there might be video posts where current employees discuss their positions or career paths with the organization, or videos that highlight current projects. These help present the organization's culture, values, and mission while giving prospective hires a sense of where they might fit into the organization. HR professionals can coordinate this strategy along with the organization's communication specialists to ensure consistent branding.

An applicant tracking system (ATS) is another way that technology has entered the recruiting process. ATS refers to a software application that creates an electronic/automated process for things like filling out a job application for candidates, searching and screening applications, referring candidates for positions, and managing applicant information for HR professionals. One major advantage of ATS is that it helps standardize applicant information in a way that is easy to search and compare with other applicants.

Employee Value Proposition (EVP)

Another way to effectively communicate a company's "brand" as an employer is by first researching the employee value proposition, or EVP. The EVP refers to employees' perception of the value of working for an organization, including not only the monetary compensation (i.e., salary and bonuses) and benefits (i.e., paid leave, retirement) but also the intangible benefits. The EVP allows employers to better understand what actually drives employee recruitment and retention, and in turn it helps HR professionals to communicate their organization's value to applicants. Examples of intangible benefits that might be important to employees include schedule flexibility (such as the option to work remotely), office design and comfort, or a sense of contributing to meaningful work. The EVP also allows HR to understand what makes their offerings different from other organizations', giving them a competitive edge at recruiting top talent.

Hiring Methods

In some cases, personality assessments such as the Myers-Briggs Type Indicator can be useful to see if a candidate is a good match for a particular job because it can reveal the person's preferences, ways of thinking, and decision-making style. A person who is classified as introverted on the Myers-Brigg assessment may not do well in a job where they often work in teams.

Reference checks are very important for companies during the hiring process. They can verify if an individual has the necessary skills, knowledge, and experience, based on prior job performance, while also validating an individual's application for employment.

Pre-Employment Screening

Reference checks are an important way for companies to protect themselves from lawsuits or damage to their reputation. For example, negligent hiring takes place when an employer hires an employee, and the employer either knew or should have known that the employee posed a risk to other employees or to customers. An example of negligent hiring is when an employee who is hired as a controller at a financial institution is later charged with embezzlement. The employer (financial institution) can ultimately be found liable for failing to conduct a proper background check on the employee if this employee did have a past history of criminal activity at a previous employer.

Employers can prevent negligent hiring claims by conducting criminal background checks, verifying employment histories and college degrees, checking on past employment gaps, and reaching out to the references of potential employees. In some industries, employers can also perform drug screenings, require physicals, perform credit checks, and check driving records for specific jobs.

A reference list is usually provided upon request, meaning the individual provides the references after a prospective employer asks for them. There are two main types of reference checks a company would need to complete: education and employment.

Education references refer to any certifications, degrees, diplomas, licenses, or any professional documents that can validate an applicant's knowledge and education. Sometimes these reference checks provide employers with specific grades or indicators of performance, but they're mostly made to verify that education was completed.

Employment references refer to feedback from past employers, co-workers, customers, or clients who can verify the individual's professional experience. The main information sought from these reference checks are on-the-job performance feedback from previous employers, as well as the individual's position(s), wages, and duration with past companies.

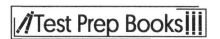

Two less common reference checks are financial and driving history. Financial reference checks relate to credit history and how an individual handles money. These are usually for positions where this would be important, such as in the banking industry, but also in the public services industry (positions in schools, hospitals, or government).

Driving history checks relate to an individual's driving record, and verify that they are able to drive safely. This is necessary for positions where driving is required, including an employee's need to use rental vehicles while conducting company business.

On-Boarding and Orientation Programs

On-boarding, also known as *organizational socialization*, is the process by which new hires obtain the knowledge, skills, and behaviors they need in order to become valued, productive contributors to the company. The success of on-boarding programs is crucial because new employees decide whether or not to stay with an organization during their first six months of work. Therefore, it is important for companies to make an effort to ensure that new employees feel supported and get adjusted to the social and performance aspects of their new roles quickly.

On-boarding can begin by having an employee's new managers and teammates reach out to them via email to welcome them even prior to their formal start date with the company. On the first day at work, the manager can introduce the new hire to the team member who will serve as their "buddy," to whom they can feel free to go to with any questions or concerns. Taking the new hire out of the office for a welcome lunch on the first day with a couple of staff members is always a nice gesture, as well as ensuring they have lunch partners for the first couple of weeks on the job.

Other aspects of successful on-boarding programs involve the new hire's manager scheduling meet-and-greet appointments to learn more about the roles that each teammate in the department plays and how the new hire will interact with them. These types of meetings can also be scheduled with individuals throughout the company who have key relationships with the department, such as members of IT, Marketing, Human Resources, etc. Additionally, providing the new hire with an on-boarding schedule that involves various team members who will train on various processes and applications can be helpful. To provide clear expectations, it is also important for the manager to meet with the new hire to discuss their performance and development plans for the first three months. Finally, to help a new hire build contacts throughout the company, it is imperative to get them involved in a cross-functional project.

There is no set time limit for on-boarding programs, but at some companies, these programs can last throughout an employee's first year.

Orientation is part of the administrative, transactional aspect of the overall on-boarding process, focused on having employees complete the following types of tasks within their first couple of days of employment:

- Have their photograph taken to create their corporate ID badge
- Take a tour of the building in which they will be working on a daily basis
- Complete I-9 verification
- Register for health care and other company benefits
- Participate in training on the company's time entry system
- Gain an understanding of the payroll process
- Review the company's history, vision, and mission, along with key policies and procedures
- Receive and sign off on a copy of their formal job description

It is also important to note that the workspace for new hires is often set up in advance with the necessary office supplies and a welcome note or card to ensure as smooth of a transition as possible.

Job Descriptions
Beyond simply attracting applicants, HR professionals are also responsible for evaluating and selecting the best hires. Again, an ATS can assist HR in searching and comparing applicant information to narrow down a list of candidates who most closely match the requirements of the job description. This also ties back to designing a job description that aligns with the organization's actual needs. Because it is not uncommon for applicants to exaggerate or even lie on resumes, it is important to conduct due diligence in confirming things like past employment and education history. Also, many organizations conduct pre-employment tests to evaluate an employee's characteristics and whether they match the organization's culture. However, hiring managers should beware of exercising unconscious bias in interviews by relying on difficult-to-define qualities like "good fit" or "matches the team"—this may lead to qualified candidates being rejected simply because of differences in age, gender, race, etc. Rather, hiring managers should rely on meaningful indicators like past job performance, personality, working style, and other qualifications.

Employee Engagement and Retention

After taking the necessary time to recruit the right employees, it is important for companies to work to retain them. Employee turnover has high costs associated with it—lost time and lost productivity. There are many different ways that companies attempt to retain staff, and not one method works for all employees. For example, some employers feel that offering a competitive benefits package that includes health care, a retirement program, and life insurance is the best way to retain employees. However, sometimes low or no cost options that improve employees' work/life balance, such as flextime, telecommuting, and allowing employees to wear jeans to work every day (unless they are attending customer-facing meetings) are the best way to go. In addition, staff can be grateful for, and tend to stay longer at, workplaces that provide perks that are meaningful to them, such as on-site childcare, tuition reimbursement, dry cleaning pickup, and free doughnuts on Fridays.

Employers can stay in touch with how their employees are feeling about the work environment by conducting what is known as *stay interviews*. During these interviews, topics including why employees came to work for the employer, why the employees have stayed at the employer, what would make the employees consider leaving, and what the employees would want to see changed are discussed. This allows management to make necessary improvements before they find themselves conducting exit interviews.

Finally, in a workplace that is serious about retention, open communication between management and employees about the company's mission and future goals is key. It is also important for management to show concern for employees' continued development and to promote from within when possible.

Surveys of Employee Attitudes and Culture
Employee surveys are a tool that management can use to determine how HR programs are being received by staff, to uncover problem areas in the organization, and to reveal employee preferences or needs. These surveys can be distributed as attitude surveys with the goal of measuring employees' job satisfaction or as opinion surveys with the goal of gathering data on specific issues. It is important that employees know they will be guaranteed anonymity in return for their participation in the survey so they will, in turn, be as honest as possible on how they view their jobs, supervisors, coworkers, organizational policies, etc. This type of employee input provides management with data on the

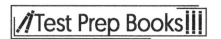

"retention climate" in the company. Collecting this data is extremely important to an organization's retention measurement efforts. It is important for management to share the results of the survey with employees, even if the feedback is negative. By continuing to administer employee surveys annually or at set intervals, management can measure improvements in responses over time.

HR and Organizational Programs

Recognition programs are used to promote a positive organizational culture by recognizing individual employees for the work they have completed. Recognition programs include personalized thank you notes for a job well done, company merchandise, and gift cards. For example, there are peer-to-peer recognition programs in place, where one employee can send a personalized thank you eCard to another employee for a job well done. In that same system, managers can acknowledge an employee for extra effort on a project by assigning a number of recognition points along with sending an eCard. Once an employee accumulates a certain number of recognition points, they can cash in the points to receive either a gift card or an item from the company store.

Program Opportunities

Companies can use special events as a way to engage employees and promote a positive organizational culture. These events can involve managers serving lunch to employees during customer service appreciation week, organizing monthly employee events such as an ice cream social on a random Friday afternoon or an after-work happy hour, or planning an annual holiday party or company picnic for employees to enjoy with their coworkers and their families at a local amusement park. Additionally, these events can incorporate an element of community service, such as employees getting together to assist a local organization (like an animal shelter or a food bank) during a "day of caring" event. Employee wellness can also be factored into these special events by scheduling yoga classes onsite for employees to participate in, or by providing monthly chair massages in a conference room at a reduced price for staff.

More companies are trying to explicitly recognize, embrace, and value the talents, backgrounds, and ideas of employees through their recruitment, training, and career development efforts. They are also working to increase the level of employee engagement by connecting colleagues across locations, generations, and functions through the formation of employee business resource groups, which further promote diversity and inclusion efforts.

Turnover and Retention Metrics

Turnover rate is the percentage of employees who leave the workforce during a period of time, typically during a calendar or fiscal year. Turnover rate is calculated by simply taking the number of employees who exited the company during the year, dividing it by the average number of employees during the year, and then multiplying that amount by 100. A high turnover rate can be a costly problem for a company and can have a negative effect on many aspects of organizational performance, such as productivity, safety, and financial performance.

Performance Management

Performance management can aid in employee retention. By establishing clear expectations for employee performance and providing frequent feedback to employees, employers can foster development of the skills and competencies necessary to achieve their goals. Meanwhile, employees can feel valued and can make progress on their own career goals. For this reason, strong employee engagement, including engagement through performance management, is tied to lower employee turnover. The elements of performance management include goal setting (related to achieving the functions of the job description, accomplishing a project, or developing certain behaviors), performance review (an assessment of how an employee has progressed toward achieving these goals, including strengths and weaknesses), and a performance improvement plan (PIP)—a plan that shows how the employer and employee can work together to progress in goal achievement.

Performance Management Systems

Although performance management is carried out by stakeholders throughout the organization, rather that only HR, it is up to HR professionals to help others understand how to use the organization's performance management system. Training and guidance from HR can help shape a performance management system that is consistent, fair, and reliable. Because many organizations include self-assessments in which employees rate their own performance, it may be necessary to train not only supervisors but also supervised employees how to use the organization's rating system. While performance management systems may vary between organizations, there are some common factors to keep in mind. First, stakeholders should have a consistent understanding of what the performance goals are for a particular position. Effective goals are summarized in the acronym SMART, which stands for specific, measurable, actionable, realistic, and timely. Also, rather than having a simple "yes/no" or "meets/does not meet expectations" assessment, supervisors are encouraged to offer assessments that recognize and foster high achievement in employees.

Satisfactory Employee Performance and Performance Management

Indeed, the purpose of performance management is not to punish or chastise employees, but to foster a culture of constant improvement and development. HR can help coach supervisors on building positive relationships with their employees, particularly when it comes to the performance review process. First, supervisors should remember to keep performance reviews focused on the future rather than on the past; for example, instead of bringing up mistakes or problems the employee has experienced during the review period, the supervisor could focus on the steps needed to avoid encountering those same problems moving forward. It is important to view coaching as an ongoing development process, rather than simply a negative reaction when something goes wrong. Also, HR professionals and supervisors can work together to establish and communicate the link between performance and rewards (if certain goals are achieved over a performance period, how will the employee be rewarded?). In this way employees can view the assessment as a chance to be recognized for their accomplishments. Indeed, communication and frequent feedback from all parties are the keys to building strong workplace relationships.

Measuring Effectiveness of Performance Management Systems

There are several outcomes of the performance management process, including:

- Disciplinary actions that can be taken for underperforming employees
- Pay increases and incentive rewards
- Opportunities for employee advancement and promotions
- Employee development plans
- Career/succession planning

Performance management gives organizations the opportunity to identify the most suitable jobs for the most qualified people. After analyzing the results of goal setting, if certain individuals possess skill sets that indicate that they would be more productive in other areas of the business, then this phase allows those transitions, or transfer assignments, to occur. Furthermore, promotions can be used to reinforce positive behavior. Another strategic use of promotions is to maximize each individual's utility by

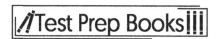

encouraging them to take positions that they may not have otherwise been interested in. These types of employment moves should be properly documented through the employees' performance appraisals to ensure that the organization is protected should any legal concerns arise.

Learning and Development

Gaps in Competencies

One essential way that HR participates in its organization's budget is by projecting human capital needs. Particularly when a new strategic plan is implemented, HR must understand how human capital requirements will evolve as a result. HR should be proactive, rather than reactive, when it comes to human capital needs (that is, it is important to anticipate workforce needs *before* they occur). In order to do so, HR professionals must have a clear understanding of the organization's current workforce and its skills and competencies (How many employees do we have? What is their experience level? What tasks are they capable of performing?). Next, they must look at the activities involved in carrying out the strategic plan and determine the activities' workforce requirements (How many employees are needed for this activity? What skills are required to perform this task?). Finally, HR compares the two, identifies any gaps (Do we have enough employees for this task? Do they have the necessary skills?), and works to fill those gaps by providing additional training, reassigning staff, or recruiting new employees.

Of course, training and recruiting cost money, so these human capital projections also aid budgeting for any new plans and projects. In anticipating workforce needs, HR helps managers get a more complete view of a project's budget requirements and avoid any surprise costs later.

Individual Development Plans (IDPs)

As the name suggests, an individual development plan (IDP) is tailored to individual employees, helping them understand their development goals and support needed to reach those goals. A well-designed IDP fosters professional development, shapes an organization's culture, and improves employee retention. An IDP grants an employee the power to direct their own learning while still giving context to what they will gain from their development and how their new knowledge will have immediate application and benefit in the workplace. HR can work with supervisors to identify ways to support IDPs such as by offering workshops, on-the-job training, online classes, or other development resources. IDPs can also be tailored to employees' individual learning styles, and they should be evaluated and modified as progress is made on gaining new skills. Overall, IDPs give employees a higher stake in their own development goals while also allowing the organization to foster essential skills for success.

Closing Gaps in Employees' Competencies and Skills

Learning and development programs can also help to close critical skills gaps for employees. For example, a science research center may have a team staffed with top specialists in engineering; however, when it comes to publishing research articles, they have difficulty with presenting their work in writing. This is a skill gap that prevents them from accomplishing their project goals. In some cases, it may be possible to hire new employees or contract out work. However, when it is more cost-effective to train current employees, HR should explore opportunities for skill development. This involves identifying the gap, establishing whether the skill is essential to the job function, and developing a learning strategy that also communicates the importance of the skill to employees. Again, investing in employees drives employee satisfaction and retention.

It can also help build an organization's culture and brand. In another instance, a retail store might have a specific vision for how it expects employees to interact with customers. While hiring managers have identified qualified and competent job candidates, they are having difficulty finding candidates who are already familiar with the store's service culture. Rather than expending resources to find candidates who come with this skill, it might be more effective to hire candidates with a strong learning potential and then incorporate these skills training into the position.

ADDIE Model

The most commonly used framework that organizations and training developers use to enhance human resource development programs is the ADDIE model. Each step in the multi-dimensional and adaptable ADDIE model is intended to bolster programs that bolster systems of personal development and training. As an acronym, each step characterizes a different phase: A denotes the Analysis phase, D denotes Design, D denotes Development, I denotes Implementation, and E denotes Evaluation. The ADDIE model is not limited to strictly training programs and is widely accepted by educators, instructional designers, industry leaders, and the U.S. Armed Forces. ADDIE is noted for being highly applicable to any project and for its flexibility in practice.

The initial phase of ADDIE is analysis wherein the course and primary learning objectives are evaluated and determined. The trainees' potential and aptitude for the subject are assessed and determined, along with any significant learning limitations. The timeline for project completion is also determined during this initial phase.

The second phase in the ADDIE model is the design phase where the principal architecture of the training course is constructed. Aside from just learning objectives, relevant subject matter is gathered and determined while exercises are planned. After these are considered, a lesson plan must be carefully fashioned that synthesizes the objectives of the course and the specific abilities or constraints of the subject.

The third phase in the ADDIE model is the development phase. After the design of the course is constructed, its methodological efficacy needs to be tested. Creating the content that is drafted in the previous phase performs this test. Development encompasses creating and distributing tangible tools or courseware for successfully engaging the program. For instance, graphics, handouts, or any other learning technologies would be circulated.

The fourth phase in the ADDIE model is the implementation phase. The implementation phase consists of establishing a procedure for training both facilitators and learners. Facilitators should continuously amend the course in order to maximize efficiency. After extensive analysis, the course should be amended and redesigned accordingly. For learners, this phase embodies preparation and gaining increasing familiarity with the course and content. In addition, learners should also develop an acute knowledge of the course materials and tools.

The fifth phase of the ADDIE model is the evaluation phase. Although the course is constantly being evaluated, this is a designated phase that empirically studies the efficiency and productivity of the course and material. Some of the questions that may be asked include: Were the course's primary objectives met? Were the learners' specified goals achieved? What (if any) were the most arduous aspects of the course or its materials, and how could any problems be appropriately addressed?

Promoting Knowledge Transfer

While many learning and development opportunities come from HR, supervisors, and other organizational leaders, it is also important to facilitate chances for learning between coworkers. When it comes to knowledge-sharing, a popular concept is "silo-busting"—that is, breaking down the separation between disparate departments and encouraging communication between offices. HR professionals can

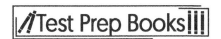

also take a role in designing coaching or mentoring programs. Mentoring programs match less experienced (often entry-level) employees with more experienced employees who can help integrate them into the organization.

Coaching also involves a transfer of skills between employees, but it can take place later in an employee's career and usually involves enhancing performance in one particular area. Finally, information and skills can be transmitted between employees (particularly from outgoing to incoming employees). Such knowledge transfer is part of succession planning, which involves preparing the next generation of workers to acquire the essential knowledge, skills, and relationships of a job position, as well as to adapt to the new demands of the field. In order to ensure seamless knowledge transfer, it is important to identify any current skill gaps between newer employees and more experienced ones, and to anticipate future gaps in institutional knowledge that might occur when those experienced employees leave the organization.

Total Rewards

Compensation and Benefits Data

In addition to attracting talent, HR professionals are also responsible for retaining talent. This can be achieved through management of total rewards plans, which include things like monetary compensation (salary, bonus, etc.) employee benefits (healthcare, vacation time, retirement, etc.), and personal growth (on- or off-the-job training, career development, etc.). Total rewards plans demand constant reevaluation to ensure that they are providing the most appropriate plan to employees—one that is in line with the organization's philosophy and comparable to those of competitor organizations. One way HR professionals can keep their total rewards plans current and competitive is by referencing total remuneration surveys, which provide market data on compensation and benefits plans from other organizations.

HR professionals can use this data for benchmarking purposes when evaluating their own organization's total rewards plans, making adjustments as necessary. In addition to consulting remuneration surveys, HR professionals also need to consider the EVP, which refers to how employees perceive the value of the organization's total rewards plan and other intangible benefits from working for the organization. EVP can be assessed by conducting internal employee surveys. HR can also conduct stay interviews, or interviews with employees to determine which factors drive retention and how they can be improved. If employees know that their input is considered in the design of their total rewards plan, they may be more likely to support the project.

The supply pool from which employers attract new hires is called the labor market. Employers must identify the labor markets (i.e., geographic, global, industry-specific, educational, and technical) from which they can recruit candidates based on the jobs that need to be filled, especially for key positions.

An analysis of labor markets during workforce planning has a number of benefits, including:

- Gaining an understanding of the unemployment rate
- Identifying where employers are competing for labor
- Researching salaries paid for certain positions
- Identifying employment trends in a particular industry

The main federal institution that measures and collates nationwide employment data is the Bureau of Labor Statistics within the US Department of Labor. This department has separate state departments that also report state-specific data. Among the data collected are market activity, average salaries, basic job duties, and working conditions.

Total Rewards Plans

Because total rewards plans represent a significant expense to any organization, they can be viewed from a return on investment (ROI) perspective—focusing on how to maximize the returns (employee satisfaction, retention, and value) from the investment (i.e., the rewards). HR professionals must ensure that plans are designed appropriately to meet the needs of employees by first assessing which benefits programs employees place the most value on as well as which benefits align with the organization's philosophy and business strategy. For example, in a sales division, annual bonuses might be aligned with employees' sales performances. Before implementing any performance-based rewards, though, the performance measures that will be appraised must first be clearly defined. In an organization that values internal advancement, an important benefit might be free employee training and educational opportunities. In designing and implementing monetary compensation rewards in particular, HR begins with a clear description of a job (its responsibilities, knowledge, and skills) and then determines the internal and external value of that position. Salary, raises, bonuses, separation, and severance pay should all be considered when designing a monetary compensation system.

Compensation and Benefits Laws

A company's total rewards strategy is used to attract, motivate, engage, and retain employees through compensation packages made up of pay, incentives, and benefits. This rewards system should be aligned with the company's mission, strategy, and corporate culture, and it must comply with all applicable laws and regulations.

Davis Bacon Act (1931)

This piece of legislation applies to contractors and subcontractors working on federally funded contracts in excess of $2,000. The act requires employers to pay all laborers at construction sites—associated with such contracts—at least the prevailing wage and fringe benefits that individuals working in similar projects in the area are receiving. Employers who fail to comply with this act risk losing their federal contracts and the ability to receive new federal contracts for a period of up to three years.

Walsh-Healey Public Contracts Act (1936)

This federal law applies to contractors working on federally funded supply contracts in excess of $10,000. Under this act, employers associated with such contracts must pay employees at least the federal *minimum wage*—currently set at $7.25 per hour—and overtime pay. Overtime pay is calculated as one and one-half times an individual's regular rate of pay for any hours worked in excess of eight hours in a single workday or any hours worked in excess of forty hours in a single workweek.

The employment of youth under the age of sixteen and convicts is also prohibited under this legislation. Additionally, the act calls for job safety and sanitation protocols. Failure to comply with this law may result in the withholding of contract payments to reimburse any underpayment of wages or overtime pay due to employees. There is also a penalty of $10 per person per day for any employer who is found to be employing youth or convicts, along with possible additional legal action. Employers may ultimately face losing their federal contracts and the ability to receive new federal contracts for a period of up to three years for non-compliance.

Fair Labor Standards Act (1938)

The Fair Labor Standards Act (FLSA) is also known as the *Wage and Hour Law*, and it covers most governmental agencies and private-sector employers. This includes companies with employees involved

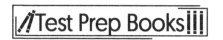

in interstate commerce, employers with $500,000 or more in annual sales or business completed, and organizations caring for the physically and mentally ill, the aging population, and educational institutions. The act does not apply to employers working in industries who are covered under other labor standards that are specific to those industries. The law was put into effect to establish employee classification and to regulate minimum wage, overtime pay, on-call pay, associated recordkeeping, and child labor, as discussed in detail below.

Employee Classification
The FLSA requires employers to classify all employee positions into two categories, exempt and non-exempt, depending on the type of work the employees do, the amount of money the employees are paid, and how the employees are paid.

- *Non-exempt* positions fall directly under the FLSA regulations. These employees earn a salary of less than $23,600 per year or $455 per week. Non-exempt positions do not involve the supervision of others or the use of independent judgment; they also do not require specialized education.

- *Exempt* positions do not fall under the FLSA regulations. These employees are paid on a salary basis and spend more than 50 percent of their work time performing exempt duties. Exempt level duties fall into three main categories: executive, professional, and administrative.

  o *Executive employees* are responsible for directing the work of two or more full-time employees. Management is a key focus of their role, and they have direct input into the job status of other employees, such as hiring and firing.

  o *Professional employees* can fall into the category of learned professionals, meaning their positions require knowledge in a specific field of science or learning, such as doctors, lawyers, engineers, and accountants. Professional employees can also fall into the category of creative professionals, meaning their positions involve the invention, imagination, originality, or talent in a recognized field of artistic or creative endeavor—e.g., writing, acting, and graphic arts.

  o *Administrative employees* are responsible for exercising discretion and judgment with respect to matters of significance, which can be directly related to management of the general business or in dealings with the customers of the business.

Minimum Wage
Under this act, employers must pay nonexempt employees at least the federal minimum wage. However, if the state in which an employee works pays a higher minimum wage than the current federal minimum wage, the employee will receive the higher state minimum wage. Additionally, employers must pay $2.13 per hour in direct wages to employees who receive tips as their form of salary. The total of the employer's wage and the employee's tips should then equal the minimum wage.

Overtime
Under this law, employers must pay nonexempt employees overtime pay at the rate of one and one-half times an individual's regular rate of pay for any hours worked in excess of forty hours of work in a single workweek. The act does not require that overtime be paid to employees for work performed on Saturdays, Sundays, or paid time-off days, such as sick days, vacation days, or holidays. Overtime pay that is earned in a specific workweek must be paid out in the pay period during which it was earned, instead of averaging overtime hours across multiple workweeks.

On-Call

Under this act, employers must pay nonexempt employees their regular rate of pay for *on-call time*—the time that they are required to remain at the employer's place of business while waiting to engage in work as required by their employer. An example of this would be medical employees who are asked by their employer to wait to engage in work in an on-call room at a hospital. Since they are not free to leave the hospital and are expected to work if called upon, they must be compensated for their time spent on-call.

Record Keeping

Under this law, employers are required to keep specific records as defined by the Department of Labor. In regard to nonexempt employees, employers must specifically keep track of the following personal information for an employee:

- Name, address, occupation, gender, and date of birth, if employee is under the age of nineteen
- Day and time of the start of the workweek
- Total hours an employee worked during each workday and for the workweek as a whole
- Employee's daily and weekly straight-time earnings
- Employee's regular hourly rate of pay for weeks when any overtime is worked
- Total overtime pay for the workweek
- Any additions or deductions to an employee's wages
- Total wages paid to an employee during each pay period
- Date the employee received payment for work performed and the pay period that payment covered

Child Labor

This legislation also put provisions in place—commonly referred to as *child labor laws*—to ensure that working youth were guaranteed a safe workplace environment that did not pose a risk to their overall health and wellbeing or prevent them from pursuing additional educational opportunities.

Youth under the age of fourteen are only allowed to perform such functions as newspaper delivery, babysitting, acting, and assisting in their parents' business, as long as that business is non-hazardous in nature. They may also perform non-hazardous agricultural work on a farm that employs one of their parents. Youth ages fourteen and fifteen are allowed to perform non-hazardous work, such as positions in retail, some yard work, and some kitchen and food service work. Youth in this age group are not allowed to work more than three hours a day or eighteen hours a week when school is in session. However, when school is not in session, these youth can work up to eight hours a day and up to forty hours a week.

Youth in this age group do have restricted work hours of 7:00 am to 7:00 pm during the school year. The evening time is extended to 9:00 pm during the period of June 1 through Labor Day. Youth ages sixteen and seventeen can work unlimited hours. However, youth in this age group are still prohibited from working on hazardous jobs, such as operating trash binders, shredders, or material-handling equipment.

Age	Legal Requirements
Under 14	Children under fourteen years of age may not be employed in non-agricultural occupations covered by the FLSA, including food service establishments. Permissible employment for such children is limited to work that is exempt from the FLSA (such as delivering newspapers to the consumer and acting). Children may also perform work not covered by the FLSA such as completing minor chores around private homes or casual babysitting.
14 & 15	Fourteen and fifteen-year-olds may be employed in restaurants and quick-service establishments outside school hours in a variety of jobs for limited periods of time and under specified conditions. Child Labor Regulations No. 3, 29 C.F.R. 570, Subpart C, limits both the time of day and number of hours this age group may be employed as well as the types of jobs they may perform. **Hours and times of day standards for the employment of 14- and 15-year-olds:** • outside school hours; school hours are determined by the local public school in the area the minor is residing while employed; • no more than three hours on a school day, including Fridays; • no more than eight hours on a non-school day; • no more than eighteen hours during a week when school is in session; • no more than forty hours during a week when school is not in session; • between 7 a.m. and 7 p.m., except between June 1 and Labor Day when the evening hour is extended to 9 p.m. **Occupation standards for the employment of 14- and 15-year-olds:** • They may perform cashiering, shelf stocking, and the bagging and carrying out of customer orders. • They may perform clean-up work, including the use of vacuum cleaners and floor waxers. • They may perform limited cooking duties involving electric or gas grills that do not entail cooking over an open flame. They may also cook with deep fat fryers that are equipped with and utilize devices that automatically raise and lower the "baskets" into and out of the hot grease of oil. They may not operate NEXCO broilers, rotisseries, pressure cookers, fryolaters, high-speed ovens, or rapid toasters. • They may not perform any baking activities.

Age	Legal Requirements
	• They may not work in warehousing or load or unload goods to or from trucks or conveyors. • They may not operate, clean, set up, adjust, repair, or oil power driven machines including food slicers, grinders, processors, or mixers. • They may clean kitchen surfaces and non-power-driven equipment, and filter, transport, and dispose of cooking oil, but only when the temperature of the surface and oils do not exceed 100 degrees Fahrenheit. • They may not operate power-driven lawn mowers or cutters, or load or unload goods to or from trucks or conveyors. • They may not work in freezers or meat coolers, but they may occasionally enter a freezer momentarily to retrieve items. • They are prohibited from working in any of the Hazardous Orders.
16 & 17	Sixteen and seventeen-year-olds may be employed for unlimited hours in any occupation other than those declared hazardous by the Secretary of Labor. Examples of equipment declared hazardous in food service establishments include: **Power-Driven Meat and Poultry Processing Machines** (meat slicers, meat saws, patty forming machines, meat grinders, and meat choppers): commercial mixers and certain power-driven bakery machines. Employees under eighteen years of age are not permitted to operate, feed, set up, adjust, repair, or clean any of these machines or their disassembled parts. **Balers and Compactors:** Minors under eighteen years of age may not load, operate, or unload balers or compactors. Sixteen and seventeen-year-olds may load, but not operate or unload, certain scrap paper balers and paper box compactors under certain specific circumstances. **Motor Vehicles:** Generally, no employee under eighteen years of age may drive on the job or serve as an outside helper on a motor vehicle on a public road, but seventeen-year-olds who meet certain specific requirements may drive automobiles and trucks that do not exceed 6,000 pounds gross vehicle weight for limited amounts of time as part of their job. Such minors are, however, prohibited from making time sensitive deliveries (such as pizza deliveries or other trips where time is of the essence) and from driving at night.
18	Once a youth reaches eighteen years of age, he or she is no longer subject to the federal child labor provisions.

Employers who fail to comply with the FLSA may face lawsuits from both the Secretary of Labor and wronged employees for the repayment of backpay of proper minimum wages and/or overtime pay. If it is found that an employer willfully violated this law, the Department of Labor can also impose a $1,100 penalty per violation for repeated offenses.

Employees and Independent Contractors
It is important for employers to be able to discern between employees and independent contractors who are performing work for them for the purpose of withholding taxes, paying overtime and on-call

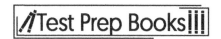

pay with regard to the Fair Labor Standards Act (FLSA), providing benefits, and granting legal protection to the appropriate individuals, all of which apply only to employees.

Employers are able to use independent contractors as a way to grow and reduce their workforce as needed while reducing their legal liability. There can also be a significant cost savings associated with having independent contractors complete work as they can typically be paid less than regular, full-time staff, and they do not receive healthcare benefits.

The Internal Revenue Service has developed a list of twenty factors that fall under three categories for employers to use to determine if an individual working for them is an employee or an independent contractor:

IRS 20-Factor Test
Behavioral Control
1. Instruction: A company-employee relationship could exist if the company dictates where, when, and how the employee works.
2. Training: A training relationship indicates the company has control over the type of work done by the employee.
3. Business Integration: Workers are likely to be considered employees if the success of the business depends on the work they do.
4. Personal Services: Independent contractors are free to assign work to anyone. Likewise, a company-employee relationship may dictate a particular person to carry out a specific task.
5. Assistants: An independent contractor may hire, supervise, and pay their own assistants, while a company-employee relationship may indicate that the company has control over the hiring, supervising, and paying of the worker's assistants.
Financial Control
6. Payment Method: Usually, hourly, weekly, or monthly payments indicate a company-employee relationship. Independent contractors are usually paid by commission or upon project completion.
7. Business or Travel Expenses: Employers who pay business or travel expenses for their employees are usually part of a company-employee relationship.
8. Tools and Materials: A company-employee relationship usually exists if the company provides the worker with tools and materials.
9. Investment in Facilities: Independent contractors usually invest in their own facilities, while employees for companies are usually provided facilities.
10. Profit or Loss: Workers who realize profits or losses are usually independent contractors.
Type of Relationship
11. Continuing of Relationships: An ongoing relationship between a company and a worker could indicate an employment relationship.
12. Set Hours: The implementation of a set schedule indicates that a company-employee relationship exists.
13. Full-Time: While independent contractors choose to work when and for whom they choose, employees sometimes must devote their schedules to full-time work for employees.
14. On-Site Services: If the work must be done on company property, a company-employee relationship probably exists.
15. Sequence of Work: A company-employee relationship is indicated if the worker must perform work in order of company preference and is not able to choose the sequence themselves.
16. Reports: If a worker is required to give oral or written reports to a company, it may indicate a level of control the company has over an employee.
17. Multiple Companies: Workers who provide services for multiple companies at one time are usually considered independent contractors.
18. Availability to Public: Workers who make their work available to the general public are often considered to be independent contractors.
19. Right to Discharge: Employers who have the right to discharge employees indicate a company-employee relationship.
20. Right to Terminate: Independent contractors are usually under contract to work, so they cannot terminate their employment as easily as employees.

Portal-to-Portal Act (1947)
This amendment to the Fair Labor Standards Act (FLSA) deals with the *preliminary tasks*—activities prior to the start of principal workday activities—and *postliminary tasks*—activities following the completion of principal workday activities.

- Examples of postliminary tasks include on-call or standby time, meals and breaks, travel time, and training time. The act requires employers to pay employees who are covered under the Fair Labor Standards Act for time spent traveling to perform job-related tasks, if that travel is outside of the employees' regular work commute.

- Employers must also pay employees for any time they spend waiting to start work when requested to do so by their employer. Additionally, employees are to be paid for hours spent in job-related training that is outside of their normal workday.

Employers who fail to comply with this law may face consequences similar to those detailed above in the FLSA section.

Equal Pay Act (1963)
This law requires employers to pay equal wages to both men and women who perform equal jobs in the same establishment. The job titles need not be identical, but rather, the content of the jobs that must be equal in nature. Equivalent jobs are required to have equal skill, working conditions, effort, and responsibility defined as follows:

- Skill: The educational and professional background of the employee performing the job, combined with their ability and training

- Working conditions: The physical surroundings in which the work is performed, along with any associated hazards

- Effort: A measurement of the physical or mental exertion that an employee needs to have in order to perform their job

- Responsibility: The employee's degree of accountability in performing their job

The act does allow for pay differentials when based on other factors other than gender, such as seniority, merit, production quantities or quality, and geographic work differentials. If brought into question, the employer is faced with the burden to prove that these types of *affirmative defenses* do indeed apply.

If there is a need to correct a difference in pay, an employee cannot be penalized by having their pay reduced. Rather, the lower-paid employee's pay rate must be increased. Employers who fail to comply with this act may face up to $10,000 in fines and/or imprisonment up to six months.

Employee Retirement Income Security Act (1974)
The Employment Retirement Income Security Act (ERISA) establishes the minimum standards for benefit plans of private, for-profit employers. It states that in order to receive tax advantages, these plans must conform to the Internal Revenue Code's requirements.

This law also established the federal agency known as the Pension Benefit Guaranty Corporation (PBGC). In return for the plans or their sponsors paying premiums to the PBGC, it guarantees payment of vested benefits up to a maximum limit to employees covered by pension plans.

Vested benefits are simply benefits from a retirement account or from a pension plan belonging to an employee that they get to keep regardless of whether they remain employed at the company. Companies have different rules regarding the number of years at which benefits vest; many are five years. Therefore, if an employee resigns after the vesting period of five years, then they can retain the benefits.

Minimum eligibility requirements were also established by ERISA. In order to participate in a plan, an employee must be at least twenty-one years of age and have completed one year of service with the company. However, company plans may be more generous concerning these minimum eligibility requirements.

ERISA established minimum vesting schedules for graded and cliff vesting. *Graded vesting* is a set schedule where employees are vested at a percentage amount less than 100 percent each year, until they accrue enough years of service to be considered 100 percent vested. *Cliff vesting* refers to employees becoming 100 percent vested after a specific number of years of service. ERISA established that employees are always 100 percent vested in their own contributions towards their retirement plans. The vesting schedules differ based on the type of retirement plan an employer is offering.

Minimum reporting standards for benefit plans were set up by ERISA. The act requires benefit plan sponsors to prepare and distribute summary plan descriptions (SPDs) to participants at least once every five years. Participants must also receive a summary annual report (SAR) that contains financial information about the plan.

Employers who fail to comply with this act may face both civil and criminal penalties. Some criminal penalties can cost companies as much as $500,000 and up to ten years in prison.

Older Workers Benefit Protection Act (1990)
The Older Workers Benefit Protection Act (OWBPA) was passed as an amendment to the Age Discrimination in Employment Act (ADEA) of 1967. Under this act, it is illegal for employers to discriminate based on an employee's age in the provision of benefits, such as pension programs, retirement plans, or life insurance. The goal is for companies to offer equal benefits to all employees, regardless of age. However, when it can be justified by substantial cost considerations, an employer can reduce benefits to older workers.

The OWBPA also prevents older workers from waiving rights when it comes to the topic of severance agreements. An older worker is to be given twenty-one days for the purpose of consulting with an attorney and considering a severance agreement, which turns into forty-five days for group terminations. An older worker then has seven days after signing such an agreement in which they can revoke the agreement if they change their mind.

The releases associated with these agreements must reference ADEA age discrimination claims. This limits an employer's lawsuit exposure should an employee decide to challenge the criteria that was used to make decisions about which employees were retained and which employees were let go. Employers who fail to comply with this act may face both civil and criminal penalties.

Retirement Equity Act (1984)
This amendment to the Employee Retirement Income Security Act (ERISA) was passed to address concerns around the needs of divorced spouses, surviving spouses, and employees who left the workforce for some period of time to raise a family. Automatic survivor benefits were now required of

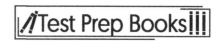

qualified pension plans in the event of a plan participant's death, and the waiver of these benefits could only occur with the consent of both the plan participant and the participant's spouse.

Additionally, pension plans are now required to make benefit payments in accordance with a domestic relations court order to the former spouse of a plan participant. Under this act, plans were no longer allowed to consider maternity or paternity leave as a break in service for the purposes of plan participation or vesting. Employers who fail to comply with this act may face both civil and criminal penalties.

Pension Protection Act (2006)
This amendment to the Employee Retirement Income Security Act (ERISA) was passed to strengthen the pension system by increasing the minimum funding requirements for pension plans, thereby eliminating existing loopholes that previously allowed missed payments for underfunded plans.

Additionally, the Pension Protection Act allows employees to be automatically enrolled in their employer's retirement plan at a default contribution rate after receiving notification. Employees are initially enrolled in default investments, typically according to the age group that they fall within, and there are provisions in place for their contributions to increase on a periodic basis.

If employees choose, they can elect to save at a different contribution rate, select different investments, or opt out of the retirement plan altogether. The automatic enrollment of employees into retirement plans allows employers to increase participation in their plans and employees to take advantage of pre-tax contributions. Employers who fail to comply with this act may face both civil and criminal penalties.

Consolidated Omnibus Budget Reconciliation Act (1986)
The Consolidated Omnibus Budget Reconciliation Act (COBRA) is an amendment to (ERISA) that allows for the continuation of healthcare coverage in the event that such coverage would end due to certain situations, such as the termination of employment, a divorce, or the death of an employee. The act covers employers with twenty or more employees.

Under this law, employees can pay to continue group medical insurance coverage for a period of up to eighteen to thirty-six months, if they elect to do so in a timely manner and pay the full costs of coverage. They can also be charged a 2 percent administrative fee. Employers who fail to comply with this act may face both civil and criminal penalties.

Patient Protection and Affordable Care Act (2010)
This act—also known as Obamacare, after President Barack Obama—was phased in over a four-year period, making access to healthcare available to several million more Americans. If individuals do not have access to employer-sponsored healthcare coverage, Medicare, or Medicaid, they are now able to purchase healthcare from an insurance exchange and possibly receive a subsidy.

One of the goals of this act is to keep the overall cost of healthcare coverage down by having individuals take advantage of preventative care, such as blood pressure and cholesterol screenings, well-woman visits, and vision screening for all children. Additionally, under this act, children are now permitted to stay under the coverage of their parents' healthcare until the age of twenty-six, and individuals with preexisting medical conditions cannot be denied coverage.

Every American citizen is now required to have health insurance each year or face paying an income tax surcharge. An employer mandate is also being enforced, which is a requirement that all companies employing fifty or more full-time employees provide at least 95 percent of those employees and their dependents with affordable health insurance or be subject to a per-employee fee, based on several factors.

Mental Health Parity Act (1996)
The Mental Health Parity Act (MHPA) was put into place to ensure that large group health plans provide coverage for mental health care in the same manner that they provide coverage for physical health care, such as surgical and medical benefits. For example, this act prevents an employer's group health plan from placing a lower lifetime limit on mental health benefits than the plan's lifetime limit on surgical and medical benefits.

This act applies to employers with more than fifty employees, as long as compliance with the act will not increase the employer's cost by at least one percent. It is important to note that this act does not require large group health plans to include mental health coverage in the benefits that they offer. The law only applies to large group health plans that already include mental health benefits in their packages.

Family Medical Leave Act (1993)
The Family Medical Leave Act (FMLA) was passed to allow eligible employees to take up to twelve weeks of job-protected, unpaid leave during a twelve-month period for specific family and medical reasons. Employees are covered under this act if their employer has at least fifty employees—full- or part-time— working within seventy-five miles of a given workplace and if they have worked for their employer for at least twelve months and for a total of 1,250 hours over the past year.

FMLA covers leave for the following reasons:

- The birth of a child, adoption, or foster-care placement

- The serious health condition of a spouse, child, or parent

- The serious health condition of the employee, one requiring inpatient care or continuing treatment by a healthcare provider

- Qualifying exigency leave, or leave to address the most common issues that arise when an employee's spouse, child, or parent is on active duty or call to active duty status—e.g., making financial and legal arrangements or arranging for alternative childcare

- Military caregiver leave or leave to care for a covered service member, such as the employee's spouse, child, parent, or their next of kin, with a serious injury or illness. Employees are to be granted up to twenty-six weeks of job-protected, unpaid leave during a twelve-month period to care for a covered service member.

Instead of taking all of their leave at once, employees can choose to take FMLA leave intermittently or in blocks of time for specific, qualifying reasons as approved by their employer. One reason for doing so would be for an employee to attend medical appointments for their ongoing treatment and testing for a serious health condition.

Spouses who work for the same employer must share the amount of FMLA time they take for the birth of a child, adoption, or foster care placement or for the serious health condition of a child or parent. The total amount of leave taken by both spouses must add up to twelve weeks for the reasons stated above or twenty-six weeks for the care of a covered service member.

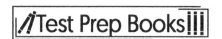

Employers also have the right to require employees to take unpaid FMLA leave concurrent with any relevant paid leave, such as sick time or vacation time, to which the employees are entitled under their current policies. In addition, a week containing a holiday still counts as a full week of FMLA, whether or not the holiday is considered to be paid time.

Employers are required to maintain an employee's group health care coverage while they are out on FMLA leave when the employee was covered under such a plan prior to leave. Once an employee's FMLA leave has ended, they are to be reinstated to their original job or to an equivalent job with equivalent conditions of employment, pay, and benefits.

Employers who fail to comply with the FMLA act may face both civil and criminal penalties. Also, if the Department of Labor finds that an employer did not post FMLA rights and responsibilities notices in the workplace, then a penalty of $110 can be assessed for willful failure to post.

Uniform Services Employment and Reemployment Rights Act (1994)
This law was passed to protect the employment, reemployment, and retention rights of civilian employees who serve in uniformed services, veterans, and members of the Reserve. The act requires covered employees to provide their employers with at least thirty days' notice of their need for leave, if possible, and covers them for up to five years of unpaid leave.

Under the Fair Labor Standards Act, exempt employees must be paid their full salary while out on leave (see 29 C.F.R. §541.602), less any compensation that they receive for serving in the military (§541.603). Employees who are out on military leave are also expected to receive the same seniority-based benefits that they would have received had they not been out of work on leave, such as vacation time and 401(k) contributions.

Additionally, if an employee's military leave will be less than one month, an employer must continue healthcare coverage under the same terms as if the employee was still actively employed. After the first month of military leave, employers are not required to continue group healthcare coverage at their expense. Instead, employers can make healthcare coverage available at the employee's expense for a period of twenty-four months or the duration of their military service, whichever is less. Employers are also not allowed to count an employee's military leave as a break in service for pension plan purposes.

The act requires covered employees returning from leave to apply for reemployment within a specific timeframe following completion of their military service:

- If an employee has been out on leave less than thirty-one days, he or she must return to work on the first workday following completion of military service.

- If an employee has been out on leave between thirty-one and 180 days, he or she must apply for reemployment within fourteen days of completing military service.

- If an employee's leave has been in excess of 180 days, he or she must apply for reemployment within ninety days of completing military service.

An employee returning from military leave is to be reinstated to a position that he or she would have been in if not out of work on leave, which may require some retraining efforts on the part of the employer. If after some period of time and retraining efforts, the employee is found not to be qualified for the new position, the employee can return to the position that he or she held prior to military leave.

Under this act, employers are also encouraged to make reasonable efforts to accommodate disabled veterans returning from military leave. Such individuals have up to two years after completing their military service to apply for reemployment.

Employers who fail to comply with USERRA may face both civil and criminal penalties, ultimately repaying any wronged employees for backpay and lost benefits.

Old Age, Survivor, and Disability Insurance (OASDI) Program

The Social Security Act (SSA) of 1935 designed this program to ensure a continuation of income for individuals who are retired, spouses and dependent children of employees who are deceased, and individuals who qualify for social security disability. This OASDI program is funded by contributions made by both employees and employers.

At a minimum, employees must work at least forty quarters or ten years to qualify for this program. A surviving spouse or dependent child's eligibility is determined by the length of time the spouse or parent has worked. The amount of benefits paid out to individuals who qualify is dependent upon the length of time the employee worked and the amount they paid into the program.

The majority of payments under this program are made in the category of Old-Age benefits. Individuals who qualify must be at least sixty-two years of age to receive partial benefits and between sixty-five and sixty-seven years of age to receive full benefits, depending on the year they were born. In most cases, a non-working spouse can expect to receive half of the amount of benefits of the working spouse.

Individuals who qualify for Social Security disability and receive benefits under this program must prove that they are unable to perform profitable work because they are totally disabled.

Federal-State Unemployment Insurance Program

Unemployment Insurance was created under the Social Security Act (SSA) of 1935 as a way to provide partial income replacement for a period of time to individuals who find themselves unemployed involuntarily. This benefit is funded primarily by employers—via a state unemployment tax—and administered by the individual states under national guidelines.

The number of weeks for which an employee can receive unemployment benefits can range from one to thirty-nine weeks, with twenty-six weeks being the most common duration. During some periods of high unemployment, the period of twenty-six weeks can be extended up to an additional thirteen weeks.

Eligibility in most states is contingent upon an employee having worked a minimum number of weeks, not being terminated for misconduct, not having left their job voluntarily, not finding him or herself unemployed due to a labor dispute, being available and actively seeking work, and not refusing suitable employment.

Medicare (1965)

This program is an amendment to the Social Security Act (SSA) of 1935 with the purpose of providing healthcare for individuals age sixty-five and older, which is not dependent on their income or ability to pay. Some individuals under the age of sixty-five who are disabled, as well as those individuals suffering from end-stage renal disease, are also eligible for coverage under Medicare. The program is funded by employees and employers paying a percentage of salaries.

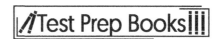

Medicare has four distinct parts:

- *Medicare Part A* is hospital insurance, which is considered mandatory, and most individuals do not have to pay for this coverage.

- *Medicare Part B* is medical insurance and covers such healthcare expenses as physicians' services and outpatient care. Medicare Part B is optional, and most individuals pay a monthly fee to have this coverage.

- *Medicare Part C* is referred to as Medicare Advantage Plans, such as HMOs or PPOs that are offered by private companies and approved by Medicare. The Medicare Advantage Plans are available to individuals who are entitled to Medicare Part A and enrolled in Medicare Part B. These plans provide participants with hospital and medical coverage, as well as with additional coverage, such as dental, vision, and hearing, and, in some cases, prescription drug coverage. Medicare Advantage Plans can provide substantial cost savings for individuals who are eligible to enroll in them once a year, during an open enrollment period.

- *Medicare Part D* is prescription drug coverage and is considered optional. Individuals who choose Part D pay a monthly fee to have this coverage. Part D is available to individuals who are entitled to Medicare Part A and enrolled in Medicare Part B.

Various Benefit Approaches
Compensation and benefits can be an essential element in retaining employees and attracting new candidates. Retaining current employees avoids the additional time and costs associated with training a new candidate altogether, as well as the risk of losing any clients or customers the individual may take along when they exit the organization.

Competitive salary and wages can be important in recruiting and retaining staff. However, unless the difference in salary is significant, it is usually not a factor—especially if the overall compensation package value is comparable. A lower take-home pay paired with a wider selection of healthcare and retirement plans may allow a company to offer a better long-term financial plan to its workers. Bonuses are yet another technique for employers to compensate and reward worthy employees.

Benefits can also assist in retention while saving the company money. Voluntary benefits help employees save money by utilizing group discounts with no added cost to the business. Retention of employees is possible with benefits such as health insurance, because many employees would not be able to afford having medical insurance if they exited their companies.

Determining Compensation
After a job analysis is performed that results in job descriptions and job specifications, a job evaluation is conducted to determine the relative worth of each job position by creating a hierarchy. This ultimately leads to the establishment of a pay structure.

- Job analysis: the process used to determine the requirements and importance of duties for a particular job

- Job descriptions: a list of general duties and responsibilities for a particular job

- Job specifications: a statement of the essential parts of a particular class of jobs. This includes a summary of the duties to be performed and responsibilities and qualifications necessary to do the job.

- Job evaluation: the ways to determine the value or worth of a job in relation to other jobs in a company

There are two main job evaluation methods: non-quantitative and quantitative.

Non-quantitative job evaluation methods are also known as *whole-job methods*. The three specific examples are job ranking, paired comparison, and job classification.

Job ranking involves a job-to-job comparison by developing a hierarchy of jobs from the lowest to the highest, based on each job's overall importance to the organization. This is a quick, inexpensive way for small organizations to compare one job to another.

Paired comparison is a process of comparing each job to every other job for the purpose of ranking all jobs on a scale from high to low. This is also an effective, low-cost job evaluation method for small companies.

Job classification involves grouping jobs into a predetermined number of grades, each of which has a class description to use for job comparisons. Benchmark jobs that fall into each class can be defined as reference points. An example of job classification put into practice is the Federal Government's use of the General Schedule classification system.

Quantitative job evaluation methods use a scaling system and provide a score that indicates how valuable one job is when compared to another job. The two specific examples are the *point factor method* and the *factor comparison method*.

The point factor method is less complex and most commonly used. This method uses specific, compensable factors, such as skill, responsibility, effort, working conditions, and the supervision of others, in order to evaluate the relative worth of each job. Each job receives a total point value, and then the relative worth of all jobs within an organization can be compared.

The factor comparison method is more complex and rarely used. This method involves a ranking of each job by each selected compensable factor and then identifies dollar values for each level of each factor to develop a pay rate for an evaluated job. It is best to use this method when wages are not frequently changed, and the organization uses a flat rate of pay for each job. This method can sometimes be used as part of a labor contract.

Organization

Structure of the HR Function

HR Service Models
There are several different HR service models; which one to use depends on an organization's needs. In a centralized HR structure, one strong corporate HR presence has authority over the entire organization. In a decentralized HR structure, autonomous HR functions operate in different business units (geographic location, department, etc.). A matrixed HR structure has a mixture of centralized and decentralized components. Finally, an organization may choose to have a largely outsourced HR structure. HR professionals should understand how the needs of the organization can be served within each structure. Smaller organizations tend to use a centralized structure, whereas larger organizations— particularly those that operate on an international scale—use either a matrixed or decentralized structure to better respond to local environments.

HR Function Improvements
HR performs several different functions. These can be divided into three main types: transactional, tactical, and strategic. Transactional HR work is largely administrative and includes individual services like payroll and benefits administration. Tactical HR work focuses on workplace solutions for employee workgroups. Finally, strategic HR work is focused on business units, or even the entire organization, by linking to the organization's strategic plan, mission, and goals. In most organizations, HR leaders increasingly focus on strategic work while often choosing to outsource transactional work. However, it is still important to facilitate communication and coordination between HR functions to ensure high-quality service to stakeholders. Each organization should determine which functions are essential to keep in house, but a general rule of thumb is that high-value skills that require in-depth knowledge of the organization are better performed in house. These include functions like performance management, strategic planning, and employee communication strategies. HR work that does not depend on workplace relationships or cultural knowledge is more appropriate to outsource if necessary.

HR Point-of-Service Contact
Particularly for organizations with a matrixed or decentralized HR structure, HR professionals serve as a point-of-service contact for stakeholders within an organizational unit. Tactical or strategic work that

affects many employees requires HR professionals to coordinate efforts with managers and other organization leaders. In decentralized HR structures, such as organizations that operate internationally, HR is the contact point for helping employees handle issues specific to their location, like understanding local labor laws, following tax codes, and analyzing local operating conditions.

Providing Consultation on HR Issues

Part of maintaining relationships with stakeholders is soliciting and responding to feedback about how to improve HR. Regular employee surveys help the HR department understand how effectively it is serving the needs of the organization's workforce. While many organizations choose to conduct annual surveys, some find it more useful to take shorter, more frequent pulse surveys to stay up to date with employees' needs. However, it is important that the results of any survey or feedback are addressed in a timely fashion so stakeholders feel that their concerns are being given appropriate consideration. For this reason, surveys should not be conducted more frequently than HR is equipped to respond to their results.

Timely Delivery of Services

In addition to receiving feedback from employees, HR should maintain a line of communication with managers and other leaders at all levels of an organization. HR concerns affect everyone from executive-level leaders to the newest employees; implementing HR strategies requires coordinated communication throughout the organizational structure. Rather than simply providing consulting at the highest levels and allowing information to trickle down, HR professionals should be engaged with employees at all levels to proactively identify and address any issues, provide appropriate guidance, and gauge how effectively HR initiatives are being implemented.

Outsourced HR Functions

Coordinating essential functions is also important when it comes to HR automation. For example, an organization may decide to automate certain HR functions like benefits administration by using a web portal where employees can enroll and manage benefits on their own. This frees up HR professionals to focus on more strategic work. However, HR still needs to ensure that the web portal is user-friendly, provides accurate and thorough information to employees, and has contact information in place if employees need help or further explanation. While HR should take advantage of opportunities to incorporate new technologies into the HR function, these need to be consistent with the established level of service provided. Automation is recommended for HR functions that are repeatable, routine, and follow a regular procedure. In some cases, automation can even improve processes and data security by ensuring that information passes through fewer hands. Augmentation is another option for streamlining routine functions. Augmentation refers to ways that technology assists employees in their job function without full automation.

Key Performance Indicators (KPIs)

Especially when it comes to measuring effectiveness, HR professionals should be able to analyze and interpret key performance indicators (KPI). KPI may vary between organizations depending on their size, location, industry, and a variety of other factors. However, some examples of KPI for HR include employee turnover rate, cost of hire, performance scores, employee satisfaction, diversity ratios, percentage of overtime hours, and percentage of job vacancies. Lagging indicators describe something that has already occurred, while leading indicators describe something that can change future performance or predict success. KPI should be objective and based on standardized measures in order to guide future development of HR. For example, if one of HR's key initiatives was committing to a diversity and inclusion (D&I) plan, relevant KPI may be diversity ratios (male to female, employees of color, age

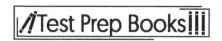

ranges), turnover rate for diverse hires, or performance ratings for diverse hires. KPI can also be used in conducting a variance analysis, which measures the degree of difference between planned performance and actual outcomes. Overall, leveraging data helps HR know what is working and what needs review.

Organizational Effectiveness and Development

Key Documents and Systems

HR helps manage an organization's structure to optimize effectiveness and implement new developments. To do so, HR professionals first need to understand the workforce's activities and make sure those are accurately reflected in job descriptions and performance management systems. This standardization ensures that talent is assigned appropriately, employees understand the key functions of their roles, and managers can give meaningful feedback to workers. Organizational development depends on observation and evaluation, so it is important to have clear standards and metrics in place for defining workforce activities.

Change Initiatives

Clear metrics for workforce activities can help HR understand areas in the organization that need change. For example, HR may find that some managers are using performance review criteria that focus too heavily on certain areas of a job while overlooking other essential job functions, causing some employees to get disproportionately high reviews. It would be up to HR personnel to help managers devise a more accurate performance management system. HR can also look at processes like promotions, team assignments, and transfers to determine if managers are following best practices. HR can periodically conduct audits of its policies, practices, and procedures to maintain an up-to-date view on their efficacy and course-correct where needed. An HR audit may focus on compliance (following applicable laws), best practices (improving competitive advantage compared to other organizations' HR), strategic planning (aligning HR with the strategic plan), or function-specific audits (focusing on a specific area like performance management, talent acquisition, etc.).

Identifying Change

Audits include evaluating the effectiveness of HR's own processes, procedures, and initiatives. In today's data-driven work environment, HR professionals have a variety of tools available to produce meaningful results from quantitative analysis. For example, in evaluating the effectiveness of a new training initiative, HR might compare before-and-after measures of worker productivity. Or the effectiveness of a high potential development program could be measured using data about retention rates, job satisfaction, or cost comparisons between developing leaders internally and onboarding external hires in leadership roles. These data-driven results will be invaluable in making recommendations to an organization's leadership and in shaping future HR practices. If HR presents meaningful information about how it can add value to an organization, it is more likely to gain support from managers and other stakeholders.

Barriers to Effectiveness

HR can also support an organization by identifying barriers to effectiveness. An organization's development may be held back by things like established cultural practices, outdated assumptions, poor communication between organizational units, fear of retaliation, and unclear job descriptions or work assignments. Once identified, HR should work with leaders throughout the organization to eliminate these barriers.

Data Analysis

In order to understand performance of initiatives, evaluate which are effective, and identify where improvement is needed, an organization must regularly analyze internal business information. Data is analyzed using **metrics** (sometimes known as key performance indicators). A metric is simply a method of measuring a particular set of data. Different metrics can be applied to different areas of an organization. Evaluation of initiatives allows HR to review the effectiveness of the program and gather data for improving future initiatives.

Workforce Management

One of HR's major responsibilities is workforce management. Workforce management refers to understanding an organization's current talent, anticipating its future needs, and implementing actionable plans to bridge any gaps.

Workforce Gaps

HR is responsible for identifying and correcting workforce gaps. A gap occurs when workforce supply and demand are misaligned. Workforce supply and demand are influenced by numerous internal and external factors. An organization's demand for talent is determined by things like its strategic plan and productivity goals, the timing of tasks (for example, seasonal work in retail or tax preparation), and the number of customers. The supply of talent can be influenced by things like worker attrition (retirement and resignation), internal transfer, and industry surplus or shortage of talent. HR professionals should be aware of organizational units that are under- or over-staffed by asking questions like, "Are there enough employees in place with the level of competency needed to achieve set goals?" or "Would productivity be impacted if this job position were removed?"

Staffing Levels

It is then HR's responsibility to fill any gaps that are detected. There are two approaches, known as buy or build. *Buy* refers to recruiting and onboarding new staff (the external approach), while *build* refers to developing the knowledge, skills, and competencies of current employees (the internal approach). Each organization needs to find the right balance of buying and building to meet its needs. Advantages of a build approach include employees' familiarity with the organization's culture and expectations, the increase in employee engagement and retention rates, and avoidance of the costly and lengthy process of hiring external candidates. However, HR professionals should also be able to judge situations in which a buy approach is preferable. For example, when major changes occur in the organization's marketplace or when an organization wants to redirect its primary goals and functions, it may be a good time to bring outside experience and fresh perspectives to the organization.

Short-Term Strategies

While workforce management generally requires long-term planning to anticipate things like retirements and industry changes, HR is also responsible for having short-term strategies to develop workplace competencies. These include measures like setting up workshops, classes, and training sessions. In order to ensure effectiveness, HR needs to start with a clear view of which competencies need to be developed, how many employees are affected, and how to measure learning objectives. If only a small number of workers need to develop a particular competency, it could be more effective to develop a self-managed learning plan or help coordinate external training. However, if there is a wider need for a skill or competency within an organizational unit or throughout the whole organization, HR can respond appropriately by designing a strategy with a wider approach.

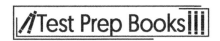

Leadership Needs

In addition to dealing with competency needs, HR also handles an organization's leadership needs. One approach is succession planning, which ensures the transfer of knowledge, experience, and relationships—both internal and external to the organization—from one generation of workers to the next. This ensures that key knowledge assets are not lost as workers retire and leave the organization. Another approach is to implement a high-potential development program. High-potential employees, sometimes known as "HIPOs," are high performing, highly productive, and highly valuable workers whom HR wants to retain and develop for the organization's future. A high-potential development program helps to identify these workers, challenge them with progressing roles and responsibilities, and provide them with development opportunities through work experience and education. This helps them to succeed in leadership positions in the future.

Restructuring the Workforce

Corporate restructuring involves the act of reorganizing a company in order to make it more profitable for its present-day situation. Corporate restructuring can take on one of two forms: financial or organizational restructuring.

Financial restructuring may be necessary due to a significant decrease in sales as a result of a poor economy. In this case, a company might make changes to its equity holdings, debt-servicing schedule, and cross-holding pattern based on the recommendations of financial and legal advisors to sustain its profitability.

Organizational restructuring may be necessary as a cost-cutting measure, in an attempt by a company to pay off debt and continue with its business operations. In this case, the structure of the organization is changed in some manner, such as through redesigning jobs and changing reporting relationships, reducing the number of hierarchical levels (creating a flatter organization), or downsizing (a workforce reduction).

Workforce reductions are the planned elimination of a number of personnel in order to make an organization more competitive through reducing costs, using technology to replace labor, mergers and acquisitions, or by moving a company to a more economical location.

Once a company realizes it has a talent surplus, Human Resources can take the following steps to avoid a workforce reduction:

- Reduce employees' hours or compensation to retain qualified staff
- Implement a hiring freeze
- Institute a voluntary separation program, also known as an early retirement buyout program

Although workforce reductions help companies cut costs in the short term, they often hurt productivity. For an organization to successfully implement a workforce reduction, it should communicate with employees throughout the entire process, and provide downsized employees with outplacement services to assist with resume writing, career counseling, and interview preparation. It can also provide referral assistance to exiting employees. Companies should strive to build the trust and commitment of the remaining employees so as to boost employee morale, especially during a downsizing situation.

Employees who are laid off are typically asked to sign a document known as a *separation agreement and general release*. This document, when signed, is a legally-binding agreement that states the employee cannot sue or make any claims against the company in exchange for agreed upon severance benefits.

Severance pay is not required by law, but most companies will pay employees who are laid off a set number of weeks of salary continuation, based upon their years of service (typically one or two weeks' pay per year of service), to ease their financial burden and to preserve the organization's image. Some companies also include a continuation of healthcare benefits for a set period of time.

An employee is given the agreement during their exit meeting and is allowed to take it home and review it with a lawyer. They have twenty-one days to sign and return the agreement for an individual separation and forty-five days to sign and return the agreement in cases of a group reduction in force. Once the agreement is signed, an employee still has seven days to revoke their signature.

Some companies have a talent shortage. Instead of hiring full-time employees, Human Resources can utilize the following tactics to manage the workforce:

- Allow existing staff to work overtime hours
- Outsource work to an external service provider
- Institute alternate work arrangements (i.e., telecommuting, job sharing, and nontraditional work schedules)
- Reemploy recent retirees on a temporary or part-time basis
- Utilize contingent workers to fill available positions and manage the extra workload (i.e., independent contractors)

Turning to alternative sources for workers can help the company save money on the hiring and interviewing process—a significant cost for many companies. Because many of the above candidates have already been screened for the job and proven themselves on the job, they may be a better match for filling short-term and even long-term staffing needs.

Employee and Labor Relations

Employee relations, as the term suggests, refers to how the people who work for a company interact, both with one another and with other external parties. The term can refer to guidelines and rules that govern these interactions, but it can also focus on the methods and strategies used to determine the rules that shape the desired relationships.

This is an important consideration for any company. People are the driving force, the fuel, and the face of the organization. Anyone who has worked in a job that requires interacting with other employees or with customers probably has an interesting story about how quickly things can break down when these relationships are not well managed. When these breakdowns occur regularly, working conditions become strained, workers are inefficient, and outside observers are left with a negative impression of the organization. This negative impression cannot only affect a business, it also can sway talented people from joining the organization.

However, perhaps even more importantly, having good employee relations does not just make good business sense—it is the law. There is legislation at the local, state, and federal levels governing workplace environments and employee interactions. Therefore, an employer who does not keep track of the state of their workplace could well be in serious legal trouble.

Interacting with a Union
In its broadest sense, a union (also known as a labor union) is simply a formally organized group of employees who work together to accomplish goals. These goals usually involve working conditions, pay,

and other aspects of a common trade, but can vary widely depending on the union and the particular situation.

A *local union* refers to either a union for a small organization or a union for a smaller geographic area. In many cases, the local union serves as a branch of the larger national union for a particular trade. A *national union* is often comprised of smaller, local unions. These groups represent a wide geographic area. A national union could represent employees of a single organization or employees of multiple organizations that happen to be working in the same trade. A *federation* is made up of different national unions representing different industries that nevertheless share some commonalities and have common goals. Finally, an *international union* represents workers in multiple countries.

Unions must go through a specific process to be officially organized and recognized as a legitimate representative for a group of workers. Employees must demonstrate an interest in participating in the union and must sign authorization cards indicating their interest in the union. At least 30 percent of eligible employees are required to sign authorization cards by the National Labor Relations Board (NLRB) before they can order an election. The union must inform the employer of the employees' desire to unionize. If at this point the employer refuses, the union may take action through the NLRB. The NLRB then holds an election where employees vote on whether to be represented by the union. Employees are eligible to vote in the election if they were on the company's payroll during the pay period directly prior to the calling of the election and during the pay period immediately preceding the election date. Any employees who were striking and then were permanently replaced are allowed to vote in an election that is conducted within twelve months following the end of the strike.

Picketing is an act of protest where a group of people (picketers) gather in front of a business to raise awareness of an issue or to discourage people from entering a building to work or do business. The NLRB outlines what kinds of picketing activities unions may legally participate in. Employees may engage in *informational picketing*, where they picket to announce to the public that they are not represented by any one authority and thus plan to organize. Employees may also engage in *organizational picketing*, where they picket to convince employees to join or support their union. Finally, employees may engage in *recognitional picketing*, where they picket to encourage the employer to recognize their union as the employees' representative.

While in disputes with an employer, unions may engage in *common situs picketing*. This is where employees picket at a location used by the targeted employer as well as other organizations. This is legal as long as the picketers make clear which employer is being protested, so that other organizations are not adversely affected by the picketing. Unions may also use *consumer picketing*, where employees picket to discourage the public from doing business with the employer in question. Finally, unions can take advantage of *double breasting picketing*, where employees picket at a location where the employer's workers are not unionized. This is only legal in certain situations.

Union-Management Activities
If a company's employees feel that their union is not doing a good enough job to represent them, they can go through the process of decertification, which strips the union of its official status as the employees' representatives. To decertify the union, 30 percent of employees must first sign a petition. Then, the employees can file the petition with the NLRB. The petition cannot be filed less than twelve months after the union was officially certified. If the NLRB approves the petition, then it holds a decertification election among the company employees. The union is decertified if a majority of the voting employees vote in favor of the decertification (a tie vote also means the union is decertified).

Deauthorization is a process of removing a union's security clause and its authority to negotiate. A security clause is basically a condition in a contract that requires employees to join a union. The deauthorization process is identical to that of decertification. First, 30 percent of employees must sign a petition in favor of deauthorization. Then, the employees file the petition with the NLRB. If the NLRB approves the petition, then it holds a decertification election among the company employees. Deauthorization is approved if a majority of the employees who are eligible to vote in favor of deauthorization. In this instance, a situation where employees who are eligible and do not exercise their right to vote equates to a vote against deauthorization.

Collective Bargaining Process

There are several strategies that are commonly employed by unions during a collective bargaining negotiation. Single-unit bargaining occurs when union representatives meet with one employer at a time and don't attempt to use the process as a springboard in separate negotiations. Coordinated bargaining takes place when unions within an organization meet with the employer to negotiate beneficial results for the groups they represent (also called multi-unit bargaining). Multi-employer bargaining occurs when a union with employees in multiple companies meets with all of those companies as a single negotiation. Finally, parallel bargaining occurs when a union successfully negotiates an agreement with a company, then uses the result of that negotiation as an example while dealing with a different company (also called leapfrogging or whipsawing).

Organization or union representatives typically use one of two approaches when engaging in a collective bargaining process. *Distributive bargaining* takes place when a group negotiates with the goal of achieving specific objectives (also called positional bargaining). *Principled bargaining* occurs when a group negotiates while remaining mindful of the key issues to each side of the process. The negotiation then becomes a process of searching for solutions from both sides in hopes that an agreement can be reached.

ADR Processes

HR professional must be able to participate and facilitate alternative dispute resolution (ADR) processes including mediation and arbitration. Mediation often serves as a precursor to the more official step of arbitration. In general terms, arbitration is sometimes thought of as a form of mediation, but legally there are important differences. Most notably, a mediator doesn't serve as a final "judge" of the dispute, but rather attempts to work with both parties to help them reach a resolution without having to take additional legal steps.

The mediation process usually begins with both parties agreeing to use a mutually acceptable mediator. The mediator sets the ground rules for the process and defines details such as what the dispute is about, who is involved, when and where the negotiations will take place, and the negotiation procedure. When the actual meeting takes place, the mediator reiterates the ground rules for the process. Both sides present their case. The mediator attempts to help both parties reach a compromise or find other solutions. If both sides agree to a compromise, a written document will be signed to ensure that both sides will follow through on the agreed-upon actions. If both sides do not agree, they may choose to pursue arbitration or litigation (court action).

Constructive confrontation is a type of mediation used in some extremely complicated or contentious disputes, particularly ones where neither party is able to agree to a compromise. Constructive confrontation can sometimes break these stalemates by temporarily skipping the main issue in dispute, and instead, focusing first on secondary issues. Sometimes, by first resolving these smaller details, a mediator can affect parties' willingness to compromise on bigger issues.

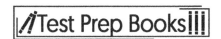

Arbitration is a way to settle disputes without taking the issue to court. In a general sense, arbitration is a form of mediation. However, arbitration typically refers to a more formal process that takes place after an initial mediation attempt has failed. In arbitration, a neutral third party (known as an arbitrator) makes a decision based on the facts presented. There are different kinds of arbitration, decisions, and arbitrators.

In *compulsory arbitration*, the disputing parties are required by law to go through the arbitration process. This could be the result of a court order, but it could also arise from a contract that dictates that arbitration take place in certain situations.

In *voluntary arbitration*, the disputing parties choose to undergo the arbitration process, usually because they cannot come to an agreement but do not want to go through a potentially expensive and time-consuming lawsuit.

In a *binding decision*, the disputing parties are required by law to follow the decision reached as a result of the arbitration process. This means that the losing party must follow the actions laid out by the decision (such as payments or reinstatement to a disputed position). In addition, a binding decision marks the end of the legal process. No party may pursue further legal action after the decision has been reached.

As the name suggests, *non-binding decisions* carry no legal weight. Either party may choose to follow or not follow the terms of the decision. In addition, a dissatisfied party may choose to follow additional legal action after the decision of the arbiter is reached.

A *permanent arbitrator* is someone who routinely judges arbitration cases for a company or other organization. An arbitrator may be trained and certified by a professional organization, but they also may simply be a person who the disputing parties trust to provide an unbiased opinion on the dispute.

An *ad-hoc arbitrator* may also be a certified professional or a mutually trusted third party. But unlike permanent arbitrators, ad-hoc arbitrators do not have a regular arbitration relationship with either party. Instead, they are chosen as a one-time solution to address only the unique dispute in question.

An *arbitrator panel* functions just like an ad-hoc arbitrator, but it is comprised of multiple arbitrators (usually three). They are sometimes called arbitral tribunals or tripartite arbitration panels.

Employee Representation

Employees may choose to be represented by a labor union. However, there are other forms of employee representation as well. The National Labor Relations Act of 1935 (NLRA; also known as the Wagner Act), administered by the National Labor Relations Board (NLRB), protects the rights of private sector workers to join labor unions; it also constrains employee representation in nonunionized companies. Nevertheless, nonunion employee representation plans can be found in many organizations where employees want a voice in the workplace. Like unions, these groups allow employees to advocate for fair treatment and improved employment conditions while also creating a channel for communication where employees can give input into the decision-making process.

However, the decisions ultimately rest with management and, unlike unions, nonunion employee representation plans keep all decisions and bargaining within the organization. One example of this type of body is a works council, which generally represents employees on a more local level than a trade union. A works council operates within an organization to improve communication between employers and employees and to increase employees' bargaining power. In the United States., a works council must be elected by employees without interference by the employer in order to be recognized as lawful. In other cases, employees may also choose to be represented by legal counsel or a governmental body to assist in negotiations or resolving disputes.

Workplace Policies and Procedures

Policies are more general in nature and serve as guidelines that focus on organizational actions. They reflect a company's philosophy, standards, or objectives. An example of a policy is how employees receive vacation time according to their years of service with a company. Procedures and rules are more specific to situations. Procedures are customary methods of handling activities. They are detailed descriptions that answer the when, what, who, how, and where. An example of a procedure is the specific method that employees use to request and authorize their vacation time. Rules are the most specific guidelines that regulate and/or restrict individuals' behavior. They reflect management's decisions in regard to actions that should be avoided or taken in situations. Employees being required to give at least a one-week notice when requesting vacation is an example of a rule.

Employee handbooks are important tools to communicate information to staff concerning the company's culture, work hours, safety, harassment, attendance, benefits, pay, electronic communication policies, and discipline policies. It is important for companies to keep employee handbooks current, simple to read, and to make accommodations for any multilingual requests. Additionally, it is important to include a disclaimer that the employee handbook is not intended to be any type of contractual agreement between the company and the employee. By making the employee handbook accessible on the company's intranet site, this eliminates outdated paper copies from floating around the office, and employees can access important policies at any time. Companies typically also require employees to sign off on a form stating that they have received and read the latest version of the employee handbook.

Conducting Investigations

Workplace monitoring is a policy that employers use in order to monitor a suspicious person and gather information. Employers may use a workplace monitoring program to discover activities that threaten the integrity and interests of the firm. Particular monitoring techniques involve wiretapping, reviewing internet content usage, GPS tracking, checking employees' social media accounts, and interviewing other employees about suspicious activity. Management surveillance programs are easier to execute if employees are required to use company phones and computers. However, before such actions are taken by an employer, all employees should be given ample documentation of rules and regulations. This will ensure that any breach of protocol is intentional and deliberate on the part of the employee.

Managing Employees and Grievances

Employee morale and team cohesion can be negatively impacted by difficult and disruptive employees. Issues with employees' behavior and other employee grievances must be managed to create a safe and productive work environment. Progressive discipline is a system that, rather than defining a single "one size fits all" response to an employee infraction, attempts to address each incident as a unique situation and then develops consequences accordingly. Typically, factors like severity and frequency (in other words, "how bad" and "how often") are key in determining the appropriate response. A system should be developed to respond to allegations of improper/illegal activities and enforce appropriate disciplinary action against employees who have violated internal compliance policies, applicable statutes, and regulations.

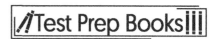

Many organizations make use of a five-stage process to address employee infractions. Coaching is the first stage, where the manager discusses the behavior problem with the employee. This stage is typically used for small or first-time infractions. Then the employee receives a first warning. This is also called the counseling stage and usually involves the employee receiving a verbal warning. Then the second warning follows, which is also called the formal warning stage. This stage progresses to the employee receiving a written warning. A disciplinary action follows. At this stage, the employee is suspended for their behavior. Finally, if the chain of progressive discipline has not corrected the behavior, the final step in the progressive discipline process is to terminate the individual's employment.

Technology Management

Technology Solutions

Nowadays, organizations rely on information technology to carry out essential business functions. Some conduct the entirety of their business via the internet. These metrics can help organizations get the most out of their IT departments.

One important category analyzes the functionality of an organization's IT resources. That is, how well are IT services working? This can be measured by looking at the number of software bugs over a given period, or the average number of hours required to resolve IT issues. If there's a large volume of IT problems, or if it takes too long to fix critical IT issues, the organization must devote more resources to improving its IT functionality.

IT metrics can also consider online business activities that examine an organization's online sales presence. If a business has a website, one important metric is the number of page views. This measures the organization's reach—how many potential customers is the organization reaching through its online marketing? How many page views lead to actual purchases? How many visitors are registered on the site or subscribed to a newsletter? If the organization isn't satisfied with this number, it's time to try new online marketing strategies. The business can also look at the ratio of online sales to sales from non-internet business (for example, over the phone or in person) in order to determine where it should focus sales and marketing efforts.

Finally, as with any department, organizations must consider the cost of IT. This metric helps the organization see what portion of its financial resources is devoted to IT services, and whether this investment adds value to the organization. For example, an organization may invest in new project management software, but this software increases productivity and helps managers keep project costs low—so the cost of the software is offset by the savings it creates.

Implementing HRIS

As organizations become increasingly dependent on technology management, it is incumbent on HR professionals to identify and implement technologies that are most beneficial to their work. Human resource information systems (HRIS) are tools for managing relevant HR data, including employee information (names, addresses, salary and job histories, etc.) and benefits administration (paid time off, benefits enrollment status, etc.). It may also include an ATS that aids with recruitment by managing resumes, applicant information, open positions, etc. In the past, such information tended to be stored in discrete databases, making it difficult to integrate data and leading to frequent duplication of information. However, with the rising trend of big data analysis, organizations—and HR departments in particular—can obtain a wealth of information from data that is properly stored and organized. Therefore, in choosing and implementing HRIS, HR professionals should consider what types of information are currently being collected and stored at the organization; what information HR needs to know, based on that data; and how data could be integrated for easier access and analysis. There is no one-size-fits-all HRIS; rather, HR professionals need to consider the unique needs of their organization.

Organizational Standards for Employee Data

Companies should maintain maximum security while possessing the personal information of customers and employees. Each organization should utilize an apparatus that monitors and reports security breaches, notifying employees, customers, and various authorities. In addition, internal privacy policies must comply with current laws and regulations. These laws are intended to deter security breaches.

A company's internal privacy policy should address sensitive information such as addresses, telephone numbers, credit reports, medical reports, employee records, company technology, and data systems that collect personal information. An effective privacy policy explains the purposes of investigations and monitors the conduct of employees. Episodic privacy tests can be useful, particularly if management has reason to believe that employee misconduct has occurred. A company should communicate regularly with its employees about security issues and technology. Additionally, written policies must exist to protect employers from employee claims of privacy invasion. Employees should be notified of these policies and agree to all conditions. An effective privacy policy will identify and monitor employees suspected of violating protocol and procure the necessary information to review the employee's practices.

Protecting Workforce Data

Identity theft occurs when a person wrongfully obtains and uses another individual's personal information, typically for financial gain. This form of fraud can be very damaging and is difficult to prevent. In order to commit identity theft, a perpetrator does not need a person's fingerprint. The criminal simply needs a Social Security number, credit card number, bank statements, or any piece of information that will allow access to personal documents. The expense of identity theft to the victim can be shocking, and in some cases, may be in excess of $100,000. Identity theft primarily occurs in public places through methods such as "shoulder surfing." This technique involves watching over somebody's shoulder when they are using an ATM machine or rummaging through someone's garbage in search of confidential material that was not disposed of properly.

Data protection is the process of securing personal information from identity theft or other corruptive activities. Data protection involves storing important materials and can be done through a variety of means, such as file locking, disk mirroring, and database shadowing. The principal purpose of data protection is to maintain the integrity and proper storage of information. Two effective means of achieving maximum data protection while ensuring availability is to pursue data lifecycle management (DLM) and information lifecycle management (ILM), which may provide better data protection in the event of a virus or hack. A feasible data protection plan is also applicable to disaster recovery and business continuity.

Technology in the Workplace

If a firm wishes to maintain competitiveness and maximize its capabilities, management should develop policies that streamline communication. These policies will allow for the freer flow of ideas and dialogue. Furthermore, the integration of electronic media will increase a firm's ability to reach out to consumers and market the company's products. Harnessing this technology can increase market share and make innovation easier.

Electronic mail, or email, is communication that occurs by exchanging digital messages. Email was developed in the early 1990s and came into widespread use by 1993. Email has become a common

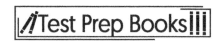

means of communication, particularly within a corporate environment. This mode of communication allows an individual to send messages to one or more recipients at once. Email has been enormously successful in streamlining the communication process while reducing the cost of using paper.

Many organizations currently integrate the use of social media into corporate strategies. Social media is online applications that allow users to share content. These sites have become so advantageous in marketing that companies hire designated employees to increase social media presence. Many firms presently require their employees to have social media skills, knowledge, and familiarity. Programs such as Twitter™, Facebook™, and Instagram™ have proven to be tremendously successful marketing tools used by companies to reach a broader audience. In addition, social media has revolutionized advertising by placing a growing emphasis on Internet marketing instead of traditional television ads. While a helpful and useful tool in many circumstances, social media may also carry unintended consequences. For example, employers often use social media to obtain personal information about a potential or current employee. Questionable social media content can influence an employer's decision to hire an individual.

As technology has increased the use of the internet, the necessity of a company website and the demand for website accessibility has grown. In order to promote equal access to websites, companies should attempt to accommodate those with cognitive, neurological, physical, visual, or auditory disabilities. In addition to disabled persons, elderly people who lack familiarity should be able to understand and navigate websites. Because the internet is an integral resource for participating in commercial activity, gaining employment, accessing health care, and finding recreational activities, equal opportunity and access to website navigation is also crucial.

Data sharing is the practice of making information accessible through public or private networks. Individuals within the network have access to the information, while those not in the network require consent for access. Data sharing usually involves varying levels of access and is generally regulated by administrators in the system.

A password is a code that is required to access restricted information. A complex password provides more security to the user and better protects sensitive information. Typically, passwords consist of letters, numbers, and symbols. This unique combination affords better protection to the user. Password sharing should be limited to those individuals who may be trusted with confidential information.

Social engineering is the act of manipulating people for the purpose of revealing sensitive information. Typically, an attacker will employ deceptive tactics to convince the target to provide information such as bank numbers, passwords, and Social Security numbers. Social engineers take advantage of a target's natural tendencies of trust. Social engineers may gain access to information by infiltrating computer systems and installing malware. Organizations should educate employees on security and the identification of untrustworthy individuals. Employees should be able to assess suspicious situations and clearly recognize red flags.

Monitoring software, also known as computer surveillance software, regulates the activity performed on a certain network. If this software detects anything that may threaten the safety and security of the network, it reports the activity to an administrator. This type of software may be employed in individual or corporate networks. Typically, monitoring software checks all information flow of network traffic on the internet. Computer surveillance software is sophisticated enough to easily detect any abnormal or suspicious action in a multitude of network information.

In the field of computer security, biometrics refers to an authentication process that requires physiological proof to validate a user. Once the measure of the user's physiology is authenticated, they will be granted access to appropriate information. Biometric identification ranges from fingerprints, facial recognition, voice recognition, hand patterns, or eye patterns. The individual's biometric information is uploaded and stored in a security system that must recognize these physical characteristics to provide information access.

HR Technology Solutions

One of the primary benefits of a well-designed and -managed HRIS is its ability to use data to develop evidence-based solutions. Traditionally, many solutions and recommendations have been based on experience, common business practices, or long-standing assumptions that may not actually be founded on objective facts. HRIS can provide HR professionals with the analytical tools necessary to answer questions that influence policy decisions. For example, by pulling data related to employee pay, retention, and future performance, HR can formulate a more compelling case for increasing an organization's standard raise structure with recommendations that are based on concrete results from the data analysis. When there is a difficult problem, data can provide something humans sometimes cannot—an unbiased perspective. For example, an organization may be committed to diversity in its upper management, and yet it still finds that it is unable to meet diversity goals in promoting employees. Conscious and unconscious biases may be influencing who managers recommend for advancement. Standardized performance metrics that are evaluated by employee management software could produce a fair and representative list of who is qualified for a particular promotion.

Technologies that Analyze Data

In selecting HR technology solutions, HR professionals need to coordinate with vendors. Because salespeople are obviously not the best source for unbiased product recommendations, it is important for HR professionals to understand their organization's technology needs and do their due diligence on industry standards. Although it is important for an organization's technology capabilities to stay current, innovation can be balanced with realistic day-to-day operational needs. The time, cost, and training needed to implement a new HRIS should be weighed against the benefits it will bring to the organization. Also, cybersecurity is of vital importance in an organization's technology plan, especially when it comes to employees' sensitive personal data. While it is impossible for any vendor to guarantee absolute security, vendors should still provide security protections that are at or above industry standard, as well as provide a response plan for how to handle any software failures.

Workplace

Managing a Global Workforce

Global Issues

From multinationals to organizations with international clients to companies that have offshore workers, there are a variety of ways that today's organizations operate in a global context. Many concerns associated with global operations fall within HR's range of responsibilities. On a basic level, HR professions need thorough and up-to-date knowledge related to global factors that influence employees. These factors are known by the acronym PESTLE, which stands for the political, economic, social, technological, legal, and environmental factors that make up the basis of required global HR knowledge. For organizations that deal with many different regions of the world, this task becomes increasingly complex and may require divisions of HR with regional expertise.

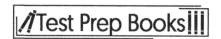

Maintaining Up-to-Date Knowledge

Whenever part of an organization's workforce is assigned to a foreign post, HR assumes responsibility for duty of care. Duty of care refers to the legal and moral obligations of an organization to provide for employees' security, health, and wellbeing when they are outside the country. For employees who travel to a foreign post with their families, duty of care extends to their family members as well. Duty of care may include a wide range of responsibilities that vary among organizations and international assignments; examples include safe housing, access to health care and emergency services, translation assistance, and access to education for children. In addition to providing for everyday needs of international workers, HR must be prepared to face emergency situations like natural disasters and terrorist attacks. During these events, HR is responsible for accounting for every employee's whereabouts as well as safely recalling them out of the country if necessary.

Particularly when it comes to emergency preparedness, HR's policies should be proactive rather than reactive. HR should provide employees with safety information and emergency training before sending them to international assignments so everyone knows how to respond appropriately in an emergency. Things like having a regular check-in procedure or knowing how to contact emergency services could save time and even lives. Organizations without appropriate emergency preparedness policies in place may face a serious legal liability known as "negligent failure to plan" if employees are vulnerable in a security incident.

Global Workforce and Stakeholders

In addition to the duty-of-care obligations that HR has to employees, there are also significant legal obligations involved in maintaining a global workforce. HR professionals must be aware of the applicable laws related to employees' immigration status and support employees in obtaining and maintaining necessary documentation. Of course, different countries have different laws, but common concerns include reporting foreign earned income and global remittances (money sent home from a foreign country), paying applicable taxes or being aware of income tax exclusions (such as totalization agreements between countries that prevent overseas workers from being taxed twice), and adhering to the permitted length of stay.

This latter concern is particularly important for employees who travel to a foreign country for a short-term business meeting that extends to a longer stay; there is the potential for these workers to become "accidental expatriates" by overstaying the permitted length of stay without declaring their worker status. Also, HR should make employees aware of potential legal risks involved with leaving and re-entering the assigned country (depending on their immigration status, for instance). Further, employees need to know how local laws differ from laws in their home country to avoid any unintended legal violations. Again, it benefits HR to be proactive in preparing employees with this information rather than waiting until a legal concern arises to address it.

Auditing Global HR Practices

Another HR concern with expatriate assignees is repatriation, or recalling employees to their home country and integrating them into their jobs at home. Employees who have been gone for extended periods may experience "reverse culture shock"; HR should provide resources for helping employees readjust to life in their home country. Related to repatriation is redeployment, when an organization moves an expatriate's assignment—either to a new country or a different location in the same country. Rather than assuming that the employee already has international experience and needs no special preparation, HR professionals should keep in mind that every assignment is different, and employees need to be provided with relevant information and training to prepare for their new assignment.

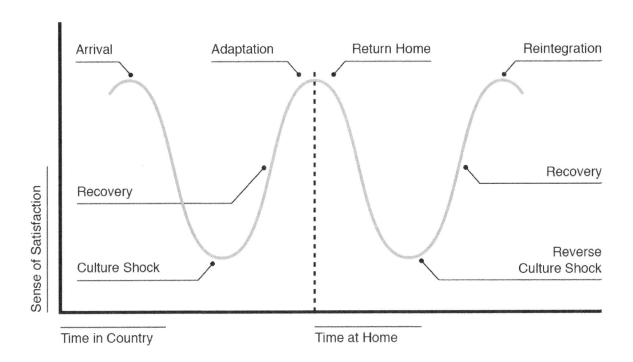

Global HR Trends and Best Practices
As with all HR practices, HR professionals also need to stay up to date on global HR trends and best practices. This can be achieved through membership in a global organization, networking with international partners, and meeting remotely or in person with global stakeholders. After implementing any policy, HR should continue to review and adjust policies as needed. This requires HR to identify clear metrics by which their global worker policies will be evaluated. When evaluating safety policies, for example, success might be quantified by evaluating data on things like the number of safety incidents (crime, injury, etc.), cost of health insurance, or payments for emergency services. An organization can also evaluate its policies through benchmarking to ensure that it is providing comparable or better services to its global workforce in comparison with other organizations.

Balance in Work Culture
As organizations expand their operations to foreign countries, they also have to maintain balance between domestic and international work culture. Although HR professionals are concerned with communicating corporate culture, values, and expectations to employees, there should also be a pragmatic understanding of how these characteristics can vary between countries. In order to avoid intercultural miscommunication, HR professionals should have a thorough understanding of local labor laws and customs, clearly defined job descriptions and explanations, and a measure of flexibility when implementing workplace policies. In these situations, it should never be assumed that anything is common knowledge or practice; such assumptions can lead to oversight and misunderstandings. Rather, expectations need to be as explicit and clearly defined as possible.

International Assignments
Finally, even organizations without employees or operations in foreign countries can be impacted by global issues. In turn, many of these impacts have relevance for HR. For example, in some industries,

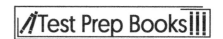

jobs continue to travel overseas through offshoring and outsourcing. As these jobs become relocated to countries with different salary standards, it can influence how that work is valued and compensated domestically. Also, if job opportunities relocate to foreign job sites, HR should implement a strategy for handling domestic employees who now need to transition to other roles within the company, perhaps through retraining or providing other education opportunities.

Diversity and Inclusion

Diversity comes in many forms. In its simplest definition, workplace diversity refers to differences in employees' characteristics. While many people may think of diversity in terms of race and gender, diversity also includes a plethora of other characteristics like age, nationality, sexuality, personality, education, family background, and socioeconomic status. While diversity refers to bringing together a team of people with different characteristics, inclusion refers to valuing, listening to, and using the products of those differences. In this way, diversity can be thought of as bringing different people to the table, while inclusion is giving them a chance to contribute to and lead the discussion.

Providing Training on Cultural Differences

For employees from the younger generation, D&I involves a more proactive mixture of diverse ideas, strategies, and backgrounds to lead an organization to innovation and modernization. From this perspective, D&I involves not only a commitment to equality, but also programs that harness the skills of a diverse workforce. One way for HR professionals to foster this is by building opportunities for mentoring and coaching between employees. For example, if an organization wants to retain and promote female employees, it might implement a mentoring program that pairs new employees with more experienced women in the company who can share their advice and insights about achieving professional success. Cross-cultural training can also be useful in creating opportunities for employees to hear about and benefit from diverse ideas. Many organizations also have employee resource groups (ERGs), which are groups created by employees who share some demographic factor(s) based on things like race, gender, or age. ERGs help diverse employees to feel represented within the organization while also helping leaders to gain insight into the needs of diverse customers and other stakeholders.

Distinguishing Between Performance Issues and Cultural Differences

While HR should work with employees at all levels, there are also specific concerns for D&I policies with managers. For example, managers may need additional training and guidance on distinguishing between performance issues and cultural differences. Culture refers to a shared set of beliefs, behaviors, attitudes, and values. Every organization has its own culture, but, particularly in organizations that have not yet developed a great deal of diversity in upper management, it can be easy to conflate the organization's culture with its leaders' demographic culture. Behaviors and customs that are assumed to be universal may not be present in every demographic, leading to conflict when a more diverse workforce is recruited. Managers may perceive their employees as "not fitting in" or "not having the right attitude" simply because they come from a different background with different expectations; this in turn can lead to conscious and unconscious biases in employee evaluations and promotions. HR professionals can anticipate and counteract this effect by providing cultural training for managers. They can also help managers to define clear, reasonable, and appropriate guidelines for clarifying performance measures.

Diversity and Inclusion (D&I) Current Trends

In addition to developing an organization's relationship with external stakeholders, a well-managed D&I program should also build employee relations and satisfaction within an organization. First, it's important to understand how employees view diversity in the workplace. For many older generation employees, diversity means equality and fairness for all workers regardless of their individual characteristics. In this view, less attention is made to what those differences actually are. Rather, employees look for policies that are defined and applied with fairness. This applies to organizational structures in particular. If it becomes evident that management- and executive-level positions are not being filled in a way that adheres to an organization's D&I principles, it is up to HR to investigate and resolve why this is happening. For example, HR may need to craft policies that remove demographic barriers to success or avoid nepotism or cronyism.

Valuing D&I Policies

Research shows that organizations with robust D&I policies are more profitable. Beyond the financial benefits, though, D&I makes sense for organizations operating in increasingly diverse environments. Many organizations say that it just makes sense to have a workforce whose makeup reflects that of the population they serve. In this way, then, an organization's commitment to diversity should be communicated to external stakeholders, helping the organization to build its relationship with clients and customers in the community. This can be accomplished by partnering with external diversity-focused programs and initiatives as well as by incorporating D&I accomplishments into marketing materials.

Fairness of Policies to All Employees

Fundamentally, an organization's D&I program needs to be all-encompassing and top-to-bottom. The commitment to and accountability for D&I need to begin with executive-level leadership and spread through leaders of all areas of the organization. However, leaders often defer to HR professionals when it comes to planning and executing D&I policies and programs.

HR professionals can also develop training programs to communicate D&I policies and model desired behavior. Again, these programs and policies should target employees from all levels of an organization, because lower-level managers will look to upper-level managers as a model for their diversity practices. Topics to cover can include things like cultural awareness, unconscious bias, generational differences, and communication styles. Research shows that employees consider things like creativity and innovation to be closely linked to diversity, so these topics can also be included in training programs.

Workplace Accommodations

Workplace accommodations fall within the scope of D&I, too. This generally relates to the Americans with Disabilities Act (ADA), which requires employers to offer reasonable accommodation to any employee with a medical condition that prevents them from performing all the functions of a job as described. Generally, it is up to the employee to request the accommodation rather than the employer to offer it first. Also, "reasonable" means that the accommodation will not place undue burden on the employer or fundamentally change the nature of its business. Examples of reasonable accommodations include installing ramps to make areas in the workplace wheelchair accessible or providing employees with additional break time. Of course, what constitutes a "reasonable" accommodation and "undue" employer burden must be evaluated on a case-by-case basis.

Also, accommodations do not only apply to physical disabilities and medical conditions. Employees might also request accommodations based on religious beliefs, for example, such as requiring time off during religious observations or refusing to perform job activities that violate their religious beliefs. Because reasonable accommodations still require employees to perform the essential function of their

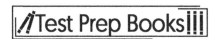

position and contribute to the overall purpose of the organization, HR professionals are responsible for reviewing job descriptions and determining whether the employees' requests can be accommodated.

Risk Management

An organization engages in risk management when it identifies, targets, and strives to minimize unacceptable risks. While a variety of different risks may arise, an organization's primary risks are generally workplace health, safety, security, and privacy. Failure to protect from these risks can result in serious consequences and may lead to negative company publicity, low employee morale, and burdensome expenses. Organizations must prioritize risk management and comply with federal laws and regulations. By doing so, employers will increase productivity and build sustainable relationships between employees and management.

Monitoring PESTLE Factors

HR professionals can monitor PESTLE factors that might have an influence on the organization and its workforce. By maintaining up-to-date knowledge on trends in these areas, HR professionals can predict upcoming changes and develop proactive strategies to handle them. For example, technological trends may indicate that some job functions will soon become automated, rendering certain worker skills obsolete. HR can anticipate where retraining may be needed for those workers. Or legal changes may affect things like hiring practices or worker benefits (health insurance, for example). HR should anticipate the potential costs this could cause the organization and plan accordingly. Economic factors that could affect the organization's profitability also closely impact HR, because any economic downturn can affect the organization's ability to attract, retain, and compensate employees.

Workplace Risk

Workplace violence is any act of physical violence, intimidation, threat, or verbal abuse that occurs in the workplace. This behavior is disruptive both physically and psychologically. Employees may demonstrate violent behavior as a result of a history of violence, a troubled upbringing, issues of substance abuse, and psychological illness. These conditions may foster violent behavior from an employee but do not make violent behavior inevitable. Workplace violence not only interrupts immediate employees, but can cause an organization to lose clients, suppliers, and advertisers. Furthermore, a firm can suffer devastating economic consequences as a result of negative publicity from incidents of workplace violence. Workplace violence attacks the foundation of trust and safety that all workplaces need to operate successfully.

Although an employer cannot completely eliminate the possibility of workplace violence, several steps can be taken to avoid these incidents. One example is a mental health program, such as an Employee Assistance Program (EAP), which provides employees the option to improve their psychological wellbeing. Additionally, offering company parties and functions in alcohol-free locations may reduce the likeliness of workplace violence. Violence may also be introduced in the workplace from the public. In areas with high crime rates, statistics show a higher probability of violence for employers who operate at night. Finally, organizations should establish and enforce a zero-tolerance policy for on-site weapons and acts of violence.

Substance abuse is a dependence on an addictive substance such as illegal drugs. This dependency not only impacts the individual but also may affect families and communities. Programs specifically designed to combat substance abuse can be extraordinarily beneficial. Because substance abuse is not limited to adults, programs may be introduced that focus on children and adolescents as well. In addition to the physical dangers of substance abuse, subsequent behavioral patterns compound issues. If treatment is not sought, the likelihood of a life of crime and poverty greatly increases.

Effective substance abuse policies protect both employers and employees in the workplace. Privacy policies generally authorize employers to conduct random drug tests if the employee has given prior consent. The employee should be clearly notified when hired that these tests may be administered by the employer. Employee substance abuse is damaging to the workplace and often results in inappropriate conduct with coworkers, insubordination, and fatal injuries due to improper use of machinery.

Through the Americans with Disabilities Act, federal guidelines exist to protect both employers and employees in regards to substance abuse. Employers do have the right to ensure a drug-free workplace by prohibiting the use of illegal drugs and alcohol. Employers may test for illegal drug use, but must meet state requirements to do so. If an employee tests positive for current drug use through proper testing procedures, employers have the right to terminate that employee.

The ADA gives protection to employees who have successfully rehabilitated from past drug use but are no longer engaged in the illegal use of drugs. Employers cannot discriminate against any employee who has either completed a rehabilitation program or is undergoing rehabilitation. Reasonable accommodation efforts should be extended to those individuals who are rehabilitated or are undergoing current treatment.

Ergonomics refers to the ability of a person to fully utilize a product while maintaining maximum safety, efficiency, and comfort. Ergonomic risk factors in the workplace can lead to musculoskeletal disorders such as carpal tunnel syndrome, rotator cuff injuries, muscle strains, and lower back injuries. In order to reduce these risks, employers should evaluate workplace ergonomics and educate employees about potential issues. An ergonomic evaluation tests a product to determine its ease of use and potential safety risks. When employers identify and address ergonomic concerns in the workplace, they protect their workers and likely prevent serious injuries.

Crisis Management

All organizations must have procedures that secure an orderly response in the event of an emergency. Emergency response plans incorporate several elements of maintaining safety and order. These elements may include practiced evacuations, reserved resources to preserve organizational function, and a plan that seeks to minimize property damage. An organization with no emergency response plan is vulnerable to instability, disorder, and distrust. An effective emergency response plan not only protects lives and property, but also provides security that management has control over the situation. This knowledge provides an element of calm in an otherwise stressful emergency situation, which can be as important as the response protocol.

An emergency response is a planned and practiced protocol used during an emergency. These strategies should be planned rationally and practiced frequently in order to mitigate the impact of a disaster. Workplace emergency responses should plan for a wide range of scenarios, such as machinery malfunctions or workplace violence. Once created, emergency response plans should be communicated to all staff, frequently tested by the organization, and kept up-to-date.

An evacuation is a coordinated and planned exit from a place that is considered to be dangerous. It is a principal component of general health and safety policies. Conditions that may prompt evacuation are fire, flood, or violence. The most effective way to orchestrate an orderly and calm evacuation is through

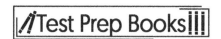

practice of an evacuation plan. This routine practice familiarizes staff with expedient exit routes and ensures that exits remain visible and unobstructed.

Hazard communication is the notification of employees concerning the noxious health effects and physical dangers of hazardous chemicals in the workplace. Workers should be clearly notified of any physical hazards (corrosion or flammability) or health hazards (skin irritation and carcinogenicity) that they will come into contact with in the workplace. OSHA created the Hazard Communication Standard (HCS) to ensure that chemical information is accessible to all individuals who may interact with the substance. In addition to the HCS, all employers are required to implement a hazard communication program that encompasses training, access to material safety data sheets (MSDS), and labeling of hazardous chemical containers.

Risk Mitigation

Injuries and illnesses are a burden for both employers and employees. The loss of productivity due to workplace injuries and illnesses can be significant, and the loss of income for employees can affect an individual and economy as a whole. Therefore, organizations must establish programs that minimize or prevent these incidents. If a workplace injury or illness does occur, workers' compensation may provide fixed payments to the employee. Workers' compensation also covers dependents of those who are killed as a result of workplace accidents. Limits do exist for these compensation benefits, such as caps on what can be collected from employers.

OSHA, a federal agency that is designed to ensure safe working conditions for employees, established process safety management standards that deal with hazardous chemicals in the workplace. If an employee could potentially come into contact with the hazardous substance during the normal course of their jobs, these substances must be properly evaluated, classified, and labeled. This information is recorded in material safety data sheets (MSDS), which must be easily accessible to individuals who work with any hazardous materials. The MSDS should state what should be done if someone has inappropriate contact with the chemicals, such as an employee who splashes a dangerous chemical in their eye.

OSHA has developed standards for employee personal protective equipment (PPE) in hazardous working environments. These items may include safety glasses, hard hats, and safety shoes. Employees are provided these items at no cost and must be paid their rate of pay for the time required to put on and take off protective equipment.

OSHA has established guidelines to assist employers in the event of a pandemic disease outbreak by utilizing proper safety equipment and procedures. The guidelines are also meant to assist the company to continue operations with a reduced workforce.

Ergonomics, or the study and design of the work environment to address physical demands placed on employees, is yet another area addressed by OSHA. In the workplace, ergonomics deals with elements such as lighting, placement of controls, equipment layout, and fatigue. OSHA examines work-related injuries that result from repetitive stress and repetitive motion, such as carpal tunnel syndrome. These are also known as cumulative trauma disorders. These workplace injuries may be reduced by redesigning workstations and improving workplace environments.

Due Diligence Investigations

Minimizing injuries in the workplace is a primary concern for employers. Accidents and injuries triggered by safety risks diminish productivity and reduce savings because of costly workers' compensation payments. Furthermore, failure to adequately protect workers can result in employer penalties and fines. Two common workplace safety risks are tripping hazards and bloodborne pathogens.

Trip hazards cause a person's foot to hit an object that does not budge, plunging the person forward involuntarily. Tripping can occur in the workplace for many reasons such as obstructed views, poor lighting, excessive clutter, uneven walking surfaces, wrinkled carpeting, or unsecure wires. Tripping may result in injuries such as sprains, broken bones, or torn ligaments. Employers should maintain an orderly workplace and arrange for bright lighting to reduce the likelihood of tripping. Accordingly, employees should pay attention and make wide turns when walking, and walk with their feet pointed outward.

Bloodborne pathogens are infectious microorganisms in human blood that can cause disease in humans. Specifically, some of these pathogens are hepatitis B virus (HBV), hepatitis C virus (HCV), and human immunodeficiency virus (HIV). One potential cause of spreading bloodborne pathogens is through improper usage and/or disposal of needles. Occupations such as nursing, healthcare professionals, medical first responders, and housekeepers who work in medical environments are the most likely to encounter a needle contaminated with bloodborne pathogens. Due to growing concerns within the medical field, The Needlestick Safety and Prevention Act of 2000 revised OSHA's Bloodborne Pathogens Standard. This law provides requirements in selecting medical devices and establishes oversight through a sharps injury log, which details all sharps-related workplace injuries.

Additional workplace safety risks with OSHA regulations are occupational noise exposure, emergency exit procedures, control of hazardous materials, lockout/tagout procedures, machine guarding, and confined space environments.

Workers' compensation laws are designed to protect employees who are injured in the workplace. The primary purpose of workers' compensation is to provide injured employees with fixed monetary sums. Worker's compensation benefits cover medical expenses due to workplace injuries. Furthermore, workers' compensation benefits are extended to dependents of employees killed by an injury or illness that occurs in the workplace. In addition to employee protection, some worker's compensation laws protect employers by limiting the amount of money that can be distributed to employees. The program also has provisions that restrict coworker liability in most workplace accidents. Most workers' compensation programs are structured at the state level by legislative bodies and agencies. However, worker's compensation exists at the federal level, where it is limited to federal employment and industries that considerably affect interstate commerce.

Obtaining a safe and secure working environment is not accomplished by simply strategizing. The staff of an organization must have adequate training to appropriately respond to diverse situations. Workplace security plans and policies address a variety of issues from a sudden crisis to an act of intentional harm. A clear understanding of security plans and policies can minimize unpredictability and panic and teach employees how to respond to a crisis.

Employees should understand security plans and how they address the physical security needs of the work environment. Workplace security plans and policies may include security measures such as control badges, keycard access systems, backup communication systems, locks on various rooms and closets, and concealed alarms. When developing workplace security plans, a team approach is vital to ensuring its success. Representatives are needed from human resources, legal counsel, security, and facilities to provide a comprehensive perspective of security needs. Once the security plans and policies are established, employees should be trained annually to review the plans and their importance.

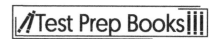

Theft is the act of taking property without the consent of the owner. Theft can occur by deception or force, with or without the knowledge of the owner. Theft can be very costly to an organization, and management should take steps to prevent any opportunity for theft. Such measures may include hidden video cameras, a private security force, and incentives for employees who disrupt incidents of theft. Theft can be accomplished by employees, management, and customers. Therefore, prevention policies should apply to all levels of the organization.

Corporate espionage is a form of spying that occurs between competitive companies. The principal purpose of corporate espionage is to obtain industrial secrets and learn about a competitor's plans, future products, business strategies, or total profits. Knowing these secrets can give a competitor an unfair advantage when trying to increase market share. A company must hire trustworthy employees, particularly employees privy to classified information. A firm should employ strategies to test employee loyalty and offer incentives that encourage employees to report suspicious activity.

Sabotage is the act of purposely weakening or corrupting a country or a company. In the workplace, sabotage is the intentional thwarting of successful planning models to create dysfunctional conditions at odds with the organization's best interests. Those who commit sabotage are known as saboteurs, and they generally conceal their identity and intentions. Sabotage is debilitating to a company, and can cultivate an environment of distrust and hostility. Therefore, management must conduct frequent tests to ensure that all members and employees act in good faith.

Safety- and Health-Related Investigations
Strict enforcement of workplace safety and security is contingent on investigative agencies. If an employer is reported, OSHA will conduct an investigation into the workplace. Throughout an investigation, OSHA works in conjunction with employers and employees to ensure greater safety and security policies are implemented. OSHA agents look beyond the immediate causes of an incident and attempt to uncover the systemic causes. OSHA investigators attempt to discover why a particular problem exists if it is determined that the issue is not a result of individual carelessness.

Following an investigation, an OSHA compliance officer can issue citations depending on the severity of the violation. If an OSHA inspector observes a violation of imminent danger, the inspector will require the employer to correct the issue immediately, as the violation will lead to serious harm or death. Other violations may be labeled serious, which means that the violation will likely cause death or physical harm. Other-than-serious is the next level of violation. This means that the condition could impact employees' safety or health but probably would not cause death or serious harm. De minimus violations are not directly and immediately related to employees' safety or health and do not require fines or citations. Willful and repeated citations are issued to employers who are repeat offenders of hazardous workplace violations. Penalties for unaddressed or intentional safety violations are very costly.

Auditing Risk Management
Risk management is especially important in human resources, which can account for a significant portion of an organization's financial risk, especially in terms of liability and legal concerns. For example, the organization can be held liable for compliance (or non-compliance) with labor laws, proper management of employee information, and legal concerns of employees like workplace safety and sexual harassment. HR can identify which risks are the most pressing for their organization and plan accordingly, perhaps through an HR audit. Like any audit, an HR audit is an inspection—in this case, of an organization's HR policies and practices. The purpose of an HR audit is to check that policies are in line with all applicable laws and regulations and are properly followed by all employees.

Workplace Health and Safety Standards

Workplace policies should strictly follow federal laws in order to legally secure a workplace that satisfies minimum health, safety, security, and privacy standards. Failure to meet federal standards can result in fines or the loss of a license. Federal laws and regulations function as minimum standards that all workplace policies must meet. Employers are allowed to pursue policies that go beyond what is legally required if they believe such policies will benefit the organization. Many employers strive to understand the delicate balance between meeting federal guidelines and maintaining high profit margins. Therefore, organizations often find innovative ways to meet federal standards while using efficient business strategies.

Five federal agencies and laws regarding workplace issues are the Occupational Safety and Health Administration (OSHA), the Drug-Free Work Place Act, the Americans with Disabilities Act, the Health Insurance Portability and Accountability Act, and the Sarbanes-Oxley Act.

The Occupational Safety and Health Act, passed in 1970, established the Occupational Safety and Health Administration (OSHA) of the federal government in 1971. This agency creates and enforces workplace safety standards. Employers who are engaged in commerce and have one or more employees must observe the regulations established by OSHA. Not only does OSHA set minimum standards, the agency ensures job training for workers in a language they can understand. Additionally, OSHA protects employees who work in substandard conditions and informs them of their rights. A critical provision of OSHA is the protection of employees who reach out to OSHA in an attempt to open an investigation of their working conditions. These employees are protected by OSHA from employer retaliation. OSHA regulations empower employees to help accomplish safety and security.

OSHA regulations focus on employer and employee rights and responsibilities. Employers must provide a safe workplace for employees. Employers are required to meet all OSHA safety standards and correct any violations. Employers are required to attempt to reduce hazards to workers and must supply free protective equipment to workers. OSHA guidelines require employers to provide safety training and to prominently display OSHA posters that detail employee rights. Employers must keep accurate records of any injuries or illnesses that occur in the workplace and notify OSHA promptly of any injuries. Furthermore, employers may not retaliate if an employee uses their right to report an OSHA violation.

OSHA regulations provide specific rights to employees. Employees have the right to demand safety on the job and obtain information concerning work hazards. Every employee has the right to file a complaint with OSHA and request a workplace inspection without fear of employer retaliation. Employees have the right to meet privately with a licensed OSHA inspector. Additionally, OSHA regulations allow employees to refuse work that may be abnormally dangerous or life-threatening.

The Drug-Free Workplace Act of 1988 requires organizations to establish a drug-free workplace, provide a copy of this policy to their employees, and institute a drug awareness program. This law applies to federal contractors with contracts of $100,000 or more and all organizations that are federal grantees. Different penalties exist for employers who do not comply with the act, including contract suspension or contract termination. Although an employer may discuss alcohol and tobacco use in its policies, the Drug-Free Workplace Act does not address the use of these substances.

The Americans with Disabilities Act (ADA) is a federal law that prevents discrimination based on disability. This law requires employers to provide reasonable accommodations to employees with a disability. For example, an employer may accommodate a disabled employee by building a wheelchair accessible ramp to enter and exit the building. Additionally, the ADA stipulates that public entities be

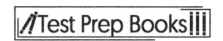

accessible for disabled persons. The ADA does include both mental and physical medical conditions, and temporary conditions may qualify as a disability. ADA protections apply to every aspect of job application procedures, employment, and promotions.

The Health Insurance Portability and Accountability Act of 1996 (HIPAA) addresses issues of healthcare access and portability as well as aspects of healthcare administration. HIPAA provisions allow workers that change jobs or become unemployed to transfer and continue their healthcare coverage. Additionally, HIPAA regulations establish standards for healthcare administration in order to reduce waste, fraud, and abuse. HIPAA laws strengthen privacy standards and provide benchmarks for medical records in areas such as electronic billing.

HIPAA is applicable to health insurance plans issued by companies, HMOs, Medicare, and Medicaid. Moreover, these regulations apply to healthcare providers who conduct transactions electronically and healthcare clearing houses that process certain information. HIPAA's Privacy Rule gives rights to the insured regarding the disclosure of medical information. Individuals may view health records and request an edit of inaccurate information. Additionally, individuals may file a complaint if rights are being denied or health information is not protected. Patient information with heightened protection is placed in the insurer's database and may include conversations about patients between medical professionals and billing information. Lastly, HIPAA creates strict rules regarding how healthcare information is disseminated and specifies who is given access.

The Sarbanes-Oxley Act of 2002, or SOX, is federal legislation that is designed to establish higher levels of accountability and standards for U.S. public institution boards and senior management. The act was passed in reaction to major global corporate and accounting scandals such as WorldCom and Enron, companies caught engaging in dubious financial practices. Sarbanes-Oxley specifically targets senior executives responsible for accounting misconduct and record manipulation. The law protects shareholders from any activity that conceals or misleads investors about the firm's finances. The firm has a mandate to transparently and accurately report financial information either to shareholders or the Securities and Exchange Commission (SEC). Moreover, SOX imposes more stringent penalties for white-collar crime and requires detailed reporting to the SEC if a company's finances significantly alter.

Level of Risk

No matter how carefully an organization conducts research, carries out analyses, and develops strategic plans, the organization will always face unknowns. There are risks that activities will fail, outside obstacles will appear, or new threats will emerge. **Enterprise risk management (ERM)** is a method of managing unknowable risks by anticipating potential risks, focusing on those with the greatest likelihood or potential impact, and planning a response strategy for when risks become realities.

An organization could choose four different responses to a particular risk: reduce the effects of the risk, share it, avoid it, or accept it. In order to reduce the effects of the risk, the organization finds ways to decrease its likelihood or to soften its potential harmful impact. If the organization wants to avoid the risk altogether, it will simply cease all activity associated with that risk. Finally, an organization might decide to go ahead and accept a risk; this might happen when cost-benefit analysis has determined that the benefits greatly outweigh all potential risk to the organization.

Corporate Social Responsibility

Corporate Social Responsibility (CSR) refers to an organization's sense of responsibility for its impact on the environment and community. CSR can be evaluated based on the three Ps of the "triple bottom line": people, planet, and profit. *People* refers to fair employment practices as well as the organization's impact on members of the community; *planet* refers to the organization's environmental impact (such as pollution, consumption of natural resources, etc.); and *profit* refers to the organization's overall contribution to economic growth. Having a CSR program encourages an organization to operate within legal, moral, and ethical boundaries. From an HR perspective, an organization's CSR program can also affect employee recruiting because the program demonstrates the organization's commitment to fair working conditions.

Community Role Model
Corporate social responsibility (CSR) refers to acknowledgement of how an organization affects the lives of its internal and external stakeholders and a commitment to work toward a positive and sustainable relationship between the organization and its environment. Sustainability, in particular, means that an organization's current needs will not compromise the needs of future stakeholders. CSR and sustainability should contribute to the "triple bottom line": economic, social, and environmental benefits. Although a strong CSR plan needs to begin with executive leadership and continue with follow-through from the everyday actions of employees, HR professionals play an important role in planning, implementing, and holding employees at all levels of an organization accountable to stated CSR goals.

Community-Based Volunteer
Because CSR relies on interactions between the organization and external stakeholders, HR professionals are tasked with representing the organization and its employees when interacting with the community. Times when HR professional might interact with community members include engaging in local, community-based programs for volunteering activities. HR professionals can help identify opportunities for the organization to give back to the local community and either partner with local organizations or develop their company's own programs for volunteering and philanthropy. For example, a tech company that operates near a low-income neighborhood may choose to provide mentoring or scholarship opportunities to students in the neighborhood to provide access to science, technology, engineering, and mathematics (STEM) education programs and future career development. Or a factory might coordinate with local environmental groups to encourage employee participation in environmental cleanup operations.

Corporate Social Responsibility (CSR) Activities
It is important to remember that CSR activities don't come from legal obligations, but rather a moral and ethical sense of responsibility. HR professionals, then, can present an organization's outward face in researching and identifying areas of local engagement. Most importantly, HR is responsible for translating those opportunities into actionable changes within the organization. HR professionals need to understand the impact of CSR activities and communicate that back to staff at all levels of the organization. This includes quantitative benefits—what financial incentives are there for participating in CSR initiatives? Because CSR activities contribute to how an organization is viewed within its community, and the level of trust that stakeholders have in an organization contributes to its ability to do business, there is indeed a strong financial incentive to commit to CSR goals and maintain the profitability of the organization. Losing customers' trust can mean losing business.

Role of CSR Activities in Impacting the Community
HR professionals also need to understand the qualitative impacts of CSR. Studies show that employee satisfaction is highly correlated with feeling that their work is meaningful and that they are making a positive impact to society. Particularly for today's generation of new employees, social impact and engagement is a crucial factor in selecting their job field. Encouraging employee involvement in CSR

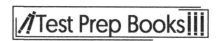

initiatives is one way that HR can improve employee satisfaction and help develop an organization's sense of culture. Also, if employees understand why they are being asked to engage in certain behaviors and are included in the process of changing workplace behaviors, they are more likely to follow through on them.

Maintaining Transparency

Communication regarding CSR planning is multifaceted. On the one hand, HR professionals need to present information to an organization's leadership to demonstrate the benefits of partaking in socially sustainable activities. Commitment to CSR must be part of the organization's overall culture, so it is impossible to move forward without executive-level support. On the other hand, HR must then also communicate those goals and behaviors to employees throughout the organization to make sure that they are carried out. One way to do this is by tying CSR initiatives to performance management. As with any HR program, it is important to determine measurable standards for employee accountability.

Environmentally Responsible Business Practices

Part of CSR is building an organization's image, brand, and reputation with the community it serves. While a company's trustworthiness may be difficult to quantify, it nevertheless has a meaningful impact on how its operations are perceived. One important factor in trust and reputation is transparency, or openness in dealings, decisions, and other information. It is an opportunity for an organization to not merely say, but to also show, that it is committed to its stated business practices and goals. For example, if an organization wants to focus its CSR activities on achieving environmentally sustainable practices, it might work on communicating those goals to external stakeholders through advertising and marketing campaigns. However, eventually those stakeholders will want to see the processes actually taking place, and it is up to the organization to share relevant information.

For example, HR might help the company share information about goals for reducing emissions, budget plans for investing in more environmentally-friendly equipment, or programs that train employees to engage in green behaviors in the office. Being transparent about these practices helps to build trust. Similarly, HR can work on building transparency about CSR within an organization. If one of an organization's CSR goals is to improve diversity in hiring, for instance, HR can provide information about how it is working toward meeting hiring goals, how its employee demographics compare with those of other organizations, or how it is supporting mentoring programs for marginalized groups. HR professionals can also work with managers to achieve appropriate levels of transparency throughout the organization.

U.S. Employment Laws and Regulations

HR professionals need to be familiar with relevant employment laws and regulations. Applicable laws may vary based on organization type, size, and other factors, but there are many regulations that apply to the majority of organizations. Several important regulations are administered by the Equal Employment Opportunity Commission, or EEOC. One of these is Title VII of the Civil Rights Act of 1964, which applies to employers with fifteen or more employees and prohibits discrimination based on race, color, religion, sex, or national origin. EEOC also oversees the Age Discrimination in Employment Act of 1967 (ADEA), which prohibits discrimination against anyone forty years old or older in terms of things like hiring, promotion, wages, termination, and denial of benefits. The ADEA also prohibits mandatory retirement in many sectors. The Equal Pay Act (EPA) prohibits wage discrimination based on sex for people in the same organization performing the same or similar jobs (in terms of skills and responsibilities) under the same or similar conditions. In addition, the EEOC administers ADA, discussed earlier in this study guide.

Domestic and Global Employment Laws

Other important regulations include the Fair Labor Standard Act (FLSA) which establishes things like minimum wage and overtime pay, standards for child labor, and defining exempt and non-exempt employees. The Family and Medical Leave Act (FMLA) outlines standards for when employees are permitted to take unpaid, job-protected family and medical leave. The Occupational Safety and Health Act of 1970 created the Occupational Safety and Health Administration (OSHA), which ensures that employers provide a safe and healthy workplace. This includes things like eliminating or reducing hazards when possible, providing free safety equipment, informing employees about chemical hazards, providing comprehensive and comprehensible safety training, keeping records of work-related injuries and illnesses, and displaying the official OSHA poster describing employees' rights and employers' responsibilities.

HR Programs, Practices, and Policies that Comply with Regulations

HR programs, practices, and policies must align and comply with these laws and regulations and others. This means staying current on local, state, and federal regulations, as well as any international laws that may be applicable. It also means being proactive and circumspect about where laws need to be applied. This ensures that the organization is providing a safe and fair workplace for employees, while also ensuring that the organization avoids any fees, fines, lawsuits, or other liabilities that may arise from not following the law. For example, when posting a job advertisement, HR must ensure that there are no references to restricting hiring based on things like age, race, or sex. The same applies to the interviewing and hiring stages and even terminating employees.

Illegal HR-Related Behaviors

Because these decisions and practices can extend beyond HR, HR professionals are also responsible for coaching employees at all levels about how to avoid illegal and noncompliant behaviors. One way to keep employees informed is by displaying posters related to applicable laws and regulations; as previously mentioned, employers are required to display certain information (related to things like OSHA and FLSA), depending on such factors as the size, location, and type of organization. The U.S. Department of Labor (DOL) offers resources to help organizations determine what information they are legally obligated to display for employees. HR can also coach employees who are responsible for things like hiring and terminating decisions in order to avoid illegal terminations, for example, or illegal questions during job interviews.

Interviewers should be sure to ask only questions that are job-related and determine qualifications that are justified by a business purpose (also known as bona fide occupational qualification, or BFOQ). If interviewers and hiring managers are screening employees based on factors that are not covered by BFOQ, it can present grounds for complaints of discrimination (for example, when an employer requires a higher level of education than is necessary for a position, and then uses this requirement as a basis to screen applicants of certain racial or socioeconomic backgrounds).

Broker Services

HR professionals can and should also consult legal experts as needed when it comes to the interpretation and application of employment laws. Whether those legal services are internal or external may depend on the nature of the organization. Smaller organizations may be more likely to consult with outside services, while large organizations are more like to have in-house legal services.

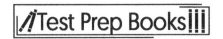

However, particularly when an organization begins operation in a new area (for example, in a new state or country), it would be a prudent move to consult with experts who have experience in local laws.

Behavioral Competency

1. SMART goals should have which of the following characteristics?
   a. Specific, Measurable, Achievable, Relevant, Timely
   b. Situational, Measurable, Action, Relatable, Timely
   c. Sensitive, Methodological, Achievable, Relevant, Timely
   d. Solid, Measurable, Automated, Reliable, Tested

2. When performing a cost-benefit analysis of a proposed project, what is a project worker's salary an example of?
   a. A stakeholder
   b. A cost
   c. A benefit
   d. A dependent variable

3. Which of the following is a tool from the Six Sigma approach?
   a. Value stream mapping
   b. HRIS
   c. SMART
   d. Flow state diagram

4. An organization's overall attitude towards dress code, working remotely, social retreats for employees, and designated break times can best be described as which of the following?
   a. Customer-centric
   b. Work-life balance
   c. Freebies
   d. Corporate culture

5. Which components of a SWOT matrix examine influences that are external to the organization?
   a. Strengths and weaknesses
   b. Opportunities and threats
   c. Strengths and opportunities
   d. Weaknesses and threats

6. Which components of a SWOT matrix examine influences that are internal to the organization?
   a. Strengths and weaknesses
   b. Opportunities and threats
   c. Strengths and opportunities
   d. Weaknesses and threats

7. Which of the following data collection methods require the services of a skilled facilitator?
   a. Paper surveys
   b. Online surveys
   c. Focus groups
   d. Classroom trainings

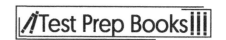

8. What does it mean when a process has been validated?
    a. That the process has been archived and no longer needs review
    b. The process has been approved by an external regulatory body, like the FDA
    c. That the process has been approved by upper management
    d. That process inputs produce the same desired output each time the process takes place

9. What is the practice of benchmarking?
    a. Using statistics to make decisions
    b. Using chalk or other removable material to mark proposed specifications on a prototype
    c. Comparing an organization's initiatives and outcomes against industry standards
    d. Holding a back-up candidate for a position in case a primary candidate rejects a job offer

10. What is confirmation bias?
    a. The human tendency to seek, favor, or influence data to match personal preferences or an established hypothesis
    b. Asking for professional help only from colleagues that are guaranteed to say yes, therefore eliminating one's networking capacity
    c. Choosing to select a random sample from a telephone book of names
    d. Promoting evidence-based research for all decision-making within an organization

11. When working with multiple stakeholders who have varied interests, what is the best way to propose and develop a new initiative?
    a. Base the initiative around the interests of the stakeholder in the group who holds the highest position within the organization
    b. Place all interests into a random generator, and allow an initiative topic to be randomly selected
    c. Via email
    d. Select an overlapping interest that could have a feasible solution

12. Self-awareness, social awareness, relationship management, and self-management are components of which of the following?
    a. Emotional intelligence
    b. Intellectual quotient
    c. Company lunch-and-learn trainings
    d. New hire training

13. What factors does a PESTLE analysis take into consideration?
    a. People, projects, and payments within an organization
    b. Political, economic, social, technological, legal, and environmental trends that influence the organization
    c. People, engagement, sustainability, time, limitations, and expectations in relation to a specific project
    d. The most proximal direct competitor

14. What is the purpose of a root cause analysis?
    a. To determine the foundation-level reason as to why an overarching issue is occurring
    b. To determine the exact employee that caused an error during a process
    c. To determine the best source of external funding
    d. To determine how to allocate fixed funds within an organization

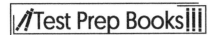

15. What are two popular search tools to find peer-reviewed, evidence-based research?
    a. CNN and FOX
    b. Medline and Yahoo News
    c. Google Scholar and PubMed
    d. People Quest and People Soft

16. Meeting, learning from, and socializing with colleagues within and outside of one's organization is known as which of the following practices?
    a. Networking
    b. Achieving work-life balance
    c. Formal education
    d. Fraternizing

17. Lisa is an HR generalist that is posting a job online. She is proud of her company's benefits system and wants to highlight some of them in the posting. What types of benefits could she include in the job posting?
    a. Company-sponsored worksite wellness program, 401(k) matching up to 5%, and an annual sponsored mindfulness retreat
    b. Job tasks, including the amount of time spent sitting each day
    c. Number of direct reports for the position
    d. An exact salary number

18. During new hire orientation, Joe wants to illustrate the company culture to new employees. What are some things he could share with them to show the organization's culture?
    a. Share that employees can choose to work remotely one day per week, that leadership sits with employees in an open workspace, and the last Friday of each month is used to celebrate an employee's personal heritage
    b. Share that new equipment will be delivered at the end of the month, and that he will follow up with each employee on assignment
    c. Share his personal career story, beginning from choosing a major in college
    d. Enroll employees in a required CPR/AED course

19. Mila is in the planning stages of an HR initiative that focuses on providing a catered healthy lunch to all employees each Monday. What is something she should focus on during the planning stage?
    I. Developing a SMART goal to determine why she wants to pursue this initiative and how she will know if it is successful
    II. Identifying stakeholders and gathering their opinions on meal types and the value of this initiative
    III. Surveying employees who attended about how they enjoyed the food served
    IV. Creating a budget proposal
    a. I and II
    b. I, II, and III
    c. I, II, and IV
    d. All of the above

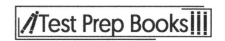

20. An HR team is developing a budget for a hiring campaign. The associated costs include marketing materials; a venue rental for a hiring fair; and the time, labor, and salaries of the staff who will work at the fair. What types of cost are these?
    a. Indirect costs
    b. Regulatory costs
    c. Direct costs
    d. Training costs

21. Each fiscal quarter within a fiscal year is an example of which of the following?
    a. Benchmarking
    b. A milestone
    c. Calendar divides
    d. Bonus assessment period

22. Ray and Nash report to team leader, Dan, who is regularly out of the office. Dan takes up to a week to respond to their emails and his phone usually goes straight to voicemail. Dan is always in the office on Tuesdays, when he checks in with Ray and Nash and answers any questions of theirs. What is a clear obstacle in this team dynamic?
    a. Ray and Nash have to share a single office
    b. Dan answers Ray's and Nash's questions together instead of individually
    c. Dan only has two reports
    d. Dan does not support a reliable communication channel

23. Which reputable approach encourages producing the most value from the least resources?
    a. Six Sigma
    b. Lean
    c. Minimalist
    d. Sustainability

24. Myra and Angela are two HR professionals who work in the same organization. Recently, Myra successfully implemented a sustainability initiative with the marketing department, where she helped them reduce the amount of paper they use. This led to saved paper, printing, and labor costs as well as reduced physical waste. Angela would like to try this initiative with the finance department, which is welcome to this idea. How can Angela begin to allocate resources for this project?
    a. Copy Myra's initiative as closely as possible, right down to the budget and timeline
    b. Use her best guess to document what she believes the finance department will need in order to reduce their paper waste, and provide a written copy to the manager
    c. Set up a meeting with Myra to discuss how she allocated resources and what went successfully, as well as what did not go successfully, and use this data to plan
    d. Ask the HR intern to devote all of his time to her initiative

25. Michael leads an HR department at a federal agency. He is in the planning stage for the new fiscal year and is thrilled that he has created initiatives that are highly detailed and comprehensive and uses the resources of contracts his agency currently has in place. He is very attached to the outcomes of these initiatives. However, a presidential election is taking place in one month that will likely affect the contracts that are awarded to his agency. What can Michael do to protect his new fiscal year plans?
a. Ensure that there is leftover money from the previous fiscal year to serve as a cushion should he not receive expected contracts
b. Create backup plans for all of the contracts that may be affected, while calmly accepting that some changes may be unanticipated and out of his control
c. Nothing, he has already distributed them to employees and archived them on the organization's servers
d. Find a new job

26. Larry manages three HR employees. Jane is in charge of compensation and benefit tasks, Ira is in charge of risk management tasks, and Samir is in charge of recruitment and hiring. Samir has an illness that takes him out of the office for six weeks, and during this time, all recruitment and hiring processes freeze. This majorly impacts two other departments that were waiting on new employees to begin. How could this situation have best been prevented?
a. Larry should have cross-trained his three employees to fill in for each other should emergencies come up.
b. Samir should have worked remotely to handle the candidates needed by the other two departments.
c. Larry should have filled in for Samir's role for the entire duration of his absence.
d. Ira should have analyzed Samir's workday operations to see if anything at work caused his illness.

27. An organization is trying to improve its parental leave policy. Who in the organization could be considered key stakeholders for this initiative?
a. Pregnant female employees
b. Male employees
c. Managers of both sexes
d. All of the above

28. What is one way to build credibility as an HR expert?
I. Pursue a master's degree in Human Resources from an accredited university
II. Take online personality surveys, such as Myers-Briggs, to determine your strengths
III. Earn nationally recognized certifications in the field
IV. Attend workshops and share key takeaways with your organization
a. I, III, and IV
b. I, II, and III
c. I, II, and IV
d. All of the above

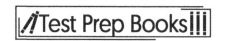

29. Tomas, an HR professional, is meeting with his direct manager, an entry-level employee in another department, and the vice-president of his organization to propose a system-wide HR initiative. What is the single most important thing Tomas can do during his proposal to promote buy-in?
   a. Wear his best suit and make sure his shoes are polished to give a solid first impression.
   b. Go to the conference room early and make sure all of his technological devices work properly for the presentation.
   c. Illustrate the value that the initiative will bring to the executive, managerial, and employee levels of the organization.
   d. Offer to pay for half of the required resources out of pocket.

30. What is the most crucial aspect of successfully implementing organizational change?
   a. Work ethic
   b. Leadership buy-in
   c. Highly compensated employees
   d. Terminating employees who do not agree

31. Jenny is an introverted individual who works best alone and behind the scenes. She is hired by a small firm to do data analysis and scientific report writing, two tasks she loves and excels at. She enjoys her first week very much and receives a great deal of praise from her colleagues and manager. However, a staffing change causes the firm to give her additional responsibilities, including organizing large team-building and training events. Jenny struggles with these responsibilities and after her thirty-day probationary period, the firm lets her go. What is the probable reason for Jenny's termination?
   a. Jenny is not a team player.
   b. Jenny has poor work ethic.
   c. Jenny was not a good fit with her new responsibilities.
   d. Jenny is not smart enough to work at the firm.

32. Lowry recently experienced the death of a loved one. While Lowry was once a stellar employee, he now begins to come to work late and is slow to finish his tasks. He appears disinterested in his work and eventually begins using up his sick days. Lowry's manager tries to support him by providing grievance resources, offering new job responsibilities, and providing the option of working from home; however, Lowry is not interested in any of these options. What lesson can Lowry's manager learn from this situation?
   a. Employees should be fired at the first sign of disengagement to avoid waste of time and resources
   b. Managers should not care too much about their employees, as it can cause emotional distress
   c. Managers should get to know their employees better outside of work, rather than only in the workplace
   d. Employee motivation is often influenced by factors that are outside of the manager's locus of control

33. What is a lean way of communicating HR programs, policies, and practices, including real-time updates?
   a. An employee handbook that is reprinted and redistributed with each new version
   b. In-person conferences that regularly review protocols
   c. An online employee handbook that is accessible to every employee and is updated online
   d. Social media

34. An employee sees a close colleague change numbers in an accounting spreadsheet to reflect incorrect values. The employee feels uncomfortable reporting the colleague, due to their friendship and close working relationship. However, the employee feels very concerned about the situation. What is one feasible resource that could help this employee in a situation like this?
    a. An anonymous and confidential HR hotline
    b. A close relationship with a superior
    c. An in-house coffee shop where the employee can go with the colleague to discuss their feelings about the situation
    d. Regular communication training sessions

35. What is the best way for HR leaders to communicate acceptable and ethical behaviors in the workplace?
    a. Provide written protocols about what constitutes as ethical and unethical behavior
    b. Relay that employees are continuously monitored with in-house cameras, so they should be especially mindful of their work behavior
    c. Model acceptable and ethical behavior themselves, as much as possible
    d. Tell employees at their new hire orientation

36. The CEO of a company holds bi-weekly meetings with his entire organization to relay new information about company performance, trends, and personal opinions relating to the industry. What is this an example of?
    a. Transparency
    b. Overshare
    c. Validation
    d. Process control

37. Where should an employee first encounter an organization's ethical standards and policies?
    a. At the new hire orientation
    b. During the first interview
    c. In the job posting for their role
    d. By reading a company press release

38. Genevieve is interviewing a new candidate, Marcus, with whom she is very impressed. He has the perfect educational background, professional experience, and cultural fit for a position she is trying to fill. She has not met any comparable candidates during the hiring campaign for this position. However, when she runs a background check, she finds that he was arrested for a DUI approximately eight years prior but was not charged. Besides this event, his background check returns clear. What is the best course of action for Genevieve to take in this situation?
    a. Eliminate Marcus from the candidate pool and continue interviewing other candidates
    b. Assume there is an error on the background check
    c. Ignore the charge and offer Marcus the job
    d. Set up an appointment with Marcus to find out the context around the charge

39. Why is networking outside of one's own organization a valuable professional experience?
    a. It can provide innovative insight that one can apply to their own organization
    b. It is nice to get out of the office once in a while
    c. It allows one to spy on the competition
    d. It allows one to learn more about their city

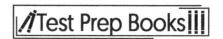

40. There is a new employee in Janelle's department. On the new employee's first day, Janelle sets up a team lunch at a nearby restaurant and asks the new employee to attend. During lunch, Janelle asks the new employee about his past work experiences and personal interests. She also lets him know that she can help him with any questions he might have during his first week. What skill is Janelle practicing?
    a. Relationship building
    b. Continuing education
    c. Empathy
    d. Critical thinking

41. During a performance review, Jordan's manager shares some concerns that Jordan does not seem to have friends at work, show interest in others, or get along well with her team members. Jordan knows that she is a shy person but would like to use this opportunity for personal improvement. How can she proactively address this opportunity?
    a. Throw a weekend party for everyone at work and force herself to socialize
    b. Schedule a couple ten-minute intervals during her workday where she actively and positively engages with her coworkers
    c. Send a flowery apology email to her coworkers
    d. Ask her best friend to apply for a job at her company so that she can prove her manager wrong

42. The vice-president of an organization has noticed that a particular employee, Ben, has been working extremely hard and has made a positive impression on a large majority of the organization's leadership. The vice-president meets with Ben and asks him about his work. Ben shares all of the accomplishments that his team has achieved in the last quarter. What is Ben displaying during this meeting?
    a. Ego
    b. Individualistic behavior
    c. Team-oriented culture
    d. Humility

43. A manager in a non-HR department is having difficultly scheduling leave for his team members in a new online scheduling system. How can an HR professional provide support in this situation?
    a. Offer to do all the scheduling for the manager
    b. Provide a training that walks through all of the steps of scheduling leave in the system
    c. Assume that the manager will eventually figure it out with time and practice
    d. Relay to the manager that the system has been easily adopted in other organizations

44. Karen is an employee in an organization's finance department who has been feeling burned out at work. She sets up a meeting with Rita, an HR employee, to discuss this issue. When Karen arrives, Rita notices that Karen looks tired and defeated. As Rita shares her issues, Karen shows empathy and observes Rita's body language. When Rita is finished speaking, Karen shares her perception of Rita's concerns and asks if she is understanding correctly. What is Karen practicing in her conversation with Rita?
    a. Active listening
    b. Conscious listening
    c. Friendly listening
    d. Passive listening

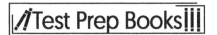

45. An organization eliminates its pension package for retirees, which causes a group of retirees to arrive in the HR department. The group is angry and yelling at the HR employees. One woman even bursts into tears at the thought of receiving less money in retirement. What is the best way for HR employees to respond to this outburst?
    a. Take it personally and feel defeated
    b. Close the doors to the HR department until the retirees leave; after all, the department is unable to change the outcome
    c. Provide the president of the company's direct line and tell the retirees to call
    d. Actively listen to the feelings of the retirees, show empathy, and try to communicate with logic and objectivity

46. Two HR staff members who are planning a worksite wellness initiative state that one of their initiative goals is to have healthier employees in their workforce. What is wrong with this goal?
    a. The goal is placing pressure on employees who are already busy
    b. The goal is pushing personal agendas on other employees
    c. The goal is too detailed
    d. The goal is ambiguous

47. Xiaoli is conducting a stakeholder meeting to review how a flu shot campaign conducted by the HR department is going. One of the stakeholders begins asking questions about the pharmacy that is providing the vaccines to the organization, and Xiaoli is unable to answer his questions. What is the best course of action for Xiaoli to take in this situation?
    a. Tell the stakeholder she doesn't know anything about the pharmacy, and move on to the next item on the agenda
    b. Tell the stakeholder information that she feels like is probably accurate, based on something she read the other day
    c. Provide the stakeholder with the pharmacy's contact information so that the stakeholder can call and get any information he needs
    d. Tell the stakeholder she doesn't know the answers to his questions, but will find out and follow-up with him within twenty-four hours

48. Maryam writes a message to her team leader to ask a question about a project. The team leader answers back with one sentence that seems terse to Maryam. What should Maryam do in this situation?
    a. Assume the team leader is angry that Maryam asked a dumb question
    b. Feel angry that the team leader did not think to add a greeting, closure, or other kind words to set the tone for the email
    c. Assume nothing, and ask the team leader about the brevity of the message when possible
    d. Assume the team leader is busy and just answered as quickly as possible

49. Soliciting feedback from stakeholders is an important part of which of the following process stages?
    a. Evaluation
    b. Control
    c. Testing
    d. Documentation

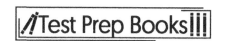

50. A company based in the United States is opening a new facility in Ireland. What will be a concern of HR professionals as the facility gets ready to launch?
    a. US foreign policy relations
    b. The assumption that the US site and the Irish site will not get along with one another
    c. The weather in Ireland
    d. Immigration laws and work visas for new employees at the site

51. An organization notices that its workforce is 78 percent females who are Caucasian. How can the organization make its workforce more diverse?
    a. Actively recruit underrepresented employees by highlighting diversity as a priority in job postings and favoring it during hiring
    b. Hire underrepresented workers even if they are not really qualified
    c. Terminate current employees and hire underrepresented employees
    d. The workforce is acceptable as is; clearly, candidates from other backgrounds are not available

52. What is one way an organization can provide benefits that cater to a diverse talent pool?
    a. Provide higher salaries to underrepresented groups.
    b. Provide progressive options like benefits for same-sex partners or paternity leave.
    c. Provide different benefit options based on employee background and interests.
    d. Ignore benefits that deal with the employee's personal life, such as family benefits.

53. If an organization has a high turnover rate among employee groups that are already underrepresented, of what is this likely indicative?
    a. All employees at the organization are actually quite dissatisfied.
    b. The competition is poaching employees to make their own workforces more diverse.
    c. Underrepresented groups are actually not qualified to do the work they are hired for.
    d. A barrier exists within the workplace that makes underrepresented groups feel uncomfortable.

54. Barbara, Cassandra, Debbie, and Enid have all worked in the same HR team for two years as generalists. Their supervisor currently left the organization to pursue another opportunity. All four employees are viable candidates for this position, and all have submitted applications. However, Barbara worked with the director of the group in another organization and has a close friendship with her. What is the fairest way to conduct interviews and selection for the supervisor position?
    a. Allow the director to have the final selection, as it is her department.
    b. Barbara should be given the position since she already has a close relationship with the director.
    c. A panel of interviewers from all parts of the company should make a selection based on merit.
    d. Allow the supervisor who resigned to provide feedback.

55. Vera is an HR generalist that works for a medical devices company. She is in charge of recruiting and hiring engineers for the research and development team; however, she knows nothing about the product that the engineers will be building. Why could this be a major problem during the hiring process?
    I. Vera may hire engineers that do not have the correct skill set
    II. Vera may provide incorrect details about job responsibilities
    III. Vera may provide compensation packages that are too high or too low for the job
    a. I and II
    b. II and III
    c. I and III
    d. All of the above

56. In a healthcare organization, which of the following might constitute as a KPI during an established fiscal period?
   a. Reimbursed payments
   b. Cash payments
   c. Revenue cycle
   d. Number of uninsured patients

57. Creating candidate profiles, updating job postings, removing filled positions, and flagging resumes can all be accomplished by which tool?
   a. HRIS
   b. HIIT
   c. HIFT
   d. CHIT

58. Quinn is an HR recruiter who has a quarterly goal of hiring 35 percent of all employees that reach the interview process. He normally meets this goal. However, one quarter found him at a rate of 10 percent. What tool can Quinn use to learn more about this poor performance?
   a. Lean
   b. Oracle
   c. Gap analysis
   d. Value stream map

59. What is a step-by-step diagram called that shows the purpose of each stage?
   a. Root cause map
   b. Value stream map
   c. Fishbone diagram
   d. Staircase diagram

60. Fiona is mapping out a process for a new initiative. She compiles the full timeline and processes of customer solutions, then brainstorms with her team about potential failures, obstacles, or setbacks that could occur at each stage. In what practice is Fiona engaging?
   a. Process mapping
   b. Negative facilitation
   c. Value stream mapping
   d. Risk identification

61. Jeremy wants to implement an HR initiative that allows department leads to swap employees for specified periods of time in order to facilitate cross-training. What sources could Jeremy share with leadership to support his case for trying this?
   a. A case study in the *New York Times* that features a Fortune500 company that did this successfully
   b. An online forum where this idea is casually referenced as something that could work
   c. Anecdotal evidence from a friend who tried it at his company of ten employees
   d. A college student's podcast that he listened to on the way to work

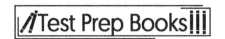

62. Lars is collecting data relating to employee productivity. He notices that facility employees are more likely to take sick days in December, while the rest of the organization have sick days scattered throughout the year. Lars hypothesizes that facility employees call out sick to have extra holiday time. What is the issue with this reasoning?

    a. The program that generated this report has not been double-checked.

    b. Lars is clearly showing confirmation bias.

    c. Facility employees often work outdoors, which could be a confounding variable.

    d. There are no issues with this reasoning.

63. Mina is conducting a professional development satisfaction survey. She needs to survey 75 percent of her organization, which has over 3,000 employees. What is the best way for her to collect detailed data from this many people?

    a. Online survey

    b. Paper survey

    c. A series of focus groups

    d. Face to face interviews

64. Elias sees a pie chart that shows about two-thirds of HR professionals hate their jobs, and only one-third find it satisfactory. What should he do before sharing this information with anyone?

    a. Ask his colleagues in the HR department how they feel about their jobs and see if it lines up with the chart.

    b. Source who conducted the research and the sample size of respondents.

    c. Review his own career choices so far.

    d. Nothing, he should feel free to share the graph because it looks professional and accurate.

65. Masao is an entry-level HR employee in an advertising agency. He is working on a project that focuses on diversity trainings offered in the workplace and is conducting preliminary research to review best practices. Masao's manager asks for a compilation of key findings. Masao sends a zip file full of every evidence-based journal article relating to diversity trainings in the workplace that he could find using Google Scholar. Masao's manager responds that he is unable to review so many articles and doesn't say anything else. What would be a better approach for this task, moving forward?

    a. Masao asks his manager the total number of articles he should send at a given time.

    b. Masao works independently from now on and leaves his manager out of his planning work.

    c. Masao pulls specific information from recently published scholarly papers that pertain to the goals to share with his manager.

    d. Masao should be moved to a different team with different communication styles.

66. Cassandra is the new HR director at a small organization. She is reviewing her company's employee handbook when she realizes that large pieces of information have not been updated in four years. As she reviews further, she realizes much of the handbook is obsolete. What should Cassandra do?

    a. Inform the head of the company, and let the head deal with the situation.

    b. Speak to her superior and offer to develop a new online handbook that can be easily updated.

    c. Return to her old company, which was much more disciplined and high-tech.

    d. Say nothing, since she is a new employee.

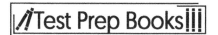

67. Ashley is conducting a workflow analysis in a patient clinic to identify sources of waste. Each day for two weeks, she sits in different areas of the clinic and examines the daily activities of each staff member. She records each task that the staff member completes, the amount of time it takes to complete the task, any obstacles that arise during the task, and anything that Ashley feels makes the task easier for the staff member she is observing. What is this type of data collection called?
    a. Focus group
    b. Work in progress
    c. Observational
    d. Transactional

68. When reviewing data or published studies, what constitutes as "recent" data collection or study?
    a. Data collection or study publication that occurred within the past two years
    b. Data collection or study publication that occurred within the past three years
    c. Data collection or study publication that occurred within the past four years
    d. Data collection or study publication that occurred within the past five years

69. Louise is meeting for the first time with a potential vendor to assist with her organization's annual wellness fair. What types of expectations should Louise discuss in person with the vendor?
    a. The vendor's role and communication timelines
    b. The vendor's work history and time in business
    c. The vendor's goods and services
    d. The vendor's personal health philosophy

70. Joelle is a new employee at an organization. She is skilled in customer service and looks forward to managing the HR needs of her organization. At her previous organization, Joelle was expected to answer all inquiries within twenty-four hours. She was taught that this was the industry standard. Her current organization uses the twenty-four-hour rule for emergencies and allows up to three business days to respond to non-urgent inquiries. What practice should Joelle follow and why?
    a. Twenty-four hours for all inquiries, as per the industry standard
    b. Twenty-four hours for all inquiries, to show her organization that she is committed to her work
    c. Twenty-four hours for emergencies and up to three days for other inquiries, per her current company's protocols
    d. Forty-eight hours, as a middle ground

71. Nate is an HR employee who works with his organization's operations departments. He is in the middle of resolving a short-term disability claim for an employee who is not present in the office. As he is working, the CFO of his organization visits his desk and asks for assistance with an urgent task that affects all employee data. This task is expected to take a full workday to complete. What should Nate do?
    a. Tell the CFO he is finishing a task for an employee, but will come help as soon as he is finished.
    b. Pause work on the short-term disability claim till the next day to help the CFO, but communicate a status update to the employee it affects.
    c. Immediately stop working on the short-term disability claim and help the CFO.
    d. Tell the CFO he is not available and refer him to another HR staff member.

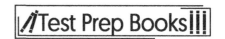

72. What is one way to eliminate job applicants who may not be a good cultural fit for an organization?
    a. List aspects that are relevant to corporate culture on the job posting.
    b. Make assumptions based on looks and body language when candidates arrive for in-person interviews.
    c. Market all jobs at in-person job fairs only where HR staff can make decisions based on their first impressions.
    d. It is difficult to pinpoint a mismatch between the organization and applicants until they are on the job.

73. Two employees who perform well individually have been placed on a project team together. However, in a team setting, they have very different work styles and attitudes and often clash angrily. How can an HR staff member help resolve this issue?
    a. Separate the two team members and put them on different projects.
    b. Put them on a probationary warning.
    c. Provide coaching to the employees to find common ground.
    d. Allow them to resolve it autonomously, as this is more empowering.

74. It is a new fiscal year, and an HR department is unsure of which initiatives to implement during the upcoming year. What is the first step they can take to target some ideas?
    a. Search online for current trends in HR initiatives.
    b. Conduct a needs assessment for the interests of the employees.
    c. Ask their friends in the organization for ideas or personal interests.
    d. Select the ideas the HR department feels most passionate about.

75. Where is a location that informal, yet effective, communication takes place at work?
    a. The break room
    b. During webinars
    c. In a conference room
    d. In a company newsletter

76. During a project meeting, Mary creates a table that includes a detailed description of every task needed for the project, a deliverable date for each task, and the owner of each task. Each member is able to access and update the table with status updates. What is Mary helping her team do?
    a. Helping each member feel accountable
    b. Micromanaging
    c. Modeling ethical behavior
    d. Collecting data

77. Why do all employees need to build a wide range of intrapersonal skills?
    a. It correlates with higher pay overtime.
    b. It is the primary factor associated with cohesive teams.
    c. It leads to better relationships at home.
    d. It allows them to work well with other employees.

78. What are the known benefits of showing concern for fellow employees at work?
    a. It correlates with higher pay over time.
    b. It builds employee morale and fosters positive working environments.
    c. It correlates with more frequent promotions.
    d. It leads to a self-reported sense of spiritual satisfaction.

79. A small business owner has hired four staff members. The business owner considers herself a fair and ethical person. However, she has hired one relative, her best friend from college, and one person from a job posting site who was previously unknown to her. All three employees are highly qualified, care about the business, have exceptional work ethic, and will be cross-trained in the same functions. What is one way that the business owner can mitigate potential bias in her treatment of the employees?

    a. Go out of her way to be extra supportive and kind to the employee found from the job board.

    b. Pay each employee the exact same salary and give the same percentage of business tasks.

    c. Try to notice when she shows bias and stop the behavior whenever she catches herself.

    d. Go out to lunch daily as a group.

80. Which term refers to an organization's identity—including mission, values, and culture—as it is communicated to current and prospective employees?

    a. Transparency

    b. Social presence

    c. Employer brand

    d. Workplace statement

HR Knowledge

81. To reduce operating costs, a company has decided to maintain its domestic headquarters but open an overseas manufacturing plant. What is the best word to describe this move?

    a. Outsourcing

    b. Downsizing

    c. Offshoring

    d. Globalizing

Read the following scenario and then answer questions 82–84.

Over the past decade, an advertising agency has steadily grown its client list in a particular foreign country, and it has decided to open a satellite office in that country to more easily handle day-to-day operation of its accounts there. Although several employees have made international business trips before, it will be the first time the organization has had a full-time presence in a foreign country. As such, the HR department is devising a strategy to prepare for expatriate employees.

82. The HR manager's first goal is to establish a clear duty-of-care policy. Which of the following best describes duty of care?

    a. The moral and legal obligations of an employer to care for employees' safety, security, and wellbeing when assigned to a foreign country

    b. International law mandating a minimum level of health insurance for expatriate workers and their families

    c. Identifying available services such as police officers, healthcare workers, and other first responders responsible for emergency response in a given country

    d. A system of compensation when employees incur health, safety, housing, and other expenses when on an international assignment

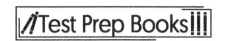

83. HR is trying to set up some learning sessions for employees who will be posted in the new satellite office. Which of the following classes would be most essential to provide for workers?

    a. An intensive language course in becoming fluent in the native language

    b. A culture class on local food, music, and famous landmarks

    c. A reminder of the company's mission, vision, and values

    d. An overview of applicable local labor laws and workplace etiquette

84. Some employees have never lived in a foreign country before and are concerned about their safety in case of an emergency. How should HR address these concerns?

    a. Prepare a presentation comparing crime statistics between the United States and other countries to reassure employees that expatriate life is safe.

    b. Monitor and share information regarding potential safety concerns in the foreign post and establish a system for employees to check in regularly.

    c. Provide employees with the numbers of local emergency response services.

    d. Only offer international assignment to employees who are confident about taking care of themselves in a foreign country.

85. An organization is considering expanding its operations to a new country and is gathering information about doing business there. Which kind of analysis would be most useful at this stage?

    a. PESTLE

    b. SWOT

    c. CBA

    d. ROI

86. What is an accidental expatriate?

    a. An employee who is detained by law enforcement for unknowingly violating local laws

    b. An employee who presents false information about their immigration status

    c. An employee who is unwillingly posted to an international assignment

    d. An employee who stays abroad too long as a business traveler

87. A retail business recently opened a store in a foreign country but has been experiencing a dispute between managers and sales staff. Managers are all expatriate employees from the home office, while sales staff are local nationals hired through a third-party vendor. Due to excessive tardiness, managers are threatening to fire sales staff who show up late to work more than two times in one week. Sales staff maintain that they have not been late to work and are angry because they feel that they are being bullied by managers. How should HR handle this conflict?

    a. Terminate the relationship with the current third-party vendor and find another agency through which to hire more reliable workers

    b. Hold a group staff meeting to discuss shared expectations and define attendance policies

    c. Replace expatriate managers with local nationals who can better understand and lead sales staff

    d. Use security camera footage to confirm employees' arrival time at work and develop an appropriate strategy based on actual punctuality rates

88. Employees need to understand the options of an organization's benefits programs and choose their enrollment plan. What is the best way for HR to present this information to employees?
    a. Schedule a mandatory presentation with a detailed overview of all the benefits options so employees can make the most informed decision.
    b. Give employees the option of allowing HR to enroll on their behalf because HR has a more thorough understanding of the benefits programs.
    c. Employ a variety of communication strategies such as email, text message, postcard, and Q&A sessions.
    d. Display benefits program posters around the building so people in different departments can see the same information.

89. What can be gained from an employee value proposition (EVP) approach to employee engagement?
    a. An organization can save money by retaining only the most valuable and productive employees.
    b. Employees can negotiate their own salary adjustments.
    c. Employees can propose changes to corporate culture.
    d. An organization can be proactive about attracting and retaining talent by analyzing what benefits it offers as an employer.

90. An organization is using a legacy HRIS because long-standing employees are comfortable with the software and feel it continues to meet their data management needs. However, several new employees are having difficulty using the outdated user interface and are pushing to adopt an entirely new platform. What is a good solution for this situation?
    a. Contract with a vendor that offers interface layer technology to develop a new user interface while maintaining the existing system.
    b. Get rid of the old system and invest in the latest HRIS before the current software becomes even more outdated than it already is.
    c. Reassign the new employees to positions that already have more cutting-edge software in place.
    d. Create an organization-wide site where employees can submit anonymous feedback about using the current HRIS.

91. An organization's HR leadership is considering switching to cloud database management. Which of the following is an important consideration in the contract with the software vendor?
    a. A plan for user training and software adoption
    b. An explanation of why cloud storage is a superior system
    c. Security standards for protecting sensitive employee data
    d. A written guarantee that the database cannot be breached by hackers

92. An organization's executives require that all HR policy recommendations be evidence-based. In this context, what is the best definition of "evidence-based"?
    a. Based on information from research studies by prominent academics outside the organization, to avoid conflict of interest
    b. Based on data from internal and external sources that is collected and analyzed in a standardized way to drive decision-making
    c. Based on conclusions made from careful observation of everyday working conditions in the organization
    d. Based on conceptual frameworks for understanding complex business trends

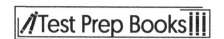

93. An organization with a commitment to diversity would like to conduct a gap analysis. What is this analysis likely to focus on?
    a. The pay gap between salaries for men and women in comparable positions
    b. How the organization has progressed in its hiring practices over the past decade
    c. The organization's current status of employee diversity in comparison to its stated diversity hiring goals
    d. How the organization's diversity statement and policies differ from those of other organizations in its field

94. HR wants to organize a training program on cultural difference in the workplace. Who should this training target?
    a. Managers and other employees in leadership positions, so they can communicate key practices to their subordinates
    b. Employees who have had problems with cultural misunderstandings in the past
    c. New employees, because they are more likely to come from diverse backgrounds
    d. Employees from all levels of the organization

95. Which organizations are more likely to have a decentralized structure?
    a. New small businesses that have not yet centralized their HR function
    b. Large organizations that operate in several locations
    c. Innovative organizations that rely on technology
    d. Family-run organizations

96. What does "systems thinking" refer to?
    a. Understanding of employee social organization
    b. Understanding of computer systems and other technology
    c. Understanding of government and other regulatory systems
    d. Understanding of how separate business units function together

97. What part of a SWOT analysis evaluates internal factors that affect an organization's performance?
    a. Strengths and weaknesses
    b. Sources and ways
    c. Output and take-in
    d. Opportunities and threats

98. What does "benchmarking" refer to in an HR context?
    a. Putting an employee "on the bench" or on the sidelines due to past performance
    b. Linking salary increases to performance metrics
    c. Identifying and setting goals relative to other organizations' performance
    d. Adhering to government regulations and other industry guidance

Read the following scenario and answer questions 99–101.

Leaders at a mid-size organization that specialize in producing car batteries are working on developing a strategic plan for the next ten years of the company. They are particularly interested in responding to the increased interest in hybrid and electric vehicles. Currently, the company's workforce is primarily concentrated in professionally licensed technicians working on the assembly floor.

99. Leadership has determined that more engineers with academic degrees will need to be added to the company. What is a first step that HR can take?
  a. Research and design meaningful job descriptions for desired new roles.
  b. Lay off enough factory technicians to offset the cost of new employees.
  c. Present a counter-strategy to maintain the current workforce as is.
  d. Canvas current employees who might be willing to change positions.

100. The factory technicians belong to a workers' union. Union negotiations have led to workers getting a 3 percent raise every year. However, to budget for the new strategic plan, company leaders cannot afford to continue this rate of salary increase; they would like to push for 2 percent or even 1 percent raises. What is an appropriate HR response?
  a. Survey employees to determine other rewards that might be valuable to workers but affordable for the company, such as flexible work scheduling.
  b. Devise a positive communication strategy for notifying employees of the new 1 percent raise policy.
  c. Transition to only hiring non-union factory technicians.
  d. Research annual raise policies at companies in other industries.

101. Part of the strategic plan involves building the company's battery research and development program capabilities. How can HR best assist with this part of the plan?
  a. Provide a budget plan for acquiring new research and development technologies.
  b. Organize a voluntary training session for employees who are interested in learning more about the projected research and development capabilities.
  c. Conduct a skills gap analysis to determine the capabilities of the current workforce and identify missing skills, and then develop a plan to fill the gap.
  d. Provide historical data about the battery research and development program's past performance.

102. What is the difference between a strategic plan and an individual action plan?
  a. A strategic plan is an end goal and an individual action plan describes the steps to achieve it.
  b. A strategic plan is conceptual and an individual action plan is concrete.
  c. A strategic plan is created by an organization's upper management and an individual action plan is created by each employee.
  d. A strategic plan describes how to reach organization-wide objectives and an individual action plan describes an employee's contribution.

103. What is an advantage of hiring from external sources rather than internal sources?
  a. It is more time- and cost-effective.
  b. It adds to workforce diversity.
  c. It has a lower interview-to-hire ratio.
  d. It leads to more rapid promotions.

Read the following scenario and answer the questions 104–105

The events planning department is having difficulty finding a capable assistant to handle their daily administrative workload. It is an entry-level, part-time job that has normally been staffed by students or recent graduates from local colleges. However, in the past five years, the position has had a high turnover rate and the department director is perpetually dissatisfied with employee performance in this position.

104. How can HR help the department overcome this problem?
a. Filling the position is taking too much time, so HR should eliminate the job and help department employees redistribute key tasks amongst themselves.
b. Students and recent graduates lack the competency for this job, so HR should update the job qualifications to require an advanced degree and several years of experience.
c. There is a clear disparity between the director's expectations and employees' performance ability, so HR should review the job description with the director and update it to reflect key skills and abilities.
d. The department director is showing poor management skills, so HR should make sure this is reflected in their performance evaluation.

105. After helping the department overcome this problem, what can HR do next?
a. Set up new employees with a mentor and proactively identify any skills gaps.
b. Discontinue its participation in the local college fair and move to online-only recruiting.
c. Enact a new policy to only hire temp employees for future administrative needs.
d. Reduce director involvement in future hiring decisions.

106. What role should social media play in HR?
a. HR can start an informational campaign warning employees that social media use is unprofessional.
b. HR can use social media to promote its organization's brand as an employer.
c. HR can create mandatory training sessions for all employees to incorporate social media communication into their job roles.
d. HR can bring all social media functions in-house for greater consistency.

107. What are primary pros and cons of using large job board websites?
a. They reach a large number of applicants, but they may end up being expensive in terms of price-per-click relative to click-to-hire ratios.
b. They take over all HR recruiting functions but leave HR professionals out of work.
c. They present a high-tech image to applicants but require too much training to implement.
d. They establish the organization's online presence, but they open it up to cybersecurity threats from hackers and viruses.

108. The employee value proposition (EVP) reflects employees' perceived valuing of the tangible and intangible rewards and benefits of working for an organization. What is an example of an intangible benefit?
a. Holiday bonus
b. Annual paid company retreat
c. Flexible schedule options
d. Retirement savings plan

109. While conducting job interviews, many hiring managers evaluate candidates based on whether they are a "good fit" with the company's culture. What is an appropriate policy to have regarding "good fit"?

a. Hiring managers should not consider it as a hiring a factor because candidates always lie about their personalities during interviews anyway.

b. Hiring managers should ensure that they are not relying on unconscious biases and determining fit based on shared age, race, socioeconomic status, or other demographics.

c. Hiring managers should make it a top priority because fitting in is the highest predictor of success.

d. Hiring managers should allow all applicants to work in the desired job for at least a day to test how well they fit into the work environment.

110. What is one of the primary benefits of an individual development plan (IDP)?

a. It gives all the development responsibility to employees, freeing up HR professionals for other strategic work.

b. It closely evaluates employees and documents mistakes to avoid wrongful termination complaints when employees are fired.

c. It provides managers with greater control over workers' daily tasks.

d. It helps workers become more invested in their professional development.

111. Why is succession planning important for an organization?

a. It assigns a quantitative value to a company's future goals.

b. It takes a proactive approach to preserving continuity in the face of worker attrition.

c. It boosts morale by reducing interdepartmental competition.

d. It creates clear lines of responsibility for effective communication.

112. What are the results of a total remuneration survey?

a. A comparison of workers' actual and desired salaries

b. A list of pay gaps within an organization

c. A report of market data on compensation and benefits plans

d. A group of employees who qualify for pay increases

113. The CEO wants to cut costs by eliminating a popular employee program that subsidizes public transportation commutes. HR is concerned about the effect this proposal will have on workers. What is an appropriate response?

a. HR does not have the authority to overrule the CEO and should avoid giving negative feedback unless it is specifically solicited by the CEO.

b. HR should engage in environmental scanning and research ways that other companies have enacted cost-cutting measures.

c. HR should eliminate the program and create a feedback survey where employees can share their feelings if they don't like the CEO's decision.

d. HR should inform the CEO of the value of the program by presenting metrics related to the ROI of the current plan, such as the ability to reach more productive and qualified workers thanks to the transportation program.

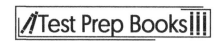

114. A large public relations firm is evaluating its HR functions to determine which tasks should be kept in house and which tasks should be outsourced. Which task are they most likely to outsource?
    a. Payroll administration
    b. Performance evaluations
    c. Recruitment
    d. High-potential development program management

115. What is an example of a factor that influences workforce supply?
    a. Worker attrition
    b. Number of customers
    c. Seasonal workload
    d. Economic downturn

116. What is the relationship between diversity and inclusion in the workplace?
    a. Diversity reflects legally-mandated equal opportunity hiring practices, while inclusion reflects company culture.
    b. Diversity refers to only hiring employees from underrepresented groups, while inclusion refers to hiring employees from all demographics.
    c. Diversity involves hiring employees with a variety of backgrounds, personalities, and working styles, while inclusion involves making sure those differences are heard and represented in the workplace.
    d. Diversity means respecting and encouraging workers to retain their individuality in the workplace, while inclusion means integrating all workers into one shared corporate culture.

117. Which of the following is true of workplace accommodations?
    a. Employers must take the lead in offering accommodations to employees.
    b. Employees need to complete legal paperwork before requesting an accommodation.
    c. Accommodations only cover conditions under the Americans with Disabilities Act (ADA).
    d. Accommodations must not place an undue burden on the employer.

Read the following scenario and answer questions 118–119.

The manager of the IT department currently conducts biannual employee evaluations. The evaluation is filled out on a single sheet of paper. On the front of the paper, employees are scored as "meets/does not meet expectations" on fifteen core skills and competencies. On the back of the paper, the manager writes more detailed feedback about areas in need of improvement. The paper is returned to employees within two weeks of the evaluation period.

118. The IT manager would like HR's feedback about how to improve this evaluation. What would be the most helpful recommendation?
    a. IT employees are used to working with cutting-edge technology, so the paper form should be replaced by an electronic one.
    b. Biannual evaluations are not frequent enough; employees should get official managerial feedback every one to two months.
    c. There should be additional evaluation standards beyond "meets expectations" to recognize and encourage employee achievement.
    d. The front page of the evaluation is too formulaic and should be eliminated; the manager can just relay the back page of feedback.

119. The IT manager has also noticed that employees seem to have negative feelings about the evaluations. What could be done to improve employees' attitudes?
    a. Replace manager-led evaluations with employee-led self-evaluations.
    b. Focus feedback on future goals rather than past mistakes.
    c. Create a competition and post evaluation results to reward top performers and motivate lower-performing employees.
    d. Schedule evaluations for the end of the day so employees can go home afterward.

120. What is an example of the qualitative impact of a well-managed corporate social responsibility (CSR) program?
    a. It improves feelings of employee satisfaction.
    b. It generates revenue by developing new customers and contacts.
    c. It reduces an organization's legal liabilities.
    d. It involves many activities that are tax-deductible.

121. Which of the following is not a law or regulation that is administered by the Equal Employment Opportunity Commission (EEOC)?
    a. EPA
    b. ADEA
    c. Title VII of the Civil Rights Act
    d. FMLA

Read the following scenario and answer questions 122–123.

> Several employees at a battery factory are concerned about their level of exposure to chemicals used on the assembly floor. One employee has read an article about how certain chemical fumes have been linked with eye disease and even blindness. This employee has been circulating the information to other workers.

122. Which agency or department is responsible for the standards that guide HR's response in this type of situation?
    a. NLRB
    b. EEOC
    c. OSHA
    d. EBSA

123. What is an appropriate HR response?
    a. HR should caution the employee about spreading rumors without first talking to their supervisor.
    b. As a preventative measure, all employees should be required to buy stronger, more advanced safety goggles if they are assigned to positions on the assembly floor.
    c. HR should combat the rumors by circulating a more detailed scientific analysis of the batteries' chemical properties.
    d. After investigating the validity of the report, HR should determine whether it is possible to work with less hazardous materials or develop improved safety measures in collaboration with factory managers.

124. In terms of closing the workforce gap, what do the terms "buy" and "build" refer to?
    a. "Buy" refers to outsourcing recruiting tasks, while "build" refers to using an organization's own HR staff to acquire new talent.
    b. "Buy" refers to acquiring talent from external sources, while "build" refers to using internal talent by reorganizing employees or developing critical skills.
    c. "Buy" refers to attracting new employees, and "build" refers to developing a mentoring program for these latest hires.
    d. "Buy" refers to offering monetary incentives to new hires, while "build" refers to attracting new workers with other benefits like on-the-job training or tuition reimbursement.

Read the scenario and answer questions 125–127.

After several high-profile cases of other large companies dealing with issues of harassment and misconduct, HR professionals at one company have decided to prioritize training to address these issues with their organization's employees.

125. Which of the following would be the most effective way to present information about workplace misconduct to employees?
    a. Give employees a checklist of workplace DON'Ts based on EEOC guidance.
    b. Show news stories of the recent high-profile cases along with commentary from legal experts about corporate liability and other worst-case scenarios concerning violations of workplace conduct policies.
    c. Set up a self-paced, remote training session to allow for greater flexibility so the information can reach as many employees as possible.
    d. Schedule mandatory in-person training with employee involvement, such as skits, role plays, and mock juries, to encourage engagement and focus on real-world implications.

126. Who would be the best featured speaker(s) for this training?
    a. A panel of employees who have made workplace misconduct complaints in the past
    b. Someone from the C-suite
    c. A Department of Justice representative
    d. The HR professionals who organized the training

127. In addition to improving training for employees, HR would also like to update its own policies to better address issues of workplace misconduct. Which of the following would be a useful measure to enact?
    a. Developing the HR workforce to handle all aspects of reporting, investigating, and addressing complaints internally.
    b. Contracting with a telecommunications group to set up a 24/7 harassment reporting phone hotline.
    c. Prioritizing diversity when hiring new HR employees.
    d. Maintaining close communication with senior-level leaders to streamline efforts.

128. What is it called when HR decides to transition manual tasks (such as completing and filing paperwork, tracking benefits eligibility) to a digital management system that completes these tasks?
    a. Restructuring
    b. Outsourcing
    c. Automation
    d. Integration

SHRM Practice Test #1

129. What does a variance analysis measure?
    a. The degree of difference between planned and actual outcomes
    b. The percentage of pay gap between employees in similar job roles
    c. The unique attributes of an organization compared to others in the industry
    d. The consistency and objectivity of performance review results

Read the scenario and answer questions 130–131.

Until recently, a company has allowed different business units to operate and organize themselves fairly autonomously. However, new corporate leadership would like to increase collaboration between departments and has come in with a "silo-busting" objective. The new leaders are also looking to create more standardization in job functions and organizational structure between departments. HR has been called on to aid with this objective.

130. In order to standardize job functions between departments, HR is conducting job analyses. Which of the following is LEAST likely to be included in the scope of these analyses?
    a. The type and frequency of tasks performed
    b. The industry standard for required competencies in this position
    c. The supervisory chain of who reports and who is reported to for the position
    d. The personal and professional qualifications needed

131. As a result of the job analysis, HR has found that identical job titles in different departments in fact have different levels of responsibility. They would like to establish an added level of responsibility for those positions that have been fallen behind. What is this process called?
    a. Job evaluation
    b. Job elaboration
    c. Job enrichment
    d. Job enlargement

132. Which of the following is an example of a short-term strategy to develop workforce competencies?
    a. Increase the academic and professional qualifications in job postings
    b. Enroll targeted employees in a high-potential development program
    c. Reassign underperforming employees to positions that better fit their skills
    d. Organize a week-long training class focused on desired skill development

133. Which of the following is true of corporate social responsibility (CSR)?
    a. It has an effect on employee recruiting and retention.
    b. It is led and organized by various community representatives.
    c. It is a form of governance based on local, federal, and other laws.
    d. It prioritizes the needs of the environment over the needs of the organization.

134. What is one way that HR can play a leadership role in an organization's corporate social responsibility (CSR) plan?
    a. Identify a pool of high-performing employees to participate in CSR activities.
    b. Collect, compile, and analyze data to demonstrate the quantitative and qualitative impacts of various CSR initiatives.
    c. Establish separate planning meetings to assign and develop CSR objectives within different business units.
    d. Devise an evaluation component to cite employees for noncompliance with stated CSR objectives.

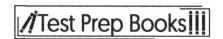

SHRM Practice Test #1

135. In accordance with the guidance of the National Labor Relations Board (NLRB), which of the following is true of labor relations?
a. The NLRB can facilitate settlements of labor disputes between employers and employees.
b. Employees can achieve lawful recognition only by working through established labor unions.
c. Employers may choose to set up a works council for their employees as a form of lawful representation.
d. Employees must select one form of representation (for example, union, nonunion, legal, or governmental).

136. What is the difference between lagging and leading indicators?
a. Lagging indicators show areas where an organization is falling behind performance goals, while leading indicators show areas where an organization is pulling ahead of performance goals.
b. Lagging indicators highlight an organization's weaknesses compared to others in the industry, while leading indicators indicate its relative strengths.
c. Lagging indicators reflect performances that happened in the past, while leading indicators reflect activity that can change future performance or success.
d. Lagging indicators show where an organization's processes are outdated or obsolete, while leading indicators show where an organization has effectively implemented cutting-edge processes and technology.

137. What would be useful key performance indicators (KPI) to consider for HR benchmarking?
a. Current time-to-hire in comparison to past timelines
b. Employee retention and turnover rates in different departments
c. Percentage of administrative costs in HR to administrative costs in the organization
d. Ratio of total employees to HR professionals within the organization and in other comparable organizations in the industry

138. HR has worked to expand its benefits package for employees, including new healthcare options. However, many employees failed to enroll before the deadline. How can HR best adjust its benefits policy for next year?
a. Remove the new benefits options, because these rewards are not highly valued by employees and present an extra cost to the organization.
b. Offer guided benefits counseling and advice leading up to the enrollment period.
c. Give employees a lump sum payment so they can purchase their own healthcare coverage outside the organization.
d. Move the deadline earlier so employees have less time to forget about completing their enrollment.

139. Which of the following is NOT a good example of useful information HR can supply during the strategic planning process?
a. Number and type of ongoing projects
b. Budget for total rewards plans
c. Number of employees
d. Education and development initiatives

135

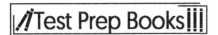

140. What is a pulse survey?
    a. An annual survey to gauge employee engagement with new initiatives
    b. An anonymous survey that allows employees to offer peer reviews of other employees throughout the organization
    c. A short, directed survey that makes it easier for employees to give feedback on a particular topic or initiative
    d. A pop quiz-like survey that evaluates gains in employee knowledge, skills, and competencies after an education and development program

141. How can HR determine ROI on total rewards package design?
    a. Consult market data on total rewards best practices
    b. Analyze relevant performance metrics (such as sales per quarter)
    c. Conduct a total remuneration survey
    d. Defer to business executives in determining employee value to the organization

Read the following scenario and answer questions 142–144.

HR at a rapidly growing tech company is in the process of selecting a new applicant tracking system (ATS) to help handle the projected increase in new hires in the next few years. There are also several hard-to-fill positions in the company that require highly specialized engineering qualifications.

142. When choosing an ATS, which of the following should HR consider a top priority?
    a. HR should evaluate the functionality of the new system from the perspective of stakeholders outside HR.
    b. As a department in an up-and-coming tech company, HR should take the lead on adopting state-of-the-art systems to hold a competitive edge over other companies.
    c. Because this is still a transition period, HR should select some functions that will remain paper based.
    d. HR should forgo dealing with a vendor and simply have employees develop the ATS themselves, since they have a high level of technical knowledge.

143. In discussions with ATS software vendors, which of the following is the LEAST important for HR professionals to focus on?
    a. Integration
    b. User experience
    c. Reporting metrics
    d. Industry usage rates

144. How can HR use the new ATS to fill the specialized job positions?
    a. Compare the qualifications of applicants with those of current employees to determine whether it is better to retrain or replace current workers.
    b. Determine essential qualifications for the job positions in order to categorize applications and help recruiters focus on a smaller pool of candidates.
    c. Use the software to design an integrated application, pre-screening test, and interview selection process that applicants complete in one session.
    d. Allow leaders throughout the organization to submit recommendations for internal hires rather than wasting resources on job posting sites.

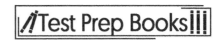

145. What does a totalization agreement between two countries do?
　　a. Mutually eliminates double taxation for expatriate employees
　　b. Establishes set exchange rates for employees' remittance fees
　　c. Sets a cap on the untaxable amount expatriate employees may earn
　　d. Relinquishes jurisdiction over tax and business fraud committed by expatriates

146. Which of the following is the best definition of an organization's stakeholders?
　　a. An organization's decision makers, including C-suite level leaders and other managers
　　b. An organization's entire workforce
　　c. An organization's workforce and its financial network, including customers and suppliers
　　d. An organization's workforce and all those affected by its social, economic, and environmental impact

147. HR has decided to conduct several stay interviews. What is a stay interview?
　　a. A type of exit interview in which fired or laid-off employees discuss the factors that led to their termination
　　b. A targeted appeal to high-performing employees in danger of being poached by competing organizations
　　c. A structured discussion to determine which factors influence employee retention and how retention efforts can be improved
　　d. A series of peer reviews to determine whether to retain an employee on a team or reassign them

Read the following scenario and answer questions 148–150.

Frederico Balzo began as a family-operated men's clothing store over fifty years ago. Fifteen years after the first store opened, the family decided to expand to a second location. Now Frederico Balzo operates over twenty stores and has expanded beyond suits to also sell shoes, watches, and other accessories. The company's latest plan is to open seven new stores within the next three years.

148. How can HR assist with the goal to open new stores?
　　a. HR can follow the steps laid out by C-suite leadership to handle workforce issues related to the expansion.
　　b. HR can participate in the strategic planning to offer input and highlight areas where workforce goals can be aligned with overall company goals.
　　c. HR can use the new stores as a testing ground to experiment with new workforce management techniques.
　　d. HR can assess and compare worker performance once all stores have opened.

149. In order to evaluate the success and effectiveness of operations in the new locations, HR needs to select the HR key performance indicators (KPI) that will be measured. How can HR best select these KPI?
　　a. Focus on long-term KPI since this is a multi-year expansion program.
　　b. Research the KPI used by HR in other men's clothing stores.
　　c. Determine the deliverables relevant to the strategic plan and identify associated HR KPI.
　　d. Track as many KPI as possible to provide the most complete picture of performance.

150. Frederico Balzo's CEO wants an idea of the effort required to staff the new stores. Which of the following would be the most useful metric for HR to provide?
    a. Time-to-hire
    b. Annual attrition rate
    c. Diversity ratio
    d. Productivity rate

151. HR feels it is not being given the opportunity to operate to its full potential. How can HR professionals make a business case for their department to present to senior leaders?
    a. Compile a timeline demonstrating how HR has grown and developed over the years.
    b. Organize a group presentation in which members of HR explain the projects they are working on and their areas of expertise.
    c. Create an information session about industry best practices in HR and highlight places where the company is falling behind.
    d. Focus on issues that matter to executives, such as recruiting and retaining top employees and increasing operational efficiency.

Read the following scenario and answer questions 152–155.

In order to free up more time for assisting with strategic objectives, the HR department of a large communications company has decided to implement new automation processes. They are currently evaluating specific functions for automating. One function under consideration is performance evaluations. Currently, the company conducts traditional annual performance reviews in which department leaders and other supervisors give feedback to subordinates. However, HR is considering adopting an employee engagement app that allows real-time, anonymous feedback between employees at all levels.

152. From an employee engagement standpoint, what would be the most important advantage of adopting the new app?
    a. It lends a game-like appeal to evaluations by allowing employees to use smartphones during work.
    b. It gives more timely and dynamic feedback to employees and helps solve performance problems as soon as they arise.
    c. It increases the appeal of working for the company by advancing its brand as a leader in modern business technology.
    d. It allows supervisors to put less effort into managing subordinates by creating a self-managed feedback system.

153. Which of the following is LEAST likely to be a drawback of using this new technology?
    a. It could create a channel for bullying and harassment.
    b. Some employees might feel overwhelmed by constant feedback.
    c. Some employees might have difficulty learning how to use the system.
    d. The app will prove to be expensive and cost prohibitive compared to traditional performance evaluations.

154. In preliminary discussions regarding plans for automation, HR has gotten pushback from some stakeholders who instead prefer augmentation. In terms of workplace technology, what is the difference between automation and augmentation?

a. Automation requires the purchase of new software, while augmentation explores ways to optimize existing software.

b. Automation allows technology to take over manual tasks, while augmentation refers to ways that technology assists employees in their job functions.

c. Automation refers to upgrades in corporate software, while augmentation refers to upgrades in corporate hardware.

d. Automation involves purchasing new software and hardware, while augmentation requires recruiting new employees.

155. How can HR encourage employee buy-in of the new performance management method?

a. Hold a demonstration of how the technology works in different situations, including information about user resources.

b. Require supervisors to phase out all traditional performance evaluation activities within the next six months.

c. Buy new smartphones for employees whose devices are not up-to-date enough to run the new app.

d. Post user testimonial videos on the company intranet.

156. What is an employee resource group (ERG)?

a. An independent review group within HR where employees can anonymously submit their complaints or concerns about workplace behavior

b. A coaching and mentoring group where new employees can meet more experienced workers from each department

c. A group created and led by employees who share common backgrounds or demographic factors

d. An extracurricular group that helps relocated employees orient themselves to their new environment

Read the following scenario and answer questions 157–158.

A successful American cosmetics retailer has decided to expand its business to overseas operations in a different country. Rather than building new stores in this location, they have decided to buy out a smaller, local cosmetics retailer and operate out of those stores. The company CEO wants to keep the same business space with some interior updates and would also like to retain as many of the existing employees as possible.

157. What would be the most productive way to manage the relationships in this new workforce scenario?

a. Suggest that the CEO significantly decrease the number of carryover employees and instead assign more of the company's American workers overseas so they can take over operations themselves.

b. Meet with local supervisors and managers to establish areas of shared goals and practices and focus on converging operations.

c. While interior renovations are underway, require all local employees to undergo a multi-week retraining process.

d. Identify high-performing local employees and assign them to newly created leadership positions.

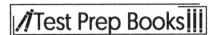

158. HR wants to assist with formalizing work processes between stores in both countries. What is the best way to accomplish this goal?
    a. Organize leadership teams in both countries.
    b. Set up an online messaging portal to handle all communications.
    c. Add the new stores to the American headquarters' meeting schedule.
    d. Arrange regular check-in meetings and agree on reporting times and methods.

159. During a job interview, asking an applicant about their childcare arrangements might be construed as discriminatory against working parents, especially working mothers. Which of the following would be a more appropriate question to ask?
    a. Which is a higher priority for you: workplace or family obligations?
    b. Do you have any commitments that will conflict with your work?
    c. Are you married or single?
    d. How old are your children?

160. Which of the following tools are commonly used by HR professionals to ensure that an applicant is a good fit for a particular job posting?
    a. An IQ test
    b. A MENSA exam
    c. Myers-Briggs assessment
    d. A logic puzzle

Answer Explanations for Practice Test #1

Behavioral Competency

1. A: The SMART acronym reminds users to ensure goals are Specific (is clearly defined), Measurable (can produce data to show evidence), Achievable (is a feasible goal within the grasp of the organization and workers), Relevant (is related to the desired overall outcome), and Timely (can be reached in a reasonable period of time). The other options do not apply.

2. B: The worker's compensation is calculated as one of the costs needed to get the project done. Without paying the worker, he or she cannot be used as a resource on the project. The worker is not necessarily a stakeholder (Choice *A*). The worker's salary is a benefit to the worker directly in return for their work, but it is not considered a benefit for the purpose of a cost-benefit analysis, making Choice *C* incorrect. The worker's pay is also fixed as a salary and is not considered a dependent variable for the purpose of the analysis, making Choice *D* incorrect.

3. A: Value stream mapping is a tool from the Six Sigma approach that shows the value added by each step within a process. HRIS (Choice *B*) refers to information systems. SMART (Choice *C*) is an acronym to guide goal setting. Flow state diagrams (Choice *D*) are not a business tool.

4. D: Corporate culture refers to the general attitude toward regular workday activities and how employees interact with one another. The categories listed have nothing to do with customers, life outside of work, or freebies, making Choices *A, B,* and *C* incorrect.

5. B: Opportunities (helpful) and threats (harmful) refer to influences that occur outside of an organization that are likely to affect the organization. Opportunities include things like an influx of skilled workers moving to the area that serve as a talent pool for the organization, or federal regulations that promote the organization's services. Threats include things like natural disasters that shut down the organization for an extended period of time, or an innovative in-home automation service that makes the organization's services redundant.

6. A: Strengths (helpful) and weakness (harmful) refer to assets and liabilities that occur within an organization. Strengths of an organization include aspects like recognition as the top leader in quality services by a credible source, or top sales received amongst all competition in the area. Weaknesses of an organization include things like a high employee turnover rate or small production facilities in comparison to the competition.

7. C: Focus groups utilize a facilitator who guides high-level, tailored discussions about a specific topic between a group of identified stakeholders. Surveys may require an administrator but are not a facilitated method of data collection. Classroom trainings are not a method of data collection.

8. D: Validated processes have tightly controlled parameters in order to produce the same desired output through each trial. This ensures consistent, high-quality products or services. The other options do not apply.

9. C: Benchmarking compares an organization's initiatives or outcomes to those of competing organizations or industry standards in order to determine efficacy and added value to the organization. The other options listed do not apply.

10. A: Confirmation bias is the tendency for researchers to select, find, or choose data that matches their personal preference or proposed hypothesis. For example, a researcher who believes adjunct college professors are mostly unhappy may gravitate toward interviewing only professors who have previously openly expressed dissatisfaction.

11. D: When working with multiple stakeholders to develop a new initiative, one should select an interest that is held by the most stakeholders in order to provide value to as many people for the least amount of resources. HR professionals should be sure not to favor one particular stakeholder's interests (Choice *A*), not to select randomly (Choice *B*), and not to make initial inquiries solely via email (Choice *C*), because it can make the process seem impersonal and unimportant.

12. A: Emotional intelligence refers to a person's capacity for positive human interaction and requires awareness of self, others, relationships, and surroundings. Higher emotional intelligence is associated with better communication and relationships.

13. B: The acronym in PESTLE stands for political, economic, social, technological, legal, and environmental. This refers to categorized trends that influence the organization and can be used to anticipate potential opportunities and risks in a variety of areas.

14. A: A root cause analysis is a systematic review of a larger issue that is broken down into smaller issues in order to determine the single "root cause" behind the larger issue. The aim of the root cause analysis is to resolve the root cause in order to have a positive domino effect on larger issues.

15. C: Google Scholar pulls all scholarly research through Google's search engine, and PubMed provides access to a wide range of legitimate medical, health, and life (including HR topics) research.

16. A: Networking refers to interacting with others who have knowledge and expertise that can provide personal and professional growth. This action does not relate to work-life balance (Choice *B*) and is not a type of formal education (Choice *C*). It is also a positive experience, whereas fraternizing (Choice *D*) normally has a negative connotation.

17. A: These are all unique benefits that would seem attractive to most employees. While job tasks and reports (Choices *B* and *C*) could be listed on the job posting, they do not fall under benefits. Salary is considered compensation and not an exact benefit; in addition, an exact salary (Choice *D*) is not usually posted in a job description.

18. A: These behaviors describe the attitudes, beliefs, and values that dictate the company's workdays. The other options are relevant to job duties or could be ways to connect with the employees but do not reflect the overall company culture.

19. C: These are all tasks that should occur during the planning stage of this initiative. Surveying employees who attended to inquire about how they enjoyed the food would be part of the evaluation stage, not the planning stage.

20. C: Direct costs refer to costs that are associated with a single project, its processes, and its outcomes.

21. B: Milestones are progressive periods by which certain business activities are expected to be completed.

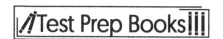

22. D: As a leader, Dan should be more accessible to his employees, either through faster email responses or through a cellphone that is answered. A single weekly meeting is not sufficient to check in with a team, especially if an urgent issue arises.

23. B: The Lean approach is a method that originated in manufacturing but is now present in almost all aspects of business across a span of industries. It aims to maximize output from the least amount of input without sacrificing safety or quality. It can be used in conjunction with Six Sigma but is an independent approach.

24. C: When implementing a new initiative, HR professionals can examine internal data from similar projects to help make their planning stage as useful and accurate as possible before beginning implementation. However, Angela should not copy Myra's initiative directly, as she is working with a different team that has different needs.

25. B: Even with the most diligent planning, HR leaders should expect the unexpected and never be too emotionally attached to outcomes. Michael should realize that all baseline plans are fluid and manage his expectations accordingly, while also preparing contingency plans for his operations. Most federal funds cannot roll over from fiscal years, and simply communicating information does not set them in stone.

26. A: Larry should have cross-trained his employees to fill in for one another in the case of emergencies. This allows normal business operations to continue, rather than halt, if an employee is absent. Samir should not have to work remotely when ill, and as a team leader, Larry should not be expected to step in and fulfill Samir's entire full-time job. Analyzing Samir's workday for causes of the illness is unnecessary unless Samir requests it.

27. D: All of these could be key stakeholders for a parental leave initiative. Pregnant mothers, male employees who have, are expecting, or want children, and managers who have to manage operations with decreased staff are all affected by decisions made to parental leave policies.

28. A: Taking online personality surveys, such as Myers-Briggs, to determine one's personal strengths is not a way to build professional credibility. Such inventories can be helpful, in certain circumstances, if administered to job candidates to determine the most appropriate fit given the job responsibilities.

29. C: Demonstrating how an initiative will bring value to each stakeholder is the best way to get buy-in for a new initiative. While looking professional and ensuring that all devices are working properly are important too, the question specifies *during the proposal* and not before. Finally, employees should not offer to pay out of pocket for company initiatives.

30. B: Leadership buy-in promotes top-down change; without leaders in the company supporting new initiatives, it is highly unlikely that subordinate employees will embrace change. They are more likely to resist if they feel those in leadership positions do not find the change valuable.

31. C: Ensuring that employees are a good fit with their job duties is a critical component of job and employee success. When Jenny is hired for a job that was a good fit, she excels. When her responsibilities were no longer a match for her strengths and interests, she did not do well. However, this does not mean she has poor work ethic, low intelligence, or is not a team player.

32. D: Managers can try a number of different avenues to help disengaged employees; however, they may not always be able to help with personal issues and should not be expected to always cater to employees outside of the workplace. Managers should try to come to a resolution before terminating an employee for major life-events.

33. C: This is a paperless method with an immediate notification system that minimizes waste yet keeps all employees informed.

34. A: An anonymous and confidential hotline can help employees report potentially unethical behaviors and feel less discomfort than if they had to do so publicly.

35. C: Modeling ethical behavior is the most effective way to show employees what is acceptable in the workplace. The other methods listed can help, but they may not be very effective on their own.

36. A: Transparency allows employees to know what is going on in most, if not all, aspects of the organization as it relates to their job. High transparency is associated with employees who feel valued, validated, and report high morale.

37. C: The job posting is the first place to share the company's mission, vision, and ethical standards. This attracts candidates with similar values to apply. Ethical standards should be reviewed again during the interview process and new hire orientation to ensure good fit and promote the values.

38. D: If Genevieve is truly impressed by Marcus and feels he could benefit the company, she should allow him the benefit of explaining any red flags, especially for events that occurred over five or more years prior.

39. A: Networking outside of one's organization allows one to witness the successes of others, a learning experience that can benefit one's own workplace. The other options listed do not directly support professional growth.

40. A: Janelle is being friendly, providing support, showing kindness, and creating a positive work environment for the new employee. These are all aspects of building a relationship which promotes better teamwork and a positive work environment.

41. B: Creating pockets of time during the course of the day to cultivate positive interactions with colleagues is an effective way to work on intrapersonal skills. The other options listed would be fairly inappropriate and socially unacceptable responses to a performance review.

42. C: Rather than speaking about all of his hard work and contributions, Ben chose to share his team's accomplishments without singling anyone out. This is a display of strong team-oriented culture in the workplace.

43. B: Taking the time to teach the manager how to use a new system is the best way to show support without taking over the manager's responsibilities or ignoring expressed concerns.

44. A: Active listening engages all of the listener's senses to communicate with the speaker, and also asks for confirmation from the speaker to ensure communication is perceived correctly.

45. D: In all HR-related matters, staff members should welcome competing points of view, remain objective, and not take attacks personally. HR professionals often have to deal with emotional topics, so they should prepare to remain calm and professional in such events.

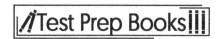

46. D: This goal is ambiguous. It provides no baseline, no definition of what constitutes as a healthy employee, no definition of what constitutes as a successful initiative, and is very subjective in nature.

47. D: Stakeholders are extremely valuable to initiatives, and their questions should be answered thoroughly, accurately, and promptly. Although Xiaoli did not know the answers to her stakeholder's questions, she offered to find out and provided a specific timeframe in which she would provide them.

48. C: HR professionals should not make any assumptions behind communications. They can make educated guesses to provide context, but if they truly cannot be objective in their reasoning, they should solicit more information from the person with whom they are communicating.

49. A: Feedback is an important part of the evaluation stage, which examines if processes were implemented smoothly, effectively, and provided value.

50. D: Depending on the candidates that apply for jobs at this new site, immigration and work visas will need to be considered based on what is required by Irish law.

51. A: In order to make workforces more diverse, organizations sometimes need to focus on actively recruiting underrepresented candidates that have qualifying credentials and experiences for the position. Workplaces that are more diverse are associated with better financial gains and higher rates of employee retention, reported satisfaction, and performance. However, qualified candidates sometimes are unaware of job opportunities or may not feel comfortable being the minority in an organization.

52. B: Organizations that consistently rank high in diverse and inclusive business practices often base business decisions on personal needs of employees, such as offering spouse and dependent benefits to same-sex partners, and offering paternity leave in addition to maternity leave.

53. D: This situation is likely to indicate that some barrier to inclusivity exists, and this is a cause for investigation, including follow-up with employees who may have resigned.

54. C: In this case, it seems as though Barbara might be favored even though all four candidates are equally qualified. Utilizing a panel of interviewers can reduce or eliminate any unconscious or conscious biases that a single leader may have during the hiring process.

55. D: HR responsibilities have a major influence on other departments within the organization. HR professionals' determination of what talent the organization needs, who is hired to fill these needs, how employees are compensated, how to mitigate personnel liabilities, and so forth should be based off internal demands of the organization. If Vera does not know this information, she cannot make appropriate hiring decisions.

56. A: Healthcare organizations need to collect payments, and reimbursements come from patients, insurance companies, and so on. The amount of payment collected is a key performance indicator that shows how much actual revenue is generated.

57. A: HRIS, or HR information systems, are a component of business technology that automates a great deal of HR-related paperwork and other tedious tasks.

58. C: A gap analysis views a process when there is a discrepancy between expected performance and actual performance, especially when milestones, goals, or benchmarks are not met.

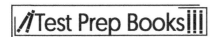

59. B: A value stream map deconstructs a procedure and defines the value each step provides in relation to an established goal. Value stream mapping clearly illustrates when a process step is wasteful or misaligned with goal achievement and allows the user to eliminate steps where possible to create a more efficient process.

60. D: Risk identification is a way for HR professionals to mitigate or eliminate all potential setbacks, especially when delivering a solution to a valued customer. By identifying risks, they are able to develop contingency plans that allow the delivery of solutions to continue uninterrupted.

61. A: The *New York Times* is a reputable publication, and the case study is an in-depth investigation at a large business. The other sources are not very credible, as they either have not successfully tried testing this initiative or utilized a very small sample size (which cannot be statistically significant).

62. C: Since facility employees often work outdoors, they could truly be sicker in December, which is a colder month. Lars cannot jump to conclusions from a single data collection without investigating all potential variables. There are no indicators in the case as described that he is showing confirmation bias or that there are issues with his data software.

63. A: Online surveys can be quickly distributed to a large group of people, can collect any type of information the researcher needs, and do not have paper waste. However, since surveys can have low completion rates, Mina may need to send regular follow up reminders or ask leadership to make the survey required in order to reach her completion goal.

64. B: Sources should always be checked for any data report. Also, visual representations of data are more susceptible to misconstrue the true meaning and should always be examined further. Elias may find out that the study only surveyed six people, or that it was conducted at a career fair, which would contribute a level of bias.

65. C: As a less experienced employee, Masao should receive clear guidance from his manager on what he expects to receive as a result of Masao's research. Additionally, they should work together to review goals for the potential initiative so that Masao can better filter his results and key findings.

66. B: This is a proactive, lean approach to find a solution for an existing problem. Cassandra also utilizes proven ways to communicate changes to her organization. The other options listed are not the actions of an engaged employee.

67. C: This is an example of observational data collection that is recording both quantitative (time spent) and qualitative (type of task, obstacles) sources of data.

68. B: Ideally, when referencing sources to drive decision-making, HR professionals should only use studies that took place within the past three years. Since innovation occurs quickly and best practices are susceptible to change, literature older than this may be obsolete.

69. A: These topics cover the relationship that Louise expects to have with the vendor leading up to the fair and during the event. The vendor's business history, work history, and services are items that should have been reviewed (such as online or over the phone) before taking the time to meet with the vendor. The vendor's personal health philosophy is not relevant.

70. C: Joelle should follow her current organization's practices to show that she is team-oriented and embraces the company culture. There may be a reason that her current company allows more time for non-urgent issues, such as other responsibilities that Joelle is expected to fulfill.

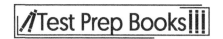
71. B: Nate should prioritize the leadership issue that will impact a large number of employees, especially since the employee with the disability claim is not physically in the office. While Nate cannot share that he is prioritizing a leadership matter over an employee matter, he can inform the employee with the short-term disability claim that he is still working on the issue and will have a resolution the following day.

72. A: The job posting should highlight aspects of corporate culture that are likely to attract the ideal applicant fit and may seem unattractive to those who are not good fits.

73. C: HR staff members should help non-cooperating employees find common ground to work together toward an end goal, rather than separating or punishing employees, whenever possible. If there are too many failed attempts at resolution, it may be necessary to escalate tactics.

74. B: Accounting for the organization's needs and interests that represent a large majority of the employees in the organization is the best way to select initiatives that will be useful, welcomed, and supported.

75. A: Break rooms are not places where formal work matters take place, such as the other options listed. However, it is an area where employees convene, relax, and often discuss work in an informal way that can often generate new and creative ideas.

76. A: Mary is providing clear, visible expectations of project tasks and completion dates. By sharing who is assigned to each task, it provides a sense of transparency and ownership. Together, these help individual members feel accountable for the role they play on the project.

77. D: Team members may be assigned by project rather than personally chosen; therefore, it is important to develop wide-ranging engagement skills that promote positive interactions. This is crucial to job satisfaction, since employees often spend full days with their team members. If they do not get along with their team, they will likely be miserable at work.

78. B: Employee morale and positive working environments are associated with compassionate and empathetic coworkers. This allows people to feel cared for and valued in the workplace.

79. B: Standardizing pay and work tasks is one way to mitigate bias in situations where bias could arise.

80. C: Employer brand. Just as a company brands itself to customers—that is, it creates and presents an image encompassing its identity, quality, and personality—employers also brand themselves to employees. Employer brand is closely related to the EVP, which encompasses all the factors—tangible and intangible—that contribute to workers' perception of value gained from working for a particular employer. Employer brand is built on things like mission, values, and work culture.

HR Knowledge

81. C: Offshoring. Offshoring refers to the relocation of some or all of an organization's processes to an international location, either internally or through third-party vendors. Choice *A* is not correct because outsourcing refers to moving an organization's processes outside the company by contracting third-party vendors; outsourcing can take place either domestically or internationally. Outsourcing and offshoring may often coincide, but they are not necessarily the same thing. Choice *B* is also incorrect; an organization downsizes when it reduces its operations and eliminates previously staffed positions.

Finally, Choice *D* is incorrect because globalizing is a very broad term for engaging in operations on an international scale; it is not the best term to describe this specific situation.

82. A: Duty of care refers to the moral and legal obligations of an employer to care for employees' safety, security, and wellbeing when assigned to a foreign country. It is important to note that duty of care encompasses both legal *and* moral obligations, so organizations should not limit themselves to only providing the minimum legal protections for expatriate workers. Choice *B* is not correct because no such law exists and, as mentioned, not all duty-of-care concerns are legal mandates. Choice *C* is not correct because, while organizations should provide employees with this essential information, it only covers an emergency response, whereas duty of care should also address day-to-day living concerns. Finally, Choice *D* is not the best answer because duty of care refers to all kinds of support offered to expatriate workers, not simply monetary compensation. Also, duty-of-care policy should be proactive, not reactive (in this case, only coming into play after employees incur an expense).

83. D: Before an organization begins operating in a foreign country, it is important to understand that laws and customs are not the same in every country. Violating local labor laws could result in excessive legal fees, fines, or even the closure of the organization's foreign office; ignorance of local workplace etiquette could create misunderstandings that lower morale and make it difficult for collaboration to occur. Choice *A* is not the best answer because, while foreign language skills can be an asset, it is unlikely that employees will become fluent in a short time; if native-level fluency is essential for the job, it would be more efficient to identify employees who already possess this qualification. Cultural understanding is another important part of adapting to a foreign assignment, but it does not eclipse the need for legal compliance in the workplace, so Choice *B* is not the best answer. Finally, Choice *C* is not the best answer, either. Although the organization may want to ensure consistency between their domestic and foreign operations, this option does not address the changes and differences that employees will inevitably encounter in their new office.

84. B: Monitor and share information regarding potential safety concerns in the foreign post, and establish a system for employees to check in regularly. As part of duty of care, HR's role is to stay informed about situations in the foreign country that may affect employees and to communicate relevant information to employees. Also, because of emergencies such as terrorist attacks or natural disasters when it is necessary to account for employees quickly, employers should establish a system for employees to check in regularly. Choice *A* is not the best answer because it downplays employees' concerns rather than addressing them. Choice *C* is too reactive; employers and employees should have a plan in place ahead of time, rather than simply waiting until after an emergency occurs to seek help. Choice *D* is also not a good choice because it causes HR to discount otherwise qualified employees. Indeed, it is HR's responsibility to provide employees with the resources they need to succeed in various roles in the organization, including international assignments.

85. A: PESTLE. The acronym PESTLE stands for the political, economic, social, technological, legal, and environmental trends that affect an organization. By conducting this kind of analysis, the organization can get a broad view of the various factors that may affect their future operation in a new country and develop a strategic plan accordingly. A SWOT analysis (Choice *B*) considers the strengths, weaknesses, opportunities, and threats of an organization, and it is useful for evaluating the organization within its current field of operation; however, in this case, the organization needs to focus on analyzing a new location, not its current operations. CBA (Choice *C*) stands for cost-benefit analysis and can be used to determine the potential costs and benefits of implementing a certain policy or making a business decision. In this example, the organization is in a fact-finding phase, not a decision-making phase, so a CBA is not necessary. Finally, Choice *D* is not the best choice because ROI stands for return on

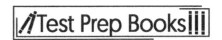

investment, or the expected yield after investing a certain amount of resources. The organization has not yet committed to investing resources in this venture, so an ROI would be premature.

86. D: An employee who stays abroad too long as a business traveler. In today's increasingly globalized world, international business trips are common for many employees. However, if a short-term business trip gets extended, an employee may be subject to taxation, immigration, or other applicable laws that they are unprepared to handle; this situation may result in a stealth or accidental expatriate. HR should closely monitor all international assignments regardless of the proposed length of travel, in case the length of stay exceeds what is expected. If a business trip develops into a long-term international post, it is HR's responsibility to ensure that the employee is in full compliance with all laws as well as the organization's policies regarding expatriate employees.

87. B: Hold a group staff meeting to discuss shared expectations and define attendance policies. The root of the conflict is managers' and staff's differing accounts of employee performance, so it is important to establish a shared understanding of events and expectations. Because there is a cultural difference to take into consideration before accusing employees of misconduct, HR should ensure that employees have a clearly defined understanding of their job descriptions. For example, if a shift starts at 9:00 AM, a manager may consider any employee who arrives after that time to be tardy. However, in some countries, arriving at 9:10 or 9:15 would still be acceptable, which may be why employees feel they are being unfairly criticized.

By clearly defining an attendance policy, future misunderstandings can be avoided. Choice A is not the best answer because the same cultural issue can arise when hiring other local nationals. Choice C is not the best answer, either, because it penalizes managers and ignores the need for collaboration between local and expatriate employees. Choice D is not the best answer because sales staff already feel they are being unfairly targeted and may react negatively to video surveillance. Also, Choice D fails to promote dialogue between managers and sales staff.

88. C: Employ a variety of communication strategies such as email, text message, postcard, and Q&A sessions. Employee benefits such as health insurance and retirement planning are important but also complex and often difficult to understand, so it is HR's responsibility to present the essential facts that employees need to know to make decisions about their benefits. The best way to accomplish this is by using a variety of different methods than can appeal to employees' different communication styles. Some employees will learn better from face-to-face sessions, while others will appreciate being able to read the information in an email. Text messages and postcards can provide a small reminder that is enough to nudge employees to enroll without being overwhelming.

For this reason, Choice A is not the best answer because it may overwhelm employees with too much information and cause them to tune out the essentials. Choice B is also not correct because, while HR professionals can make recommendations, only employees themselves can make the final decision about what options are best for their lives. Choice D is also not the best answer because there is no way to ensure that employees are actually reading the information; similarly, there is no interactive interface for employees to ask questions if they want clarification or more details.

89. D: An organization can be proactive about attracting and retaining talent by analyzing the benefits it offers as an employer. An EVP approach allows an organization to understand how employees perceive the benefit of working for their employer, in turn enabling HR to develop a strategy for recruiting and retaining talent.

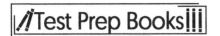

90. A: Contract with a vendor that offers interface layer technology to develop a new user interface while maintaining the existing system. Because the main issue is the user interface—that is, the part of the software that employees use to access and manage the data—interface layer technology can help to extend the usefulness of the system. Although it is important to stay on top of technology developments, it is impractical and costly to make major system changes that may not be necessary.

91. C: Security standards for protecting sensitive employee data. HR must ensure that industry-standard security practices are in place when it comes to protecting sensitive employee records. Choice *A* is something that HR professionals should develop within their organization, and it does not need to be provided by the vendor. Choice *B* is also part of the organization's due diligence to fully understand the platform it is adopting. Choice *D* is not a good choice because it is impossible to fully guarantee that any storage system is completely invulnerable; it is more important to ensure that the vendor is complying with the latest security standards and is equipped to deal with security threats.

92. B: Based on data from internal and external sources that is collected and analyzed in a standardized way to drive decision-making. Rather than simply basing decisions on current practice or "the way it's always been done," evidence-based decision making requires factual data collection and analysis to support key decisions. Choice *A* is not the best answer because, while this could be one source of evidence, it is also possisble to gather evidence from within the organization. Choice *C* is also not the best answer because it only focuses on qualitative data rather than incorporating quantitative analysis as well. Choice *D* is also incorrect because it doesn't reference data.

93. C: The organization's current status of employee diversity in comparison to its stated diversity hiring goals. A gap analysis is a method of studying a current state in order to determine how to move to a desired state. In this case, the organization is trying to meet its stated diversity goals, and it must first understand its current diversity status.

94. D: Employees from all levels of the organization should be included. Diversity and inclusion (D&I) should be part of an organization-wide policy that involves all employees. Choice *A* is not the best answer because key training messages may get lost in translation as they travel from leadership-level employees to their subordinates. Choice *B* is also not the best answer because it reacts to past problems rather than working to proactively create a workplace culture that avoids such conflict. Choice *C* is also not a good choice because long-standing employees also need training to adapt to changing workplace conditions.

95. B: Large organizations that operate in several locations. In a decentralized HR structure, separate HR offices operate largely autonomously, based on separate business units such as different departments or locations. This is useful for organizations with regional or international operations, where HR professionals benefit from having local knowledge of business operations and employee needs. In fact, small businesses are the most likely to have a centralized HR structure. As organizations grow larger, they are more likely to outsource or decentralize certain HR functions.

96. D: Understanding of how separate business units function together. When HR professionals look at an organization from the perspective of systems thinking, they consider how separate business units work together and impact each other. This systems thinking influences HR's recommendations for the workforce organization best suited to achieving the strategic plan.

97. A: Strengths and weaknesses. The acronym SWOT stands for strengths, weaknesses, opportunities, and threats. The strengths and weaknesses a SWOT analysis reveals are internal factors that put the organization at an advantage or disadvantage compared to other organizations in the industry.

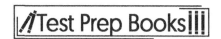

Opportunities and threats are external factors that can positively or negatively influence an organization's performance.

98. C: Identifying and setting goals relative to other organizations' performance. Benchmarking involves doing environmental scanning, locating leaders in the field, and determining what those organizations have done to achieve success. Through benchmarking, an organization can learn from others' success in setting and reaching performance goals.

99. A: Research and design meaningful job descriptions for desired new roles. Whenever new job positions are added to an organization, HR is responsible for creating the job descriptions for them. The job descriptions serve as a blueprint for hiring and organizing the expanded workforce. Particularly because these positions play an innovative and cutting-edge role in the organization, HR may need to conduct research by looking at similar jobs in other organizations to determine what to include in the scope of the job description. Choice *B* is not a good choice because laying off experienced employees to make way for unfilled positions is premature and will lead to staffing instability. Choice *C* is also not a good choice because HR should present workable solutions to help achieve future goals, and changing management is part of that. Finally, Choice *D* is not the best answer because, while some internal transfers may be possible, there is a difference between technical and academic skills. And again, the job descriptions must be in place before filling any roles.

100. A: Survey employees to determine other rewards that might be valuable to workers but affordable to the company, such as flexible work scheduling. HR is responsible for designing fair and competitive total rewards packages; however, not all rewards are monetary or tangible. HR should work to determine what rewards are most valuable to employees and may find that some of these come at a lower cost to the organization. Choice *B* is not the best answer because HR should be more proactive about advocating for fair employee compensation. Choice *C* is also incorrect because it would take too long to carry out this transition and might also make it hard to hire qualified workers in the future. Also, while Choice *D* might be a good step in designing employee rewards, it does not present an overall solution to the current situation.

101. C: Conduct a skills gap analysis to determine the capabilities of the current workforce, identify missing skills, and develop a plan to fill the gap. Strategic planning involves determining where an organization currently stands, where it wants to be, and the steps it needs to take to move from the present to the future. The same is also true of its workforce—HR needs to know the current capabilities of employees and plan how to fill any gaps that impede future performance. Choice *A* is something that would be handled by staff in the new department, not by HR. Choice *B* might be a good idea, letting employees know about the future of the organization, but it does not present actionable solutions for achieving the strategic plan. Finally, Choice *D* is not the best answer because it focuses on past trends rather than future goals.

102. D: A strategic plan describes how to reach organization-wide objectives and an individual action plan describes an employee's contribution. Choice *A* is not correct because both a strategic plan and an individual action plan describe the steps needed to achieve a goal; they simply differ in the scope and level of responsibility. Similarly, Choice *B* is also incorrect because both types of plans include concrete, actionable steps. Choice *C* is not correct because, while an individual action plan is carried out by individual employees, it is created under the guidance of managers and other leaders.

103. B: It adds to workforce diversity. Internally-sourced hires such as internal transfers can lead to employees who are already familiar and comfortable with workplace culture, but external hires are

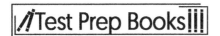

more likely to add diversity in terms of demographics, backgrounds, personalities, and working styles. Choice *A* is not correct because far less time and money are needed to recruit internally sourced hires. Also, internal hires have a lower interview-to-hire ratio, so Choice *C* is also incorrect. Choice *D* is also not an advantage of external hires.

104. C: There is a clear disparity between the director's expectations and employees' performance ability, so HR should review the job description with the director and update it to reflect key skills and abilities. HR needs to make sure that a capable candidate is selected for this position, and that begins with outlining the key responsibilities of the job. Job descriptions should be reviewed and updated regularly to ensure that they align with the actual skills and abilities needed to perform the essential job functions; since wrongly-qualified people keep getting placed in the job, it is likely that the job description is outdated and is attracting the wrong candidates.

Choice *A* is not the best answer because while it may save time on filling the position, it could also overburden other employees. Choice *B* is also not a good choice; the job is described as entry-level, part-time work, so experienced workers with advanced degrees would be overqualified. Choice *D* is also not the best answer because, while management may play a role in the assistant's success, it is impossible to determine without further review. Also, were that the case, HR should work to provide guidance to the manager rather than simply adding a negative note to their evaluation.

105. A: Set up new employees with a mentor and proactively identify any skills gaps. Mentoring can help aid employee satisfaction and retention, and it can help aid their integration into a new workplace. Also, by identifying skills gaps, HR can provide timely training opportunities for improved employee performance. Choice *B* is not a good choice because it cuts off an important external relationship for the organization. Choice *C*, hiring temporary workers, would only exacerbate the problem of high turnover. Finally, Choice *D* is not a good choice because clearly communicating with the director regarding department staffing needs is important for selecting the appropriate candidate.

106. B: HR can use social media to promote its organization's brand as an employer. In today's society, there are countless ways organizations and HR can use social media. Branding is an important way to communicate to customers, applicants, and other stakeholders, and social media is an appropriate platform for reaching them. Choice *A* is not a good choice because social media is incredibly widespread already and there are appropriate, professional ways to use it, depending on each industry. Choice *C* is also not necessary because not all job functions require social media posting on behalf of the organization. Finally, Choice *D* depends on the needs of the organization and isn't a requirement of social media use.

107. A: They reach a large number of applicants, but they may end up costing more in terms of price-per-click relative to click-to-hire ratios. Large job sites like Monster, Indeed, Career Builder, and others help HR to reach a far larger applicant pool than other face-to-face recruiting strategies. However, the larger applicant pool also means that many more people click on job ads than will actually apply, and more will apply for jobs than will actually be hired. When devising a recruiting strategy, HR should consider the price of advertising on these sites.

108. C: Flexible schedule options. Tangible benefits and rewards include things with monetary value like salaries and bonuses. Intangible benefits, by contrast, may not have a quantitative value, but are still important to employees. These include things like flexible schedules, telework options, and a sense of contributing to meaningful work.

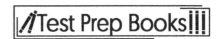

109. B: Hiring managers should ensure that they are not relying on unconscious biases and determining fit based on shared age, race, socioeconomic status, or other demographics. Although fit is always an important factor for ensuring a positive workplace dynamic, hiring managers should be conscious of how they determine fit, balancing it with an organization's D&I policies.

110. D: It helps workers become more invested in their professional development. Although many development programs may be extended throughout an organization or limited to specific business areas and departments, an IDP is tailored to an employee's specific needs and created with their input and objectives in mind. This makes workers more invested and involved in their own future success. Choice *A* is not correct because HR should still be involved with helping employees create and manage their IDPs. Choices *B* and *C* are not correct because the purpose of an IDP is to give employees a roadmap for their own development, not to create opportunities for punitive measures or micromanagement.

111. B: It takes a proactive approach to preserving continuity in the face of worker attrition. Succession planning refers to the process of planning for future leadership in an organization to ensure that key knowledge, relationships, and other valuable assets are not lost when leaders resign or retire.

112. C: A report of market data on compensation and benefits plans. A total remuneration survey helps HR to design total rewards plans for their organization that are fair and competitive based on available market data about rewards for similar jobs, industries, companies, etc.

113. D: HR should inform the CEO of the value of the program by presenting metrics related to the ROI of the current plan, such as the ability to reach more productive and qualified workers thanks to the transportation program. HR wants to demonstrate the importance of the program; however, the CEO is mostly interested in its cost. In this case, HR should translate the program's value into monetary terms by analyzing its ROI. Choice *A* is not a good choice because HR has a responsibility to provide input regarding changes that affect workers. Choice *B* is also not the best choice because, while it can be part of an overall fact-finding strategy, it does not present actionable results for decision making now. Also, Choice *C* is not a good strategy because it seeks worker feedback after the decision has already been made.

114. A: Payroll administration. There are many factors that determine which, if any, HR functions an organization chooses to outsource. Overall, though, it is easier to outsource transactional tasks that are largely administrative in nature, such as payroll administration. HR functions that are more likely to be kept in house are those that require working knowledge of the organization's culture or relationships between employees (things like Choice *B*, performance evaluations, or Choice *D*, high-potential development program management).

115. A: Worker attrition. Workforce supply may refer to the number of workers available for a specific position or for the industry as a whole. Worker attrition, or the number of workers who leave due to things like retirement or resignation, affects the workforce supply. The other choices all refer to factors that influence workforce demand, or the number of workers needed by an organization at a given time.

116. C: Diversity involves hiring employees with a variety of backgrounds, personalities, and working styles, while inclusion involves making sure those differences are heard and represented in the workplace. Choice *A* is not the best answer because, while some aspects of an organization's diversity program may be guided by EEOC regulations, it does not include other diversity considerations like a variety of personality types, working styles, and backgrounds. Choice *B* is also incorrect because inclusion refers to integrating the contributions of diverse employees into the workplace. Finally, Choice

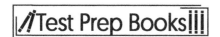

D is not the best answer because diversity and inclusion are complementary rather than competing ideals.

117. D: Accommodations must not place an undue burden on the employer. Employers are required to provide reasonable accommodations to employees as long as these do not place an undue burden on the employer. There is room for interpretation in the meaning of "undue burden," however; generally, it refers to anything that would be cost-prohibitive or would go against the nature of the organization's work. The other choices are incorrect because employers are not required to offer any accommodation that employees do not ask for themselves; however, employees are allowed to ask in plain language without necessarily using the legal or technical terminology. Also, accommodations cover more than just the ADA; employees can also request accommodations on religious grounds, for example.

118. C: There should be additional evaluation standards beyond "meets expectations" to recognize and encourage employee achievement. The purpose of an employee evaluation is to give meaningful feedback that leads employees to set and achieve new goals. If employees are simply scored on whether they meet expectations, they may not be given the impetus they need to set and achieve high performance objectives. Choice *A* is not the best answer because, while HR should work to incorporate new technologies where appropriate, this is not the most meaningful change that the process needs. Choice *B* is not the best answer because evaluations that are too frequent can be just as harmful as evaluations that are too infrequent; they might increase employee stress, feelings of micromanagement, or feelings that evaluations are not very meaningful. Finally, Choice *D* is not the best answer because the back page of the evaluation only focuses on areas of improvement and doesn't recognize any positive areas of performance.

119. B: Focus feedback on future goals rather than past mistakes. Evaluations should be presented as a chance for employees to focus on their achievements. If they didn't achieve their goals to their full potential, how can they reach their goals next time? Future-focused evaluations give employees a concrete action plan moving forward. Choice *A* is not the best answer because, while self-evaluations are a useful tool, they should be used alongside evaluations from someone in a supervisory role. Choice *C* is also not a good choice. Rewards for performance may work well in some organizations; however, publicly posting the results of employees' evaluations would violate their privacy, and many employees react negatively to competition. Finally, Choice *D* is not the best way to make a meaningful change.

120. A: It improves feelings of employee satisfaction. Employee satisfaction is closely linked to feelings of contributing to meaningful work. Particularly for the younger generation of workers, employees want to feel that they are making a positive impact on society. CSR is one way that an organization can allow employees to feel that they are helping others, the environment, and/or their community. The other choices refer to things with a monetary benefit, which would be quantitative rather than qualitative.

121. D: FMLA. This acronym stands for the Family Medical Leave Act, which outlines standards by which employees are granted unpaid time off for family or medical leave without being terminated from their jobs. All the other choices refer to things covered by the EEOC: EPA (Equal Pay Act, which prohibits salary discrimination based on sex), ADEA (Age Discrimination in Employment Act, which prohibits age discrimination for workers who are forty and older), and Title VII of the Civil Rights Act (which prohibits discrimination based on race, color, sex, religion, or national origin).

122. C: OSHA. OSHA refers to the Occupational Health and Safety Administration, which administers workplace safety standards. The other choices are incorrect: NLRB stands for the National Labor Relations Board, which provides standards for unions and other employee relations. EEOC stands for

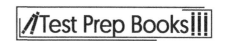

Equal Employment Opportunity Commission, which oversees cases of workplace discrimination. EBSA stands for Employee Benefits Security Administration, which administers and enforces standards for employee benefits like retirement and health plans.

123. D: After investigating the validity of the report, HR should determine whether it is possible to work with less hazardous materials or develop improved safety measures in collaboration with factory managers. HR should conduct due diligence into any employee's claims of workplace hazards. If the concerns are valid, OSHA guidance indicates that employers should look for ways to eliminate hazards completely before enacting other measures like improved safety practices or protective equipment. Choice A is not the best answer because employees should not feel punished or silenced for raising safety concerns. Choice B is also not a good choice because OSHA standards prohibit employers from requiring employees to buy necessary safety equipment; this should be provided by the employer. Finally, Choice C is not the best choice because health and safety information should be presented in a way that can be easily understood by employees. Not all factory workers can be expected to understand a highly technical report about chemicals.

124. B: "Buy" refers to acquiring talent from external sources, while "build" refers to using internal talent by reorganizing employees or developing critical skills. Basically, "buy or build" refers to external or internal sourcing of talent to close an organization's workforce gap. Different strategies can be appropriate in different situations, and a combination of both may prove effective for many organizations.

125. D: Schedule mandatory in-person training with employee involvement, such as skits, role plays, and mock juries, to encourage engagement and focus on real-world implications. Workplace conduct is a topic that HR should emphasize for all employees with a high level of engagement. HR has made the right first step in deciding to proactively address workplace harassment and misconduct; however, establishing clear guidance and creating a culture of civility comes from true engagement with employees. For this reason, Choice C is not the best choice, because employees will be passive learners. Also, while Choice A might be a good supplementary resource, employees also need positive modeling and information about how they *should* behave in the workplace, rather than just negative information about how they *should not* behave. Finally, Choice B is not the best choice because abstract legal implications may not have a strong connection to employees. Instead, Choice D gives employees a chance to explore situations that affect their everyday workplace interactions.

126. B: Someone from the C-suite. An organization's culture of civility must be rooted in its leadership. If employees sense that rules about workplace conduct do not apply to an organization's executives, or are applied inconsistently, standards of civil behavior are less likely to take hold throughout the organization. It is important to engage leaders from the C-suite to lead by example. Choice A is not the best choice because some employees may prefer to keep their complaints confidential; experience with harassment may be personal and hurtful to share with a large audience. Choice C is not the best choice because, while guidance from the Department of Justice could be helpful, it is better to begin with leadership from inside the organization. Finally, while HR should be involved with all levels of this training, it is important to reach outside HR to leaders in other areas of the organization.

127. C: Prioritizing diversity when hiring new HR employees. Particularly in cases of workplace harassment based on sex, race, religion, or other factors, employees need to know that their concerns are taken seriously by HR and that their needs are reflected in the makeup of the HR department. Ensuring that HR follows the same D&I hiring standards as the rest of the organization can set the stage for building rapport with employees and helping them feel represented. Choice A is not the best choice

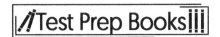

because there are situations in which HR should seek external help, especially in cases of a conflict of interest or high legal liability. Choice *B* is not the best choice, either, because many employees are unaware of hotline numbers, and the reporting may go through outside channels before returning to HR. Moreover, there could be significant lag time between the incident, the reporting, and the HR response. As for Choice *D*, while it is important for HR to keep an organization's leaders on the same page with regards to workplace conduct, it is also important that HR maintain a level of objectivity, in case complaints are lodged against senior leaders themselves.

128. C: Automation. Automation helps HR reduce time-consuming busywork, paperwork shuffling, and redundant tasks by transitioning manual tasks to automatic digital functions.

129. A: The degree of difference between planned and actual outcomes. A variance analysis helps to evaluate the effectiveness of strategic planning and other workplace initiatives while also helping to identify where and how the gaps occurred between planning and execution. Choice *B* is incorrect; the percentage of pay gap between employees in similar job roles is not what a variance analysis measures. Choice *C* is incorrect as well; this refers to an organization's competitive advantage.

130. B: The industry standard for required competencies in this position. Because this effort is intended to standardize positions within different departments of the same organization, HR is less likely to consider outside evaluation criteria. Looking at industry standards for job positions is relevant when crafting new job descriptions, which is not the objective in this case. All the other choices refer to important criteria about the qualifications, type of work, and organizational structure essential to the function of the position.

131. C: Job enrichment. Job enrichment refers to increasing a job's depth by adding new responsibilities to an existing job title. Choice *D*, job enlargement, refers to broadening the scope of a job by adding new tasks. Job evaluation and job elaboration are not established HR terms.

132. D: Organize a week-long training class focused on desired skill development. Although building the skills, knowledge, and competencies of the workforce is an ongoing responsibility of the HR department, sometimes there are short-term skills gaps that need to be closed. In this case, organizing a class or workshop to directly target the missing skill is a practical and effective approach. For example, if many employees are struggling with adopting new workplace software, a few training courses can help them get up to speed. Choice *A* is not the best choice because interviewing and onboarding new employees is very time-consuming and not the best short-term strategy. Choice *B* is also not the best choice because a high-potential development program should carry employees throughout the time at an organization until they are positioned to become leaders; again, this is a long-term rather than short-term development strategy. Finally, Choice *C* is not the best choice because, while internal reassignment can help employees to find positions that best fit their competencies, this choice does not solve the problem because it removes underperforming employees without replacing them or building the skills of remaining workers.

133. A: It has an effect on employee recruiting and retention. A well-managed CSR program helps improve the organization's reputation and relationship with various stakeholders, including potential and current employees. Many employees value ethical and meaningful work; the perception of making a difference in the community and environment tends to reflect positively in employee satisfaction. CSR programs also act as part of an organization's branding and advertising, which influences the reach of HR's recruitment efforts. Choice *B* is not the best choice because, while any CSR program involves interaction with external stakeholders, it should ultimately be guided by internal leaders. Choice *C* is also

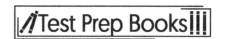
incorrect. Some elements of an organization's CSR initiatives may be influenced by legal regulations (for example, laws that regulate pollution or emissions may shape an organization's environmentally-friendly policies). However, organizations are also influenced by moral and ethical responsibilities, not just legal ones. Finally, Choice *D* is incorrect because ideally CSR will balance the needs of the organization and the environment, rather than prioritizing one at the expense of the other.

134. B: Collect, compile, and analyze data to demonstrate the quantitative and qualitative impacts of various CSR initiatives. HR can assist with communication and planning within CSR, and this involves analyzing metrics to understand how the CSR plan is functioning. This information is then communicated to various internal and external stakeholders and can influence CSR decision making moving forward. Choice *A* is not a good choice because CSR initiatives depend on the participation of all employees at every level. Choice *C* is also not the best choice because, while different business units may have different contributions to make to an organization's overall CSR efforts, they should be united by a common vision and interdepartmental communication should be facilitated. Choice *D* is also not the best choice. Incorporating CSR participation into evaluations is one way to emphasize its importance in the workplace. However, any such evaluation should include ways to recognize and reward employees for their contributions, rather than simply punishing them for not participating.

135. A: The NLRB can facilitate settlements of labor disputes between employers and employees. Although disputes can often be settled within an organization, some situational factors may require external assistance. Factors like the level of the complaint, the number of people involved, the size of the liability, etc. can influence whether an organization chooses to seek external settlement or mediation. Choice *B* is not correct because there are various forms of nonunion representation for employees. Choice *C* is also incorrect because, in order to be recognized as lawful, works councils must be elected by employees without employer interference. Choice *D* is incorrect because employees may choose different forms of representation for different situations. For example, union representation can aid with collective bargaining for employees across many different organizations with an industry. However, nonunion representation like a works council can help employees handle situations specific to their workplace. Unions sometimes help with the election of works council representatives.

136. C: Lagging indicators reflect performance that happened in the past, while leading indicators reflect activity that can change future performance or success. Leading and lagging indicators both include KPI that help an organization evaluate its performance relative to strategic planning objectives and make adjustments to optimize future performance.

137. D: Ratio of total employees to HR professionals within the organization and in other comparable organizations in the industry. There are various KPI that can be of use to HR professionals in evaluating and improving the HR function. However, this question specifically asks about benchmarking, which involves measuring an organization's performance against industry best practices. All the choices except for Choice *D* refer to KPI that only consider the internal performance of the organization, not how it stands relative to other organizations.

138. B: Offer guided benefits counseling and advice leading up to the enrollment period. While employees are attracted by an organization's benefits package, realistically, many employees get overwhelmed by the wealth of options and the decision-making factors that go into benefits enrollment. HR should offer accessible, plain-language information to employees, including offering personal guidance to walk employees through their benefits selection. Choice *A* is not the best choice because, while HR should constantly evaluate whether it is offering meaningful benefits to employees, HR should first consider whether poor communications rather than unpopularity of options is preventing people

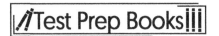

from enrolling. Choice *C* should also be eliminated because employees generally need more—not less—assistance when it comes to understanding their healthcare options; this choice removes all HR guidance from the process. Choice *D* is also not the best way of addressing the underlying problem.

139. A: Number and type of ongoing projects. All the other choices indicate relevant metrics from HR that can influence and inform the strategic planning process. However, Choice *A* refers to information that should be supplied from many different areas of the organization, not just from HR.

140. C: A short, directed survey that makes it easier for employees to give feedback on a particular topic or initiative. A pulse survey is intended to take the "pulse" of employee opinion without being as lengthy or thorough as other surveys conducted by HR. The purpose of a pulse survey is to gather immediate responses from employees, which HR professionals can quickly act on. For this reason, pulse surveys can be conducted more frequently than other types of surveys. They are appropriate when quick feedback is needed.

141. B: Analyze relevant performance metrics, such as sales per quarter. When it comes to total rewards design, ROI is determined by taking the value an employee adds to the organization and comparing it to the amount that is spent to retain that employee. In this case, metrics that can demonstrate this added value help HR and other stakeholders to develop a rewards package that fairly compensates employees. Choices *A* and *C* can both be eliminated because best practices and total remuneration surveys both consider standards for compensation throughout the industry, but they do not reflect rewards relative to the value that employees add to the company. Choice *D* is also not the best choice because HR should take the lead in determining and communicating employee value.

142. A: HR should evaluate the functionality of the new system from the perspective of stakeholders outside HR. Whenever HR is considering adopting new processes, such as selecting a new ATS, it has to consider the needs of all stakeholders, including those outside HR. The purpose of ATS software is to help recruit the best employees to work throughout the organization, so HR needs to communicate with relevant stakeholders to determine which software functionalities will improve their experience. HR can also consider the ATS from the perspective of stakeholders outside the organization (i.e., applicants). Choice *B* is not the best choice because each organization may have unique needs for its ATS; serving the needs of the organization is more important than trying to outpace others. Choice *C* is also not a good choice because it will create confusion to maintain two systems at the same time. Choice *D* can also be eliminated because, while employees may have technical capabilities, they are not necessarily HR specialists, and this could detract from the overall goals of the organization.

143. D: Industry usage rates. Again, it is most important for HR to choose a product that fits their organization's and stakeholders' needs, rather than seeking a "one-size-fits-all" solution based on others in the industry. Choice *A* is important because any new software will have to integrate well with other systems already in use. Choice *B* is also important because any system is only as effective as the people who use it; if it is too difficult for stakeholders to use the ATS, it will not be effective. Vendors should also be able to devise a plan for user support after the software purchase. Finally, Choice *C* is also essential in selecting an ATS. The advantage of using a digital applicant management system is that it can easily generate reports and metrics to inform HR and organizational decision-making.

144. B: Determine essential qualifications for the job positions in order to categorize applications and help recruiters focus on a smaller pool of candidates. An ATS can help HR to sort and screen candidates' qualifications, which can be very useful when looking for highly specialized skills. Choices *A* and *D* can both be eliminated because they don't present solutions that increase the workforce; based on the scenario, the company is expanding, so hiring new employees is inevitable. Choice C is not a good choice either because, while all those functions may be possible through an ATS, it is not advisable to lump them all together for applicants. The application process should be easy to navigate and complete. Many job seekers report not completing their applications due to the length or complexity of some online job applications.

145. A: Mutually eliminates double taxation for expatriate employees. This prevents employees from being taxed in both their home country and their country of work during an international assignment. This is an example of one of the many situations HR needs to be prepared for when sending employees to other countries; in this case, it translates into significant financial savings for employees if they take advantage of this tax agreement where available.

146. D: An organization's workforce and all those affected by its social, economic, and environmental impact. Stakeholders include everyone, both internal and external, influenced by an organization's operations. Choice A limits itself only to leadership, so it is incorrect. Choice B limits itself to the workforce, but stakeholders include people outside the workforce. Choice C is also incorrect because it considers only those influenced by the organization's economic impact.

147. C: A structured discussion to determine which factors influence employee retention and how retention efforts can be improved. A stay interview is a chance for HR to gain insight into why employees decide to stay at their jobs. Things like culture, leadership, professional development, job satisfaction, and other factors can all drive this decision. HR can use stay interviews to determine which areas are working well for employees and which areas need improvement.

148. B: HR can participate in the strategic planning to offer input and highlight areas where workforce goals can be aligned with overall company goals. HR participation is essential from the earliest stages of the strategic planning process to provide insight and predict challenges and solutions related to HR. Choice A is not the best choice because HR should contribute to the planning process; senior-level leaders might not be able to anticipate all the workforce challenges involved with the expansion. Choice C is also not the best choice. HR should always work to improve and innovate its processes. However, when opening new stores, the company first wants to establish a consistent brand and culture with existing stores. It would not make sense to introduce too many uncertainties to the new project. Finally, while Choice D might be a good step for HR to take in reviewing and evaluating the strategic plan, it is not the best choice because there are many other proactive measures that HR should take first.

149. C: Determine the deliverables relevant to the strategic plan and identify associated HR KPI. Before deciding what to measure, HR needs to have an idea of what the objectives and deliverables of the strategic plan are. Is the company looking to increase profits? Develop their brand? Improve operational efficiency? Different objectives should be measured by different KPI. For example, if the strategic plan calls for increasing profits, then HR should identify KPI related to costs and revenue such as cost-per-hire and sales numbers. Choice A is not the best choice because both long- and short-term metrics can be relevant here. Choice B is also not the best choice because, although environmental scanning is always useful in strategic planning, it's important to focus on the specific goals relevant to this company. Finally, Choice D could result in a muddle of information in which the data is not focused enough to provide answers to company leaders' questions about performance.

150. A: Time-to-hire. This is the KPI most closely related to filling the positions at the expanded locations. Knowing the current time-to-hire helps the company budget for how long it will take to recruit

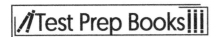
and onboard new employees based on the number of vacancies and available HR staff. The other choices do not refer to KPI that measure things related to hiring.

151. D: Focus on issues that matter to executives such as recruiting and retaining top employees and increasing operational efficiency. In making a business case, it is important to target the things that matter to stakeholders and decision makers, not just to HR. By showing how HR can help the organization achieve its goals, HR professionals can make a better case for why senior leaders should value HR's contributions. Choice *A* is not a good choice because it focuses on past performance and not on the issue at hand (namely, that HR should be given increased scope of operations). Neither Choice *B* nor Choice *C* is an appropriate choice because they are based on HR-specific practices that may not be relevant to outside stakeholders. HR professionals need to remember to approach issues from the perspective of those who might be asking, "What does this have to do with me?"

152. B: It gives more timely and dynamic feedback to employees and helps solve performance problems as soon as they arise. One of the drawbacks of conducting annual performance evaluations is that they may take too long to address critical issues with performance; in other words, the damage has already been done or inefficient work practices have already been established. This app provides more opportunities for feedback from more perspectives. Choice *A* is not the best choice because encouraging phone use at work does not really contribute to productivity or engagement. Choice *B* could be a potential advantage to this new program, but technology for technology's sake is not the primary objective of any new processes in the workplace. Choice *D* is not the best choice, either, because the program should encourage better engagement, not allow supervisors to disengage from the workers they manage. In other words, it presents an opportunity for a different type of feedback rather than removing supervisors from the feedback process altogether.

153. D: The app will prove to be expensive and cost-prohibitive compared to traditional performance evaluations. Generally, most moves toward automation present opportunities to cut costs and operate more efficiently by removing hours of manual labor and paperwork, so this is least likely to be a major drawback of adopting an automated system. Choice *A* represents a major potential problem that HR should work to address: How can they prevent constant feedback from turning into an opportunity to bully or overly criticize some employees based on personal feelings? The same applies to Choice *B*. Choice *C* is also a potential hurdle HR should overcome because any new technology requires some time for users to learn how to operate and optimize the system's functionality.

154. B: Automation allows technology to take over manual tasks, while augmentation refers to ways that technology assists employees in their job function. Both automation and augmentation are terms related to incorporating new technology into existing work processes. However, whereas automation refers to instances in which digital processes can fully replace employee functions or actions, augmentation looks at areas where employees can continue to perform tasks with the help of new technologies. For people who fear that automation will lead to replacing entire groups of workers, augmentation is a more attractive way to approach bringing technology into the workplace.

155. A: Hold a demonstration of how the technology works in different situations, including information about user resources. With any new workplace technology, employees need to fully understand how to use the new system before they can engage with it. Holding a demonstration that addresses different scenarios can give employees ideas of how to integrate it into their work; offering user resources gives employees a way to find answers and solutions afterward. Choice *B* is not the best choice because it doesn't consider the needs of all stakeholders; for example, some supervisors may prefer to use both performance evaluation methods, or some employees may need longer than six months to adjust to a

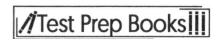

different management style. Choice C is also not the best choice because it isn't very practical and doesn't address engagement for employees who already have phones. Choice D is not a good choice because the videos are not likely to reach all employees who are using the app.

156. C: A group created and led by employees who share common backgrounds or demographic factors. An ERG is often part of an organization's D&I plan. It allows employees to meet similar coworkers (in terms of things like age, race, gender, socioeconomic background, and other factors), build rapport, represent the needs of external stakeholders, and give feedback to the organization.

157. B: Meet with local supervisors and managers to establish areas of shared goals and practices and focus on converging operations. Successful international operations are those that balance the parent company's culture with that of local operations. Especially when opening new stores, it is more productive to identify areas of similarities and overlapping objectives rather than only emphasizing differences. This enables the local employees to add value where their skills can contribute to the parent company's goals. Choice A is not the best choice because it defeats the purpose of buying an existing company—that is, to use their established practice and experience. Choice C is also not the most productive choice; again, if all employees require extensive, costly retraining, it does not make sense to retain experienced cosmetics salespeople. Finally, Choice D is not the best choice because, while it is definitely important to assess the capabilities of the new workforce, this choice does not fully explain how to integrate their skills into new ownership.

158. D: Arrange regular check-in meetings and agree on reporting times and methods. Constant coordination and communication with clearly defined objectives and performance measures is the best way to ensure that shared goals are being met. Choice A is not the best choice for addressing this particular issue because it doesn't mention how the leadership groups in each country will be communicating with each other. Choice B is also not the best choice; online messages (such as email and instant messenger) are important, but other forms of communication should be incorporated as well. Choice C is not a good choice because it doesn't consider possible time zone problems that could arise from simply putting local stores on American schedules; mutually agreed upon meeting times should be established instead.

159. B: Do you have any commitments that will conflict with your work? Employers are prohibited from asking applicants any questions that may lead to hiring discrimination based on things like age, gender, nationality, and religion. Questions about family, children, and marital status are particularly likely to target women. Interviewers must ensure that they are asking the same or similar questions to all applicants, and that the questions remain relevant to the job function. In this case, Choice B is the best because it approaches the important issue for the employer—how much availability does the applicant have?—without introducing needlessly personal or discriminatory factors. All the other choices include topics that would be inappropriate to ask about during an interview.

160. C: The Myers-Briggs Type Indicator is a personality test that shows people's preferences, ways of thinking, and decision-making style. These factors are important when matching a person to a job. For example, a person who is classified as extroverted on the Myers-Brigg assessment may not do well in a job where they often work alone.

Behavioral Competency

1. Which of the following attributes is NOT an element of effective leadership?
    a. Managing time in a financially responsible manner
    b. Solving problems as they arise
    c. Strategic thinking
    d. Carrying out the requirements of the job

2. Laura has been hired to complete multiple human resources (HR) personnel tasks. These tasks can include which one of the following?
    a. Developing job postings
    b. Completing workplace investigations
    c. Establishing a benefits program
    d. Filing paperwork

3. Which one of the following statements is true regarding developing jobs within an organization?
    a. Jobs are developed based on an individual's particular skill set and background.
    b. Jobs are developed based on goals and objectives established by leadership to ensure that qualified employees perform duties that contribute to the overall interests of the organization.
    c. Jobs are developed based on the budget and what level of job responsibilities that budget can afford.
    d. Jobs are developed based on the supervisor's discretion and the responsibilities that individual wants performed.

4. Amy and Michelle work in HR and are very passionate about the work they do. They work directly with the lower levels of the organization to influence the culture, set the tone for behavior, and communicate the goals and achievements of the organization. When a survey is conducted to determine how effective their efforts have been, the results are not positive. What could Amy and Michelle have done differently to have better results?
    a. Hire a third party to create a specific marketing plan for employees.
    b. Work with and engage the leaders of the organization to directly interact with their teams to influence the culture and communicate the goals of the organization.
    c. Meet with employees more often and require participation at all group meetings.
    d. There is nothing that could have been done differently—the plan was appropriate and the employees were just not interested.

5. Which of the following is NOT an element of navigating an organization to effectively implement HR initiatives?
    a. Facilitating communication and decision making
    b. Using an understanding of process, systems, and policies
    c. Using awareness and understanding of the political environment and culture
    d. Demonstrating an understanding of the formal HR work roles only

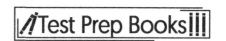

6. When setting goals and milestones, it is important to ensure they exhibit SMART qualities. Which of the following characteristics does SMART stand for?

    a. Specific, Methods, Achievable, Relatable, and Tests

    b. Significant, Measurable, Assessable, Reasonable, and Timely

    c. Specific, Measurable, Achievable, Relevant, and Timely

    d. Strategic, Momentum, Achievable, Resounding, and Tests

7. Which of the following statements is true regarding a vision and mission statement?

    a. A vision statement focuses on the future goals; a mission statement focuses on the values, standards, and organizing principles.

    b. A vision statement focuses on the values, standards, and organizing principles; a mission statement focuses on the future goals.

    c. A vision statement asks questions about what the organization wants to accomplish; a mission statement answers the questions about what the organization wants to accomplish.

    d. Vision and mission statements should be indirect, with high-level information.

8. David has been an HR manager for six months with his new organization. When setting up his professional goals and milestones for the next year, he used the exact list from his previous position at another organization. He received an outstanding performance rating from his work and believed that by doing the same work at his new organization, he was setting himself up for success. His supervisor, however, did not agree and asked him to redo his goals and milestones. Why would David's supervisor ask him to do this, and what should David do?

    a. The supervisor was simply exerting control over his subordinate. David should go to the next-level supervisor for support.

    b. The supervisor clearly did not read the list of goals and milestones that was submitted, and David should request another meeting to review the original list.

    c. The list of goals and milestones was not specific and applicable to the new organization's goals and achievements.

    d. The list of goals and milestones was not on the proper form, and David should just copy and paste the list to the new form and resubmit the original list.

9. Patrick was involved in a lengthy and complex project to relocate office staff to a new building. At the end of the project, management reviewed the metrics and determined that not only was the project over budget, it took much longer than anticipated to complete and employees still had concerns, such as ergonomic issues and technology breaks. What should Patrick do?

    a. Communicate to the manager that the issues won't happen again and move to the next project.

    b. Conduct a gap analysis and a root cause analysis to determine why milestones were not met.

    c. Hold a team meeting to determine what the team members think should be done.

    d. Prepare an in-depth PowerPoint presentation of the items that were successful in the project.

10. Tools from which of the following approaches can be used to determine resources needed at each step of a project?

    a. Six Sigma

    b. Quality control

    c. Quality assurance

    d. Lean manufacturing

11. Sometimes there are many things that are out of a team's control, such as funding changes, new or updated regulations, and personnel changes. Which of the following concepts is important to understand when building milestones and objectives for a project?
    a. Rigidity
    b. Discipline
    c. Austerity
    d. Flexibility

12. Emily and Chris have worked in the HR department for five years. They have wanted to launch a wellness program since they started working for the company and finally prepared a plan to roll out to the employees. After meeting one-on-one for months, they created all of the documents necessary to communicate the new program to employees. They created sign-up sheets, a summary sheet, a summary plan description that outlined the benefits of participating in a wellness program, and a lengthy frequently asked questions (FAQ) document. After emailing the documents to all employees, Emily and Chris were disappointed to see that very few employees were interested in the program. Which one of the following choices is best in describing what Emily and Chris could have done differently to get a better outcome?
    a. Made participation in the program mandatory.
    b. Conducted an employee survey to get direct feedback on employees' needs.
    c. Communicated program details to leadership to have them instruct employees to participate.
    d. Added a new line item of "wellness program participation" to employees' performance evaluations to ensure participation.

13. Which of the following is NOT an acceptable standard when ensuring an organization has clear and enforceable ethical standards?
    a. Establishing a code of conduct
    b. Conducting HR audits
    c. Establishing a values statement
    d. Requesting that employees promise they will behave appropriately

14. The HR department is starting to see an increase in employee complaints, specifically regarding inappropriate behavior, such as foul language, racist and sexist jokes, and inappropriate statements regarding personal and religious beliefs. Which of the following should the HR department immediately engage in to resolve these issues?
    a. Send out the code of conduct and applicable policies to all employees, requiring them to submit a notice of acknowledgment.
    b. Require employees to attend training related to workplace behavior.
    c. Investigate all complaints fully and take corrective action immediately.
    d. Communicate the current climate of the organization to leadership and request their support.

15. A company may decide to outsource which of the following functions to free up staff time, reduce costs, improve compliance, and avoid fines related to Internal Revenue Service (IRS) filings or incorrect payments?
    a. Payroll
    b. HR
    c. Information technology
    d. Marketing

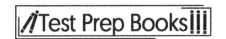
16. Stephanie has worked in the HR department for seven years. She has a full personal life and prefers to keep it private. She comes to work on time, takes her breaks, and leaves on time. She does her work with minimal direction or interaction with others and prefers to eat her lunch alone. Stephanie was recently assigned a project that requires her to interact with her team and engage with them to ensure that multiple opinions and expertise are considered; however, she has not received the most welcoming reception, and her peers do not seem to want to participate or engage with her on the project. What can Stephanie do to turn this situation around?

a. Talk to her supervisor to let him know that the team is not working with her and ask that they be directed to do so.

b. Do the project on her own to the best of her ability, without the team's input.

c. Network with her colleagues and converse with them to gain trust and build interpersonal relationships.

d. Continue to behave in the same manner, schedule more meetings, and hope the team will come around.

17. What is a useful method to implement that can ensure HR staff and leadership have the same expectations of an initiative?

a. Stakeholder mapping that avoids the initiative value

b. A project proposal lacking financial analysis of the return on investment of the initiative

c. The Myers-Briggs Type Indicator to predict leadership's expectations

d. A written project proposal that outlines the timeline, milestones, needed resources, and dates for deliverables

18. Which of the following is the most crucial component of fostering collaboration among a team?

a. Maintaining a positive attitude

b. Open communication

c. Showing appreciation

d. Building interpersonal skills

19. Which of the following are the components of emotional intelligence (EI)?

a. Relationship awareness, social management, team management, self-awareness

b. Supporting team culture, team leadership, identifying team roles, conflict management

c. Social awareness, resource management, time management, performance management

d. Social awareness, relationship management, self-management, self-awareness

20. Eric is a team leader in the HR department and supervises HR professionals at various levels, including analysts, administrators, and supervisors. He is struggling with the team's motivation to go above and beyond in providing customer service. Although the team answers questions and handles situations appropriately, Eric wants to elevate the team's performance to deliver even better results. What should he do to effect this change in the team?

a. Eric should work to display these characteristics in his daily work, verbally communicate expectations to the team, and recognize when an employee goes above the standard.

b. Eric should immediately deliver performance reviews to the entire team to formally communicate the new level of service expected.

c. Eric should work with finance to budget a new position and hire an energetic individual who goes above and beyond in their work to motivate the team.

d. Eric should email the team to communicate the new expectations for customer service.

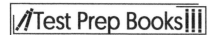

21. Julia has been working with her union representative regarding discipline for performance issues. Her supervisor has issued multiple disciplinary notices for her lack of attention to detail, which has resulted in errors and additional work to correct the mistakes, thus costing additional money. The latest discipline included an unpaid suspension for three days. Julia does not believe the discipline is warranted and has filed a grievance to have it removed from her record and the suspension reversed with pay. She claims she never received the appropriate training necessary to be able to perform at the level required; however, the grievance has been denied at the supervisor, management, and executive levels due to the documentation, which includes training records. A grievance arbitration ruled in favor of upholding the discipline. Does Julia have any additional options?
   a. Yes. Julia can appeal the grievance arbitration decision.
   b. Yes. Julia can resubmit her original grievance and go through the process again.
   c. No. Grievance arbitration is enforceable and cannot go to court to be changed.
   d. No. Julia needs to find another job with a new organization.

22. Graham is the chief executive officer (CEO) of a reputable company that provides transportation services to local businesses. A customer service representative filed a complaint with the Equal Employment Opportunity Commission (EEOC) charging that she has been subjected to discrimination and harassment by a supervisor for a number of years. An attorney has taken the case, and a lawsuit has been filed. Graham has reviewed the claim and is weighing a settlement to close the claim so that the company can move forward. Which of the following factors is NOT an influencer Graham should consider when deciding to settle?
   a. Damage to the company's reputation
   b. New systemic problems
   c. Financial cost of an investigation and trial
   d. Graham's personal financial concerns

23. Which of the following is money awarded to an individual in a workplace discrimination case, generally equal to lost earnings?
   a. Retroactive pay
   b. Front pay
   c. Back pay
   d. Specialty pay

24. Which of the following statements is false regarding collective bargaining?
   a. All changes that management wants to implement, regardless of the subject, are required to be negotiated through the collective bargaining process.
   b. Collective bargaining is the act of negotiation between the employer and employees, with a union representing the employees' interests.
   c. The goal of collective bargaining is to develop a mutual agreement.
   d. There are several strategies that can be used during a collective bargaining process, including single-unit bargaining, coordinated bargaining, multi-employer bargaining, and parallel bargaining.

25. Lisa is the chief negotiator for her organization and will be negotiating with four union groups that each represent a different group of employees—public safety, management, administrative and clerical, and skilled trades. Each group has a special and unique skill set, with employees each having their own needs specific to training, wages, specialty pay, time off, work schedules, and personal protective equipment. One of the memorandums of understanding (MOUs) is expiring soon, and therefore Lisa is working on her bargaining strategy and wants to ensure that her method is appropriate for the situation. Which strategy should she employ when working on her overall negotiations strategy for the upcoming discussions?
    a. Multi-employer bargaining
    b. Single-unit bargaining
    c. Parallel bargaining
    d. Coordinated bargaining

26. James is the new leader of an organization that employs many individuals in various disciplines and locations. He has initiated multiple methods to ensure that all employees receive communication that is relatable and appropriate. He sends out frequent email announcements and newsletters to discuss what is happening in the organization, hosts town hall meetings and informal brown bag lunches, and frequently walks around each location to engage with employees directly. What else can James do to make sure all employees have opportunities to engage with him directly and ensure open lines of communication?
    a. Host and pay for a Christmas party.
    b. Establish an open-door policy.
    c. There is nothing he can do.
    d. Take donuts to every location every Friday.

27. Jennifer meets regularly with her team members, both as a group and individually, to ensure that each employee understands expectations and current projects and issues are handled timely and effectively. In each group meeting, she makes sure time is allocated for each individual to communicate concerns or ideas. During this time, she engages with the speaker, takes notes, responds with body language, and asks questions. What type of listening is Jennifer engaging in?
    a. Functional
    b. Operational
    c. Active
    d. Empathetic

28. Which one of the following is a crucial component of program evaluation, guiding and sustaining initiatives, and providing valuable customer service?
    a. Soliciting feedback
    b. Interpreting the context of received communications
    c. Seeking further information
    d. Responding to communications

29. Karen has recently been hired in the HR department for a company that operates in twenty-four countries and fourteen US states. In addition to learning about her individual role and the functions of her HR team, what should she seek to understand to ensure successful HR initiatives?
    a. The organization's line of business from a global perspective
    b. Financial customs
    c. Immigration work laws
    d. Competitors' policies and procedures

30. How can a site's geographic location affect business operations?
   a. All locations should be managed the same to ensure equity and that one location does not receive more attention and resources than another.
   b. Each location will have a separate management team that will run the operations differently based on their own unique experience and background.
   c. Some locations may require additional resources or plans to address specific needs, such as climate change, harsh weather conditions, and coastlines.
   d. The home-base location should allocate resources equally, with management distributing them as appropriate.

31. Which of the following is vital when operating in a global environment?
   a. Responding promptly to and fully addressing all stakeholders' needs
   b. Soliciting feedback from leadership concerning the HR functions
   c. Seeking further information to clarify any ambiguous issues
   d. Understanding and respecting differences in regulations and accepted business operations

32. Robert is working on a performance evaluation project with several managers from locations across the country. His primary goal is to roll out one comprehensive program to ensure alignment and consistency across the organization, regardless of the location. He is struggling with the information and feedback he is receiving from each manager because they are focusing on their individual location's needs versus the overarching organization's needs. What can Robert do to ensure agreement among the locations while achieving his goal of a comprehensive performance evaluation program that meets the organization's goals?
   a. Robert should continue on his structured path to roll out the program, with or without the managers' buy-in or participation.
   b. Robert should discuss the concerns with his supervisor and ask to get the location managers on board.
   c. Robert should clearly define the expectations of the project and establish aligned values.
   d. Robert should develop separate programs for each location to meet their specific needs.

33. Which of the following benefits is associated with a diverse workplace?
   a. Higher employee retention
   b. Higher employee complaints
   c. Increased training needs
   d. Higher employee turnover

34. Rachel is responsible for the campus recruiting program in her organization. She routinely attends hiring fairs and events at the university campuses in the surrounding area. These events always provide a more than adequate number of applicants for the open positions. What should Rachel consider adding to this campus recruiting program for even stronger results?
   a. Submit a request to the career centers for candidates to be sent directly to the organization to minimize expenses related to attending the hiring fairs.
   b. Expand the list of campuses she visits to outside of the area to include candidates from different backgrounds and locations, ensuring a more diverse candidate pool.
   c. Request candidate referrals from current employees while offering a candidate referral bonus program.
   d. Continue attending these specific hiring fairs and events because the candidate pool is adequate for the organization's hiring needs.

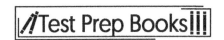

35. Which of the following is a way to learn more about the business operations, functions, products, and services of an organization?
    a. Read all of the job descriptions for every position within the organization.
    b. Review available internal documents, external literature, and customer service surveys.
    c. Send out an email to the department leaders asking them to respond to specific questions.
    d. Meet with employees to ask them questions about their goals, objectives, and work product.

36. PESTLE is a structured tool used to learn about trends that can influence an organization's goals, processes, and employees. What does PESTLE analyze?
    a. People, Environmental, Society, Teamwork, Legal, and External trends
    b. Political, Environmental, Social, Teamwork, Logistics, and External trends
    c. People, Engagement, Sustainability, Technological, Legal, and Environmental trends
    d. Political, Economic, Social, Technological, Legal, and Environmental trends

37. Mark is concerned with the number of employees leaving the organization. He believes they are resigning due to the company not paying a competitive salary. What can Mark analyze to determine if his belief is accurate?
    a. Exit interview data
    b. Job descriptions
    c. Cost-of-living index
    d. External salary data

38. Which of the following should NOT be used to inform business decisions?
    a. Organizational metrics
    b. Key performance indicators
    c. Political trends
    d. Cost-benefit analysis

39. Jake prepared a cost-benefit analysis as part of a presentation to pitch a new HR training program that would provide all employees an opportunity to enhance their interpersonal and communication skills. He focused on equipment, materials, time, and the corresponding benefits related to training employees. Management was impressed but concerned that this proposal was not holistic and complete. What did Jake forget?
    a. Legal fees
    b. Labor costs
    c. Marketing costs
    d. Nothing. Jake provided a complete analysis with no missing information.

40. Anna is responsible for tracking all of the HR information for the department. She uses multiple spreadsheets to keep track of merit increases, performance evaluations, addresses, emergency contacts, and other important information. Anna also uses a complex document to track job postings, recruitment, and hiring procedures. What tool would make her work easier to manage and allow for a more timely and accurate method of tracking employee information?
    a. Microsoft Access
    b. HR Information System (HRIS)
    c. Online business dashboard
    d. Document mapping system

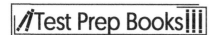

41. Sylvia is working to establish a new policy related to parental leave. The organization has not historically practiced consistent procedures relative to maternity, paternity, and ongoing family leave. Although there are many federal and state laws, Sylvia needs to ensure the organization is not only in compliance with these laws but that consistent, fair, and equitable practices are put in place that align with an overall policy that addresses the process, time frames, exceptions, and other issues that could arise. Sylvia would like to survey employees to receive feedback as to what they would like to see in this new policy. Who should she survey?
    a. All employees
    b. Female employees
    c. Female employees who have used maternity leave
    d. Managers and supervisors

42. Which of the following statements about strategic plans is inaccurate?
    a. Strategic plans involve objectives, analysis, looking at strengths and weaknesses, and implementation.
    b. Strategic plans are executed by employees and HR professionals to ensure these employees have the necessary skills to accomplish the plans.
    c. Strategic plans are a one-time activity that should always guide the organization toward the overall goals and objectives.
    d. Strategic plans should maximize the organization's strengths, take advantage of industry opportunities, and regularly be improved.

43. A SWOT (strengths, weaknesses, opportunities, threats) analysis is a comprehensive tool that assists an organization in defining internal and external factors that can impact the entire organization. Which of the following identify internal factors an organization must consider?
    a. Strengths and weaknesses
    b. Strengths and opportunities
    c. Weaknesses and threats
    d. Opportunities and threats

44. A SWOT analysis is a comprehensive tool that assists an organization in defining internal and external factors that can impact the entire organization. Which of the following identify external factors an organization must consider?
    a. Strengths and weaknesses
    b. Strengths and opportunities
    c. Weaknesses and threats
    d. Opportunities and threats

45. Sarah has created an informational document for managers regarding all of the new state and federal regulations that impact the organization. She included the actual legislative language and what will change regarding day-to-day practices. Additionally, she added resources, such as external websites, for managers to have as much information as possible. Sarah sent the document to all managers along with an extensive email detailing the responsibilities of understanding this information. What should Sarah do to ensure that managers are fully aware of and have a complete understanding of the new regulations?
    a. Send out weekly emails with reminders to review the material.
    b. Conduct specialized trainings and reach out directly to managers to address questions.
    c. Require managers to respond to the email that they have received and understand the material.
    d. Print the document and place it in all of the managers' personnel files.

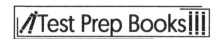

46. Which of the following is a fundamental component of an initiative's effectiveness?
    a. Fiscal responsibility
    b. Sustainability
    c. Environmental impact
    d. Employee satisfaction

47. Why is it important to collaborate with business partners who provide different strengths and experiences?
    a. Because these individuals can provide innovative solutions to problems that apply to other circumstances and situations an HR professional may not be aware of.
    b. Because the solutions should be provided by non-HR managers and HR should simply facilitate and manage the changes.
    c. Because HR professionals are in charge of writing overall policy, not developing solutions to address specific concerns.
    d. HR should not collaborate with professionals outside of HR.

48. According to the 1961 text *The Planning of Change* which of the following is NOT a strategy for managing change?
    a. The normative-reductive strategy
    b. The power-coercive strategy
    c. The technology-innovation strategy
    d. The empirical-rational strategy

49. Which strategy assumes individuals are rational and will naturally follow a path that benefits their self-interest?
    a. The power-coercive strategy
    b. The empirical-rational strategy
    c. The technology-innovation strategy
    d. The normative-reductive strategy

50. Lucas is preparing to roll out several new HR programs that will change how employees receive their benefits. The organization has not updated these programs since their inception, and therefore has fallen behind the industry standards and seen substantial cost increases. Lucas is determining which strategic method to use to roll out these changes to ensure the best reception from employees. Which of the following should he consider when determining which strategy to deploy?
    a. Lucas should consider the overall employee makeup of the organization as well as the sensitivity of the changes being implemented.
    b. Lucas should consider having the CEO deliver the message and implement the power-coercive strategy, with the message being delivered by the highest level of leadership.
    c. Lucas should consider sending an email to all employees to avoid conflicts.
    d. Lucas should consider showing employees how expensive the programs were and implement the empirical-rational strategy, with employees having the information as to how costly this would continue to be.

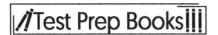

51. Amelia is responsible for sending out Consolidated Omnibus Budget Reconciliation Act (COBRA) notifications when an employee exits the organization. Regardless of the reason for separation, she must adhere to the notification requirements to ensure compliance. When is Amelia required to send out the initial COBRA notice regarding continuation of coverage options?
    a. On the day the separation notice is received
    b. Within ninety days of separation
    c. Within two weeks of separation
    d. On the day of separation

52. Deidre is new to the HR field, and she has made it a priority to attend conferences and social events, participate in workplace events such as wellness walks, and engage in meaningful conversations with individuals and teams. She is committed to building valuable relationships that will allow her to receive and give support to others in the HR field. What activity is Deidre engaging in?
    a. Team building
    b. Networking
    c. Benchmarking
    d. Socializing

53. Monica is interviewing interested vendors for services related to administering and managing the company's retirement program. Each vendor has submitted a cost proposal with specific details on the services provided along with a sample service agreement, which includes a cost breakdown. Which one of the following items should be discussed in the interviews to gauge which vendor will be the best selection?
    a. Retirement services and options available
    b. The company's retirement plans for their employees
    c. Communication and rollout plans
    d. Fixed and variable costs

54. Soleil is working to implement a new payroll and time-tracking program that will be a large undertaking, involving numerous departments and costing a substantial amount of money. In order to ensure that all of the key stakeholders are on board and have their concerns addressed, she is conducting one-on-one and department meetings; sending status emails while soliciting feedback and documenting comments, ideas, and concerns raised; and compiling survey responses from employees. What practice is Soleil engaging in?
    a. Recordkeeping
    b. Project management
    c. Milestone tracking
    d. Strategic planning

55. Which skill helps to recognize the feelings and communication styles of both one's self and others, resulting in being able to build better relationships?
    a. Intelligence quotient
    b. Athletic abilities
    c. Cognitive dissonance
    d. Emotional Intelligence skills

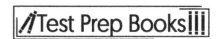

56. Which of the following is an inaccurate statement regarding grievances?
    a. Grievances allow management to respond appropriately through proper methods.
    b. Grievances follow a specific process that is identified by the organization's contract.
    c. Grievances are informal and should be resolved verbally by the supervisor.
    d. Grievances are complaints made formally and in writing.

57. Amalia is a member of the negotiations team and is preparing for the upcoming round of bargaining. The union has a long history with the organization, and most negotiations end up extending way past the end of the current contract. Amalia personally does not believe unions are necessary due to the numerous and strict federal and state laws that protect employees. She decides to start speaking directly with employees to let them know what the organization would be able to do for the staff if there was no union. What practice is Amalia engaging in?
    a. Negotiating in bad faith
    b. Negotiating in good faith
    c. Collective bargaining
    d. Unfair labor practice

58. The local union and company representatives are beginning the negotiation process for the upcoming year. There are legitimate concerns on both sides, including wages, benefits, schedules, workload, and retirement costs, that must be addressed in the successor contract. Before presenting proposals, each side takes the floor to discuss their issues and relate their concerns. Both parties agree to negotiate in good faith and work together to find solutions for each item. Which bargaining practice are these groups engaging in?
    a. Parallel bargaining
    b. Principled bargaining
    c. Distributive bargaining
    d. Coordinated bargaining

59. Which method of communication can spread information quickly but often becomes misinterpreted, misunderstood, and incorrect?
    a. Emails
    b. Newsletters
    c. Town hall meetings
    d. Word of mouth

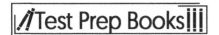

60. Raphael has been asked by senior leadership to give a presentation at the next board meeting. He is to present information concerning the recent customer service survey that was sent out to new customers from the last year. Raphael is excited about the opportunity to present to the senior leadership, for both the experience and the exposure to the team. He spends a significant amount of time preparing the presentation, his talking points, and handouts. He delves into the history of the department, the current staff, issues they are dealing with, and compensation information. Raphael's information is very detailed, but he finds that after fifteen minutes, he is losing the team's attention. What could be the reason for this?

    a. The leadership team is simply not aware of this information, and Raphael needs to keep to his presentation.

    b. Raphael was not mindful of the leadership's time and did not address the specific item requested.

    c. The leadership team should have been offered the ability to ask questions throughout the presentation.

    d. Raphael's presentation is not clearly conveying the information that was compiled, and he should request a quick break.

61. For several weeks after payroll is done, the payroll coordinator goes to HR to let them know an employee has been regularly using leave he has not yet accrued. What can HR do to address this concern?

    a. Contact the supervisor and allow for an in-person discussion to address the issue.

    b. Provide the employee with a formal, written reprimand.

    c. Monitor the situation and see if it occurs a few more times, and then address.

    d. Roll out mandatory training to all employees on proper leave usage and tracking.

62. Davina is conducting an analysis to determine the organization's next product launch. The launch must be successful to ensure the well-being of the organization, employees, customers, and community. What analysis should Davina conduct to make sure she takes into account all of the information that could influence this product launch?

    a. SWOT

    b. PESTLE

    c. Cost-benefit

    d. Risk assessment

63. Karen is working on preparing a report that outlines how her organization will benefit from a new purchasing system. Within the report, she outlines the short-term and long-term benefits that will be realized. Additionally, she presents how these benefits compare to the costs of the new system. These costs include projected labor, equipment, materials, time, and other potential costs, such as a contingency budget to address unforeseen issues that arise. What type of analysis has Karen conducted?

    a. Key performance indicators analysis

    b. Needs assessment analysis

    c. Cost-benefit analysis

    d. SWOT analysis

64. Which of the following functions is NOT performed through an HRIS?

    a. Initiate and run payroll functions, such as issuing paychecks and tax-related documents.

    b. Store data related to employee performance and job satisfaction.

    c. Manage and store employee documents and create reports.

    d. Manage, update, and store candidate profiles during a recruitment process.

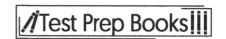

65. When a strategic plan calls for changes in employee skills, knowledge, behaviors, and/or work deliverables, what is the role of HR?
    a. HR holds multiple meetings and initiates various types of communication to reach out to managers, ensuring they are on the same page and personally training their employees.
    b. HR works with the legal team to ensure that the organization has the authority and management right to make the changes requested to the strategic plan.
    c. HR prepares exit strategies and severance packages for employees who do not meet the new requirements necessary to accomplish the plan.
    d. HR facilitates these changes by implementing updated policies, procedures, training, and other appropriate plans to ensure employees have the necessary skills to deliver the plan.

66. Adam has recently finalized a new MOU with his union. One of the areas that had various changes made was standby pay. Each department was engaging in a different practice, resulting in different standards, procedures, protocols, and wages. Prior to negotiating with the union, Adam met with each department that employed the practice of standby pay to discuss their current practices, concerns, and ideal future situations. Now that the new MOU is finalized with a standardized practice for standby pay, what should Adam do to ensure that all departments are aware of, understand, and are in compliance with the new terms?
    a. Communicate the changes with the highest level manager and charge him with training the departments.
    b. Meet one-on-one with every department manager and supervisor to communicate the changes made.
    c. Provide specialized training to all departments and offer individual training if needed.
    d. Send an email with the MOU, highlighting the section of standby pay so it is easily noticed.

67. When using the empirical-rational strategy to initiate change, what is the best way to accomplish the change successfully?
    a. Provide an employee lunch when communicating the change.
    b. Educate employees with new information on the change.
    c. Incentivize the change to relay the benefit employees will experience.
    d. Have the leader of the organization communicate the change.

68. Which of the following is an accurate statement about ambiguity?
    a. Ambiguity can cause conflict and distress for employees.
    b. Ambiguity is always preventable and should be avoided.
    c. Ambiguity will not affect business practices or processes.
    d. Ambiguity allows for creativity and innovation.

69. Lori has recently worked with her HR team and the organization to recruit and hire a large number of new employees. With production increases and the customer needs changing, the organization set a strategic goal to increase the workforce by 50 percent. With such a dramatic increase in newly hired employees, the workforce culture has changed substantially. Lori wants to ensure that the newly hired employees, as well as the tenured employees, are engaged, involved, and have a positive and inclusive work environment. What should Lori establish to make sure all employees are provided with these opportunities?
    a. Employee satisfaction survey
    b. Employee business resource groups
    c. Department and organization meetings
    d. Performance evaluation meetings

SHRM Practice Test #2

70. Monique has recently seen an increase in employee resignations within one particular department. Upon analyzing the demographics, she sees that a large majority of employees who left are minorities. Although the organization has established policies specific to diversity and inclusion, a barrier could still exist that is causing employees with a specific background to leave. What can Monique do to work with the leadership to identify and eliminate this barrier?
   a. Conduct internal interviews with employees to ask why others left.
   b. Audit the programs, practices, and policies regarding diversity and inclusion.
   c. Conduct mandatory diversity and inclusion training for all employees.
   d. Contact the employees who left and ask them to consider returning.

71. Which process administers, manages, and supports significant transitions related to resource allocation, operations, business processes, and other large-scale changes?
   a. Risk management
   b. Strategic planning
   c. Critical evaluation
   d. Change management

72. Phoebe is working on a salary review an employee requested. The employee believes new work has been assigned that changes the job being done and therefore a higher pay rate should be applied. Phoebe wants to get this review completed today so that she can relay the results to the manager and come to a resolution for the employee. Halfway through her work, her director pulls her into a meeting and asks her to work on a special task that was requested by the vice president. How should Phoebe manage her workload?
   a. Phoebe should attend to the special task first and then finish the salary review.
   b. Phoebe should finish the salary review first and then attend to the special task.
   c. Phoebe should request that the special task be assigned to another team member.
   d. Phoebe should request that another team member finish the salary review.

73. When an HR professional shows and demonstrates an understanding of the importance of using data to make informed business decisions and propose solutions, which of the following is being exhibited?
   a. Service quality
   b. Customer service
   c. Data advocacy
   d. Critical thinking

74. Which of the following is a vital component of communication that builds trust?
   a. Empowerment
   b. Courage
   c. Collaboration
   d. Transparency

75. Stephanie is conducting research into employee satisfaction surveys. She has been tasked with researching industry standards, samples, and communication plans. Which of the following should guide the type of research design and data Stephanie collects for this project?
   a. Customer service complaints
   b. Benchmarks and HR metrics
   c. Exit interview information
   d. Strategic goals and objectives

176

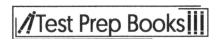

76. Which of the following data collection method requires a skilled facilitator?
    a. Focus groups
    b. Paper and online surveys
    c. Customer satisfaction surveys
    d. Observational groups

77. Rebecca is working to develop metrics and key performance indicators that measure how effective the new marketing programs are in driving new business to purchases. She is researching how other organizations measure this data to show how the marketing initiatives compare with the competition. Which of the following practices is Rebecca engaging in?
    a. Comparable review
    b. Statistical analysis
    c. Six Sigma
    d. Benchmarking

78. Which of the following are the two primary methods to examine HR programs, practices, and policies objectively for effectiveness and sustainability?
    a. Risk analysis and evaluation
    b. Risk analysis and process evaluation
    c. Program and process evaluation
    d. Program and risk analysis

79. When a process is tightly controlled and the results produced are the same each time the process is duplicated, which of the following can be said about the process?
    a. The process has no confirmation bias.
    b. The process is statistically valid.
    c. The process is validated and consistent.
    d. The process has been approved by management.

80. Maia is completing her annual objectives and determining the proposed time frames for accomplishing each item. She identifies one objective to complete per fiscal quarter within the fiscal year. Which of the following best represents these fiscal quarters?
    a. Key performance indicators
    b. Milestones
    c. HR metrics
    d. Fiscal calendar

HR Knowledge

81. Rebecca is responsible for ensuring that the organization's recordkeeping processes and systems are in alignment with and meeting compliance requirements for the FLSA. Which of the following items is NOT a standard piece of information that Rebecca is responsible for monitoring?
    a. Performance evaluations and professional growth plan
    b. Personal information, such as address, date of birth, and position
    c. Work schedule, including day and time of the start of the work week
    d. Total wages paid during each pay period, including additions or deductions

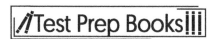
Read the following scenario and answer questions 82–85.

Liz is working on hiring a large group of individuals under the age of eighteen for a youth employment pilot program. Several departments are interested in participating to bring in a group of young individuals to assist with certain jobs that will support the full-time staff. The departments have all identified a specific need and job that will be assigned to the new employees. After the first six months, Liz will evaluate the program to determine if it should continue, be expanded, be altered, or conclude.

82. Liz has received many applications for the youth employment program. She wants to sort the applications into groups by age. What are the age groups she should use?
 a. Ages 14 and under, age 15, age 16, ages 17 and 18
 b. Under 14, age 14, age 15, age 16, age 17, age 18 and over
 c. Under 14, ages 14 and 15, ages 16 and 17, age 18 and over
 d. Ages 14 and under, ages 15 and 16, ages 17 and 18

83. Liz required departments to submit a requisition for the number of youth employees required along with the specific work that would be performed and the hours scheduled to work. If the work and hours aligned with the FLSA standards, Liz approved the request; however, if the work and hours were outside of the scope of the FLSA requirements, the requisition was denied and returned to the department to update for reconsideration. Once approved, Liz determined which age group would be most appropriate for the request to match up the candidates with a position. Which of the following positions would not be suitable for an employee who is fifteen years of age?
 a. Cashier representative—tallying sales and collecting payments via cash or credit
 b. Waitress—taking and delivering food orders to customers as well as collecting payments
 c. Maintenance crew—cleaning office space, including vacuuming, dusting, or other cleaning
 d. Warehouse dock worker—loading and unloading products to or from the conveyor line

84. Liz received several applications from individuals who are eighteen years of age. How do the FLSA child labor laws apply to this group of candidates in the youth employment program?
 a. Youths who are eighteen years of age may not drive on the job or operate a company vehicle.
 b. The FLSA child labor laws do not apply to youths once they reach eighteen years of age.
 c. The FLSA child labor law of specific hours and times of day standards apply.
 d. Youths who are eighteen years of age may perform cashiering, shelf stocking, and bagging.

85. When evaluating the youth employment program, Liz realized there were numerous candidates aged eighteen and over. What should she consider adding to the program details to deter this and ensure that only candidates under the age of seventeen apply?
 a. Nothing, as Liz can use the pool of candidates over the age of eighteen for other full-time positions with the company.
 b. Hire those over the age of eighteen to ensure that the organization has increased flexibility regarding scheduling.
 c. Only accept applications from internal employees' children to ensure the candidates are under the age of eighteen.
 d. Update the applicant requirements to indicate that only individuals under the age of eighteen will be considered.

86. Which of the following categories is not used to determine if an individual is an employee or an independent contractor?
    a. Relationship type
    b. Financial control
    c. Social control
    d. Behavioral control

87. Michael contacts HR to assist with a question regarding how to code a timecard. His employee, Jack, attended a training session for four hours outside of his normal workday. The training was conducted after hours and was provided to increase knowledge related to new tools and reports available in the payroll system. How should HR instruct Michael to report this time?
    a. Because the training was after hours and did not alter his usual work schedule, the timecard should reflect the training but with no pay.
    b. The training should be reported similar to stand-by pay and paid out at this same rate for the time he attended.
    c. The training was voluntary and not required as part of his job or assignment, so this time is not payable.
    d. The training should be reported per the standard process regarding payable hours and, if necessary, the overtime policy.

88. Which of the following laws establishes the minimum standards for benefits plans of private, for-profit employers?
    a. Pension Protection Act
    b. Employee Retirement Income Security Act
    c. Equal Pay Act
    d. Health Insurance Portability and Accountability Act

89. What term refers to employees becoming 100 percent vested in their retirement program after a specific number of years of service?
    a. Cliff vesting
    b. Graded vesting
    c. Immediate vesting
    d. Eligibility vesting

Read the following scenario and answer questions 90–92.

> Susan is responsible for administering the benefits program at her organization. Several employees have recently left the organization to take positions with other organizations or to retire. During their exit interview, she reviews the benefits coverage and ending date, retirement programs and options, and vacation leave payouts. Because the employees all indicated they would have health insurance with their new agencies or be covered under Medicare, Susan did not send out the applicable paperwork to select the option to continue the health care coverage at their own cost.

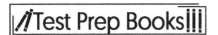
90. What ERISA amendment is Susan's organization in violation of by not sending out the paperwork for former employees with information on the options to continue the group health care coverage?
    a. Family Medical Leave Act
    b. Uniform Services Employment and Reemployment Rights Act
    c. Consolidated Omnibus Budget Reconciliation Act
    d. Health Insurance Portability and Accountability Act

91. If a former employee decides to select the option to continue the health care coverage, how is the premium paid?
    a. The organization pays the full cost of coverage.
    b. The organization and former employee both pay 50 percent.
    c. The organization pays 25 percent, and the former employee pays 7 percent.
    d. The former employee pays the full cost of coverage.

92. Because Susan's organization did not comply with the requirement of communicating with former employees their options to continue the group medical insurance coverage, what could the organization face?
    a. Civil and criminal penalties
    b. OSHA investigation and audit
    c. Civil penalties only
    d. FEHA investigation and audit

93. Which of the following laws is also known as Obamacare, named after President Barack Obama?
    a. Americans With Disabilities Act
    b. Patient Protection and Affordable Care Act
    c. Mental Health Parity Act
    d. Family Medical Leave Act

94. Which of the following statements regarding the Family Medical Leave Act is accurate?
    a. Employers are required to maintain employees' group health insurance coverage while they are out on FMLA leave.
    b. Spouses who work for the same employer each receive twelve weeks of FMLA time for the birth of their child.
    c. Employers cannot require employees to take their paid leave, such as vacation or sick leave, when using FMLA.
    d. FMLA only covers leave for the birth or adoption of a child or a serious health condition of the employee or child.

95. The Old Age, Survivor, and Disability Insurance Program was designed by the Social Security Act of 1935 to ensure a continuation of income for retirees, spouses and dependent children of employees who passed away, and those who qualify for Social Security disability. How long must an employee work to qualify for this program?
    a. 20 years, or 80 quarters
    b. 5 years, or 20 quarters
    c. 10 years, or 40 quarters
    d. 30 years, or 120 quarters

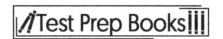

96. Which part of Medicare is hospital insurance, considered mandatory, and generally at no cost to qualifying individuals?
    a. Medicare Part A
    b. Medicare Part B
    c. Medicare Part C
    d. Medicare Part D

97. Which part of Medicare is prescription drug coverage, considered optional, and provided for a monthly fee to those enrolled?
    a. Medicare Part A
    b. Medicare Part B
    c. Medicare Part C
    d. Medicare Part D

98. Which part of Medicare is medical insurance that covers health care expenses such as outpatient care and physician's care, considered optional, and provided for a monthly fee for those enrolled?
    a. Medicare Part A
    b. Medicare Part B
    c. Medicare Part C
    d. Medicare Part D

99. Judy is reviewing several positions within a department to ensure that the pay structure is accurate and appropriate. She conducted a job analysis of each of the positions to determine the requirements and importance of each job duty. Once she completed the job analysis, she then reviewed the job descriptions to ensure that each one was an accurate listing of the general duties and responsibilities for each job. Judy is now creating a statement of the essential parts of these jobs that includes a summary of the duties performed, responsibilities, and qualifications necessary to complete the job. What did Judy create?
    a. Job specification
    b. Job evaluation
    c. Classification review
    d. Compensation study

100. Job ranking, paired comparison, and job classification are all forms of which type of job evaluation method?
    a. Quantitative job evaluation method
    b. Qualitative job evaluation method
    c. Nonquantitative job evaluation method
    d. Factor comparison evaluation method

101. Which of the following quantitative job evaluation methods is less complex and commonly used to evaluate the relative work of a job?
    a. Point factor method
    b. Factor comparison method
    c. Whole-job method
    d. Job classification method

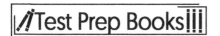

102. What can an organization achieve by implementing a strong employee value proposition (EVP) to encourage employee engagement?
    a. A strong EVP allows an organization to realize a 100 percent retention rate with no turnover among employees.
    b. A strong EVP allows an organization to proactively attract and retain top talent by ensuring an understanding of the benefits offered.
    c. A strong EVP allows new employees to engage in stronger negotiations for their benefits and compensation.
    d. A strong EVP allows employees to provide feedback and suggestions to change and improve the corporate culture.

103. Which categories of a SWOT analysis evaluate the internal factors that can impact an organization's performance and achievement of goals?
    a. Opportunities and weaknesses
    b. Opportunities and threats
    c. Strengths and opportunities
    d. Strengths and weaknesses

104. Stephanie is beginning her preparation for the upcoming negotiations with the bargaining unit. The previous three-year contract allowed for 4.5 percent cost-of-living increases annually for each year of the contract. In reviewing the financial forecasts for the next three years, Stephanie sees that the organization will be facing a budget deficit and unable to offer salary increases. What can Stephanie do as a proactive measure to address this concern in the preparation process?
    a. Identify several lower-level positions that, if eliminated, could fund a cost-of-living increase for the remaining employees.
    b. Create an internal memo to send to all employees communicating the status of the financial forecast and budget deficits.
    c. Conduct a survey asking for feedback regarding rewards and benefits that are affordable to the company and valued by employees.
    d. Ask the bargaining unit to push negotiations to the next year until the budget deficits can be addressed and the organization is in a better financial position.

105. What does a total remuneration survey provide a report on?
    a. Salary ranges, including the minimum and maximum, for all positions in an organization
    b. Annual financial report showing personnel costs, including total budget versus expenditures
    c. Total rewards data, including compensation and benefits, for the market
    d. Satisfaction levels of employees regarding wages, benefits, programs, and culture

106. Tom is the engineering manager and has recently provided annual performance evaluations for his entire team. He noticed that the employees all seemed disengaged and unenthusiastic with the process. What can he do to improve employee engagement with the annual performance evaluations?
    a. Focus on a self-evaluation tool versus a manager evaluation tool.
    b. Focus on future goals and professional development.
    c. Focus on a 360 evaluation tool for coworkers to evaluate each other.
    d. Conduct evaluations on a Friday at the end of the day so they can head home right after the evaluation.

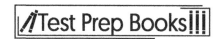

107. Human Resources and Payroll will be implementing a new timekeeping and payroll system. This new system will require employees to enter their time worked and leave time directly into the system versus writing out a paper timesheet. Supervisors will therefore need to approve the timesheets of their direct reports within the system for Payroll to process paychecks. What can HR and Payroll do to encourage support and engagement with the new system?

    a. Provide in-person training complete with demonstrations on how to use the system, pointing out the efficiencies and available information.

    b. Create a train-the-trainer program and require these individuals to meet with employees and provide training as needed.

    c. Prepare an in-depth communication and training guide to send out to all employees and supervisors.

    d. Provide employees with the customer service contact information of the provider and direct them to the provider.

108. What is the primary difference between strategic planning and individual action planning?

    a. Strategic planning refers to an employee's goals and objectives, whereas individual action planning refers to an organization's specific long-term goals and objectives.

    b. Strategic planning refers to the plan that evolves from understanding the talent needs of an organization, whereas individual action planning refers to the recruitment plan for each need.

    c. Strategic planning refers to an organization's long-term goals and objectives, whereas individual action planning refers to the performance management evaluation process.

    d. Strategic planning refers to an organization's long-term goals and objectives, whereas individual action planning refers to an individual's goals and objectives that achieve the strategic plan.

109. Which of the following is an important aspect of both strategic plans and individual action plans?

    a. Both plans involve the outlining of steps needed to transition from current to future status.

    b. Both plans break down the roles and responsibilities associated with each action item.

    c. Both plans allow for ongoing evaluation to ensure objectives are met and goals are achieved.

    d. Both plans inform business decisions with knowledge of the goals and objectives.

Read the following scenario and answer questions 110–112.

> Evelyn is new to the HR team at a software company. One of her primary job responsibilities is to manage the performance management process for the organization. Annual performance reviews are due for all employees, and she is working with the management and supervisory staff to ensure that all employees receive an annual review. Evelyn is struggling to get participation from staff, and many managers and supervisors are not aware of the forms, process, or time frame to complete the performance evaluations.

110. What should Evelyn immediately do to engage the management and supervisory staff in the performance management process?

    a. Provide training, forms, required timeline, (including due dates), and coaching on delivering employee evaluations.

    b. Implement a new policy that requires evaluations be conducted by the annual due date or disciplinary actions will be taken.

    c. Discuss the situation with the HR director and CEO and request their immediate attention to the issue.

    d. Continue to send out emails and communications requesting the documents within the time frame needed.

111. A newly promoted supervisor asks Evelyn what the purpose of performance management and evaluation actually is so that he can complete the documents thoroughly and accurately. What should Evelyn tell him?
 a. The purpose is to coach and counsel employees in areas of improvement.
 b. The purpose is to rate employees' performance and identify areas of growth.
 c. The purpose is to offer encouragement and recognition of performance.
 d. The purpose is to foster a culture of constant improvement and development.

112. Sharon is working on the department's new objectives. She was successful in meeting all of the established objectives for the previous two years, and therefore wants to branch out and identify some new, creative, and different objectives to take the department in a new direction. What should Sharon do first to identify some new ideas?
 a. Work with leadership and employees to conduct a needs assessment.
 b. Discuss the idea with her LinkedIn network of colleagues to get their thoughts.
 c. Revamp the previous years' objectives with new results and time frames.
 d. Conduct an industry analysis to see what competitors are doing.

113. What federal institution measures and collates nationwide employment data, such as market activity, average salaries, and working conditions?
 a. Bureau of Labor Statistics
 b. Internal Revenue Service
 c. Department of Labor
 d. Equal Employment Opportunity Commission

114. When conducting the IRS 20-Factor Test to determine if an individual is an employee or an independent contractor, which of the following factors is considered a "type of relationship" factor?
 a. Personal services
 b. Profit or loss
 c. Public availability
 d. Business integration

115. Under the Equal Pay Act, what are the four areas that must be equal to establish whether jobs are equivalent to each other?
 a. Qualifications, job duties, supervision, responsibility
 b. Skill, working conditions, effort, responsibility
 c. Qualifications, working conditions, teamwork, education
 d. Skill, education, qualifications, effort

116. Heather has experienced a higher than usual turnover rate with employees leaving the organization for other opportunities. During her exit interviews, the employees are consistently communicating that the positions they have accepted are paying salaries comparable to what they are earning. What topics should Heather consider asking about during the exit interviews to determine why employees are leaving the organization?
 a. Recognition programs
 b. Promotion opportunities
 c. Training opportunities
 d. Health care options

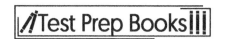

117. What term is defined as when an organization's current needs do not compromise the needs of future stakeholders?
   a. Sustainability
   b. Responsibility
   c. Feasibility
   d. Cooperation

118. Which of the following is a crucial factor in the new generation of employees selecting their job field?
   a. Compensation and benefits
   b. Retirement programs
   c. Flexible staffing schedules
   d. Social impact and engagement

119. Layla is responsible for increasing her company's diversity among all positions and within all departments of the organization. This objective aligns with the organization's corporate social responsibility plan to reflect the social demographics of the metropolitan area. She has been diligently working toward this goal with every recruitment, and the HR director has requested a report to determine the status of this initiative. Which of the following should Layla focus her attention on in this report?
   a. Key performance indicators for all HR metrics
   b. Employee demographics compared to other organizations in the area
   c. Recruitment concerns from the previous five recruitments
   d. Campus recruitment initiative program status

120. What term is defined as a qualification that is determined to be justified by a business purpose?
   a. Bona fide occupational qualification
   b. Minimum required qualification
   c. Preferred qualification
   d. Essential job functions

121. Which of the following laws applies to employers with fifteen or more employees and prohibits discrimination based on race, color, religion, sex, or national origin?
   a. Age Discrimination in Employment Act of 1967
   b. Fair Labor Standard Act
   c. Title VII of the Civil Rights Act of 1964
   d. Equal Employment Opportunity Commission

122. Which of the following laws prohibits the discrimination against any individuals who are over the age of forty related to hiring, firing, promotions, changes in wages or benefits, or other employment-related decisions?
   a. Age Discrimination in Employment Act of 1967
   b. Fair Labor Standard Act
   c. Title VII of the Civil Rights Act of 1964
   d. Equal Employment Opportunity Commission

123. Martin is hiring an entry-level accountant. This position is newly created due to the increasing workload. Martin would like to hire a seasoned individual who has earned a master's degree in the field of accounting and has ten years of experience. He reaches out to the HR analyst, Ally, to discuss his needs and ensure that he has a pool of candidates who are highly qualified and ready to take on this position. Which of the following responses would not be appropriate?

    a. Ally should schedule a meeting with Martin to discuss the position, qualifications, and needs of the department as well as the current positions, qualifications, and salaries.

    b. Ally should accept Martin as the subject matter expert on his needs for the position and proceed with the posting as Martin has described, including the qualifications.

    c. Ally should provide other options as to the position requirements, specifically the qualifications, to ensure that the best-fitting candidates will apply and interview.

    d. Ally should conduct market research to determine comparable positions with other agencies and provide a benchmark analysis to Martin to revise his position description and qualifications.

124. Rita is establishing an orientation session for several employees who will be transferred to a new international location. Which of the following topics would be most critical to these employees?

    a. Learning the language, cultural norms, and translation services

    b. Scenic and tourist locations, including historical sites and establishments

    c. The organization's vision, mission, and values that will be applicable to the new location

    d. Specific local labor laws, workplace etiquette, and cultural differences

Read the following scenario and answer questions 125–126.

> Monica's distribution company recently expanded operations into a new international country. To ensure the company's standards are established with the new workforce, senior leadership selected high-performing managers across the organization to be transferred to the new location. These managers are tasked with hiring the workforce from the local talent pool and working to train potential managers for future installation. After six months, Monica has received numerous complaints from employees regarding inappropriate behavior from several of the managers who were placed to lead the new location. Several of the complaints are similar in that they focus on managers disciplining employees for tardiness, taking excessive breaks, and frequently extending lunch breaks.

125. What should Monica do first to address these complaints?

    a. Provide a template for disciplinary memos to be placed in each of the employee's files.

    b. Terminate the employees who have been violating the attendance policy.

    c. Schedule a meeting with the managers to discuss the specific concerns and details.

    d. Coordinate a transfer of several employees for training purposes.

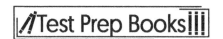

126. Once Monica has a clear understanding of the issues, she realizes the root cause is a difference of understanding related to expectations. Additionally, after researching culture norms and labor laws of the country, she realizes the managers do not have a clear understanding of these elements. What should Monica do next?
    a. Work with senior leadership to replace the managers and course-correct the entire location's workforce.
    b. Conduct a training session for the managers and then hold a group staff meeting to discuss expectations and attendance policies.
    c. Continue with the course of action the managers have initiated and proceed with progressive discipline.
    d. Close out the complaints with responses that indicate the management has the right to discipline employees for policy violations.

127. Which of the following statements is true regarding workplace accommodations?
    a. Accommodations must be reasonable, not place an undue burden on the organization, and be initiated by the employees.
    b. Accommodations must be initiated by the employer and supported by medical paperwork prior to implementation.
    c. Accommodations must be initiated by the employers and not place an undue burden on the organization.
    d. Accommodations must be initiated by the employee and supported by legal paperwork prior to implementation.

128. There are many quantitative and qualitative benefits from an efficient and productive corporate social responsibility program. Which of the following is a quantitative benefit of a robust CSR program?
    a. Improved employee engagement
    b. More positive workplace
    c. Reduction of legal liabilities
    d. Increased employee satisfaction

129. Gabriel has heard that several employees are concerned for their safety in the working environment due to hazardous materials. Although he has not received an official report, he believes he has an obligation to look into the concerns. After Gabriel conducts an investigation, he provides his findings and recommendations to senior leadership. What should Gabriel's recommendation include?
    a. Counseling and potential discipline to the employees who began the rumors and caused other employees to be unnecessarily concerned
    b. Options to work with less hazardous materials that will address the employees' concerns and implementation of improved safety measures
    c. Requirement for all employees to purchase new personal protective equipment (PPE) to ensure their safety when working in the environment
    d. Ceasing operations immediately until OSHA can be contacted to address the issue and provide resolutions to implement

130. Which of the following is an accurate statement regarding corporate social responsibility?
    a. CSR is championed by local community representatives and leaders.
    b. CSR is a mandatory requirement and governed by federal statute.
    c. CSR identifies the environmental needs and prioritizes these over profitability.
    d. CSR has a positive impact on employee recruiting, retention, and overall satisfaction.

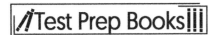

131. Which of the following focuses on creating opportunities for employees to learn about, engage in, and benefit from diverse ideas?
    a. Group assessments
    b. Mentoring program
    c. Cross-cultural training
    d. Diversity and inclusion

132. Organizations that prioritize risk management and the safety of their workforce will experience which of the following?
    a. Increased productivity and sustainable relationships
    b. Increased costs and extensive protocols and regulations
    c. Decreased productivity and lower employee satisfaction
    d. Decreased costs and increased training requirements

133. Hector has seen a recent increase in employee complaints that specifically relate to behavior that is inappropriate for the workplace. Although not a violation of the harassment or bullying policy, Hector believes the behavior is not contributing to a positive work environment. What program should Hector consider implementing to provide some opportunities and benefits to his employees, such as counseling and conflict resolution?
    a. Life insurance plan
    b. Employee Assistance Program
    c. Education assistance
    d. Smoking cessation program

134. Which of the following statements is NOT accurate regarding the Americans with Disabilities Act?
    a. The ADA only protects employees who have physical medical conditions.
    b. The ADA protections apply to every aspect of job application procedures.
    c. The ADA requires employers to provide reasonable accommodations to employees.
    d. The ADA is a federal law that prevents discrimination based on disability.

135. Which of the following agencies ensures safe working conditions for employees by establishing process safety management standards?
    a. ADA
    b. OSHA
    c. HIPAA
    d. SOX

136. If OSHA cites an organization with a violation that a condition is not directly or immediately related to employees' safety or health and does not require fines or citations, the organization has been served with which type of violation?
    a. Other-than-serious
    b. Near miss
    c. De minimus
    d. Willful and repeated

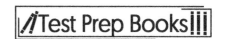
137. If OSHA cites an organization with a violation that indicates the condition raised could impact employees' safety or health but probably not cause death or serious harm, the organization has been served with which type of violation?
    a. Other-than-serious
    b. Near miss
    c. De minimus
    d. Willful and repeated

138. Kyle has recently been investigated by the organization based on an anonymous complaint received by the HR tip line. After conducting an investigation, the HR director concluded that Kyle had taken multiple pieces of hardware from the IT department. The recommended action is to terminate Kyle immediately with which of the following rationale?
    a. Kyle has committed a felony act against the organization.
    b. Kyle has violated the theft policy of the organization.
    c. Kyle has committed sabotage against the organization.
    d. Kyle has violated the workplace security program.

139. One of the primary responsibilities of HR is to coach employees at every level of the organization on how to avoid illegal and noncompliant behaviors. Ensuring that employees are aware of and understand what is appropriate and inappropriate is vital to ensure that the organization and individual employees are protected. What is a best practice that should be implemented to keep employees up-to-date and informed?
    a. Send an introductory email of all applicable laws and regulations when employees are hired.
    b. Provide employees all policies and procedures during the new-hire orientation.
    c. Direct employees to the internal website where all policies and procedures are located.
    d. Display posters related to applicable laws and regulations in common areas.

140. Which of the following terms is described as the process of removing a union's security clause and authority to negotiate?
    a. Deauthorization
    b. Arbitration
    c. Mediation
    d. Confrontation

141. Which of the following terms refers to the formal process used to settle a dispute?
    a. Deauthorization
    b. Arbitration
    c. Mediation
    d. Confrontation

142. Angel is working through an employee dispute that has resulted in an impasse between parties. Neither side is willing to consider compromise or accept anything other than their specific resolution. What should Angel consider next to attempt to work toward a resolution?
    a. Mediation process
    b. Compulsory arbitration
    c. Constructive confrontation
    d. Arbitration process

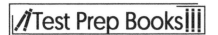

143. Joseph is updating his organization's employee handbook. The handbook has not been reviewed or updated in years, and he finds that many policies are outdated and not in compliance with new state and federal regulations. Which of the following is NOT something Joseph should consider when updating the employee handbook?

a. Update the policies regarding harassment, discipline, attendance, safety procedures, work hours, and compensation and benefits to include in the handbook.

b. Create an acknowledgement of receipt and understanding for employees to sign saying they received, read, and understand the content of the updated handbook.

c. Provide the updated handbook to current employees to ensure they are aware of the policies, procedures, and requirements.

d. Include a disclaimer indicating that the handbook is intended to be the contractual agreement between the employer and employee.

144. What process deals with employee infractions, addressing each incident as a unique situation and developing consequences accordingly?

a. Coaching and counseling

b. Progressive discipline

c. Consecutive discipline

d. Employee reviews

Read the following scenario and answer questions 145 and 146.

Susan is the HR analyst responsible for investigating employee complaints and then determining the appropriate level of discipline to deliver. The organization uses a four-stage process of progressive discipline and issues discipline appropriate to the employee behavior. The first stage is coaching and an informal warning; the second stage is a formal warning and a written reprimand; the third stage is a suspension for a period of time (between three days and one week); and the fourth stage is the final stage in the process resulting in termination. Susan investigates each specific incident completely and thoroughly, reviews disciplinary history, and consults with the manager before making the disciplinary decision. The policy does state that although progressive discipline is preferred, a decision can be made to override the consecutive stages and move to a specific stage of discipline based on the incident.

145. Susan is currently investigating an incident regarding an employee not arriving to work on time. Sam did not follow appropriate procedures to call in late on several occasions. Over the past month, he has been late to work five times and only called his supervisor once. The attendance policies specifically outline the procedures and requirements to call in late, and Sam did not follow these. Susan reviews Sam's file and finds that he has been given numerous informal warnings, but due to the time frames between the previous incidents and the fact that the supervisor has been delinquent in reporting these incidents, Sam has not progressed to the second stage of the disciplinary process. What is the best disciplinary action for Susan to initiate?

a. Formally provide a written warning and review the policies and procedures regarding attendance and calling in late.

b. Initiate one last coaching session with an informal warning and indicate to Sam that the next infraction will result in moving to stage three.

c. Provide a coaching session with an informal warning; additionally, write up the supervisor for failure to report the incidents in a timely manner.

d. Skip the second stage of discipline and initiate the third stage, with Sam receiving a three-day suspension for the numerous infractions.

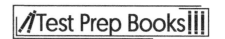
146. Susan begins investigating a complaint from Mary against Hank for sexual harassment. After conducting a thorough investigation, she confirms that Mary was in fact sexually harassed by Hank. Multiple witnesses corroborate Mary's claims of inappropriate comments and physical exchanges. After reviewing Hank's file, Susan finds no disciplinary history of any kind. Hank is a high-performing employee with excellent performance evaluations. What is the best disciplinary action Susan should initiate?

    a. Initiate an informal warning and coaching session regarding Hank's behavior and review the policies specific to harassment.

    b. Move immediately to the fourth stage of the disciplinary process and terminate Hank's employment due to the severity of the infraction.

    c. Initiate stage two of a formal warning and written reprimand regarding Hank's behavior.

    d. Initiate stage three of a five-day suspension regarding Hank's behavior.

147. Which of the following is the process of securing personal information from identity theft or other corruptive activities?

    a. Workplace monitoring

    b. Surveillance techniques

    c. Internal monitoring

    d. Data protection

148. Which of the following is a policy employers implement that allows the organization to monitor a suspicious person and gather information that will be used to conduct an investigation?

    a. Workplace monitoring

    b. Surveillance techniques

    c. External monitoring

    d. Data protection

149. Why is technology management so important to the HR department?

    a. Technology management identifies and implements effective technology solutions that are most beneficial to the HR department.

    b. Technology management invests in project management software that increases productivity and maintains cost increases to a manageable level.

    c. Technology management implements and uses technology solutions that support, facilitate, and deliver effective HR services and critical employee data storage.

    d. Technology management analyzes the functionality of the organization's technology resources to ensure that the most effective systems are deployed.

150. Sandra is working on getting her information technology (IT) department to select a new Human Resources Information System (HRIS). The HR department needs an updated system that will allow for managing employee data, administering benefits, tracking leave time, and initiating recruitments. Which of the following is NOT something Sandra should consider?

    a. The types of information that are currently being collected and stored

    b. A one-size-fits-all system that provides general resources across the HR spectrum

    c. The information that will need to be collected and stored in the future

    d. How data can be integrated for easier access, reporting, and analysis

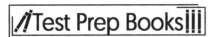

151. If an organization strives to maintain competitiveness and maximize capabilities, which one of the following should management develop?
   a. Policies that streamline communications
   b. Free break room lunches
   c. Walking paths on site
   d. Update technology once a year

152. Which of the following refers to the act of manipulating people for the purpose of revealing sensitive information?
   a. Software monitoring
   b. Biometric identification
   c. Data sharing
   d. Social engineering

153. What is the primary benefit of a well-designed and well-managed HRIS?
   a. The ability to run generalized reports
   b. The ability to use data to develop evidence-based solutions
   c. The ability to provide subjective perspectives
   d. The ability to meet goals and objectives specific to hiring

Read the following scenario and answer questions 154 and 155.

Kevin is the HR director for a fulfillment center. He has recently undergone a complete review of the HRIS and determined that a new software program should be identified and implemented. Part of his review included speaking to employees to gain insight and feedback directly from the end users. He found that although many long-term employees were satisfied with the current system, newer employees struggled to work within the system and access information. He discovered that most employees spent inordinate amounts of time accessing information, entering information, and preparing reports. A new software package has been identified and is being tested to implement within the next quarter. This new package will address all of the concerns and deficiencies from the previous system.

154. What should Kevin ensure is part of the transition plan with the vendor to guarantee a seamless and effective transition when implementing the new platform?
   a. A dual interface between the existing, legacy program and the new, updated software program to ease the transition
   b. A clean break with the legacy program ending effective at midnight and the new software beginning effective at 12:01 a.m.
   c. An opportunity for employees to provide feedback and look at other vendors and software platforms to provide this service
   d. Allowing both systems to be functional so that employees can choose which software they prefer to use

155. The new HRIS platform is a cloud database management system. Which of the following should Kevin ensure is provided in the new vendor's contract regarding employee data?
   a. Reporting metrics
   b. Written guarantee
   c. Security standards
   d. Password protocols

156. Larry is working to enhance his organization's brand as an employer of choice. Which of the following is the best initiative Larry should incorporate into his plan?
    a. Implement a career day with local universities.
    b. Enhance the organization's social media presence.
    c. Create open houses for the community to attend.
    d. Hire a coordinator to focus on marketing and branding.

157. Jennifer has been conducting a work study within the accounting department. She has noticed that many employees spend a large amount of time creating and preparing reports from information that was downloaded from the payroll system. The payroll system was implemented more than a decade ago, and although system updates have been installed, the system does not appear to be very effective. When preparing her report, she includes these findings along with recommendations to address the issues. Which of the following would be the most appropriate recommendation to address this issue?
    a. Transition to a new system that automates the task of report creation and preparation.
    b. Restructure the department to allow employees with experience in Excel to create reports.
    c. Outsource the tasks of report creation and preparation.
    d. Continue to operate as usual because employees are familiar with the current method.

158. How does augmentation differ from automation?
    a. Augmentation allows technology to take over manual tasks, and automation allows technology to assist employees.
    b. Augmentation looks at new ways of becoming more efficient, and automation looks at new software platforms for efficiencies.
    c. Augmentation works to recruit and hire new staff to take on more responsibility, and automation works to increase the work being done by the system.
    d. Augmentation allows technology to assist employees, and automation allows technology to take over manual tasks.

159. Which of the following HR work is focused on multiple business units or the entire organization, with the main focus being the vision, mission, and goals of the company?
    a. Transformational
    b. Strategic
    c. Tactical
    d. Transactional

160. Which of the following is NOT an effective communication method when working with employee and management survey feedback?
    a. Allowing information to trickle down
    b. Engaging with employees at all levels
    c. Providing appropriate guidance as needed
    d. Implementing initiatives to address needs

Answer Explanations for Practice Test #2

Behavioral Competency

1. D: Although it is necessary for all employees to carry out the requirements of the job, it is not a component of being an effective leader. Effective leadership skills include managing time in the most financially responsible manner (Choice A), solving problems as they arise (Choice B), and strategic thinking (Choice C).

2. A: Common HR personnel tasks include developing job postings. Although workplace investigations (Choice B), benefits programs (Choice C), and paperwork (Choice D) are all responsibilities performed within the HR function, usually these tasks are performed at a higher level.

3. B: Jobs within an organization are developed based on goals and objectives established by leadership to ensure that qualified employees perform duties that contribute to the overall interests of the organization. Establishing jobs with this criterion helps to establish a robust candidate selection pool as well as ensuring that the selected individual is performing tasks and duties that align with the organizational, departmental, and divisional goals.

4. B: HR personnel should work with those in leadership roles to ensure maximum participation, effort, and involvement from employees. Employees will mirror what they see in their leadership, and efforts should be rolled out starting at the top of the organization.

5. D: In order to navigate an organization to successfully implement HR initiatives, it is important to demonstrate an understanding of formal and informal work roles across the organization, not just limited to HR. Additionally, having an understanding of leadership goals and interests as well as employee relationships will assist in the successful implementation of initiatives.

6. C: SMART is a commonly used acronym when setting goals and milestones. SMART stands for Specific (detailed); Measurable (able to produce data showing effectiveness); Achievable (feasibly attainable); Relevant (applicable to the overall goals and objectives); and Timely (reachable in a reasonable amount of time).

7. A: A vision statement focuses on the organization's future goals and answers questions about accomplishments. A mission statement focuses on the values, standards, and organizing principles, with a focus on why the organization exists. Both statements should be clear and direct, and a vision statement should focus on specific future goals and steps that will be taken to accomplish these goals.

8. C: The list of goals and milestones was not specific and applicable to the new organization's goals and achievements. David should review the list and determine which items align with his new organization's strategic plan as well as the vision and mission statements. Each organization has specific goals that every employee should be working toward achieving at all levels. Although some of the items David was successful in implementing at his previous organization may be appropriate at his new organization, he should review how these items align with the overall strategic plan and goals and resubmit a list that is more appropriate.

9. B: A gap analysis or root cause analysis can be used to determine when and why projects go off track. Understanding this is important to future tasks and projects so that issues can be managed before they become a problem. Although communicating issues (Choice A), holding a team meeting (Choice C), and

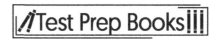

a PowerPoint presentation of successful items (Choice *D*) are important, it is vital to understand what exactly will be done to correct the areas that were not completed successfully in the original project as well as to not repeat these in the future. Without knowing what needs to be done differently, these errors are likely to be repeated.

10. A: Six Sigma is the approach that has many tools available to determine the resources a project may need. From process mapping to value stream mapping, these tools can be instrumental in the success of a project.

11. D: When establishing a project's milestones and objectives, flexibility is important to understand. Conditions may change outside of the team's control that need to be accounted for, which could result in making updates and changes to the project's status. Additional resources could be needed, team members could need more training, or the budget may have been constricted due to financial changes. All of these issues could result in the need to allow flexibility in the project, milestones, and achievements.

12. B: By conducting an employee survey to get direct feedback from employees, HR can focus efforts on what employees want, need, and ultimately, will use. Although the program may have been perfectly designed according to Emily and Chris's needs and wants, they failed to learn what other employees needed and wanted.

13. D: An organization should be diligent when ensuring they have clear and enforceable ethical standards. Asking an employee to "promise" they will behave in a certain way, however, will not ensure this is accomplished, nor will it protect the organization from liability. Additionally, each employee may define appropriate behavior differently, and therefore organizations should make sure all employees abide by the same guide of ethical standards.

14. C: Although the HR department should take all of these actions, it is important to first investigate the complaints received and do whatever is necessary to resolve the issues. Once this has been done, the department should then engage in the other three actions quickly. When HR takes all of these actions, employees will be able to see that the organization is transparent in its work and policies and takes complaints seriously. These actions can increase morale and ultimately create a workplace environment that fosters increased efficiency and productivity among employees.

15. A: Payroll functions are vital to the success of an organization and can be costly to maintain in-house. Organizations may make the decision to outsource this function to reduce costs and improve compliance and resource allocation.

16. C: Stephanie needs to build rapport and relationships with her team before asking them for support and help with a project. She can maintain a private, personal life while interacting with others. Being kind, open, helpful, and engaging in small talk can assist in establishing relationships necessary to ensure a positive work environment.

17. D: A written project proposal that outlines the timeline, milestones, needed resources, and dates for deliverables is a useful method to make sure all stakeholders have the same expectations. Choice *A* is incorrect; stakeholder mapping should identify initiative value, not avoid it. Choice *B* is incorrect; a project proposal should include a financial analysis. Choice *C* is incorrect, as this would not be helpful in clear communication and getting everyone on the same page.

18. B: Open communication is the most crucial component of fostering collaboration among a team because it minimizes resistance, offers opportunities for individuals to lead, promotes an encouraging environment, and can eliminate a fear of retribution. Maintaining a positive attitude (Choice *A*) and showing appreciation (Choice *C*) are elements of open communication, and building interpersonal relationships (Choice *D*) is a by-product of having open communication.

19. D: Social awareness, relationship management, self-management, and self-awareness are the four components of EI. EI requires an individual to be aware of self, others, relationships, and surroundings and equates to better communication and relationships.

20. A: Eric should work to display these characteristics in his daily work, recognize when an employee goes above the standard level of service and award this behavior, and clearly communicate expectations to the team. Although he can indicate these performance levels in future reviews (Choice *B*), he first needs to ensure that his behavior models the characteristics he wants from his team and that the team is aware of these expectations. Hiring a new individual to motivate the team (Choice *C*) is not the best answer, as Eric can work to motivate his own team members without stretching the budget. Eric can communicate these expectations in an email (Choice *D*), but it would be better to verbally communicate the expectations first to allow for a dialogue and questions.

21. C: No. Julia does not have additional options. Grievance arbitration decisions are enforceable and cannot be challenged or taken to court. She has exhausted all options through the grievance process, and the decision reached by the third-party arbitrator is final.

22. D: When deciding whether to accept a settlement regarding a discrimination or harassment charge, the decision maker should consider damage to the company's reputation (Choice *A*), new systemic problems that could be uncovered (Choice *B*), and the financial cost of an investigation and trial (Choice *C*). Personal financial concerns should not be a consideration when reviewing and making a decision to move to settlement.

23. B: Front pay is money awarded to an individual that is generally equal to potential lost earnings and is usually required when a position is not available or an employer has not made any effort to address ongoing issues. Front pay could also be warranted if the employee would be forced to endure a hostile work environment if returned to the original position.

24. A: Management does not have to collectively bargain all subjects and/or changes. Specific subjects are defined as mandatory and must be bargained, including working conditions and terms, hours, wages, benefits, and safety concerns. Many subjects are considered voluntary and can be discussed within the collective bargaining process but are not required.

25. B: Lisa should employ the single-unit bargaining strategy when negotiating with each union group. This will allow each group to bargain on behalf of the unique needs of the group of employees represented. It should be noted, however, that the union representatives for each group could be parallel bargaining at the same time. Union representatives could strategically use what each group bargains separately to promote their requests and wants. Although parallel bargaining is usually used by one union group with each organization they have agreements with, it can also be used between union groups within one organization.

26. B: James is doing a great job in establishing various methods of communication to ensure that all employees are engaged and have an opportunity to connect. Establishing an open-door policy gives employees the opportunity to meet with James one-on-one outside of their normal work environment.

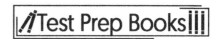
Employees may not feel comfortable bringing up issues in front of other coworkers or even a supervisor, and therefore this gives them another venue to communicate freely.

27. C: Active listening is when the participants are engaged in the discussion and using senses beyond just hearing, such as body language. Active listeners engage in the discussion but allow the speaker to fully communicate their thoughts and concerns without interruption.

28. A: Soliciting feedback from senior leaders is a crucial component of program evaluation, guiding and sustaining initiatives, and providing valuable customer service. HR professionals serve all areas of the organization, including employees at all levels. Without this feedback, HR professionals are unable to fully gauge the success of initiatives and will not be able to provide the best programs, policies, and customer service for their employees.

29. A: Understanding an organization's line of business from a global perspective can allow an HR professional to communicate to other employees how they fit into the larger goals and achievements of the organization. Having this understanding will also allow HR professionals to tailor unique and appropriate HR initiatives for employees that will make a difference and have an impact.

30. C: Geographic locations can impact business operations, requiring different resources from each other. Circumstances such as climate (extreme heat or cold weather) or naturally occurring disasters (hurricanes or tornados) can require a location to tailor a specific disaster plan and identify resources to provide. Some locations may require additional financial resources or extensive plans to address location-specific needs.

31. D: When HR professionals are operating in a global environment, it is vital to conduct business with an understanding of and respect for differences in rules, laws, regulations, and accepted business operations and practices. Operating with this global mindset allows HR professionals to adhere to legal requirements as well as creating and fostering a healthy and productive workplace for employees.

32. C: HR professionals often have to manage contradictory practices or needs to ensure alignment within a project. Robert should communicate the overall objective with the location managers while working to understand their individual, specific needs. He may be able to work within the planning process to address these needs or discuss how they can be addressed in other ways.

33. A: Organizations that have a more diverse workplace experience higher rates of employee retention. Additionally, employees are generally more satisfied and perform at a higher level than employees in workplaces that lack diversity.

34. B: By expanding the list of campuses Rachel visits to outside of the area, she will be able to include candidates from different backgrounds and locations, ensuring a more diverse candidate pool for selecting recruits.

35. B: The most appropriate method for learning about the business operations of an organization is to review available internal documents, external literature, and customer service surveys.

36. D: The PESTLE analysis tool specifically looks at the Political, Economic, Social, Technological, Legal, and Environmental trends. Using the PESTLE tool requires an HR professional to be able to think critically about how these trends will impact the organization reaching the goals and accomplishments established.

The image shows the Test Prep Books logo.

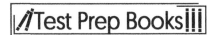

37. D: External salary data is the best source of data to review and analyze when determining if a company is paying their employees a salary that is competitive against the industry standard.

38. C: Although politics has been a subject that has infiltrated every aspect of life, it is important to make business decisions based on organizational metrics (Choice *A*), key performance indicators (Choice *B*), and cost-benefit analysis (Choice *D*).

39. B: Jake failed to add in the costs of labor, such as the costs of the employees delivering the training as well as the employees taking the training and being backfilled with overtime by other employees. When preparing a cost-benefit analysis, it is vital that all costs are included to ensure the entire cost is accounted for.

40. B: Anna and the organization would greatly benefit from implementing a robust HRIS that can manage, track, update, and report on employee information. It is critical that organizations embrace technology and new ways of being productive, efficient, and accurate.

41. A: Sylvia should survey all employees because anyone could have a need for parental leave, not just female employees who have used maternity leave. Additionally, although some employees may not need parental leave, they may have ideas that could be useful to consider when developing the policy.

42. C: Strategic plans are an ongoing and continuous process. Plans should be evaluated to determine effectiveness and whether new strategies or resources should be considered to accomplish the identified goals. Strategic plans should be regularly reviewed and updated as necessary to ensure the mission and vision of the organization are met.

43. A: Internal factors considered by a SWOT analysis are strengths and weaknesses. An organization's strengths are helpful, and weaknesses are harmful to the overall goals and initiatives.

44. D: External factors a SWOT analysis considers are opportunities and threats. An organization's opportunities are helpful, and threats are harmful to the overall goals and initiatives.

45. B: HR professionals can provide specific and specialized training to make sure managers understand any new regulations, laws, or policies. It is especially important for managers to understand how these changes will impact them on a daily basis. Offering an opportunity to ask questions and discuss specific situations can also ensure that managers fully understand the changes. HR professionals should also be available on an as-needed basis to answer questions and offer advice on situations that arise.

46. B: Sustainability of a new initiative is a fundamental component to determine its effectiveness. Positive results that are immediate are always fantastic; however, these positive results should be sustained over a period of time to determine the overall effectiveness of an initiative, program, or solution.

47. A: When HR professionals collaborate with business partners outside of HR, they are bringing to the table different strengths and experiences that can provide diverse and innovative solutions to concerns HR may not be aware of or understand. HR professionals do not typically work in the same environments as other employees and may not have an understanding of the daily operations and issues employees face. By bringing individuals who have this experience to the table, a more holistic solution can be considered because multiple perspectives and expertise are being taken into account.

48. C: The text *The Planning of Change* outlines three strategies for managing change. The technology-innovation strategy is not a strategy for managing change.

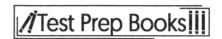

49. B: The empirical-rational strategy assumes that individuals are, in general, rational and will follow a path that benefits them. This strategy to effect change works well when individuals are presented with the benefits that will be experienced by embracing a specific change.

50. A: When rolling out changes, especially ones that are sensitive or important, it is vital to ensure an understanding of the employees within the organization and the culture. Understanding these factors will assist in selecting the best strategy to use when rolling out changes, especially substantial changes. Small changes should be considered in the same light as substantial changes because the subject matter, although seemingly small in the scope of the larger business, may be a substantial change to an individual employee.

51. B: Although the length of time an individual can be eligible for COBRA coverage will differ based on the circumstances, to be in compliance, employers are required to provide an initial COBRA notice within ninety days of the individual's separation.

52. B: Deidre is engaging in networking by interacting with others in both formal and informal settings. Networking is a means to build valuable relationships and create support systems among peers and colleagues.

53. C: During the interview process, Monica should ask questions about the communication and rollout plans should she be selected as the retirement administrator. Retirement services and options (Choice A), retirement plans for employees (Choice B), and fixed costs (Choice D) should have been included in the cost proposal provided.

54. A: Soleil is practicing recordkeeping to ensure there is documentation showing the involvement, discussions, and acceptance of items during the process. Recordkeeping can be instrumental in communicating why certain decisions were made during the process while also allowing multiple opportunities for stakeholders and leadership to be involved, regardless of their busy schedules.

55. D: Emotional Intelligence (EI) skills allow one to recognize the feelings and communication styles of others as well as one's self. EI includes being socially aware, managing relationships, managing one's self, and being self-aware. The components of EI all allow for building and maintaining better relationships.

56. C: Grievances are not informal and are handled in a prescribed and methodical manner. Once a grievance is filed, all communications and remedies should be made in writing, not verbally.

57. A: Amalia is engaging in the practice of negotiating in bad faith. Regardless of her own feelings about unions or how long it takes to negotiate a successor contract, she is putting the organization at risk by attempting to negotiate directly with employees. Amalia should work within the guidelines of negotiating in good faith and discuss any actions she believes are necessary with her negotiations team before taking action.

58. B: Principled bargaining occurs when both sides that are negotiating understand each other's concerns and agree to search for solutions together in order to reach an agreement.

59. D: The word-of-mouth communication can spread information quickly; however, individuals may inaccurately represent the information, which can lead to misinformation and misunderstandings. The individual who initiated the information can quickly lose control over the message, its accuracy, and its effectiveness.

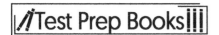

60. B: In this situation, it does not seem as if Raphael is being mindful of the senior leadership's time. At fifteen minutes, he should have concluded his presentation and allowed for discussion time. Additionally, although his presentation may have been fantastic with the data he put together, he was specifically asked for the recent customer service survey data. Raphael should have focused only on the requested item instead of adding unnecessary data and information, regardless of how good it is.

61. A: HR should first reach out to the supervisor. The issue could easily be remedied with an in-person discussion to be sure the supervisor is aware of the situation and has an understanding of how to ensure the employee is not using leave that has not yet been accrued.

62. B: Davina should conduct a PESTLE analysis to ensure she is aware of the Political, Economic, Social, Technological, Legal, and Environmental trends that could influence or impact her product launch. The analysis can assist her with identifying anticipated opportunities as well as mitigate potential risks. Davina's product launch has a higher probability of success if these trends are identified during the planning process.

63. C: A cost-benefit analysis works to outline in specific detail costs related to a project regarding labor, equipment, materials, time, and other costs. This analysis shows how both short-term and long-term benefits will outweigh the costs and can be instrumental in gaining support from key stakeholders in agreeing to proceed with a new program or project where there are financial requirements.

64. A: Payroll functions are typically managed through a separate information system. Although there will most likely be connectivity between the HRIS and payroll system, they are separate systems that manage technology specific to the function. HRIS manages historical data (Choice *B*), employee documents (Choice *C*), and candidate and employee profiles (Choice *D*), among other important information.

65. D: HR is responsible for facilitating the changes needed by implementing new training programs, updating policies and procedures, and ensuring the workforce has the needed knowledge, skills, and behaviors to accomplish the goals outlined in the new strategic plan. Additionally, HR may need to recruit new employees if the strategic plan calls for specific expertise or additional workload.

66. C: Providing training to all of the departments and offering specialized individual training as needed is the most effective way to communicate the changes to a practice.

67. C: In order to effectively manage change with the empirical-rational strategy, it is important to incentivize the change. If employees undergo a change but understand how it can positively impact them, they are more likely to accept it and agree with it.

68. A: Ambiguity should be avoided when possible because it can cause conflict, affect business processes, and create distress for employees. When it cannot be avoided, it is important to use clear communication methods and practices to ensure any ambiguity is resolved with clarity.

69. B: Employee business resource groups are an excellent tool that can increase employee engagement by connecting employees to others outside of their usual working environment. These groups allow for new connections to be made between employees and opportunities for them to be more diverse and inclusive in their daily work and interactions.

70. B: Monique should audit the programs, practices, and policies regarding diversity and inclusion to ensure they are appropriate and being implemented. Choice *A* is incorrect because the remaining

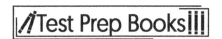

employees may be part of the issue or contain bias that an audit would otherwise uncover. Choice *C* is incorrect; diversity training could be part of the solution to this issue, but it does not identify the issue. Choice *D* is incorrect because it still does not identify the issue at hand.

71. D: Change management is the process that seeks to support significant transitions within an organization and could include large-scale changes, resource allocation, operations changes, and an updated business process. Effective change management can help an organization to be effective even while undergoing changes.

72. A: Phoebe should attend to the special task first and then finish the salary review. Specific tasks and individuals within an organization may need a higher and faster level of customer service. If Phoebe believes the special task will not allow her to complete the salary review within a reasonable amount of time, she should contact the employee and let them know the status and that she is working to finalize her review.

73. C: Being a data advocate allows for the use of data to make informed business decisions and propose appropriate recommendations. It also allows for a number of benefits and additional credibility to the HR professional proposing the changes.

74. D: Transparency is a vital component of communication that builds trust within an organization and between employees.

75. B: Benchmarks and HR metrics should always guide the types of research design and data collection that are being used. Using the benchmarks and HR metrics will ensure that the most appropriate and applicable data is collected for the assessment.

76. A: Focus groups use a skilled facilitator to organize, administer, and manage the sessions. These facilitators solicit feedback and opinions about specific topics and questions identified by the organization prior to the sessions.

77. D: Benchmarking involves developing metrics for key items that can be used to determine the effectiveness of a program as well as how the initiatives compare to the competition and the industry.

78. C: Program evaluation and process evaluation are the two primary methods HR professionals should use to determine if programs, practices, and policies are effective and sustainable.

79. C: A process is considered validated and consistent when, after a tightly controlled process is completed multiple times, the same results and output are produced each time.

80. B: Milestones are specific periods of times that mark a start and end point for objectives, projects, or delivering a work product. Regardless of whether an organization adheres to a fiscal year or calendar year, breaking up a larger time frame into smaller time frames to accomplish specific items are considered milestones.

HR Knowledge

81. A: Although it is important and necessary for HR professionals to track performance evaluations and growth plans, these items are not regulated under the FLSA to be included in the record-keeping system. Generally, they are tracked and monitored in a Human Resources Management System (HRMS) because

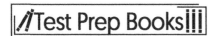

there are no federal regulations that need to be maintained. FLSA record keeping pertains to personal information (Choice *B*), work schedules (Choice *C*), and total wages paid (Choice *D*).

82. C: Liz should categorize the applications by age and use the same categories as FLSA to ensure accuracy and compliance when assigning work tasks and scheduling hours. These age categories are under 14, ages 14 and 15, ages 16 and 17, and age 18 and over.

83. D: Employees hired at the age of fifteen are not allowed to perform any work related to loading or unloading products to or from a conveyor line or a truck. Additionally, there are other limitations regarding the work employees aged fifteen can perform. They may not operate power-driven lawn mowers, work with any hazardous materials, work with freezers or meat coolers, or conduct any work with a power-driven machine.

84. B: Once youths reach eighteen years of age, the FLSA child labor laws no longer apply because they are now legal adults. Work, hours, and wages would now be regulated by the standard FLSA regulations, not the child labor law regulations.

85. D: When evaluating the program, if Liz sees that there is a higher number of candidates who are over eighteen, she should consider updating the applicant requirements to specifically indicate that only individuals under the age of eighteen will be considered. If an applicant is over the age of eighteen at the time of application, the application will not be considered.

86. C: Social control is not one of the three categories identified by the IRS to determine if an individual is an employee or an independent contractor. The three categories are type of relationship (Choice *A*), financial control (Choice *B*), and behavioral control (Choice *D*).

87. D: The training should be reported as time worked because this is considered a postliminary task per the Portal-to-Portal Act, which is an amendment to the FLSA. Because the training is job related and was recommended by the supervisor, this time should be paid at the employee's normal rate of pay and, if necessary, the overtime rate.

88. B: The Employee Retirement Income Security Act (ERISA) establishes the minimum standards for benefits plans of private, for-profit employers. ERISA also established the Pension Benefit Guaranty Corporation, which guarantees payment of vested benefits. The Pension Protection Act (Choice *A*) is an amendment to ERISA that strengthened the pension system by increasing minimum funding requirements. The Equal Pay Act (Choice *C*) is a law that requires employers to pay equal wages to both men and women who perform equal jobs in the same organization. The Health Insurance Portability and Accountability Act (HIPAA) (Choice *D*) is an amendment to ERISA that improves the continuity and portability of health care coverage and addresses preexisting conditions.

89. A: Cliff vesting refers to employees becoming 100 percent vested after a specific number of years of service. Cliff vesting has one eligibility point related to years of service, and once that is met, the employee is fully vested in the benefit. Graded vesting (Choice *B*) refers to a set schedule in which employees become vested at a certain percentage for each year of service. A typical graded vesting schedule would be 20 percent for each year, up to five years of service at which time the employee would be 100 percent vested. Immediate vesting (Choice *C*) refers to being automatically vested in 100 percent of the benefit—this would always apply to an employee's contributions regardless of a cliff vesting or graded vesting schedule. Eligibility vesting, Choice *D*, is also an incorrect answer choice.

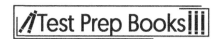

90. C: The Consolidated Omnibus Budget Reconciliation Act, commonly known as COBRA, is the amendment to the ERISA law that requires an organization employing twenty or more employees to allow for the continuation of health care coverage after separating from employment. Regardless of an individual communicating that they will not take advantage of the continuation of coverage option, this does not alleviate the organization from their responsibility to send out the paperwork to allow the individual to have the information to make this choice.

91. D: If a former employee decides to continue the group medical insurance coverage with their previous employer, the individual is responsible for paying the entire cost of the coverage. Organizations may also impose an administrative fee of 2 percent to cover the costs of keeping the former employee on the roster.

92. A: Because the organization did not comply with the COBRA requirements, they could face both civil and criminal penalties. Choice *C* is incorrect because the choice of criminal penalties is left out. Although there may be audits and investigations conducted to determine policy, procedure, and protocols (Choices *B* and *D*), these would most likely be conducted by the Department of Labor, not OSHA or FEHA.

93. B: The Patient Protection and Affordable Care Act is also known as Obamacare. This act made access to health care available to more Americans along with health care purchase options and subsidies to ensure affordability.

94. A: Employers are required to maintain group health insurance coverage for an employee who is out on FMLA leave. The coverage must be the same as prior to the FMLA leave. Spouses who work for the same employer receive a TOTAL of twelve weeks of FMLA time for the birth of their child, making Choice *B* incorrect. Employers can require employees to take their paid leave, such as vacation or sick leave, when using FMLA, and this requirement must be stated in the company policies, making Choice *C* incorrect. FMLA covers leave for the birth or adoption of a child; placement of a foster child; the serious health condition of the employee, spouse, child, or parent; and additional needs related to military servicemembers and caregivers, making Choice *D* incorrect.

95. C: In order to qualify for benefits under the Old Age, Survivor, and Disability Insurance Program, an employee must work at least 40 quarters, or 10 years.

96. A: Medicare Part A is mandatory hospital insurance coverage that most individuals do not have to pay for once qualified.

97. D: Medicare Part D is voluntary prescription drug coverage that individuals pay a monthly fee for. Part D is available to those who are eligible for Part A and also enrolled in Part B.

98. B: Medicare Part B is voluntary medical insurance that covers health care expenses, such as outpatient care and physicians' services. Individuals pay a monthly fee for this coverage.

99. A: Judy completed a job specification. A job specification is a detailed statement of the essential parts of a particular class of jobs. It includes a summary of the duties to be performed and responsibilities and qualifications necessary to do the job.

100. C: Non-quantitative job evaluation methods, also known as whole-job methods, include job ranking, paired comparison, and job classification.

101. A: The point factor method is a less complex and commonly used quantitative job evaluation method. This method uses specific, compensable factors, such as skill, responsibility, effort, working conditions, and supervision, to evaluate the worth of each job. The factor comparison method (Choice *B*) is more complex and used less frequently because it involves a much more complex process to determine pay rates using factors and values. Whole-job methods (Choice *C*) is another term for non-quantitative job evaluation methods, and the job classification method (Choice *D*) is one example of a non-quantitative job evaluation method.

102. B: Organizations that have a strong employee value proposition (EVP) relative to employee engagement are more proactive when attracting and retaining top talent. Having a robust EVP allows an organization to have full understanding of the benefits needed and offered to employees.

103. D: The internal factors that are evaluated in a SWOT analysis are strengths and weaknesses. The external factors that are evaluated in a SWOT analysis are opportunities and threats.

104. C: During the preparation process prior to bargaining, Stephanie should focus on data and information that can be used to prepare offers and ideas to propose to the bargaining unit. Based on the financial status of the organization, an excellent tool Stephanie can deploy is a survey for employees. This survey can ask employees how they value different rewards and benefits so that the organization can come up with unique, valued rewards that are cost-effective and affordable to propose to the bargaining unit for the next contract. These rewards could help offset a salary expectation if they are valued by employees.

105. C: A total remuneration survey provides an analysis of total rewards information, including compensation and benefits plans, for an entire market. These data can be used to determine competitiveness and equity against competitors and other agencies to ensure that employees are paid appropriately.

106. B: Tom should focus performance evaluations on future goals and professional development to engage employees with the process.

107. A: The best response to rolling out a new system, regardless of the function, is to provide in-person training that demonstrates the new system, uses, and functions. Additionally, pointing out the efficiencies and how the new system will positively impact the employee can increase engagement with the new system. Although a train-the-trainer program can be useful (Choice *B*), it is best to have one consistent training program to ensure the message and delivery are consistent. Additionally, an in-depth communication and training guide (Choice *C*) may work to ensure that all employees have information available to them in an easy-to-use guide, but it is not the best response out of the choices. This training guide could include the customer service contact information (Choice *D*), but if questions arise as to the functionality of the new system, an internal contact should be provided to employees. Choice *D* is not the best response to the new system.

108. D: Strategic planning refers to an organization's overall long-term goals and objectives, whereas individual action planning refers to an individual's goals and objectives that work to achieve the strategic plan.

109. C: Strategic plans and individual action plans both allow for ongoing evaluation to ensure objectives are being met and goals are achieved. These evaluations allow for course correction and an opportunity to make changes to ensure that the organization and employees are meeting the objectives. Individual action plans involve outlining steps needed to move from the current state to a new proposed future

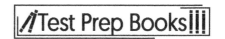
state as well as break down the roles and responsibilities tied to each action. Strategic plans specifically inform business decisions with knowledge of the overall goals and objectives.

110. A: Although all of these actions may be appropriate at particular times to address the issue, the first thing Evelyn should do is to provide training to the managers and supervisors. This training should include information on the process, forms, and timeline as well as coaching on how to deliver an effective evaluation. Evelyn should respond to questions and provide real-life examples to situations that may arise during the process.

111. D: The overall purpose of a performance management and evaluation process is to foster a culture of constant improvement and development. Although the evaluation may include coaching, counseling, recognition, and encouragement, the sole purpose is to enhance the organizational culture by consistently growing and developing employees.

112. A: Conducting a needs assessment with leadership and individual employees will help Sharon identify the organization's needs—either new or ongoing. These needs can then assist her in tailoring initiatives to support them. Although it is a great idea to solicit ideas from peers outside of the organization, it is critical to first understand the organization's overall objective and goals. This will ensure that any objectives identified, including new and innovative ideas, support the overall mission of the organization.

113. A: The Bureau of Labor Statistics is a division of the Department of Labor that measures and collates nationwide employment data. These data include market activity, average salaries, job duties, and working conditions. The BLS also provides state-specific data, with each state having its own department.

114. C: Public availability is a factor under the "type of relationship" factors when determining if an individual is an employee or an independent contractor. Personal services and business integration (Choices A and D) are considered behavioral control factors, and profit or loss (Choice B) is considered a financial control.

115. B: The four areas the Equal Pay Act require to be equal when establishing if jobs are equivalent are skill, working conditions, effort, and responsibility. These factors allow for a clear comparison of positions to make a determination.

116. D: If Heather is seeing a large number of employees leaving for offers from a competitor at a comparable rate, she may want to start asking about the health care options provided by the competitor. Although asking about the company's recognition programs (Choice A), promotion opportunities (Choice B), and training opportunities (Choice C) may provide some insight into enhancing these programs, it is important to have a broad understanding of why employees chose to take a new position if the salary is not substantially higher than they are currently making.

117. A: Sustainability exists when an organization's current needs do not compromise the needs of future stakeholders. By being able to sustain the current commitments, an organization will not lessen their obligation to the economic, social, and environmental commitments made.

118. D: A crucial factor for the future generation of new employees to determine their job field is the social impact and engagement of the work they will do and the organization that will employ them. Although compensation and benefits (Choice A), retirement programs (Choice B), and flexible work options (Choice C) are important when joining an organization and picking a career, they are not the primary focus on the next generation coming into the workforce.

119. B: Layla needs to focus her report on the requested subject matter—how the organization is making a difference in the diversity relative to the hiring activity across the organization. She should ensure that her report identifies the employee demographics compared to other organizations in the area. Additionally, she can discuss how the department is working toward meeting the hiring goal. This may be one key performance indicator that she can address (Choice A), but she should stay focused on the subject matter and not delve into all of the HR metrics. Discussing recruitment concerns (Choice C) and a campus recruitment initiative (Choice D) may be valid because they are related to the overall objective, and they will ensure transparency because they are part of the process to achieve the objective, but they should not be the main focus of the report.

120. A: A bona fide occupational qualification, or BFOQ, is a qualification that has been determined to be justified by a business purpose. Minimum qualifications should be related to the job and established to reflect what experience would be needed in order to do the job being recruited for.

121. C: Title VII of the Civil Rights Act of 1964 prohibits discrimination based on race, color, religion, sex, or national origin. The EEOC administers and oversees this law along with the Age Discrimination in Employment Act of 1967.

122. A: The Age Discrimination in Employment Act of 1967 prohibits discrimination against anyone forty years of age or older regarding hiring, promotions, wages, benefits, termination, and other actions. The EEOC administers and oversees this law along with Title VII of the Civil Rights Act of 1964.

123. B: An inappropriate response to this situation would be to simply accept Martin's recommendations and proceed forward with his excessively high qualifications for an entry-level position. Martin is setting up unrealistic qualifications that do not match an entry-level position. He may not realize that he is establishing an artificial recruitment barrier and potential discriminatory hiring practice. Additionally, with such high qualifications for an entry-level position, Martin may not get many candidates, which is a much lesser concern than having a discriminatory hiring practice. Ally should meet with Martin to discuss equitable positions within the organization (Choice A) and comparable positions to benchmark against outside the organization (Choice D) as well as to provide options for him to establish qualifications that better align with the position (Choice C).

124. D: Although all of these topics would be important for employees who are transferring to a new country, the most critical and essential would be the specific local labor laws, workplace etiquette, and cultural differences. Violating labor laws in other countries may result in fines, closure of the office, or even consequences specific to the individual. Many countries have severe penalties for violating cultural norms, and it is important for employees and their families to understand these to ensure compliance.

125. C: Monica should first schedule a meeting with the managers to discuss the concerns and complaints filed. She should ask specific questions to get as much information and details regarding the situation as possible.

126. B: The best course of action is for Monica to first train the managers regarding cultural norms and local labor laws and how the company's policies align with these. She should then conduct a group staff meeting to ensure that the entire workforce, including management, is on the same page regarding expectations and attendance policies.

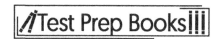

127. A: The statement that is accurate regarding accommodations is that they must be reasonable, not place an undue burden on the organization, and be initiated by the employee. Employers are not responsible for initiating accommodations (Choices *B* and *C*); however, they are responsible for responding to and working with the employee to ensure they are considered and, if appropriate and reasonable, implemented. Employers may request medical paperwork that supports the request of accommodations to ensure that the requests adequately address the employee's needs, making Choice *D* incorrect.

128. C: A reduction of legal liabilities is considered a quantitative benefit of a robust CSR program because it is a metric that can be measured, or quantified. Qualitative benefits include improved employee engagement (Choice *A*), a more positive workplace (Choice *B*), and an increase in employee satisfaction (Choice *D*). These benefits, although critical and important, are not measured in the same manner and are considered qualitative.

129. B: The best recommendation for Gabriel to include in his report is options to work with less hazardous materials and implement improved safety measures. It is unacceptable to counsel and discipline employees who are concerned about their safety and discuss these concerns with other employees, making Choice *A* incorrect. Additionally, even though new PPE may be required based on the new safety measurements, it would be the responsibility of the organization to purchase this equipment for employees, making Choice *C* incorrect. Although it may be prudent to notify OSHA depending on the safety concern, it will be the responsibility of the organization to propose and implement resolutions to address the concern, making Choice *D* incorrect.

130. D: The statement that is accurate is that CSR has a positive impact on employee recruiting, retention, and overall satisfaction. CSR can be the defining factor for new and current employees to come to or stay with an organization. Although CSR involves and engages with local community representatives and leaders, CSR is guided and championed by internal leadership, making Choice *A* incorrect. Additionally, there may be federal statutes regarding specific environmental practices, and a CSR program is not regulated by federal or local statutes, making Choice *B* incorrect. Finally, even though environmental needs are a priority for the CSR program, they do not take priority over profitability and organizational success, making Choice *C* incorrect.

131. C: Cross-cultural training allows for employees to engage in opportunities that broaden their experience. This training allows for hearing about others' experiences so they can benefit from these ideas. Group assessments (Choice *A*) are a way to evaluate candidates in a group setting with exercises and sample issues to gauge how individuals respond to and resolve issues. Mentoring programs (Choice *B*) match two individuals for learning and growth opportunities. Cross-cultural training (Choice *D*) is a component of diversity and inclusion programs.

132. A: Organizations that prioritize risk management and engage in robust safety programs will experience increased productivity and sustainable relationships. Organizations who value employees and their safety will experience higher employee satisfaction, which will in turn result in higher productivity, lower retention, and relationships with stakeholders that are sustainable and enduring.

133. B: Hector should consider implementing an Employee Assistance Program, which provides various resources to employees to handle situations, such as mental health, work-life balance, difficult situations, conflict resolutions, personal concerns, financial issues, and many other issues an individual may deal with. An Employee Assistance Program is considered a flexible benefit program and should be a part of an organization's offerings to employees.

134. A: The ADA not only protects employees who have a physical medical condition but also applies protections to those with a mental medical condition. The ADA protections apply to every aspect of the job application procedure, employment, and promotions. The ADA also requires employers to provide reasonable accommodations to employees and is a federal law that prevents discrimination based on disability.

135. B: OSHA, the Occupational Safety and Health Act, is responsible for creating and enforcing workplace safety standards. OSHA sets minimum standards, provides job training in multiple languages to ensure understanding, and protects employees.

136. C: OSHA issues multiple types of violations, including the de minimus violation. This violation is issued when a condition is investigated to show that it is not directly and immediately related to an employee's health or safety and no fine or citation is required.

137. A: OSHA issues multiple types of violations, including the other-than-serious violation. This violation is issued when a condition is investigated to show that it could impact an employee's health or safety but probably would not result in death or serious harm.

138. B: The HR director's recommendation to terminate Kyle is based on the violation of theft policy of the organization. Although Kyle has in fact committed a felony act (Choice A), this is for the police to investigate if the agency decides to press charges. The rationale for termination should be the policy violation. Choices C and D are incorrect.

139. D: A best practice organizations can implement to keep employees up-to-date regarding applicable laws and regulations is to display posters in common areas, such as breakrooms, meeting areas, or employee information boards. It is a best practice to provide employees the actual policies and procedures during new-hire orientation and show employees where to find this information (Choices A, B, and C); however, these answer choices are incorrect because they do not refer to keeping employees up-to-date but rather deal with employees being introduced to compliant behaviors.

140. A: Deauthorization is the official process to remove a union's security clause and negotiating authority. Deauthorization removes the requirement that employees must join the union; the process is identical to decertification. Arbitration (Choice B) is a form of mediation that is a formal process to settle disputes prior to going to court. Mediation (Choice C) is generally the precursor to arbitration through a less formal process to resolve concerns and issues. Confrontation (Choice D) is also a form of mediation that is used when a stalemate occurs and neither side is willing to consider resolving the matter.

141. B: Arbitration is a form of mediation but is the more formal process. Arbitration is a way to settle disputes using a third-party mediator without going to court. Deauthorization (Choice A) is the official process to remove a union's negotiating authority as well as the requirement that employees must join the union. Mediation (Choice C) is generally the precursor to arbitration through a less formal process to resolve concerns and issues. Confrontation (Choice D) is also a form of mediation that is used when a stalemate occurs and neither side is willing to consider resolving the matter.

142. C: Angel should consider constructive confrontation as the next step in the process. Constructive confrontation is a form of mediation that is used in specific circumstances, such as the example provided. This process can break stalemates by working through secondary or tertiary issues instead of focusing on the primary issue.

143. D: Joseph should not consider including a disclaimer that indicates the employee handbook is intended to be the contractual agreement between the employer and employee. In fact, he should consider the exact opposite of this by including a disclaimer that the handbook is NOT intended to be an agreement between the employer and employee. Updating policies and including these in the handbook (Choice *A*), incorporating an acknowledgement form (Choice *B*), and providing this information to current employees (Choice *C*) are all considerations Joseph should incorporate with the new employee handbook.

144. B: Progressive discipline is the process by which employee infractions are responded to, with each incident identified as a unique situation with appropriate consequences delivered. Coaching and counseling (Choice *A*) may be used as a form of progressive discipline to address certain behaviors, if appropriate. Consecutive discipline (Choice *C*) is a made-up term, and employee reviews (Choice *D*) are typically scheduled evaluations of individual performance that may include training and other coaching opportunities to address behaviors.

145. A: The best option for Susan to initiate is to formally provide Sam with a written warning, the second stage in the disciplinary process. Additionally, she should review the policies and procedures regarding attendance and calling in late to ensure that Sam understands the expectations of the organization. Susan could initiate further coaching sessions, but at this point, it appears that these have done little to change Sam's behavior in the past, making Choice *B* incorrect. Writing up Sam's supervisor for failure to report the incidents seems excessive, especially if this is the first time the supervisor has been made aware of the issue, making Choice *C* incorrect. Although skipping to stage three of the discipline process may seem reasonable, every opportunity should be made to address and change Sam's behavior before progressing to a suspension, making Choice *D* incorrect.

146. B: Due to the severity of the incident and clear violation of policies as well as the illegality of the behavior, Susan should move immediately to the fourth stage of the disciplinary process and terminate Hank's employment. He may have no disciplinary record, but there are certain behaviors and actions that warrant immediate termination, and sexual harassment is one of them.

147. D: Data protection is the process of securing personal information from identity theft or other corruptive activities. This process involves storing important materials, such as employment data that includes social security numbers, dates of birth, dependent information, and other highly sensitive data. The principle purpose of data protection is to maintain the integrity and proper storage of information. Workplace monitoring (Choice *A*) refers to a policy employers use to monitor suspicious activity within the organization and gather information to investigate. Surveillance techniques (Choice *B*) refer to particular methods, such as wiretapping or Global Positioning System (GPS) tracking, to monitor an employee's actions. Internal monitoring (Choice *C*) is a different term that could be used to describe workplace monitoring.

148. A: Workplace monitoring is a specific policy employers use to monitor a suspicious person within the organization and gather information to investigate the activity. Surveillance techniques (Choice *B*) refer to particular methods, such as wiretapping or GPS tracking, to monitor an employee's actions. External monitoring (Choice *C*) is not a correct answer. Data protection (Choice *D*) is the process of securing personal information from identity theft or other corruptive activities.

149. C: Technology management is important to the HR function because it implements and employs technology-focused solutions that support, facilitate, and deliver effective services. Additionally, technology management stores critical employee data. Technology management does identify and

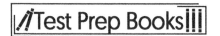

implement technology solutions that benefit HR as well as invests in software that increases productivity; however, these are standard functions of technology management and not specific to the HR function, and therefore Choices *A* and *B* are incorrect. Choice *D* is incorrect because HR professionals are responsible for analyzing the functionality of the resources to ensure effectiveness and then work with the IT professionals to prepare a technology management plan to address.

150. B: When Sandra is considering a new HRIS with her IT department, she should consider the information that is currently being collected and stored as well as the information that will need to be collected and stored in the future, Choices *A* and *C*. Additionally, she should consider how the data stored within the system can be integrated with other systems for easier access, reporting, and analysis, Choice *D*. Sandra should not consider a one-size-fits-all system because no two agencies are alike and each has its own unique methods, processes, and pieces of information that need to be collected.

151. A: The best way for an organization to maintain competitiveness and maximize capabilities is to develop and implement policies that streamline communications. These policies may specifically delve into areas of electronic media, social media, and the internet; however, it is vital for each policy to tie back to an overall communications policy to ensure each is streamlined and they all work together. It is also vital to ensure each method of communication is properly addressed within one primary communications policy to ensure that they are each streamlined and working together.

152. D: Social engineering is the act of manipulating people for the purpose of revealing sensitive information. This concept has become more prevalent among hackers looking for personal information to steal identities. Software monitoring, Choice *A*, refers to regulating activities performed by employees on a network. Biometric identification, Choice *B*, refers to using a physiological method, such as fingerprints or facial recognition, to prove identity. Data sharing, Choice *C*, refers to the practice of making information accessible through public or private networks.

153. B: The primary benefit of a well-designed and well-managed HRIS is the ability to use data to develop evidence-based solutions. Choice *A* is incorrect; a benefit of HRIS is that it can run unique and specialized reports. An effective HRIS provides objective, not subjective, perspectives by removing the human factor from the information, making Choice *C* incorrect. Additionally, although the system will provide insight and data, it will not meet goals and objectives by itself but will provide the data in order for the HR team and departments to achieve success, making Choice *D* incorrect.

154. A: The best way for Kevin to ensure a seamless transition is to work with the vendor to guarantee that a dual interface between the current and new programs is offered. This will allow employees to gain a better understanding of the new system and how it relates to the legacy system. A clean break of turning off the legacy program will eventually need to occur; however, it is best to not do this immediately, making Choice *B* incorrect. Additionally, although it is important to continue to receive employee feedback on the new system, it should not be used to look at other vendors and software platforms, making Choice *C* incorrect. The feedback could, however, be used to improve the new platform. It is not in the best interest of employees or employers to have two functional systems. This can create confusion, errors, and overall an unproductive and inefficient working environment, making Choice *D* incorrect.

155. C: Kevin should ensure that the new vendor's contract addresses security standards for protecting and safeguarding employee data. Reporting metrics and written guarantees, Choices *A* and *B*, are usually standard items within a contract, but these items do not specifically address employee data security. Password protocols, Choice *D,* are typically not part of a vendor contract but may be required as part of the operating procedures for the software.

156. B: The best initiative Larry can incorporate into his plan to enhance the organization's brand is to increase its social media presence. There are a wealth of platforms that will allow Larry to have a huge impact in pushing out the organization's message of being an employer of choice. Career days and open houses, Choices *A* and *C,* are ideas that have worked in the past to create an organization's positive messaging; however, they are less effective than social media. Although hiring a coordinator, Choice *D,* may be an effective strategy in the short term, once programs are in place, it may not be the most effective strategy in the long term. Additionally, this would cost money an organization may not have.

157. A: The best recommendation to propose would be to transition to a new system that would allow for the automation of report creation and preparation. This would minimize errors, create efficiencies, and increase productivity among employees. Restructuring the department to shift the work or outsourcing the report creation would not address the underlying issue of working with a system that is deficient in providing accessible information, making Choices *B* and *C* incorrect. Although it may be appealing to continue to operate as usual because there is no change associated with this, it is not in the best interest of the organization or employees, making Choice *D* incorrect.

158. D: Augmentation differs from automation in that augmentation allows technology to assist employees, whereas automation allows technology to take over manual tasks. Both processes are meant to create more efficiency and productivity, with augmentation focusing on employees taking on more tasks with the help of technology and automation focusing on replacing employee actions relative to manual tasks.

159. B: Strategic HR work focuses on multiple departments, or even the entire organization, with an emphasis on the company's vision, mission, and goals. Although this work may be transformational, Choice *A,* it is primarily defined as strategic in nature. Tactical HR work, Choice *C,* focuses on workplace solutions for the day-to-day operations, whereas transactional HR work, Choice *D,* focuses on the administrative tasks.

160. A: The LEAST effective communication method listed is allowing information to trickle down. This method places the burden on each level of the organization to not only communicate the information but to do so in a manner that is consistent each and every time. HR should own the message by engaging with employees at all levels, providing guidance as needed, and implementing initiatives to address the needs identified within the survey feedback.

Behavioral Competency

1. Which of the following terms refers to the "mood" of an organization?
    a. Environment
    b. Values
    c. Climate
    d. Culture

2. What is the difference between a mission statement and a vision statement?
    a. A mission statement focuses on day-to-day work, and a vision statement focuses on future goals.
    b. A mission statement focuses on future goals, and a mission statement focuses on day-to-day work.
    c. A mission statement focuses on day-to-day work, and a vision statement focuses on the process for this work.
    d. A mission statement focuses on future goals, and a vision statement focuses on the process for these goals.

3. Susan is preparing her team's department objectives that will be used to create individual goals and accomplishments for her employees' performance reviews. What should Susan ensure that each of these objectives includes?
    a. Well-written, clear, concise, and specific language to ensure understanding
    b. Specific, measurable, achievable, relevant, and time-bound aspects
    c. Professional growth, development, training, and learning opportunities
    d. Recognition and appreciation for previous performance and accomplishments

4. Which of the following tools would NOT be used to determine why goals were not achieved or why there was a discrepancy between expected outcomes and actual outcomes?
    a. Six Sigma
    b. Gap analysis
    c. Root cause analysis
    d. Cause-and-effect diagram

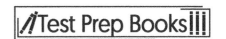

5. Karen is recruiting a new software engineer and is looking for a candidate that has experience as well as motivation and passion for the job. She has narrowed the candidate pool down to two candidates. Candidate A has ten years of progressive experience, has worked as a supervisor, and is highly recommended by references. Candidate B has four years of progressive experience, has not worked as a supervisor, and is highly recommended by references. Both candidates meet the required qualifications, and Karen must make a decision after her interviews. During the final interviews, she notices a fundamental difference between the candidates relative to their passion and motivation. Candidate A answers questions specifically and directly, with little passion or motivation to go above and beyond. Candidate B answers questions with passion and specific details as to going above and beyond the expectations as well as seeking out additional opportunities for growth. What should Karen decide to do?

    a. Create two positions and hire both candidates A and B because each individual brings necessary skills and experiences needed by the department.

    b. Delay making a decision and request that the department director interview both candidates and make the decision on which candidate should be hired.

    c. Hire candidate A because the individual's experience is more extensive and includes supervision, and Karen can work to engage and motivate the individual later.

    d. Hire candidate B because the individual's passion, motivation, and experience align with what Karen is seeking for the department and this position.

6. What can HR specifically do to alleviate employees' fears and concerns about reporting unethical behavior and possible retaliation?

    a. Provide annual training regarding the policies and expectations.

    b. Provide confidential and/or anonymous reporting methods.

    c. Provide all employees with the handbook to ensure knowledge of the policy.

    d. Provide frequent updates to the policies and procedures.

7. An organization that has a lack of transparency will experience which of the following?

    a. Innovation and higher satisfaction

    b. Increased productivity and lower turnover

    c. Decreased morale and higher turnover

    d. Increased promotion rates and innovation

8. Jessie has recently joined a new organization as the HR manager responsible for labor relations and negotiations. One of the first items she wants to accomplish is understanding what each department does and what they need in order to ensure that future negotiations and day-to-day decisions are reflective of the departments' overall needs. How can Jessie best accomplish this in the most effective manner?

    a. Send out an introductory email with Jessie's background information and an invitation to visit any time to discuss concerns and needs.

    b. Review the current union contract and policies to establish a list of needed items that should be changed in upcoming negotiations.

    c. Survey current employees to determine satisfaction levels with compensation, benefits, leave programs, and retirement.

    d. Establish one-on-one and group meetings to engage in two-way dialogue that fosters information sharing.

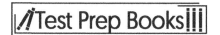

9. Olivia has a broad professional network she engages with frequently. She attends conferences and networking events and frequently assists other agencies with survey data and interview panels. She has met numerous individuals who have mentored her and assisted with her professional advancement. What is another benefit of networking and building relationships Olivia can specifically bring back to her organization?

    a. External networking should be solely about career advancement and personal growth.

    b. She can learn about successful HR initiatives with other agencies and implement them at hers.

    c. She can determine which specific HR area she wants to move into at her organization.

    d. She can obtain vendor recommendations to eliminate the need to request service proposals.

10. Josie is struggling with her workload. Numerous employees have retired, and a lot of the mandatory work has been given to her to handle while HR recruits new employees. She wants to be successful and help the team, but she is overwhelmed and not sure what to do. Josie reached out to HR to discuss her concerns and see what could be done. What should HR do to assist Josie with this situation?

    a. Approve the removal of the extra work and assure her that employees will be hired soon.

    b. Immediately bring in Josie's manager and instruct them to hire a contractor.

    c. Listen to Josie and work with her to find resolutions that would help with the situation.

    d. Expedite the recruitment process and hire a new employee by the end of the week.

11. Which of the following tools is used to identify an initiative's value to a stakeholder along with the investment and influence that specific stakeholders have in promoting and supporting the initiative?

    a. Stakeholder mapping

    b. Stakeholder analysis

    c. Stakeholder diagramming

    d. Stakeholder review

12. What benefit can be gained by serving as a team leader?

    a. Communicating with other team leaders and directors.

    b. Being able to supervise and direct the work of others.

    c. Reaching the endpoint of professional learning and growth.

    d. Gaining knowledge about the business and operations.

13. Bill filed a complaint with the Equal Employment Opportunity Commission (EEOC) alleging that the company he works for has engaged in unfair, unethical, and discriminatory practices related to internal promotions. He has been passed over for a promotion multiple times and believes he is being unfairly targeted due to his age. He submits his paperwork to the EEOC to be investigated. The EEOC conducts an investigation and finds there is no probable cause and dismisses the case. What can Bill do next?

    a. Nothing; Bill has exhausted his rights and has no further recourse.

    b. Bill can file a grievance with his union representative for a new investigation.

    c. Bill can request a right-to-sue letter and sue the employer in the court of law.

    d. Bill should quit because he will not be able to return to his position now that the employer is aware of his claims.

14. What type of bargaining occurs when groups negotiate terms for a contract while being mindful of the key issues to each side in the process?

    a. Distributive bargaining

    b. Principled bargaining

    c. Positional bargaining

    d. Coordinated bargaining

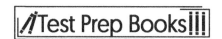

15. All except for which of the following terms refers to when a union successfully negotiates an agreement with a company and then uses these results to deal with another company?
    a. Whipsawing
    b. Multi-employer bargaining
    c. Leapfrogging
    d. Parallel bargaining

16. Which of the following statements is inaccurate regarding employee newsletters?
    a. Newsletters are not always useful for communicating urgent or immediate information.
    b. Newsletters are labor-intensive and infrequent.
    c. Newsletters have the potential of providing information in a welcoming manner.
    d. Newsletters allow for formal two-way communications between the employer and employees.

17. Amber receives an email from a department leader in her organization that outlines a new program that will be implemented as a pilot program. As a member of the team that will be creating the implementation plan, she is confused about the intent and reasoning for the program. Multiple pieces of information are missing, and there are various conflicting messages throughout the memo. What should Amber do?
    a. Proceed forward with her specific duties and tasks related to the program and allow the leader and her manager to address the issues.
    b. Forward the email to the department leader's direct supervisor to ensure they are aware of the discrepancies and can address them.
    c. Respond directly to the department leader with clear and specific questions to ensure the entire team is on the same page.
    d. Take no action and await further instruction from her supervisor because most of the misunderstanding will most likely be cleared up.

18. Employee business resource groups help to further promote which of the following efforts?
    a. Diversity and inclusion
    b. Professional growth and learning
    c. Relationships and communications
    d. Development and training

Read the following scenario and answer questions 19 and 20.

> Veronica is the HR manager for an accounting firm that employs individuals across the country. Each site maintains a separate operational structure and aligns their business practices to the customers they serve. Veronica has noticed that each site has specific needs and concerns, and she is working to align policies and procedures to establish a more consistent HR presence between sites.

19. What is Veronica addressing by establishing consistent policies and procedures?
    a. Behavioral concerns
    b. Workplace climate
    c. Resource allocation
    d. Mini-cultures

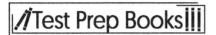

20. What should Veronica consider when establishing consistent policies and procedures?
    a. Employee demographics and turnover
    b. Specific state laws and regulations
    c. Supervisory complaints and concerns
    d. Customer demographics and sales

21. Which of the following is a way to ensure that diversity and inclusion practices are sustainable for an organization?
    a. Troubleshooting
    b. Recruiting
    c. Auditing
    d. Brainstorming

22. Cynthia is initiating a new benefits program in the organization that will be deployed in the next calendar year. What can she do to best ensure that this program favors all employees equally and does not cater to one group of employees over another?
    a. Communicate the process used to choose the new program.
    b. Standardize the benefits program and make it equally accessible to all employees.
    c. Provide assurance to employees that the program is for everyone.
    d. Request the program be rolled out by executive management.

23. Which of the following is NOT a trend that is investigated by the PESTLE analysis?
    a. Economic
    b. Social
    c. Environmental
    d. Process

24. Which of the following is NOT an accurate statement regarding the PESTLE analysis?
    a. A PESTLE analysis is an informal tool used to learn about trends that could influence an organization.
    b. A PESTLE analysis should be used by HR professionals to assist in guiding their work.
    c. A PESTLE analysis should include both internal and external resources.
    d. A PESTLE analysis often indicates process improvement needs to mitigate risks.

25. What term refers to the software, online systems, applications, or innovations that automate or simplify tasks within an organization?
    a. Information systems
    b. Business technology
    c. Workplace resources
    d. Reporting systems

26. A SWOT (strengths, weaknesses, opportunities, threats) analysis should be used at which step in the strategic planning process?
    a. Plan formation
    b. Objectives and goal setting
    c. Review and evaluation
    d. Internal analysis

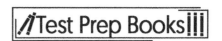

27. Which of the following statements is inaccurate regarding a SWOT analysis?
   a. A SWOT analysis should only be used to analyze large, organizational-level issues.
   b. A SWOT analysis reviews internal factors, specifically strengths and weaknesses.
   c. A SWOT analysis is a comprehensive yet flexible tool reviewing external and internal factors.
   d. A SWOT analysis reviews external factors, specifically opportunities and threats.

28. Tommy is reviewing the milestones of the HR department to determine if the new recruitment process is effective and provides departments with quicker turnaround to fill open positions. Which of the following metrics should Tommy review to assess the success of the new process?
   a. Percentage of open positions compared to total headcount, or attrition rate
   b. Direct feedback from supervisors on the quality of the candidate pools for open positions
   c. Comparison of the current number of days needed to fill positions with the former process
   d. Number of open positions per department across the organization prior to the new process

29. Edison is the chief financial officer (CFO) for a large accounting firm. He has recently been briefed on new legal regulations that require the company to change and update financial policies. If the organization does not comply with the new requirements and within the designed time frame, it could face substantial fines. Which of the following change management approaches would be the best option to use in this situation?
   a. Normative-reeducative strategy
   b. Empirical-rational strategy
   c. Environmental-adaptive strategy
   d. Power-coercive strategy

30. Processes should be audited regularly to ensure they are providing the same results and outcomes consistently. What method monitors a process from start to finish to ensure the same results occur every time?
   a. Transparency
   b. Validation
   c. Data collection
   d. Risk management

31. Self-awareness, social awareness, relationship management, and self-management are all equally important elements of which of the following skills?
   a. Emotional intelligence
   b. Psychological intelligence
   c. Intelligence quotient (IQ)
   d. DISC personality

32. Thiang and Sarah work in HR as specialists, supporting separate departments within the organization. Thiang recently distributed an employee survey to the finance department to gauge employee satisfaction in various areas, including work-life balance, leave procedures, communication, and resources. Thiang received an excellent response and was able to tailor new initiatives for the group to further increase satisfaction. He also received multiple new ideas for decreasing expenses and increasing efficiency, which yielded even further success. Sarah read about the success of the survey and departmental changes in the employee newsletter and wants to use the same technique in the IT department. How should Sarah begin this endeavor?

a. Sarah should request that Thiang duplicate the process in the IT department and reply back with the final results, next steps, and recommendations.

b. Sarah should work to re-create the survey for the IT department and initiate it immediately in order to capitalize on the momentum of the newsletter.

c. Sarah should submit a proposal to her manager to hire an external vendor for the purpose of surveying the IT employees to gain the insight and information necessary for proposing new initiatives.

d. Sarah should reach out to Thiang to discuss the survey, including the creation of the questions and finalizing the results as well as lessons learned, before implementing the survey in IT.

33. How can HR leadership best communicate appropriate and acceptable behaviors within the workplace?

a. Specifically communicate this information to employees during orientation.

b. Hang posters with federal and state regulations in break rooms and lunchrooms.

c. Consistently display ethical, reliable, and acceptable behaviors.

d. Communicate the required behaviors via email and newsletters on a regular basis.

Read the following scenario and answer questions 34 and 35.

Adam is a benefits specialist for his organization and is preparing his annual objectives for the upcoming year. One of his objectives is to have healthier employees across the organization. This objective is the overarching goal, with specific tasks identified as a wellness fair, benefits expo, free flu shots, and a free smoking cessation program.

34. Adam's main objective to have healthier employees is a lofty goal to achieve. What could be problematic with this objective?

a. It is vague, with no measurable data points to indicate achievable success.

b. It is unachievable because employee health is not the business of an organization.

c. It is too specific, and there are too many defined tasks that will most likely not occur.

d. It should be a departmental objective, not an individual objective.

35. What can Adam do to correct this objective?

a. Eliminate the objective and replace it with the defined tasks he identified.

b. Rewrite the objective to reflect the SMART principles.

c. Keep the objective as written because it is a philosophical objective.

d. Keep the objective and add more defined tasks to accomplish the goal.

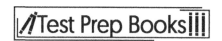
36. The accounting manager recently retired, and several employees within the department are interested in applying for this position. The finance director will be making the hiring decision for this position, and it has been brought to HR's attention that he knows several of the employees on a personal basis. One employee is a member of the same church, one employee has children in the same school and grade, and one employee is a member of the same softball league. How can HR work to ensure an unbiased and fair recruitment and selection process?

    a. Employees who have a personal relationship with the finance director should not be allowed to apply for the position because they will not be interviewed fairly.

    b. Nothing; a finance director should be able to conduct himself in a professional, ethical, fair, and unbiased manner regardless of personal relationships outside of the workplace.

    c. Establish an interview panel with stakeholders from across several departments who will interview all candidates and select the most qualified candidate.

    d. Restructure the position to report to a different director to ensure there is no bias or unfairness in the recruitment and selection process.

37. Michelle is working with the sales department to initiate a recruitment for a new sales representative. She is new to the organization and industry and wants to ensure that she conducts an effective and successful recruitment. Michelle meets with the hiring manager and other employees in this position to gain insight and a full understanding of the position before initiating the recruitment. Why is it important for Michelle to have this information?

    a. It is not important to the recruitment because Michelle should proceed with the most recent job description for the recruitment process.

    b. It is important so that Michelle can provide correct details about the position in the recruitment brochure and hire a candidate with the right skill set.

    c. It is not important to the recruitment because Michelle should conduct the process with complete subjectivity, which will allow for an unbiased process.

    d. It is important so that Michelle can have a good working relationship with the hiring manager and employees beyond the recruitment for this position.

38. Jose works for a small organization that employs approximately one hundred individuals. He wants to learn more about how the employees feel about their salary, benefits, and work. The organization does not have the budget to assist with this project. Additionally, his employees are skilled labor mechanics and do not have much experience with the computer. Which method of data collection should Jose use to gather this information?

    a. Paper survey

    b. Focus group

    c. Individual meetings

    d. Online survey

39. When including data from publications and studies, what time frame would be considered "recent?"

    a. Data or studies from the past ten years

    b. Data or studies from the past twenty years

    c. Data or studies within the past one year

    d. Data or studies from the past three years

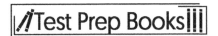

40. Blair has recently joined a new organization that maintains a policy regarding customer service. The policy requires that all requests and inquiries be responded to within 24 hours. Blair has always prided himself on his customer service skills and used a personal guideline of 48 hours to allow for time to research and educate himself on the issue. How should Blair proceed when responding to customers?
    a. Institute a new personal guideline of a 12-hour response time to exceed expectations.
    b. Abide by the organization's policy requiring a 24-hour response time.
    c. Continue working within his own personal guideline of a 48-hour response time.
    d. Institute a new personal guideline of a 36-hour response time.

41. George is recruiting for several positions and is working on updating the job descriptions. In addition to the specific roles and responsibilities of the open positions, he wants to add information specific to the organization's mission, values, vision, culture, and working environment. What is George describing to prospective employees?
    a. Employer brand
    b. Corporate culture
    c. Work-life balance
    d. Total rewards

42. Why are interpersonal skills so important for all employees to develop?
    a. They allow employees to be ready for promotion opportunities.
    b. They allow employees to have a higher level of satisfaction with their work-life balance.
    c. They allow employees to work more effectively and productively with others.
    d. They directly correlate to a higher level of job satisfaction.

43. When a project goes over budget and exceeds the proposed time frame, what analysis should be conducted?
    a. SWOT analysis
    b. Gap analysis and root cause analysis
    c. PESTLE analysis
    d. Outcome and needs analysis

44. Why is it important for HR professionals to have an understanding of and ability to work with statistics?
    a. This skill is not important for HR professionals to have because the finance department typically employs individuals who are experts in this field.
    b. This skill allows HR professionals to promote to higher levels of responsibility more quickly than those who do not have this skill.
    c. This skill is not important for HR professionals to have because their sole responsibility is policy, process, and protocols.
    d. This skill allows HR professionals to identify trends and use the data to support initiatives while also seeing errors or flaws in the data.

45. What can ambiguity, or being vague, cause when communicating with employees?
    a. Opportunities for employees to go above and beyond
    b. Innovation, productivity, and motivation
    c. Confusion, conflict, and distress
    d. Lower turnover and increased job satisfaction

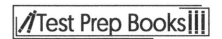

46. An HR professional who understands how important data is and uses data to make recommendations or decisions is displaying which of the following attributes?
    a. Data advocacy
    b. Statistical analysis
    c. Customer service
    d. Business sense

47. Which of the following policies encourages openness and transparency with employees?
    a. Communications policy
    b. Social media policy
    c. Open-door policy
    d. Code of conduct policy

48. What can an HR professional implement to gain insight into why employees resign from an organization?
    a. Classification review
    b. Exit interviews
    c. Employee surveys
    d. Compensation review

Read the following scenario and answer questions 49 and 50.

Klaus is working on a compensation study for several departments within his organization. He has requested that employees respond to a position analysis so that he can review the accuracy of the current job descriptions and ensure that he takes into account all of the actual duties being performed when comparing salaries against the industry standard. He has located several data sources that provide information on various positions that he can use in his study.

49. What factors should Klaus confirm about the data sources before using the information?
    a. They are recent (within three years) and relevant to the positions being reviewed.
    b. They are from an online source that seems reputable.
    c. They are available online and at no cost to the organization.
    d. They support the current compensation levels set for the positions.

50. At the conclusion of the compensation study, Klaus makes recommendations for several positions to receive an increase to the compensation rate. One employee believes their position should also receive an increase and that the study was not accurate. What should Klaus do?
    a. Communicate to the employee that the decision is final and that when the next compensation study is conducted, the position will be reviewed again.
    b. Ask the employee's manager to discuss the study and provide the employee with the position analysis that was completed.
    c. Nothing; the study was completed and the findings are complete, so there is no further action for Klaus to take.
    d. Schedule a meeting to discuss the study, including the position analysis the employee completed and the data used to make the determination.

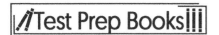

51. Louise is an HR director for a company that provides heating, ventilation, and air conditioning (HVAC) equipment and services to independent contractors. She routinely works with the executive leadership team to ensure the HR programs, policies, and practices are appropriate and necessary for the employees. Louise responds to every call, concern, and question, regardless of the level of the employee. She takes pride in her ability to communicate with all levels of the organization and in the relationships she has built with employees. During her performance review, the CEO admonishes her for not being available to him regarding a question he had because she was in a scheduled meeting with a line worker. How should she respond?

a. Louise should apologize and offer to have her staff schedule meetings with employees to address concerns.

b. Louise should offer to schedule daily check-in meetings with the CEO to ensure that he does not have any needs.

c. Louise should take the feedback and not respond during the meeting.

d. Louise should communicate to the CEO that all employees are her customers, and she provides the same level of customer service to a line worker as she does to the CEO.

52. Which of the following is the first necessary step in the risk management process?

a. Mapping the full timeline and customer service processes

b. Communicating with the team on the deliverables needed

c. Identifying the potential risks

d. Preparing a mitigation plan to eliminate any setbacks

53. What can accurate data tell an HR professional about the internal organization, specifically the employees?

a. Consumer trends

b. Customer preferences

c. Productivity trends

d. Client engagement

54. Which of the following statements is an inaccurate representation of the importance of evidence-based decision making?

a. It provides credibility and logical support for initiatives.

b. It allows the process to be contained to one or two individuals.

c. It provides transparency as to why certain decisions are made.

d. It can be easily communicated and shared with others.

55. Edward has been tasked with preparing a proposal for a new benefits program. The proposal will be presented to the leadership team for final approval before moving to implementation. He has reviewed the employee demographics, current trends and analysis from the marketplace, current benefits usage, best practices, costs, and benefits. Additionally, he assembled several employee panels to ask questions, receive input, and gain insight into what is important to employees. All of this information has been put together to make a final recommendation for a new benefits program. What will the likely result be from the leadership team?

    a. The leadership team will most likely approve the new benefits program because a decision needs to be made quickly and to ensure implementation begins immediately.

    b. The leadership team will most likely deny the new benefits program because the current program meets the needs of the employees and there have been no complaints.

    c. The leadership team will most likely not make a decision because they will need more data and information along with additional options to consider versus one recommendation.

    d. The leadership team will most likely approve the new benefits program because Edward prepared the recommendation on relevant and current data as well as employee feedback.

56. Kate has been given an assignment to prepare a trend analysis looking at multiple pieces of data, such as wages, medical costs, retirement costs, fringe benefit costs, and other employee-related costs. The analysis should take into account the organization's current position as well as industry standards and their primary competitor's current position. What is the first thing Kate should do before compiling the data?

    a. Kate should determine if there is any data or published documents available.

    b. Kate should gather all of the organization's current data and create her analysis.

    c. Kate should create her analysis and then gather the data to support the analysis.

    d. Kate should seek out third-party vendors who prepare this information.

57. Which of the following is the process of establishing a relevant, unbiased system of data collection?

    a. Benchmarking

    b. Validation

    c. Quality assurance

    d. Quality control

58. Sophia is collecting data to complete a compensation analysis. This data will help the organization determine if salaries need to be increased or if they are appropriate and in alignment with the industry. Sophie has discovered a website that has information available on practically every job she needs to assess; however, she is hesitant to use the information. What factors should she rely on when determining whether to use this data?

    a. The data goes back several years.

    b. The data is recent and relevant.

    c. The data supports the recommendation of providing salary increases.

    d. The data supports the recommendation of not providing salary increases.

59. Leroy is working on an employee satisfaction survey. He wants to measure how satisfied employees are with the organization in areas such as salary and benefits, supervisory relationships, leadership, communications, and culture. Which of the following is the best method for collecting this type of information?
    a. Sending out a survey
    b. Establishing focus groups
    c. Initiating observational data collection
    d. Reviewing performance evaluations

60. Which of the following data collection methods has a risk of low engagement or facilitator bias?
    a. Surveys
    b. Classroom training
    c. Focus groups
    d. Exit interviews

61. Which of the following strategies is the comparison of an organization's initiatives and outcomes against competitors, industry standards, or industry goals?
    a. Best practices
    b. Data collection
    c. SWOT analysis
    d. Benchmarking

62. David is conducting a salary survey for the engineering department. Several engineers have left the organization for a competitor, and management wants to determine if the salary is a reason for the departures. Although several engineers have indicated in their exit interview that compensation was a factor, David has reviewed the data and it does not support this reason. He has looked at base salary, overtime opportunities, car allowances, and bonus opportunities. What information is he missing?
    a. Benefits costs, vacation time, and retirement costs
    b. Promotional opportunities for future growth and salary increases
    c. Salary bands for starting pay and maximum pay
    d. Number of recognized holidays and time-off opportunities

63. Jessica recently received her performance review, and as part of her learning and development opportunities, a course in statistics and data analysis was recommended. Because Jessica has never been strong in this subject, she is hesitant to attend. Why is it important for her to have a working knowledge and understanding of statistics even though she works in HR?
    a. Jessica will be able to add this certification to her resume.
    b. Jessica will become more marketable as a candidate.
    c. Jessica will be able to promote to a higher-level position within the company with this higher skill set.
    d. Jessica will be able to identify flawed, misleading, or misrepresented data.

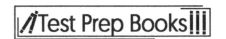

64. Joe has conducted a paper survey to assess the effectiveness of the HR department. After entering and reviewing all of the data, he is surprised to see that most employees are not happy with the services and customer support they have received. He is certain that he has implemented programs and policies that are beneficial to employees and is quite upset over the results. What should Joe do?

a. Disregard the information because it is clearly biased and inaccurate.

b. Treat the information as a learning opportunity and implement rational and effective change that addresses the issues identified.

c. Hold employee meetings to discuss how the department actually operates versus what the survey results indicated.

d. Hire an outside vendor to conduct the survey again to ensure there is no perceived bias or misunderstanding in the questions being asked.

65. In order to promote an organization's benefits program, which of the following details should be included in a job posting?

a. Salary range, including when increases will be considered during the calendar year

b. Alternate work schedules, flexible spending accounts, and wellness programs

c. Specific daily responsibilities and tasks of the position

d. Supervisory responsibilities as well as who this position reports to

66. Michael wants to update the organization's wellness policy, specifically the programs related to weight loss and smoking cessation. Who should he reach out to in order to gain insight and feedback regarding these programs?

a. Female employees at all levels

b. Male employees at the supervisory level

c. All employees at all levels

d. Female and male managers

67. Which of the following is the most effective, streamlined, and lean method to communicate policies, programs, procedures, forms, and information?

a. A secure online portal where employees can find updated information

b. A printed manual distributed to each employee annually

c. An in-person employee orientation delivered annually

d. An electronic newsletter delivered via email to all employees monthly

68. Heather is an HR director who holds biweekly one-on-one meetings, monthly team meetings, and biannual recognition lunches with all of her employees. During these meetings, she provides organizational updates, industry news, issues and concerns, and project statuses. She also goes around the room to ensure that all employees have an opportunity to discuss any issues, ask questions, or offer feedback. What is Heather displaying to her team during these sessions?

a. Transparency and innovation

b. Leadership and team-oriented culture

c. Leadership and innovation

d. Transparency and team-oriented culture

69. Ling is presenting to the leadership team on a value-based wellness program that will engage employees and require them to take a more active role in their wellness. The program has been shown to decrease insurance rates, and Ling believes this program could also help with future costs as well as promote employee wellness, decrease sick leave usage, and create a more productive workforce. During the presentation, the marketing director asks about the materials provided by the vendor to advertise this initiative to employees or if the organization will have to develop and fund the advertisements. Ling is not prepared for this question and does not have the answer. How should she respond?

a. Indicate that she does not have this information but will reach out to the vendor to get the information and send it to the team.

b. Indicate that the vendor will provide all marketing materials and then reach out to the vendor to ask them to do so.

c. Indicate that she does not have this information and then move on to the next section in her presentation.

d. Indicate that the vendor will not provide the materials and then reach out to the vendor to see if they can.

70. During the evaluation stage, which of the following is vital information to seek from stakeholders?

a. Documentation
b. Feedback
c. Questions
d. Costs

71. Which of the following is a step-by-step diagram that shows each stage's purpose?

a. Cost-benefit analysis
b. Value stream map
c. Gap analysis
d. Process map

72. Rita is sourcing data and publications for research on her new program. She wants to gather various sources and different opinions to create a unique proposal that will interest multiple stakeholders within the organization. How far back in time should she consider data from to ensure her proposal is relevant and timely?

a. Three years
b. Five years
c. Ten years
d. No time limit

73. Jose is hiring a new analyst and has a robust candidate pool. Each candidate is highly recommended, with specific and extensive experience in the duties that will be performed in the position. Jose needs to ensure that he selects a candidate who fits well within the organization, department, and team. He will be interviewing each candidate using a behavioral interview style but wants to also have a better understanding of each candidate's personality, specifically how they communicate and interact with others. Which of the following tools should Jose initiate within the interview process to determine this information?

a. SWOT analysis
b. Skills assessment
c. Writing exercise
d. Myers-Briggs assessment

74. Elise is preparing the annual performance reviews for her team. Each team member submitted recommendations of initiatives they would like to individually focus on. Michelle submitted four items she would like to focus on in the next calendar year. Which of the following is NOT a standard initiative for the HR team to focus on and should therefore be replaced with a more appropriate initiative?
    a. Review, update, and implement a robust and flexible recruitment process.
    b. Audit the payroll processing to ensure that bills are being paid in a timely manner.
    c. Establish a new exit interview process with specific questions based on the employee's tenure.
    d. Conduct an annual salary survey to ensure salaries are aligned with the industry.

75. Nancy is preparing a budget for the training and development conference. The conference, which is held every year for all employees to attend, is a full day of events that provides information related to the organization's success and accomplishments, future goals and objectives, and training sessions to teach key skills and techniques. Nancy has budgeted for the site location, food and beverages, employee salaries, materials, external facilitators' fees, giveaways, and emergency issues that may arise. These types of costs are which of the following?
    a. Training
    b. Indirect
    c. Direct
    d. Tax-deductible

76. Carol was tasked with researching, initiating, and implementing a new online training module for employees. The module would allow all employees, regardless of level and position, to complete mandatory training related to compliance, ethics, and regulatory topics. Unfortunately, the project did not meet the established goals regarding training offerings, budget, and timing. Certain regulatory trainings were not included, the final costs were over budget, and the rollout was more than three months late. Which of the following methods should Carol apply to this situation to determine why the objectives were not met?
    a. Process mapping
    b. Cause-and-effect diagram
    c. Value stream mapping
    d. SMART objectives

77. When gaining buy-in for large-scale projects that impact the entire organization, which of the following terms describes the concept of finding values or interests across multiple departments that would encourage support?
    a. Leadership support
    b. Work-life balance
    c. Employee morale
    d. Umbrella goals

78. An organization's policies that govern employees' actions, describe acceptable and unacceptable behaviors, and guide employee behavior with specific details is referred to as which of the following?
    a. Code of conduct
    b. Values statement
    c. Ethical standards
    d. Employee handbook

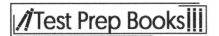

79. Natalia, Lisa, Julian, and Louis are members of the HR team, and each has a different discipline they are responsible for. Natalia manages recruitment; Lisa manages employee benefits; Julian manages employee relations; and Louis manages risk management and workers' compensation. Their manager, Hannah, receives a call that Natalia was involved in a car accident and will be out of the office for at least two months recovering. She pulls together the team to discuss the plan for managing Natalia's workload during her absence and discovers that neither Lisa, nor Julian, nor Louis is familiar with the recruitment process or where Natalia keeps her recruitment documents. What should Hannah have done to ensure that this precarious situation did not occur?

    a. Familiarize herself with each discipline and serve as the secondary resource for all areas.

    b. There was nothing Hannah could have done to foresee an emergency such as this.

    c. Keep a consultant on retainer to come in and pick up the duties in situations like this.

    d. Ensure that each HR discipline has an assigned primary and secondary resource.

80. When should an employee be introduced to an organization's ethical standards and policies?

    a. During the interview process with the hiring manager

    b. During the onboarding and new-hire orientation

    c. When reading the job posting to apply for the position

    d. When a complaint arises against them and HR begins the investigation

HR Knowledge

81. Which of the following concepts uses the perspective of systems thinking to understand how an organization operates?

    a. Professional development

    b. Key performance indicators

    c. Individual action plan

    d. Strategic planning

82. Which of the following conditions should Human Resources consider in order to make recommendations regarding strategic planning and alignment?

    a. Internal and external conditions

    b. Industry standards and metrics

    c. Internal conditions only

    d. Workforce trends

Read the following scenario and answer questions 83–85.

> Amelia is conducting a recruitment for a new position within the organization. The new position requires a specific certification, undergraduate degree, and one year of experience. When Amelia reviews the applications submitted, she identifies those with these specific requirements and schedules an initial round of interviews. She prepares the questions to focus on the work the organization will need done to ensure the best candidates are selected to move to the second round of interviews with the hiring managers. At the conclusion of the initial interviews, she is disappointed in the results. Although the majority of the candidates provided answers to the questions, none of the answers were in-depth and lacked real-world experience.

83. What should Amelia do immediately following the initial interviews?
    a. Notify the candidates that the organization will not be proceeding with this recruitment.
    b. Prepare a new plan for the recruitment and present it to the HR team for feedback.
    c. Communicate the results and concerns regarding the candidates with the hiring manager.
    d. Repost the recruitment to engage a new group of candidates and conduct interviews.

84. What should Amelia consider changing in the required qualifications to ensure candidates with the right background and job experience apply?
    a. Nothing, as the qualifications are appropriate for the position.
    b. Eliminate the years of experience necessary and only require the degree and certification.
    c. Increase the years of experience and allow for experience to substitute for the degree.
    d. Add supervisory experience to the qualifications to attract candidates who have more experience.

85. If Amelia and the hiring manager decide to move forward with the highest-ranking applicants from the initial recruitment, which of the following would be an appropriate step to add to the recruitment process?
    a. No additional steps
    b. Written exercise similar to the work performed
    c. Additional interview with the entire team
    d. Longer interview with specific and difficult questions

86. Which of the following is the keystone of HR's value to an organization?
    a. Talent acquisition
    b. Strategic planning
    c. Training and development
    d. Recruitment and retention

87. What exercise determines the knowledge, skills, abilities, and experience necessary to perform a job?
    a. Classification study
    b. Job analysis
    c. Skills gap assessment
    d. SWOT analysis

88. What is the strongest advantage of external sourcing?
    a. Encouraging connections with job seekers
    b. Cost-effective, as the costs are generally low
    c. Candidate familiarity with the organization and culture
    d. Support of building diversity and bringing fresh perspectives

89. Which of the following is not a method of internal sourcing?
    a. Employee referrals
    b. Promotions and transfers
    c. Walk-in applicants
    d. Recruiter-sourced hires

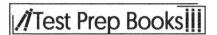

Read the following scenario and answer questions 90–92.

Joseph is working on a recruitment for his marketing team. The team comprises employees who have been with the organization for at least five years, with the most tenured employee having more than twenty years of experience. The department manager has made it a priority to promote internally to ensure that employees are provided opportunities to grow and develop within the organization. The organization also has a robust employee referral program that many employees, including the marketing team, have taken advantage of. The open position is now vacant due to an employee retirement.

90. When proposing a recruitment plan to the department manager, which sourcing method should Joseph suggest as the most appropriate method for this position?
   a. Internal sourcing first and then external sourcing
   b. External sourcing first and then internal sourcing
   c. Internal sourcing only
   d. External sourcing only

91. After Joseph posts the position, he receives complaints from current employees that they should have been considered first for the position instead of external candidates. What should Joseph do to mediate this situation?
   a. Follow up with the individuals who complained and communicate the sourcing strategy for this position and the importance of sourcing externally to the entire team.
   b. Discuss the situation with the department manager and consider allowing internal candidates to be considered along with external candidates.
   c. Close the posting and initiate an internal promotion-only recruitment for the position to appease the current employees.
   d. There are no actions Joseph should take regarding this situation because the recruitment is appropriate for the organization and the manager should handle the complaints.

92. Joseph is concerned about the new team member fitting within the current workgroup dynamic. The team has been together several years and works extremely well together. What could Joseph add to the recruitment process to address the chemistry and fit of the potential new hires?
   a. Written exam and sample work assignment
   b. Myers-Briggs personality assessment
   c. Workgroup interview with the entire team
   d. One-on-one interview with the most senior team member

93. Which of the following would be considered an inappropriate preemployment screening?
   a. Marital and parental history
   b. Criminal background check
   c. Medical and drug screenings
   d. Financial and credit history checks

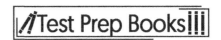
94. Julia has recently extended an offer to a potential new hire. She is requesting feedback from past employers, coworkers, and individuals who know the new hire and can attest to the work ethic, past performance, and overall behavior exhibited. What is Julia conducting?
    a. Educational reference check
    b. Emotional intelligence test
    c. Performance review
    d. Employment reference check

95. Onboarding is the process for new hires to learn about the knowledge, skills, and behaviors needed to become valued and productive contributors to the company. This process is also known as which of the following?
    a. New-hire orientation
    b. Organizational socialization
    c. Preemployment screening
    d. Organizational orientation

96. How long should onboarding programs typically last?
    a. The employee's first week
    b. The employee's first day
    c. The employee's first year
    d. Ongoing throughout employment

Read the following scenario and answer questions 97–98.

> Margaret has recently hired several new employees in various positions across the organization. She has conducted individual new-hire orientations for each employee to address the specific personal needs of each employee as well as a group orientation to facilitate a speedier entrance into the workplace. Margaret has trained the new employees in the payroll system, provided each with a copy of the employee handbook, and communicated the organization's vision, mission, and values.

97. Margaret wants to stay in frequent contact with the new employees to ensure they are acclimating well to the new organization and position. How should Margaret engage with each new employee?
    a. 360 feedback
    b. Stay interviews
    c. Exit interviews
    d. Satisfaction survey

98. Margaret receives the resignation from one of her recent hires. The employee indicates they are leaving the organization due to receiving an offer for a position of the same level but at a higher salary. Margaret reviews the offer and sees that the amount would equate to a 10 percent increase. What should Margaret do?

a. Nothing. If the employee wants to leave the organization, Margaret should accept the resignation letter and move forward with a new recruitment.

b. Attempt to negotiate with the employee directly and provide an immediate counteroffer to work to keep the employee with the organization.

c. Conduct an exit interview when the resignation letter is received to gather the information needed as to what could have retained the employee.

d. Communicate with the department manager and determine if there is flexibility in the current process and budget to provide a counteroffer.

99. What type of programs are used to promote organizational culture by identifying and rewarding individual employees for the work done?

a. Special event programs
b. Recognition programs
c. Inclusion programs
d. Incentive programs

100. Elyse has experienced a high number of employees leaving the organization. The senior leadership would like a presentation given to provide current information and a plan to address the issue. What data piece should Elyse ensure is included in her presentation?

a. Turnover rate
b. Days to hire
c. Number of openings
d. Recruitment budget

101. Which of the following is NOT an outcome of the performance management process?

a. Salary increases and promotions
b. Growth and development opportunities
c. Employee satisfaction and morale rate
d. Disciplinary actions and training needs

102. ADDIE is the most commonly used framework organizations use to enhance human resource development programs. What are the phases of the ADDIE model?

a. Analysis, Development, Distribution, Implementation, Engagement
b. Administration, Design, Delivery, Innovation, Evaluation
c. Analysis, Design, Development, Implementation, Evaluation
d. Administration, Development, Design, Instrumentation, Engagement

103. Which of the following is a direct benefit of analyzing labor markets during workforce planning?

a. Recruiting top talent for open positions
b. Identifying where employers are competing for labor
c. Gaining insight as to why employees are leaving
d. Benchmarking with other competitors

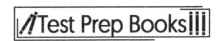

Read the following scenario and answer questions 104–106.

Marisa is evaluating her organization's total rewards plan to ensure that employees are earning a fair and competitive salary against the competition. Additionally, Marisa is interested in learning if employees are satisfied with the benefits package and noncompensatory programs, such as the alternative work schedule.

104. Which of the following should Marisa implement to begin her review of how employees view the current benefits package and noncompensatory programs?
    a. Classification review
    b. Compensation study
    c. Remuneration survey
    d. Employee satisfaction survey

105. Once Marisa has collected the data internally, she needs to compare the data to external data and information to determine comparability, equitability, and competitiveness. Which of the following should Marisa consult to make this determination?
    a. Classification review
    b. Compensation study
    c. Remuneration survey
    d. Employee satisfaction survey

106. Once Marisa has concluded her study of the internal data collected from employees and communicated the results to leadership, what should she do next?
    a. Formally report the results to executive leadership to see what they would like to do next in the process.
    b. File the results and refer to them only to compare to any remuneration surveys available.
    c. Coordinate with the Bureau of Labor Statistics to upload the data received and report the information.
    d. Communicate with employees to ensure they know their input is valued and important to the process.

107. Which of the following federal laws established employee classification and regulated minimum wage, overtime pay, on-call pay, recordkeeping, and child labor?
    a. Family Medical Leave Act
    b. Fair Labor Standards Act
    c. Davis Bacon Act
    d. Walsh-Healy Act

108. Which of the following positions falls under the Fair Labor Standards Act (FLSA) regulations?
    a. Nonexempt positions
    b. Exempt positions
    c. Professional positions
    d. Administrative positions

109. PESTLE is a structured tool used to learn about trends that can influence an organization's goals, processes, or employees. What does PESTLE analyze?
    a. People, Environmental, Society, Teamwork, Legal, External trends
    b. Political, Economic, Social, Technological, Legal, Environmental trends
    c. People, Engagement, Sustainability, Technological, Legal, Environmental trends
    d. Political, Environmental, Social, Teamwork, Logistics, External trends

110. When an organization assigns employees to foreign countries, what is the legal and moral obligation HR assumes responsibility of for these employees and their families?
    a. Tax accountants
    b. Housekeeping
    c. Duty of care
    d. HR advocates

111. Michael is sent to the Germany office to attend several business meetings over the course of a week. After the meetings conclude, he decides he wants to fly over to his spouse to enjoy the sights of Munich and other tourist areas for a couple of weeks. What could Michael's worker status now be considered?
    a. Employee on leave
    b. Accidental tourist
    c. Illegal immigrant
    d. Accidental expatriate

112. When an employee transfers to a new country for an assignment and then returns home, which of the following is a factor for both transitions that can result in a low level of satisfaction?
    a. Recovery
    b. Adaptation
    c. Culture shock
    d. Arrival

Read the following scenario and answer questions 113–115.

Bruce has been working in Sweden for his organization over the past three years. His assignment is ending, and he has requested a transfer for a new assignment in Hong Kong. The new assignment has recently been approved, and he has been given three months to transition to the new country. His HR contact, Cecilia, worked with him during his initial move to Sweden and has provided excellent support to him and his family. Bruce receives his initial transfer paperwork and is surprised to see that a new HR contact has been assigned to him for his transition out of Sweden and then into Hong Kong. He is uncomfortable working with a new HR contact because Cecilia has gotten to know the family, and he will need to go over all of his needs and requirements again with the new contact.

113. What should Bruce do first regarding the change in HR support?
    a. Contact Cecilia to understand why the change in contact was made.
    b. Contact the HR director to request a change back to Cecilia.
    c. Send an email to his supervisor with a formal complaint about the change.
    d. Cancel his request to relocate to Hong Kong.

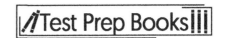
114. There could be many reasons why the new HR contact was assigned to Bruce to assist him with his new assignment. Which of the following would NOT be a reason for the new HR contact assignment?
    a. Cecilia is on maternity leave and will not be available during the time frame.
    b. Cecilia does not have experience with Hong Kong laws and requirements.
    c. Cecilia has transferred to a new department and no longer handles global assignments.
    d. The HR director implemented a new policy to reassign all expatriates to new contacts.

115. Bruce is not comfortable working with the new HR contact to handle his transition out of Sweden and into Hong Kong. What could he request?
    a. To work with Cecilia on both transitions because he is confident in her skills and abilities for both locations
    b. To work with Cecilia on his transition out of Sweden and the new contact for his transition into Hong Kong
    c. To handle the transition to his new assignment on his own and only communicate with the new contact as needed
    d. To have his new assignment terminated and to work with Cecilia to transition him and his family back to the United States

116. What term refers to the differences in employees' characteristics?
    a. Workplace diversity
    b. Workplace inclusion
    c. Workplace culture
    d. Workplace dynamics

117. In addition to developing strong relationships with external stakeholders, what can an organization's diversity and inclusion programs accomplish as its primary focus?
    a. Provide thorough investigations of complaints.
    b. Ensure a strong training and development program.
    c. Ensure compliance with federal and state statutes.
    d. Build employee relations and satisfaction.

118. Tim has recently provided Human Resources with permanent restrictions due to a documented medical disability. He is an accountant, and the majority of his work relates to payroll processing, accounts receivable, and accounts payable. The restrictions address physical concerns as well as limit Tim's ability to work a full 8-hour shift. Tim has requested accommodations for each physical concern that includes installing better ergonomic-specific equipment, such as a keyboard tray, special chair with lumbar support, and a footrest. Additionally, he has requested an accommodation to limit his workday to no more than a 6-hour shift, resulting in a maximum 30-hour work week. How should HR respond to Tim regarding his accommodation requests?
    a. Automatically deny the accommodations because they were not received from his doctor.
    b. Automatically approve the accommodations to ensure compliance with the Americans With Disabilities Act (ADA).
    c. Review the accommodations and determine which are reasonable and which are not and then prepare a response to address each request.
    d. Lay off Tim and eliminate his position so that he will be eligible for severance and unemployment benefits.

119. When an organization identifies, targets, and strives to minimize unacceptable dangers or threats, what process are they engaging in?
    a. SMART goals
    b. Myers-Briggs Type Indicator
    c. Risk management
    d. Corporate social responsibility

120. Which of the following terms refers to a planned and practiced protocol used during an emergency?
    a. Strategic plan
    b. Emergency response
    c. Evacuation plan
    d. Hazard communication

Read the following scenario and answer questions 121–122.

> A fulfillment center recently opened to support the distribution needs of a growing city. The center hired more than a thousand employees quickly to ensure the staffing levels would be appropriate to handle the workload when the facility began operations. In addition to coordinating group orientations to navigate the hiring process, group meetings were also scheduled to familiarize employees with the benefits and programs offered by the company. Human Resources also wants to schedule group meetings to review the safety protocols and emergency response plans to ensure employees are aware and understand their role and responsibility if an emergency was to occur.

121. The plant manager does not support holding another set of group meetings to discuss the emergency response plans. He wants the staff to focus on the distribution operations for the first year and then would consider providing an hour or two to provide this training. How should HR respond to this situation?
    a. Communicate to the plant manager that these plans protect lives and property, provide a level of security to employees, and ensure compliance with safety standards.
    b. Schedule the group meetings to occur immediately, ensuring that employees receive this training and information promptly.
    c. Create a formal memo that outlines the entire program and request that supervisors distribute the memo to each employee and post it in the break rooms.
    d. Schedule the group meetings to occur exactly one year from the date of opening to align with the direction from the plant manager.

122. During the group meetings to train employees on the emergency response plan, HR also emphasizes the evacuation plan for the facility. Visual aids are provided with exit routes mapped out for the entire facility along with meeting places and procedures. In addition to providing this information to employees, what else can HR do to ensure employees effectively evacuate the facility in the case of an emergency?
    a. Require employees to sign an acknowledgment statement at the end of the training.
    b. Post special posters throughout the facility that showcase the exit routes.
    c. Request that supervisors frequently quiz employees on the exit routes.
    d. Coordinate a scheduled and unscheduled practice evacuation.

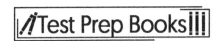
123. OSHA requires that organizations adhere with specific regulations regarding hazardous chemicals, including providing training, labeling hazardous chemical containers, and providing access to MSDS information. What does MSDS stand for?
    a. Mandatory Substance Data Sheets
    b. Measurable Safety Detailed Slips
    c. Material Safety Data Sheets
    d. Menacing Safety Data Slips

124. Veronica is assessing Janine's workstation to ensure that the workspace is efficient and comfortable and makes the best use of space. Additionally, Veronica asks Janine specific questions regarding her physical comfort in the space, including her comfort levels with the keyboard, monitor height, and lighting, to determine if there are any special needs that must be accommodated. What practice is Veronica engaging in?
    a. Safety and risk appraisal
    b. Ergonomic evaluation test
    c. Physical risk assessment
    d. Illness and injury report

125. When preparing a workplace policy, which of the below statements is accurate?
    a. If there is a federal regulation regarding a program, a workplace policy is not needed.
    b. If there is a federal regulation regarding a program, the policy should mirror the regulation.
    c. Workplace policies should provide equal or greater benefits than the federal regulations.
    d. Workplace policies should provide equal or less benefits than the federal regulations.

126. Which of the following laws is designed to establish accountability and standards regarding accounting misconduct, record manipulation, and inappropriate financial practices?
    a. Employee Retirement Income Security Act (ERISA)
    b. Generally Accepted Accounting Principles (GAAP)
    c. US Government Accountability Office (GAO)
    d. Sarbanes-Oxley (SOX) Act

127. Which of the following is not a standard function of the Occupational Safety and Health Act?
    a. Develop standards for employee personal protective equipment.
    b. Provide fixed payments to injured employees and their dependents.
    c. Establish guidelines to assist employees in the event of a pandemic disease outbreak.
    d. Ensure safe working conditions for employees and establish safety management standards.

128. What are the two most common workplace safety risks?
    a. Bloodborne pathogens and tripping hazards
    b. Lockout/tagout and confined space hazards
    c. Noise exposure and bloodborne pathogens
    d. Lockout/tagout and tripping hazards

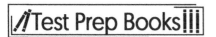

Read the following scenario and answer questions 129–131.

Rosie is new to the organization and working to update the workplace security plans. After reviewing the security plans, she identifies several areas that need to be addressed to protect the organization. In addition to expanding the plan's language to include specific plans and policies that minimize exposure, she is working on a communications plan to ensure that all employees are aware of and understand the new security plan.

129. In addition to addressing theft and corporate espionage, what other topic should Rosie ensure is addressed in the security plan?
    a. Illness prevention
    b. On-the-job injuries
    c. Sexual harassment
    d. Sabotage

130. Rosie is preparing a training class for all employees to attend to adequately prepare the organization in the case of a security issue. In addition to corporate espionage and theft, Rosie is also focusing on training employees on important security details that include security measures. Which of the following items would not be addressed regarding security measures?
    a. Emergency communication systems
    b. First aid and AED locations and procedures
    c. Alarms locations, secure rooms, and security guard location
    d. Employee badges and facility security protocols

131. How often should Rosie train employees on the security plans and policies?
    a. Annually
    b. During new-hire orientation
    c. Every other year
    d. Every six months

132. Corporate social responsibility (CSR) refers to an organization's sense of responsibility for its impact on the environment and community. Which of the following are the evaluation factors for CSR?
    a. People, purpose, proceeds
    b. Public, process, profit
    c. People, planet, profit
    d. Public, purpose, proceeds

133. The three evaluation factors identified in question 24 that show how effective an organization's CSR is are known as which of the following?
    a. The hat trick
    b. The triple bottom line
    c. The triple play
    d. The social responsibility scale

134. Which of the following service models allows Human Resources (HR) to have a presence within different business units?
    a. Centralized
    b. Matrixed
    c. Outsourced
    d. Decentralized

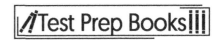
135. Which of the following service models allows HR to have one corporate presence over the entire organization?
   a. Centralized
   b. Matrixed
   c. Outsourced
   d. Decentralized

136. Lucy is the HR director for an organization that employs individuals across the country. A majority of the employees are located in the corporate headquarters; however, many work in service centers located in large metropolitan areas. Although the majority of her HR team supports and works at the corporate headquarters, she also has team members stationed at each of the service centers to allow all employees to have access to HR support. Which service model is Lucy using?
   a. Centralized
   b. Matrixed
   c. Outsourced
   d. Decentralized

137. What are the three primary areas of functions HR performs?
   a. Transactional, provisional, supervisory
   b. Educational, training, supervisory
   c. Educational, provisional, strategic
   d. Transactional, tactical, strategic

138. What type of HR work is administrative and includes payroll and benefits administration?
   a. Tactical
   b. Personnel
   c. Transactional
   d. Strategic

139. Which of the following statements is true regarding outsourcing of HR work?
   a. HR work that is dependent on having knowledge of workplace relationships, organizational culture, or team dynamics is not appropriate to outsource.
   b. Performance management, strategic planning, and employee communications are all appropriate examples of HR work that should be outsourced.
   c. A general rule of thumb is to always perform HR work in-house through a centralized, decentralized, or matrixed service model.
   d. A general rule of thumb is to outsource HR work as much as possible to free up valuable time and resources to train and problem solve.

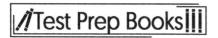

Read the following scenario and answer questions 140–142.

Phoebe has recently joined a software company that employs hundreds of individuals across the country. She has been tasked with reviewing the current HR team and how services are provided to employees. She reviews the organizational chart and understands the department is structured in a centralized way, with all staff located at the corporate headquarters on the East Coast. The majority of employees are stationed at locations in the central Midwest and on the Pacific coast. She begins her work with an employee survey to gain insight into how the HR professionals are viewed by the employees. She asks questions about how knowledgeable the HR staff has been, how helpful each staff member was during issues such as taking leaves of absence or changing benefits, and how the HR staff could improve to provide better service.

140. Once the data was compiled, Phoebe saw a clear pattern of HR staff not being available to employees when needed. Although the HR staff always responded with accurate information and were helpful with issues, the delays in response times varied from more than 24 hours to three days. Phoebe compiles a list of recommendations to improve this concern. Which of the following options should NOT be a potential recommendation?

a. Propose a flexible work schedule for HR staff to be available during the different time zones, ensuring that staff is available in the office when needed.

b. Propose a new policy that all calls will be returned within 24 hours (no exceptions) and that HR staff will be disciplined when not followed.

c. Propose that HR staff be provided with an on-call program that includes a company cell phone to respond to concerns from employees when needed.

d. Propose relocating HR staff or hiring new staff at each location across the country to ensure that resources are available where needed.

141. Phoebe presents her recommendations along with a list of positives and negatives for each option to the leadership team for consideration. The team votes to initiate a flexible work schedule to align the work schedules with other time zones. Which of the following would be a negative element of this recommendation?

a. Cost and budget

b. Disruption to service

c. Staffing and resources

d. Participation and lack of volunteers

142. Which of the following should Phoebe consider when rolling out this proposal to the HR staff and then to the employees?

a. Define the program as a pilot program with a check-in for a secondary survey after six months to assess its effectiveness for both HR staff and employees.

b. Establish a new policy that defines all parameters and implement the program permanently, with a new survey to be conducted after a year.

c. Communicate the new program to the HR staff at the same time as the employees so one less communication is sent out, eliminating any possible confusion.

d. Communicate to the HR staff that if this program is not successful after six months, the leadership team will be moving staff to other locations.

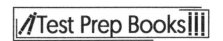
143. Which of the following is an accurate statement regarding employee surveys?
    a. Employee surveys should only be conducted to determine if employees are satisfied with their compensation and benefits.
    b. Employee surveys should be conducted as frequently as possible because this allows employees to continually provide feedback.
    c. Employee surveys are only effective when a response is provided and actions are taken as a result of the feedback.
    d. Employee surveys should be conducted with managers and supervisors, who can provide feedback on behalf of their subordinates.

144. Employee turnover rate, cost of hire, performance scores, employee satisfaction, diversity ratios, and percentage of overtime hours are all examples of which of the following?
    a. Interview techniques
    b. Wellness program training
    c. Technology implementation
    d. Key Performance Indicators (KPIs)

145. HR is responsible for understanding an organization's current talent, anticipating future needs, and implementing actionable plans to bridge gaps. This major responsibility is known as which of the following?
    a. Organizational development
    b. Workforce management
    c. Succession planning
    d. Strategic planning

146. What are the two approaches used by HR to fill skills gaps within an organization?
    a. Buy and build
    b. Attract and retain
    c. Recruit and build
    d. Train and develop

147. Julian is working with the leadership team to ensure that the organization's employees have the skills and competencies needed to achieve the goals and objectives. He is conducting a skills gap analysis and discovers that a majority of the mid-level managers lack conflict resolution and team-building skills. What would be the best option for Julian to implement?
    a. Research training programs provided by external vendors and provide information to the employees.
    b. Require these employees' managers to indicate this lack of skill in the upcoming performance evaluation.
    c. Conduct a specific training program for these employees that provides an opportunity to learn these skills.
    d. Conduct a recruitment to hire new mid-level managers who specifically have this skill set.

148. Which approach handles an organization's leadership needs by ensuring the transfer of knowledge, experience, and relationships from one generation of workers to the next?
    a. Exit interviewing
    b. Skills gap assessment
    c. Workforce management
    d. Succession planning

149. Miguel is working with the leadership team to reorganize the organization to ensure profitability based on the current economic situation. This action is a direct response to the company experiencing significant decreases in sales over a period of several quarters. What type of action is Miguel conducting?
   a. Financial restructuring
   b. Workforce reduction
   c. Organizational restructuring
   d. Corporate restructuring

150. Lisa is working with her team to address a talent surplus. She has identified multiple areas to focus on, such as a reduction in work hours, implementation of a hiring freeze, and creation of a voluntary separation program. By focusing on these items, what is Lisa working to avoid?
   a. Financial restructuring
   b. Workforce reduction
   c. Organizational restructuring
   d. Corporate restructuring

Read the following scenario and answer questions 151–153.

Samantha's organization has made the decision to move forward with a workforce reduction due to costs and expenses exceeding sales and profits. Samantha has experienced being laid off with a previous organization and is bringing that experience to this circumstance. She wants to make certain that employees receive the necessary information to ensure a successful implementation of the workforce reduction.

151. What should Samantha focus on immediately?
   a. Communicate with employees about the decision, process, and timeline.
   b. Create separation agreements and general releases for employees to sign.
   c. Implement a hiring freeze across all departments.
   d. Attempt to change the decision of the executives by preparing a proposal.

152. Samantha is working on creating a benefits package for the employees who will be separated. One of these benefits will include resume writing, career counseling, and interview preparation. What benefit is Samantha offering with these services?
   a. Severance
   b. Separation agreement
   c. Employee assistance
   d. Outplacement services

153. Once the workforce reduction is complete, what should Samantha and the executive team focus on?
   a. Checking in frequently with the separated employees to ensure they gain employment
   b. Reporting out on the new profit and loss statements to show the new productivity rate
   c. Boosting the morale of the remaining employees to ensure productivity does not suffer
   d. Discussing potential future reductions in case more are needed

154. Which of the following is NOT an immediate solution used to address a talent shortage?
a. Provide employees with an opportunity to work overtime.
b. Hire temporary employment staff to manage extra workload.
c. Maintain current workload while recruitments are conducted.
d. Reemploy recent retirees as part-time employees.

155. One of Janet's objectives is to work to improve the organization's employee relations. She is focusing on several items to accomplish this goal. Which of the following is NOT something that Janet can affect when implementing change in employee relations?
a. How employees interact with each other and with external customers or partners, specifically how they work together, communicate, and accomplish their goals
b. Local, state, and federal regulations that govern workplace environments and interactions, specifically laws that relate to harassment and workplace environments
c. The methods and strategies used to determine the rules that shape relationships, specifically interpersonal skills and communication—verbal and nonverbal
d. The guidelines and rules that govern how interactions between individuals take place, specifically the organization's policies and procedures

156. Which of the following is a formally organized group of employees who work together to accomplish goals?
a. Labor union
b. Employee resource group
c. Department team
d. Work group

157. Which of the following labor unions are made of up national unions representing different industries that share some similarities, such as common goals?
a. National unions
b. Partnerships
c. International unions
d. Federations

Read the following scenario and answer questions 158–160.

Employees at a manufacturing company have recently gone through the organizing process to form a labor union. After many years of little to no salary increases, no changes to benefits such as medical insurance or retirement, and an increase in safety concerns, employees reach out to the National Labor Relations Board (NLRB) to begin the process of forming a union to protect their interests. After employees work through the process of gaining signatures and establishing enough interest in the formation of a union, the process will continue on to formalize an election to vote on representation.

158. Which one of the following steps should the employees have engaged in prior to the election?
a. Identify and hire a professional labor negotiator.
b. Reach out to other local unions that offer representation.
c. Notify and inform the employer of the desire to unionize.
d. Coordinate a picketing event to ensure the union is established.

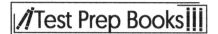

159. The employer has refused to accept the request to form a union and does not believe employees want to be represented by a union. The employees reach out to the NLRB to move to the next step of the organizing process. What will the NLRB do next?
 a. Hold an election for employees to vote on whether to be represented by a union or not.
 b. Negotiate with the employer directly to establish the union for employees.
 c. Establish the goals and objectives of the new union for employees to consider.
 d. File a petition under the National Labor Relations Act (NLRA) to protect employee rights.

160. Once the employees established the union and negotiated for higher wages, better benefits, and safer working conditions, they find that after a period of time, the organization has stepped up and followed through on even more positive impacts for employees. The employees also begin to feel that the union is not doing an adequate job of representing them and it's not worth the union dues they are paying. What process can employees begin in order to strip the union of its official status as their representative?
 a. Avoidance
 b. Decertification
 c. Deauthorization
 d. Picketing

Answer Explanations for Practice Test #3

Behavioral Competency

1. C: An organization's "mood" refers to the organizational climate, which can be directly affected by the environment, policies, behaviors, and process. Choice *A* is incorrect because environment is a general term that refers to the actual surroundings or conditions in which employees work. Choice *B* is incorrect because values refer to the ideas that guide an organization's actions. Choice *D* is incorrect because an organization's culture refers to the overall working environment, employer standards, interactions, and how work is accomplished.

2. A: A mission statement focuses on the day-to-day work that is being performed, and a vision statement focuses on the future goals and accomplishments. The mission statement supports the vision statement. Choices *B*, *C*, and *D* are all incorrect because the mission statement focuses on what is being done now, and the vision statement focuses on what will be done in the future.

3. B: Susan should ensure that each objective includes the SMART aspects: specific, measurable, achievable, relevant, and time-based. Without these aspects, an objective may not be met or the status could be unknown. By including the SMART aspects, there can be a clear understanding of performance expectations. Choice *A* is incorrect because all language should be well written, clear, concise, and specific, but without SMART aspects, there could still be misunderstandings as to what is to be accomplished. Choices *C* and *D* are inaccurate because professional development and recognition should be separate items contained within a performance review but separate from performance objectives. If a training opportunity is to be an objective for an employee, the item should be written as an objective, containing the SMART aspects.

4. A: Six Sigma is a specific technique that works to improve business processes by implementing various tools and concepts to reduce errors and eliminate waste. Gap analysis, root cause analysis, and cause-and-effect diagrams, Choices *B*, *C*, and *D*, are incorrect because they are all tools that would be used to determine why goals were not achieved or if there was a discrepancy between the expected results and actual results.

5. D: The best decision for Karen to make is to hire candidate B based on the passion, motivation, and experience aligning with the needs of the department and position. Choice *A* is not a feasible option because budgets are set and staffing determined well in advance of recruitments. Choice *B* is not an appropriate option because Karen is the hiring manager and therefore tasked with making this decision. She should not push this decision up to the next level in the organization; this is part of her responsibilities. Choice *C* is not the best option because if an employee is not motivated and passionate prior to starting with a new organization, these qualities probably cannot be instilled later on.

6. B: HR can specifically alleviate employees' fears and concerns about reporting unethical behavior and possible retaliation by providing them with a confidential and/or anonymous reporting method. This will protect their identity while still allowing for a proper and thorough investigation to occur. Although Choices *A*, *C*, and *D* are all appropriate actions to take to ensure a robust policy that is compliant with the law and is understood by employees, these actions may not specifically address employees' concerns about making a report.

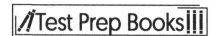

7. C: An organization that has a lack of transparency will experience decreased morale and higher turnover among employees. Choices *A, B,* and *D* are incorrect because they all align with a higher level of transparency. Organizations that are transparent with employees will experience higher levels of innovation, productivity, and promotion rates and lower turnover.

8. D: The best way for Jessie to fully understand the organization's needs as well as individual departmental needs is to establish one-on-one and group meetings. These meetings will assist in facilitating a two-way dialogue that fosters the sharing of information that will yield more successful contract negotiations. Although Choices *A, B,* and *C* are all best practices that would be beneficial to include in the overall process when preparing for negotiations, they do not provide specific departmental needs and wants. Choice *A* does not specifically provide a set meeting to discuss issues, and it places the burden of initiating the communication on the managers. Choice *B* does not provide insight into departmental knowledge and needs. This task may be necessary after meeting with the departments to gain knowledge and insight into how the contract can be changed. Choice *C* would provide insight as to how employees are satisfied with the total rewards package but would not provide the information needed to address department needs.

9. B: A major benefit of HR professionals networking outside of the organization is to learn about successful HR initiatives that have been implemented at other agencies and work to bring those initiatives into their own organization. External networking provides an excellent source of ideas from others who have wide and diverse experience. Choice *A* is incorrect because although career advancement and personal growth are benefits of external networking, there are numerous benefits for those who engage in networking. Choice *C* is incorrect because although networking may expose Olivia to new ideas and thoughts, which could in turn move her toward specific HR areas of work, this is not a specific benefit to the organization. Choice *D* is incorrect because although vendor recommendations may be provided by a professional network, this should not replace the formal process to review potential vendors.

10. C: The best thing for HR to do to assist Josie with this situation is to listen and work with her to find resolutions that may address the situation. This discussion may bring up new ideas and thoughts on how to move forward that HR can then discuss with Josie's manager to see if they are feasible. Choice *A* is incorrect because HR does not usually have the authority to remove work from another department's employees. Additionally, it is not appropriate to ensure when new employees will be hired with a current employee because if it doesn't occur, it could cause new problems. Choice *B* is not correct because although it may be a recommendation after speaking with Josie, HR should make recommendations and work to assist, not instruct, on specific actions for other departments. Choice *D* is incorrect because, based on the evaluation and background processes, it may not be possible to hire a new employee this quickly.

11. A: Stakeholder mapping is the official term that refers to a tool used to identify the value an initiative would have for a stakeholder as well as the investment and influence the stakeholder would have in promoting the initiative. Choices *B, C,* and *D* are incorrect; although they are other terms similar to mapping, they are not the actual defined term.

12. D: Gaining knowledge about the business and operations, such as financial information, is a benefit of being able to serve as a team leader. This can be rewarding—both personally and professionally. Choices *A* and *B* are incorrect because communicating with others, supervising, and directing work are specific job duties a team leader would engage in and not examples of a benefit gained by serving in this

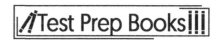

role. Choice *C* is incorrect because an HR professional should never reach the endpoint of their professional development but should always strive to continue learning and growing.

13. C: Bill's next steps can be to request a right-to-sue letter and sue the employer in court. Although Bill does not have to proceed with these steps, he does have this option available to him. Choice *A* is inaccurate because he does have further options. Choice *B* is also inaccurate because filing a grievance should have been done prior to filing the complaint with the EEOC; however, Bill could have immediately filed with the EEOC and skipped filing a grievance. Choice *D* is also inaccurate because, based on Bill's claims and allegations, he is protected from retaliation from his employer or fellow employees.

14. B: Principled bargaining occurs when groups negotiate a contract while being aware and mindful of the key issues to each side. Principled bargaining is a process of finding solutions so that both sides gain from the agreement. Choices *A* and *C*, distributive bargaining and positional bargaining, both refer to bargaining that takes place to achieve a specific objective. Choice *D*, coordinated bargaining, refers to bargaining that occurs when multiple unions within one organization meet to negotiate as one group to benefit all employees.

15. B: Multi-employer bargaining specifically refers to bargaining that occurs when a union with employees at multiple companies meets with all of the companies in one negotiation. Choices *A, C,* and *D*, whipsawing, leapfrogging, and parallel bargaining, all refer to when a union successfully negotiates an agreement with a company and then uses these results to deal with another company.

16. D: Newsletters do not allow for a formal two-way communication between the employer and employees. Newsletters are static and created by certain employees, conveying information deemed appropriate at that time. Choices *A, B,* and *C* are all incorrect because they are accurate statements regarding newsletters. Newsletters are not the best method to relay urgent information to employees and can be labor-intensive and infrequent. Additionally, newsletters can provide information in an engaging and welcoming manner.

17. C: Amber should respond directly to the department leader, asking specific questions and requesting clarity regarding the discrepancies she noted. This will ensure the entire team is on the same page and the pilot program is implemented to address the actual issues. Choice *A* is incorrect; by moving forward with the role, she may end up needing to redo her work because there is ambiguity in the information provided. If she is unclear about any element, she should ensure this is cleared up before moving forward. Choice *B* is incorrect because this action could be seen as a passive-aggressive action and tattling on the department leader. Choice *D* is also incorrect because Amber assumes others will clarify the issues and provide her with direction later.

18. A: Employee business resource groups help to specifically promote the diversity and inclusion efforts of an organization. These groups help to connect employees and facilitate a positive working environment. Choices *B, C,* and *D* are incorrect because professional growth, better relationships, increased communication, and training opportunities are possible outcomes or products of employees engaging in a resource group.

19. D: Veronica is specifically addressing the "mini-cultures" that have been created within each site. By establishing consistent policies and practices, she can work to align the sites in how operations are conducted. Choice *A* is incorrect because individual concerns regarding behavior should be addressed separately and specifically in alignment with policy. Choice *B* is incorrect because workplace climate refers to the mood and pulse of the employees within an organization. Choice *C* is incorrect because resource allocation refers to the personnel who are conducting the work needed.

20. B: Veronica should ensure that she is fully aware of and understands all applicable state laws and regulations when establishing new policies and procedures. State laws could provide additional benefits or require additional levels of compliance, and the policies and procedures should reflect this to ensure alignment. Choices *A, C,* and *D* are all pieces of information that may prove to be helpful when reviewing which policies to update or specifically address, but policy should not be created specific to employee demographics, supervisory complaints, or customer sales.

21. C: Auditing diversity and inclusion practices provide an organization the ability to ensure they are sustainable. Choice *A*, troubleshooting, is a term that refers to solving an issue or discovering the reason behind a problem. Choice *B*, recruiting, is a term that refers to the hiring process of new employees. Choice *D*, brainstorming, refers to the process in which ideas are discussed among a team to deliver new options to accomplish a task.

22. B: The best way for Cynthia to ensure that this new benefits program favors all employees equally and does not cater to any particular groups is to standardize the program and make it equally accessible to all employees. Although Choices *A, C,* and *D* are options that can be included in the rollout of the program, they do not actually ensure equality and accessibility of the benefit for all employees. Communication of a process used when making a decision, assurance of equity, and support from executive leadership are all best practices that could assist in the support and implementation of the program but would not ensure equity of the program itself.

23. D: The PESTLE analysis tool investigates the Political, Economic, Social, Technological, Legal, and Environmental trends that influence an organization. Process is not a trend analyzed by this tool. Choices *A, B,* and *C* are therefore incorrect because they are trends within the PESTLE tool.

24. A: Choice *A* is the inaccurate statement because a PESTLE analysis is a formal, structured tool used to determine trends that could influence an organization. Choices *B, C,* and *D* are not correct because they are all accurate statements regarding a PESTLE analysis. A PESTLE analysis should be used by HR to guide work, should include internal and external resources, and often indicates process changes to mitigate risks.

25. B: Business technology is the formal term that refers to the software, online systems, applications, or innovations that automate or simplify tasks within an organization. Choices *A, C,* and *D* are incorrect because information systems, workplace resources, and reporting systems are all components of business technology and work together to further automate process.

26. D: A SWOT analysis, which reviews the strengths, weaknesses, opportunities, and threats of an organization, should be used during the internal analysis step of strategic planning. Choices *A* and *C* are not correct because plan formation and evaluation both occur after the internal analysis step. Choice *B* is not correct because setting objectives and goals should be the first step in the strategic planning process.

27. A: Although a SWOT analysis can be used to analyze large, organizational-level issues, this analysis is also extremely helpful to assess issues at any level, including individual, departmental, or team issues. Choices *B, C,* and *D* are incorrect because they are all accurate statements about a SWOT analysis. A SWOT analysis is a comprehensive and flexible tool that assesses internal factors (strengths and weaknesses) as well as external factors (opportunities and threats).

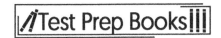

28. C: Tommy should review the current number of days needed to fill a position with the new process against the number of days needed to fill a position with the previous process. In doing so, he is comparing the metrics between the current and baseline data to show if there has been an improvement in filling positions faster with the new process. Choices A and D are important pieces of information but are specific pieces of data at a particular point in time. The attrition rate and number of openings do not show a trend or the effectiveness of a process. Choice B is an excellent source of information because it is always important to gauge the satisfaction of employees regarding specific processes and programs; however, this data would be subjective and could not be measured.

29. D: In the case presented, the best change management approach would be the power-coercive strategy to implement these changes. This strategy would be appropriate because the CFO will give the instruction as to what is expected and what could occur if these changes do not happen. Employees will need to be compliant in making these changes to ensure the organization is not placed in a position of risk. Choice A, normative-reeducative strategy, is the change management technique used when a change is related to cultural norms and social values. Choice B, empirical-rational strategy, is the technique used to educate individuals with the alternative options that will incentivize them to move to the new change. Choice C, environmental-adaptive strategy, is the technique used when there is an organizational change such as layoffs or retirements and the remaining employees need to adapt.

30. B: Validation is the auditing method used to ensure that a process delivers the same outcomes each time it is used. Validation looks at each step within a process to ensure consistency and predictability. Choice A, transparency, is a vital component of communication that builds trust. Choice C, data collection, refers to the specific process of sourcing information. Choice D, risk management, is the process that identifies potential risks within a process.

31. A: Emotional intelligence refers to the ability to identify and manage one's own emotions. It includes four equally important elements: self-awareness, social awareness, relationship management, and self-management. Choices B and C are incorrect because psychological intelligence and intelligence quotient (IQ) are both terms used to describe how smart an individual is based on particular testing results. Choice D is incorrect because a DISC personality is the result provided to individuals who participate in the DISC personality test.

32. D: Sarah should reach out to Thiang to discuss the survey, specifically how the survey was created and how results were tallied to understand the data. It would also benefit Sarah to ask Thiang what didn't quite work or what should have been done differently in order to address these issues prior to initiating the survey. Choice A is incorrect because Sarah should not ask Thiang to do this same process with her department. Thiang may offer to assist, but Sarah should not expect another individual to conduct work that is within her scope of responsibilities. Choice B is incorrect because Sarah is working blindly and trying to figure out what was done so that she can attempt to re-create the process and products. Choice C is incorrect because it is highly unlikely that funding would be approved for a survey such as this, especially since one was just conducted in-house at a low, or even no, cost.

33. C: The best way for HR leadership to communicate appropriate and acceptable behaviors within the workplace is to consistently behave in an ethical, reliable, and acceptable manner. Choices A, B, and D are all acceptable best practices to ensure that the message of what is appropriate behavior is communicated frequently; however, the best way to communicate this is to model the behavior on a daily basis.

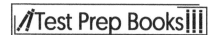

34. A: Adam's objective of having healthier employees is vague and ambiguous, with no measurable data points to successfully achieve this goal. Healthy employees are most definitely the business of an organization and can be achieved if done properly, making Choice *B* incorrect. The objective is not specific and the defined tasks are all achievable, making Choice *C* incorrect. Finally, the objective should be defined further with specific measurements and data points before moving forward as either a departmental or individual objective, making Choice *D* incorrect.

35. B: To correct the objective, Adam should rewrite it using the SMART principles. The objective should be smart, measurable, achievable, relevant, and time-based. The SMART principles allow for measured success versus not knowing if an objective has been achieved. Choice *A* is incorrect because each of the tasks would still need to be written in a SMART manner; otherwise, the same issue exists. Choice *C* is incorrect because objectives should not be written as philosophical objectives but rather as tangible and achievable goals. Choice *D* is inaccurate because by keeping the original objective, the same problem of not being able to measure success exists regardless of how many tasks are identified to support the goal.

36. C: HR can work to ensure an unbiased and fair recruitment and selection process by establishing an interview panel with stakeholders from other departments who interact with this position. This panel can interview all candidates and make a selection based on the qualities of the individuals. Although the finance director may be a part of this panel or have the final decision of who will be selected, incorporating this step in the process will help to ensure an unbiased process. Choice *A* is incorrect because all employees should have the ability to apply for any position within an organization regardless of relationships outside of the workplace. Choice *B* is incorrect because although it should be expected that a director will always act with the best intentions, employees may not have this same understanding and think there is bias. Any actions that can be taken to eliminate even the perception of bias will help to ensure all parties are happy with the process. Choice *D* is incorrect because restructuring the reporting relationship or a position due to external relationships is not a realistic option.

37. B: It is important for Michelle to have this insight and information prior to the recruitment so that she can provide accurate information about the position in the recruitment flyer. This will also help to ensure that the best candidate is hired with the right skill set to accomplish the objectives of the position. Choice *A* is not the best choice because without gaining the insight from the department manager, Michelle may be working with an outdated job description that does not fully describe the work or reflect new work. Choice *C* is incorrect because although subjectivity can be important to a recruitment process, it should align with the importance of understanding the needs of the department and position. Choice *D* is incorrect because although having a good working relationship with the hiring manager beyond the recruitment is important, it should not be the primary reason for discussing the current recruitment needs.

38. A: The best data collection method for Jose to use to gather employee satisfaction information would be a paper survey. Because there are no resources available, he could prepare a paper survey and send it out to employees to complete and submit. Choice *B* is incorrect because focus groups are targeted discussions, usually conducted by a facilitator, to discuss specific issues and gain insight about a process. Choice *C* is not the best option because meeting with individuals would take an extreme amount of time and not allow for any level of confidentiality and may not produce the best results. Choice *D* is also incorrect because without resources, Jose may not be able to produce the tools necessary to initiate a survey and employees may not be receptive to taking an online survey.

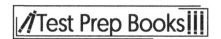

39. D: Data collection and studies that are included in publications are considered "recent" when they occur within the past three years. Choices *A* and *B* are incorrect because ten or twenty years is much too long of a time frame, and there can be many changes within that period of time. Choice *C* is also incorrect because although one year is very recent, it limits the amount of research available.

40. B: Blair should abide by his new organization's policy of requiring a 24-hour response time for customer service inquiries. Although he may not be able to answer all the issues at this time, he can let the customer know he is aware of the issue and working toward resolution. Choice *A* is incorrect because although it is commendable that Blair wants to exceed expectations, he may be putting himself in an unrealistic and unachievable position. Choices *C* and *D* are incorrect because both time frames, 36 hours and 48 hours, are outside of the policy and Blair would be in violation of the required 24-hour response time.

41. A: George is specifically describing the organization's employer brand when discussing the mission, values, vision, culture, and working environment. Choices *B*, *C*, and *D* are incorrect because these elements—culture, work-life balance, and total rewards—are all incorporated in the employer brand.

42. C: Employees are encouraged to develop interpersonal skills because these skills allow for a more effective and productive working relationship with others. Choices *A*, *B*, and *D* are incorrect because these circumstances rely on multiple factors, not just an employee's interpersonal skills, that would need to be considered relative to an employee's readiness for a promotion and their satisfaction with work-life balance and the job.

43. B: When a project goes over budget and exceeds the proposed time frame, the team leader should conduct a gap analysis and root cause analysis to determine the reasons the milestones and objectives were not met and how to address these in the future. Choice *A*, a SWOT analysis, is not correct because this analysis determines the strengths, weaknesses, opportunities, and threats of an organization. Choice *C*, a PESTLE analysis, is not correct because this analysis determines factors associated with political, economic, social, technological, legal, and environmental trends that influence an organization. Choice *D*, an outcome and needs analysis, is incorrect because it is not an actual analysis.

44. D: It is important to have an understanding of and ability to work with statistics because this skill allows HR professionals to identify trends and use the data to support initiatives while also seeing errors or flaws in the data. Choices *A* and *C* are incorrect because this skill is vital to ensuring that data is incorporated into effective and productive HR initiatives. Choice *B* is incorrect because although this skill may make an HR professional more marketable in their career goals, it does not specifically equate to a faster career progression.

45. C: Ambiguity, or being vague, when communicating with employees can cause confusion, conflict, and distress. When employees do not have a clear direction, they will not be motivated or engaged to do their best work, and therefore, Choices *A*, *B*, and *D* are incorrect. When an organization's leader is ambiguous in their communications, results will not include employees going above and beyond, innovative and productive work, or lower turnover and higher satisfaction.

46. A: An HR professional who understands how important data is and uses data to make recommendations or decisions is displaying the attribute of data advocacy. Choices *B, C,* and *D* are incorrect because they each refer to a different attribute that is important to being an effective HR professional. Statistical analysis is the ability to review and understand data and trends; customer service is working with those who are being served; and business sense is a general term that refers to an understanding of situations that will arise within an organization.

47. C: An open-door policy specifically encourages openness and transparency with employees. Managers and leadership often implement an open-door policy to ensure that employees know they are welcome to provide insights and feedback without fear of recourse. Choice *A* is incorrect because a communications policy is a broad policy that encompasses all areas of communication, which could include an open-door policy as well as a social media policy, which is Choice *B*. Choice *D* is incorrect because a code of conduct policy is written to ensure employees are aware of and understand ethical and appropriate behaviors in the workplace.

48. B: An HR professional can incorporate exit interviews to the process when individuals resign from an organization to gain insight into why they are leaving. Exit interviews can include questions specific to compensation, job benefits, retirement, leave benefits, training, supervisory relationships, and other items that can help HR determine if there is a root cause that needs to be addressed. Choices *A, C,* and *D* are incorrect because they are all tools that can be used to provide other important information separate from when an employee resigns.

49. A: Klaus should confirm that the data sources are recent (within three years) and relevant to the positions he is reviewing within his own organization. Choices *B, C,* and *D* are incorrect because they do not support the actual validity or relevancy of the data, and Klaus should not be seeking data that supports a predetermined conclusion.

50. D: Klaus should schedule a meeting to discuss the study, including the position analysis the employee completed and the data used to make the determination. By providing the employee with this information, there may be an understanding of why the decision was made. Additionally, if there was information that Klaus missed or misunderstood, he may want to take this into account and revise the recommendations. Choice *A* is not correct because this is not the best way to communicate this type of decision and could create a negative working environment for the employee and coworkers. Choice *B* is not correct; this message should be owned by Klaus because this was his survey. By passing the responsibility to the manager, there is an increased opportunity for misinformation that could cause further issues. Choice *C* is not correct; Klaus should follow up with the employee because this is the professional thing to do. Although there may not be an opportunity for Klaus to make revisions to his study and recommendations, follow-up is important to ensure good working relationships and customer service.

51. D: HR professionals have numerous customers, including everyone who works within the organization. They should strive to communicate with and assist all employees, regardless of their position and level. Respecting and making a commitment to all employees is vital to ensuring robust relationships and establishing a positive work environment.

52. C: The risk management process begins with identifying the potential risks that may need to be mitigated in a process. Without establishing the risks, it is impossible for the team to map a timeline, communicate deliverables, or develop a plan to address them, making Choices *A, B,* and *D* incorrect.

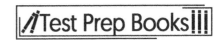

53. C: Internal data can provide HR professionals with information about employees, specifically productivity trends, job satisfaction, and turnover rates. External data can provide the organization with information about consumer trends, customer preferences, client engagement, and advertising techniques, making Choices *A, B,* and *D* incorrect.

54. B: Evidence-based decision making allows the process to be collaborative, involving leadership, employees, stakeholders, and others who may be impacted by a decision. This process provides credibility and logical support for initiatives, provides transparency as to why certain decisions are made, and can be easily communicated and shared with others, making Choices *A, C,* and *D* incorrect.

55. D: The leadership team will most likely approve the new benefits program being recommended. Edward has based his recommendation on current data, both internally and externally, as well as input from current employees, and therefore the leadership team can have confidence in the analysis. The first step that should be taken when a decision needs to be made is to examine relevant data and research. Edward has done this and gone further in his analysis by conducting the sessions with employees.

56. A: Kate should first determine if there is existing research or data available before embarking on the task of locating the necessary data. If this resource exists, she can then begin pulling in the organization's data and then create the analysis. If this resource does not exist, Kate can then pull the organization's data and create a plan to source the outside data as needed.

57. C: Quality assurance is the process of establishing a relevant, unbiased system of data collection. Quality assurance ensures that the data collected is applicable and appropriate to the outcome. Without quality assurance, an HR professional may be looking at data that is not relevant to the subject matter and, as a result, making decisions based on inaccurate conclusions.

58. B: Data should be recent and relevant while answering questions the organization may have regarding the analysis. If the data cannot be confirmed as to when it was collected or how it was collected, it should not be used, making Choice *A* incorrect. Furthermore, data should not be used simply because it supports or does not support a particular recommendation because this creates bias, making Choices *C* and *D* incorrect.

59. A: Sending out surveys is the data collection method that gathers individual feedback from a wide group of employees. Surveys can be completed in numerous ways to ensure maximum participation, including entering answers online or completing a paper copy of the survey.

60. C: Focus groups work to solicit feedback and opinions about certain topics while engaging the group through a facilitator. Unfortunately, focus groups run the risk of low participation or engagement and could have an issue with facilitator bias.

61. D: Benchmarking is one way for HR professionals to determine the effectiveness and values of programs by comparing the initiatives and results against competition, industry standards, and other outside standards.

62. A: When conducting a salary survey to make a determination about compensation, it is important to look at all components. This includes not only wages, overtime opportunities, car allowances, and other items specific to monies payable but also benefits costs, retirement costs, and vacation time. Benefits plans may be more expensive, with higher out-of-pocket costs for the employee. Retirement plans may not be funded at the same rates, also costing an employee more out of pocket. When conducting a salary survey, it is vital to consider all of the items that affect an employee's compensation.

63. D: HR professionals regularly review, analyze, and interpret data. Being able to understand when the data does not make sense is vital to ensuring that appropriate recommendations are made based on the data. If one cannot recognize when there is an issue with a data set, improper results and decisions could be made, having far-reaching negative impacts. Although having this knowledge does mean Jessica can add it to her resume (Choice A), be more marketable as a candidate for future jobs (Choice B), and potentially be considered for a promotion opportunity (Choice C), this should not be the sole motivation for adding this skill set to her resume.

64. B: Joe should treat the information as a learning opportunity. He should review and understand the results objectively and without emotional bias. Then, after reviewing the information and options available, he should implement rational and effective change that addresses the issues identified.

65. B: Benefits programs, such as alternate work schedules, flexible spending accounts, and wellness programs, are all excellent examples to highlight in job postings. Candidates should have a clear understanding of the programs available to employees.

66. C: Michael should reach out to all employees for information related to wellness programs, such as weight loss and smoking cessation. Employees at all levels of the organization could be considered a stakeholder in these programs, and each individual may have different insights or experiences that could greatly maximize the effectiveness of a program.

67. A: A secure online portal where employees can find updated information is by far the most efficient, streamlined, and lean way to communicate information. Employee handbooks, benefits forms, direct deposit forms, safety policies and forms, and other important information can be made available and updated as needed. Although it would be great to provide all employees a manual (Choice B), in-person training (Choice C), or a newsletter (Choice D) with this information, these options could be costly. Updates are sometimes needed frequently, and employees can be in a classroom for lengthy periods of time versus doing the job.

68. D: By engaging the team via meetings and recognition, providing information, and offering the ability to have a dialogue, the HR director is exhibiting characteristics of transparency and team-oriented culture. Employees who have this type of leadership often feel more valued, are more productive, and have greater satisfaction with their job and organization.

69. A: Ling should indicate to the leadership team that she does not have this information. Ling should then let the team know that she will reach out to the vendor to get the information and send it to them for their consideration. She should ensure that she responds to any and all questions, even those she is unable to answer.

70. B: During the evaluation stage, it is vital to gain feedback from all stakeholders. This feedback will allow for a more aligned, cohesive, effective, and robust plan.

71. B: A value stream map shows the purpose of each stage and defines the value of each step of the process. Value stream maps help to show where there is waste or unnecessary actions within the entire process to allow a more streamlined and efficient process.

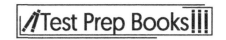

72. A: To ensure her data and research are relevant and recent, Rita should only consider data collection or publications from the past three years. Looking at research older than three years would most likely not yield innovative, creative, and different ideas.

73. D: A Myers-Briggs assessment provides insight into an individual's personality and can be a useful tool for supervisors to assess how a candidate would fit within an organization, department, and team. Additionally, this assessment also provides helpful information as to how a candidate would respond to certain tasks and duties related to specific positions. For example, if a candidate identifies as an introvert in the assessment, positions that are responsible for tasks specific to outreach, networking, and public speaking may not be the best match.

74. B: Appropriate HR initiatives generally focus on the recruitment process (Choice A), interview processes (Choice C), and annual salary surveys (Choice D). Although auditing the payroll processes to ensure timely payment is an ambitious initiative, it is not usually assigned to the HR function.

75. C: Costs related to a single project or program, such as an event put on by the organization, are considered direct costs and should be budgeted accordingly. Regardless of the different costs associated with an event, such as materials, labor, salaries, and locations, they are direct costs because they are all related to one event.

76. B: Carol should initiate a cause-and-effect diagram to determine why her project did not meet the established objectives. She can also use a gap analysis or root cause analysis to pinpoint where the process deviated from the plan.

77. D: Umbrella goals, or interest overlaps, can be extremely helpful when presenting a large-scale project to leadership for their buy-in and support. Identifying goals that will extend beyond and reach into other departments will increase the likelihood that the project will be supported.

78. A: An organization's policies that govern employees' actions, describe acceptable and unacceptable behaviors, and guide employee behavior with specific details is referred to as the code of conduct.

79. D: In order to ensure that all disciplines have appropriate resources and work could continue when a team member must be out of the office unexpectedly, Hannah should have identified not only a primary team member to be responsible for the discipline but also a secondary team member. Having this backup allows the knowledge to be transferred and shared with more than one team member and alleviates situations that could arise and jeopardize getting the work done.

80. C: Employees should be introduced to the organization's ethical standards and policies prior to being employed. This information should be included in the job description and available to all candidates prior to submitting an application. In doing so, the recruitment process is working to identify the most suitable and best-fit candidate, beginning with the first interaction as an applicant.

HR Knowledge

81. D: Strategic planning refers to the process of determining where an organization wants to be in the future and the steps needed to get there. Strategic planning uses systematic thinking to gain an understanding of how an operation works. Professional development (Choice A) refers to a process that is employee-specific to continue learning and growth. Key performance indicators (Choice B) refer to metrics an organization uses to determine effectiveness, efficiency, productivity, and other performance measurements. An individual action plan (Choice *C*) refers to a documented plan that outlines what an employee needs to do to reach certain milestones and achievements.

82. A: Being aware of both internal and external conditions will help an HR professional make the best recommendations through a planning process as well as ensure alignment with the overall goals and objectives. Although having an understanding of industry standards and metrics (Choice *B*) will be a part of the external conditions as well as the workforce trends (Choice *D*), it is important to have an overall understanding of all the internal and external conditions to ensure complete understanding of the conditions that should be considered. Choice *C* is incorrect because it leaves out external conditions.

83. C: Amelia should immediately meet with the hiring manager and discuss the results from the interviews. This meeting should include ideas for a new plan for the recruitment, options for moving forward with the current applicant pool, and other ideas to ensure the best candidate is identified and selected for the position.

84. C: Amelia should consider increasing the years of experience with an allowance for experience to substitute for the degree. Many organizations will substitute two years of additional experience for a degree so that candidates with different backgrounds and career paths still qualify for the position. Eliminating the experience (Choice *B*) would most likely not yield more qualified candidates and may result in fewer candidates with the ability to perform the job functions. Similarly, adding supervisory experience (Choice *D*) may not yield more qualified candidates but could actually deter qualified candidates. Some positions prioritize work experience over a degree, and Amelia should consider this when preparing job descriptions and minimum requirements.

85. B: Amelia and the hiring manger should consider adding a step to the process that involves a written exercise that is similar in nature to the work that would be performed. Many organizations conduct typing tests, report writing, presentation delivery, or other methods to determine the most qualified candidate. Although adding another interview to the process (Choice *C*) with the entire team may provide more information, it may not provide the most appropriate and applicable information necessary to select the best candidate. The same could be said about adding more questions that are difficult to answer (Choice *D*).

86. A: Talent acquisition is the keystone of HR's value to an organization. HR is instrumental in strategic planning (Choice *B*) and in charge of training and development (Choice *C*) and recruitment and retention (Choice *D*); however, ensuring that the organization's needs are met with the human capital required to perform the job is a keystone to the HR function.

87. B: A job analysis is an exercise used by HR professionals to determine the knowledge, skills, abilities, and experience required for a job to be performed successfully. A job analysis can also identify physical and environmental factors that could affect job performance. A classification study (Choice *A*) is an exercise used to determine if work currently being performed by an employee is appropriate based on the written job description. A skills gap assessment (Choice *C*) is an exercise to determine the skills and training needed by an employee to be successful in their current position or future positions. A SWOT analysis (Choice *D*) is an exercise that reviews an organization's strengths, weaknesses, opportunities, and threats to assist with strategic planning and setting objectives.

88. D: One of the strongest advantages of external sourcing for recruitment is that it supports building a diverse workforce and brings fresh perspectives to an organization. Although any recruitment should encourage connections with job seekers, external sourcing can be more costly than internal sourcing, making Choices *A* and *B* incorrect. Additionally, candidates who are sourced externally with no

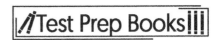

connection to an internal source will most likely not have familiarity with the organization and culture, making Choice *C* incorrect. This is a strength of internal sourcing.

89. C: Walk-in applicants are considered a method of external sourcing. Employee referrals (Choice *A*), promotions and transfers (Choice *B*), and recruiter-sourced hires (Choice *D*) are all methods of internal sourcing. All methods have pros and cons regarding timeliness, cost, and quality of candidates.

90. D: Based on the current demographics of the team, the most appropriate sourcing method would be external sourcing. By sourcing candidates externally, the team will be provided with a new employee who will bring new experiences and ideas to the group, which could produce better team and individual results, including new perspectives and ways to work. Although it may be prudent to also include an internal sourcing method at some point in the process, an external sourcing method would be the best approach.

91. B: The best course of action is for Joseph to discuss the complaints with the department manager and consider allowing internal candidates to apply for the position along with the external candidates. Although Joseph could follow up with employees to communicate the sourcing strategy and its importance (Choice *A*), the complaints were specific to not being allowed to apply for the position, and therefore this action will not address the main issues. Joseph should work with the department manager, and HR should own any communications to employees regarding a recruitment strategy (Choices *C* and *D*).

92. B: A Myers-Briggs personality assessment or an equivalent personality test may be a great option for Joseph to add to the process. This test will show personality differences as well as communication styles, leadership styles, and other important pieces of information that could help Joseph and the department manager make the best candidate selection. Although written exams, sample work assignments, and additional interviews could provide important information, they generally will not allow for specific personality traits to be displayed.

93. A: Preemployment screenings generally include criminal background checks, medical and drug screenings, financial and credit history checks, and other background information reviews. An inappropriate screening would be checking the marital and parental history of a candidate, which would include asking questions regarding these subjects during the interview process.

94. D: Julia is conducting an employment reference check. This type of reference check gathers feedback from former employers, supervisors, coworkers, and other contacts regarding the performance, behaviors, and work ethic exhibited by the potential new hire. Educational reference checks (Choice *A*) are specific to degrees, certifications, diplomas, or other specific educational achievements. Emotional intelligence tests (Choice *B*) are preemployment screenings some organizations use to test leadership and interpersonal skills. Performance reviews (Choice *C*) are a formal process an organization conducts annually or as needed to communicate how employees are performing in their jobs.

95. B: Onboarding, also known as organizational socialization, is the process for new hires to learn about the knowledge, skills, and behaviors needed to be valued and productive members of the team and organization. New-hire orientation (Choice *A*) refers to the administrative process of reviewing benefits, creating a security badge, and training on payroll processing, time-card management, and other important processes that all employees participate in. Preemployment screening (Choice *C*) is conducted prior to the actual hiring of a candidate, and organizational orientation (Choice *D*) is a term that combines several of these concepts.

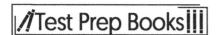

96. C: Typical onboarding programs should last for the employee's first year to ensure there is ample time and opportunity for full orientation to the organization. Although there are some specific items, such as payroll processes or timekeeping management, that should be delivered on the first day or during the first week, the organization should make a concerted effort throughout the employee's first year of employment to ensure full orientation to the culture.

97. B: Stay interviews are conducted to stay in touch with employees to gauge how they feel about the organization, position, and culture. These interviews allow HR professionals to assess if there are changes that need to be made and to address any needs that are raised before issues arise that may be more complicated to correct. 360 feedback (Choice A) is a term that refers to employees rating their supervisors to provide insight into the supervisory and leadership skills. Exit interviews (Choice C) are conducted with exiting employees to understand why they are leaving the organization, and satisfaction surveys (Choice D) are conducted with all employees to gauge how they feel about certain topics, such as leadership, communication, salary, and benefits.

98. D: Margaret should immediately communicate with the department manager to identify if the manager wants to work to retain the employee. If the answer is yes, a discussion should occur to determine if there is an opportunity within the budget to provide a counteroffer. Although the other options could be acceptable, the best option is to work with the department manager first. If the employee cannot or should not be retained, an exit interview should be conducted and a new recruitment established.

99. B: Recognition programs are programs used to promote a positive organizational culture by recognizing individual employees for the work they have done. Recognition programs can be formal or informal and can have a large impact on employees. Special event programs (Choice A) are designed to promote a positive culture; they generally do not reward employees for their work. Inclusion programs (Choice C) are incorporated into day-to-day operations to ensure that all employees' voices are heard. Incentive programs (Choice D) provide financial rewards to those employees who perform at a higher level than others and have a larger impact on the organization.

100. A: Although all of the data options are excellent pieces of information, one of the most important pieces of data is the turnover rate. The turnover rate is the percentage of employees leaving the workforce during a specific period of time. Turnover rates should be calculated at an organizational, departmental, and divisional level to determine specific pockets of the organization that may be experiencing a higher turnover than others.

101. C: Employee satisfaction and morale rate (Choice C) is not an outcome of the performance management process. This rate is determined by an employee survey to establish what the organization does well and what needs to be improved. Standard outcomes of the performance management process are salary increases and promotions, growth and development opportunities, and disciplinary actions and training needs (Choices A, B, and D).

102. C: The ADDIE model has five phases: Analysis, Design, Development, Implementation, Evaluation. It is vital to follow these steps in sequence. ADDIE is highly effective and can be applied to any project or program and is extremely flexible.

103. B: Identifying where employers are competing for labor is a benefit of analyzing labor markets during the workforce planning process. Additionally, other benefits include gaining an understanding of the unemployment rate, researching salaries paid for certain positions, and identifying employment trends. The remaining choices may be indirect benefits from this analysis but are not direct benefits.

104. D: An employee satisfaction survey is an excellent tool to establish how employees feel about internal programs, such as benefits and flexible work schedules.

105. C: In order to establish how the organization aligns with other agencies and competitors, a remuneration survey can be consulted to determine if the current salaries, benefits, and programs are in alignment with other agencies. Remuneration surveys are excellent sources to use as benchmarks.

106. D: It is vital to communicate with employees after requesting their participation in a survey. This ensures they know they are important to the process and that their feedback is vital to ensuring that proper programs are implemented.

107. B: The Fair Labor Standards Act (FLSA) is also known as the Wage and Hour Law. The FLSA established employee classification and regulated issues related to wages and child labor. The Family Medical Leave Act (Choice *A*) allows eligible employees in an organization unpaid leave time to care for themselves and family while protecting their jobs. The Davis Bacon Act (Choice *C*) applies to contractors working on federally funded contracts over $2,000. The Walsh-Healy Act (Choice *D*) applies to contractors working on federally funded contracts over $10,000.

108. A: Non-exempt positions fall directly under the regulations of the FLSA. Non-exempt positions do not involve the supervision of other employees, require specialized education or training, or use independent judgment for decision making. Positions that are exempt, which include professional and administrative positions, do not fall under the regulations of the FLSA, so Choices *B, C,* and *D* are incorrect.

109. B: The PESTLE analysis tool specifically looks at the Political, Economic, Social, Technological, Legal, and Environmental trends. Using the PESTLE tool requires an HR professional to be able to think critically about how these trends will impact the organization reaching the goals and accomplishments established, especially when dealing with global issues.

110. C: Duty of care is the term used to describe the legal and moral obligation HR is responsible for when employees are assigned to foreign countries. This duty of care extends to the families of the employee as well and can include safe housing, health care access, translation service, emergency care, and education.

111. D: Michael could now be considered an accidental expatriate for overstaying the permitted length of his stay without declaring a worker status. Although he would be considered an employee on leave (Choice *A*) relative to payroll purposes, this would not have an impact on his worker status. Choices *B* and *C*, accidental tourist and illegal immigrant, are incorrect.

112. C: Culture shock occurs after arriving in a new country and upon returning home, resulting in a low level of satisfaction for both stages. Recovery (Choice *A*) also occurs in both processes but results in increasing the level of satisfaction for the individual. Individuals experience the highest level of satisfaction during this process when they first arrive (Choice *D*) as well as during the adaptation phase (Choice *B*), both in the new country and at home.

113. A: Bruce should first contact Cecilia to understand why a new contact was provided to him. Once he has an understanding of the reason behind this change, he can then determine next steps, such as requesting a change with the HR director, emailing his supervisor, or cancelling his request to relocate to Hong Kong, if that is his decision.

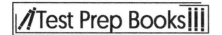

114. D: Assigning new contacts to expatriates due to a new policy is the least likely to occur within an organization that routinely has employees on international assignment. The goal is to have consistent and reliable customer service, and maintaining one point of contact ensures this. There may be several reasons, however, for the new assignment, including that Cecilia is on an approved leave of absence or has been transferred to a new position within the organization (Choices *A* and *C*). Most importantly, if Cecilia does not have specific experience with Hong Kong laws and requirements (Choice *B*), it may be in the best interest of Bruce, his family, and the organization to transfer his contact to an HR representative who does have this experience.

115. B: The best option for Bruce is to request that he works with Cecilia on his transition out of Sweden and then works with the new HR contact for his transition into Hong Kong. Depending on the factors, Cecilia may not be available or have the necessary knowledge to assist with his relocation to the new country (Choice *A*). It would be unwise for Bruce to request that she handle the transition if she does not have the appropriate experience or to handle his own transition because this could result in many legal issues for him as well as the organization. It is not wise for Bruce to handle the transition on his own (Choice *C*). Although he could request that his new assignment be terminated, it is not necessary and would be quite extreme for Bruce to decline the career opportunity due to having a new HR contact (Choice *D*).

116. A: Workplace diversity refers to the differences in employees' characteristics, which can include race, gender, age, nationality, sexuality, personality, education, family background, and socioeconomic status. Workplace inclusion (Choice *B*) refers to bringing these individuals together to contribute as a group. The two elements of diversity and inclusion work to create the workplace culture (Choice *C*). Workplace dynamics (Choice *D*) is simply another term that can describe the culture, values, and principles of an organization.

117. D: A strong diversity and inclusion program will not only develop relationships with external stakeholders but will also build employee relations and satisfaction. Although it is important to ensure that any program, including diversity and inclusion, meets all federal and state regulations (Choice *C*), this should not be a primary focus of what the program will accomplish. Providing thorough investigations of complaints (Choice *A*) and ensuring a strong training and development program (Choice *B*) are important but may fall outside the scope of diversity and inclusion programs.

118. C: The best course of action for HR to take is to review each individual accommodation and determine if it is reasonable or not. If the request will create an undue burden on the organization, it is appropriate to deny an accommodations request. In this case, requesting the position to be reduced to a 30-hour work week would most likely create an undue hardship based on the workload and importance of the job responsibilities. Although the ergonomic requests appear to be reasonable and appropriate, the reduced work schedule does not appear to be reasonable. It is perfectly appropriate to approve some accommodations and not approve others based on how reasonable they are.

119. C: Risk management is the process an organization engages in when identifying, targeting, and striving to minimize unacceptable dangers, threats, or risks. Choice *A*, SMART goals, are steps used in future planning and goal setting. Choice *B*, the Myers-Briggs Type Indicator, is an assessment that shows the differences in how people make decisions based on their personality. Choice *D*, corporate social responsibility, is when a corporation aims to contribute to charitable, activist, or philanthropic practices involving the community.

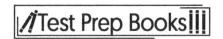

120. B: An emergency response specifically refers to a planned and practiced protocol to be used in the event of an emergency. A strategic plan (Choice A) is an overall organizational plan specific to goals and objectives. An evacuation plan (Choice C) is a part of the emergency response and is a coordinated and planned exit from a specific location. A hazard communication (Choice D), also part of the emergency response, notifies employees when there is a physical danger regarding a hazardous chemical in the workplace.

121. A: HR should immediately communicate with the plant manager about the importance of an emergency response plan. By ensuring these plans are understood by all employees, the organization is protecting lives and property as well as providing a sense of security to employees. The organization will also be in compliance with safety standards.

122. D: The most effective way to ensure that an evacuation plan will be implemented in the best way possible is to coordinate scheduled and unscheduled practice evacuations from the facility. Although acknowledge statements, special posters, and quizzes (Choices A, B, and C) will promote retention of the information, the best way to ensure that an evacuation plan will be effective is to practice the evacuation.

123. C: The acronym MSDS stands for Material Safety Data Sheets. These sheets are required to include any potential hazards of the product and how to work with the product safely. Material Safety Data Sheets are vital to having a complete and effective health and safety program.

124. B: Veronica is utilizing the ergonomic evaluation test to ensure that Janine's workspace does not pose any physical risks, is an efficient space to work productively, and meets Janine's needs. Ergonomic evaluation tests protect employees and help to prevent serious injuries.

125. C: Workplace policies should strictly follow federal laws in order to legally secure a workplace that satisfies minimum standards regarding health, safety, security, privacy, and benefits. The policy should provide equal or greater benefits than the federal regulations in order to be in compliance. Benefits can never be less than what the federal regulations mandate. Additionally, organizations must create policies that align with federal as well as state regulations, so mirroring federal laws may not align with the state laws.

126. D: The Sarbanes-Oxley Act of 2002 is federal legislation designed to establish a higher level of accountability and standards for public institution boards and senior management. SOX was established to ensure high-level executives are held responsible for accounting misconduct, record manipulation, or inappropriate financial practices.

127. B: OSHA is not responsible for providing fixed payments to employees who have suffered from an injury in the workplace. This function is provided by workers' compensation programs administered by organizations and their risk management departments.

128. A: Although all of the hazards listed can occur in a workplace and employers should have a plan to address each, the most common workplace safety risks employees are exposed to are bloodborne pathogens and tripping hazards.

129. D: Rosie should ensure that, in addition to theft and corporate espionage, the workplace security plan addresses sabotage. Although the other three options are important as well, they should each be addressed separately within the safety program or personnel policies.

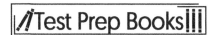

130. B: First aid and AED locations and procedures should be addressed during safety training and new-employee orientation. Although it may be prudent to review this information within the security plan training, it is vital to address specific items related to security measures during this training. These include emergency communication systems (Choice *A*); alarm locations, secure rooms, and security guard location (Choice *C*); and employee badges and facility security protocols (Choice *D*).

131. A: Employees should be trained annually to review the security plans, their importance, and the roles and responsibilities each employee has to the plan. Although it is a best practice to also provide this training during new-hire orientation, the best answer is annually.

132. C: An organization's CSR can be evaluated on the three P's: people, planet, profit. Although the public, the organization's purpose and process, and overall proceeds will be important to the CSR, they are not the evaluation factors used to determine how effective an organization's CSR is.

133. B: The three factors that evaluate an organization's CSR—people, planet, profit—are known as the triple bottom line. The hat trick (Choice *A*) is a term used in hockey, the triple play (Choice *C*) is a term used in baseball, and the social responsibility scale (Choice *D*) is a made-up term.

134. D: When the HR department has a presence within different business units, the service model being used is a decentralized model. A decentralized model focuses on having HR individuals assigned to specific areas and working within that specific department, unit, or location.

135. A: When the HR department has one corporate presence over the entire organization, the service model being used is a centralized model. A centralized model focuses on having HR employees from a main office oversee management functions in a separate unit.

136. B: A matrixed service model is one that uses both a centralized and decentralized service model. Matrixed service models can be instrumental in ensuring that an organization employing individuals in various locations gives all its employees access to HR support while also ensuring one HR message, or vision, is implemented.

137. D: The functions HR performs can be divided into three main types of work: transactional, tactical, and strategic. Within each of these areas, HR provides support in education, training, supervision, and other areas.

138. C: Transactional HR work is administrative in nature and includes services such as payroll and benefits administration. Transactional work can include preparing and processing new-hire paperwork, employee benefits enrollment or updating benefits selections, and entering performance evaluations into a tracking system.

139. A: The best type of HR work to outsource is work that does not depend on knowledge specific to workplace relationships, organizational culture, or team dynamics. This knowledge, which typically only individuals within the organization have, should be used as much as possible to ensure the best results. The best rule of thumb is to outsource work that does not require in-depth knowledge of the organization or internal dynamics.

140. B: Although a policy recommending how quickly staff should respond to calls may be an option, there should always be exceptions based on the specific circumstances, including vacations or other leaves and complex questions that require research. Phoebe should be prepared with various recommendations for consideration, including flexible work schedules to align with the different time

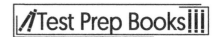

zones of other employees (Choice *A*), an on-call program to allow for additional availability outside of the normal work hours (Choice *C*), and potential relocation of staff or recruitment of staff at each of the other locations (Choice *D*).

141. D: One potential negative to initiating a flexible work schedule that aligns better with other time zones is the lack of participation and volunteers to work different hours. One major positive attribute to this recommendation is the cost and budget (Choice *A*); there would be limited costs associated with implementing this practice. Additionally, there would be very little, if any, disruption to services (Choice *B*), with employees most likely seeing an immediate increase in services. Another positive element would be that the organization could use current staffing and resources (Choice *C*) to implement this change.

142. A: The best option for Phoebe to consider when communicating and rolling out the new program is to define it as a pilot program. This allows HR staff and employees to understand that changes can still be implemented to ensure the program is effective. Additionally, initiating a second survey after six months will allow for feedback that could make the program work more efficiently. Although Phoebe should eventually establish a new policy that defines the flexible work schedule (Choice *B*), it should only be done when the program is fully vetted. Making it immediately permanent does not allow employees to be included in the process to make changes.

Phoebe should also communicate first with HR staff because these individuals will be impacted by the schedule changes. The employees supported by HR should understand the changes, but HR should receive the first notification, making Choice *C* incorrect. It is important to be open and honest with the team about the success of this program; however, it is unnecessary to communicate that staff will be relocated if the program is not successful, making Choice *D* incorrect. This step would need to be fully vetted and considered before being implemented because communicating too early would just create fear and confusion among employees.

143. C: Surveys are an excellent way to collect feedback from employees on a variety of subjects. They are only effective, however, when employees receive a response and see that actions are being taken as a result. When this does not occur, employees do not feel engaged and will usually not participate in future surveys due to the inaction. Surveys should be conducted to determine employee satisfaction with numerous items, including compensation, benefits, training, supervisory relationships, communication, culture, departmental services, and any other topic where information is needed, making Choice *A* incorrect. Surveys should only be conducted as frequently as they can be responded to with definite action items, making Choice *B* incorrect. Additionally, surveys should be provided to all employees, not just supervisors or managers, making Choice *D* incorrect.

144. D: Key Performance Indicators (KPIs) are types of performance measurements. KPIs include numerous points of data, such as employee turnover rates, cost of hires, performance scores, employee satisfaction, diversity ratios, and percentage of overtime hours. Choices *A, B,* and *C* are incorrect.

145. B: Workforce management is one of HR's major responsibilities. This includes understanding an organization's current talent, anticipating future needs, and bridging any gaps with specific actions and plans. Organizational development and succession planning (Choices *A* and *C*) are elements of workforce management because they allow for the growth and internal promotion of current employees, which is vital to managing the workforce. Strategic planning (Choice *D*) is the process of identifying and working toward goals and objectives, of which workforce management is a vital component.

146. A: Buy and build are the two approaches used by HR to fill skills gaps within an organization. Buy refers to recruiting and onboarding new staff with specific skills, and build refers to developing the knowledge, skills, and abilities of the current employees. The buy approach is the external method, and the build approach is the internal method.

147. C: The best option for Julian is to conduct a specific training program for the mid-level managers who lack the identified skills. He should ensure that the employees have an opportunity to learn these skills prior to taking any further actions. Julian may want to research external training programs (Choice *A*); however, it is his responsibility to roll out this training to the employees, not to simply make them aware of the training. Although indicating the need for this skill in performance evaluations (Choice *B*) may be necessary in the future, it is important to ensure that employees have the opportunity to increase their knowledge and skills in these areas first. The same is true regarding recruiting new employees with this skill set, Choice *D*.

148. D: Succession planning is the process by which the HR department ensures the transfer of knowledge, experience, and relationships—both internal and external—from one generation of workers to the next. This process ensures that key knowledge is not lost when employees leave an organization. This is exceptionally important when long-term employees retire and take the historical knowledge with them.

149. A: Financial restructuring is a form of corporate restructuring that is specific to when an organization has experienced significant decreases in profits primarily due to a poor economy. Workforce reductions (Choice *B*) are the planned eliminations of personnel to make an organization more competitive. Organizational and corporate restructuring (Choices *C* and *D*) are terms that refer to realigning a company's departments and workflows to make processes more efficient and cost-effective.

150. B: Workforce reductions are the planned eliminations of a specific number of positions and therefore personnel to make a company more competitive. When a workforce reduction is being considered, HR can focus on several factors, such as reducing hours, implementing a hiring freeze, or creating a voluntary separation program, to avoid having to lay off personnel. As indicated earlier, financial restructuring (Choice *A*) is a form of corporate restructuring specific to addressing decreases in profits due to economic conditions. Organizational and corporate restructuring (Choices *C* and *D*) are terms that refer to realigning a company's departments and workflows to make processes more efficient and cost-effective.

151. A: Once the decision to implement a workforce reduction has been made, it is critical to immediately communicate with employees. This communication should include information such as the specific decision, process moving forward, and timeline. Although it will be important to create separation agreements (Choice *B*), this is not an immediate need and can be addressed further along in the process. Additionally, a hiring freeze (Choice *C*) may be necessary across all departments, but communicating first to current employees to ensure productivity continues during the process is crucial. Attempting to change the decision (Choice *D*) at this point in the process is usually not worthwhile because by this stage, all other avenues have been reviewed and there are no other options to resolve the matter.

152. D: Outplacement services provide career counseling, resume writing, and interview preparation to assist separated employees with future employment.

153. C: Samantha and the executive team should immediately focus on boosting the morale of the remaining employees to ensure that productivity does not suffer as a result of the reductions. Samantha may want to implement a new best practice by checking in with the separated employees to see if they have been employed (Choice A); however, this is not mandatory and should only be done when all other checkpoints have been completed. Although new reports (Choice B) will eventually be created to show the new profit and loss information, it should not be the initial focus of leadership. Although future reductions may be necessary (Choice D), it should not be an immediate concern to address but only looked into after a new, thorough review of the organization's productivity and profitability.

154. C: Although initiating recruitments will need to be conducted to address a talent shortage, this process can take time and will not address the issue in the quickest and most efficient manner. Immediate solutions should be deployed to address the workload issue so that the organization does not lose customers. Solutions such as allowing employees to work overtime, hiring temporary employees, and reemploying retirees (Choices A, B, and D) can be quick to implement and address the workload need right away.

155. B: Employee relations is specifically defined as how the people within an organization interact with others—both internally and externally. To improve the organization, Janet needs to focus on how employees work together, communicate, and accomplish goals (Choice A). Employee relations can also refer to the methods and strategies used to determine the rules that shape relationships as well as the guidelines and rules that govern interactions between individuals (Choice C). She also needs to focus on the company's policies, procedures, and training methods to ensure they have the skills necessary to accomplish working together effectively (Choice D). While local, state, and federal regulations are vital to understand and apply to all of these areas, and the laws should be adhered to and complied within each of the areas above, Janet cannot affect the laws. However, she can affect change within her organization and how each of the employee relations items are applied.

156. A: A labor union is simply a formally organized group of employees who work together to accomplish goals. These goals can include working conditions, salary, benefits, safety concerns, and other issues. An employee resource group (Choice B) is a voluntary, employee-led group fostering a diverse and inclusive workplace that aligns with the organization's mission and values while supporting the goals and objectives. Department teams and work groups (Choices C and D) are simply terms that describe units of employees within specific groups.

157. D: Federations are labor unions made up of national unions that represent different industries. These industries share specific common interests and goals. National unions (Choice A) are large entities made up of smaller, local unions. Partnerships (Choice B) is a term used to describe relationships between entities. International unions (Choice C) represent employees in various countries.

158. C: Prior to establishing an election to select representation, the employees should notify and inform the employer of the desire to unionize. This is vital to the process because if the employer does not agree and refuses, the union has rights within the NLRB that it can exercise. It is always important to follow every step within this process to ensure that no rights are lost due to a technicality. At this stage of the process, hiring a professional negotiator (Choice A) is not necessary, although it may be during actual negotiations with the employer in the future. Reaching out to other local unions (Choice B) that offer representation may be a good idea to benchmark and gain insights into working with a union but is not part of the official process of establishing a labor union. Coordinating a picketing event (Choice D) is a protected act in which represented employees protest to raise awareness.

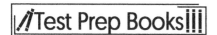

159. A: If an employer refuses to accept that employees want to be represented by a union, the employees can then take further actions with the NLRB. The NLRB will hold an election in which employees will vote on whether they want to be represented by a union or not. This vote will then determine what the next steps are in moving forward to establish the union. Employees do not have to negotiate with the employer to establish a union (Choice *B*). Although employees will eventually establish goals and objectives of the new union (Choice *C*) as well as by-laws and elected positions, this will take place after the union has been officially created and not at this point in the process. It is not necessary to file a petition with the NLRA to protect employee rights (Choice *D*) because these rights are already protected under this act.

160. B: Decertification is the process by which employees vote to strip a union's official status as their representative. This process starts with a petition that is filed with the NLRB and continues to a decertification election among employees. If a majority of employees vote in favor of the decertification, the union is officially disbanded. Avoidance (Choice *A*) is a process an organization works through to communicate with employees who are considering forming a union. Deauthorization (Choice *C*) is the process to remove a union's security clause and negotiations authority. Picketing (Choice *D*) is an act of protest to raise awareness of issues and discourage individuals from entering the building to work or do business.

Dear SHRM-CP Test Taker,

We would like to start by thanking you for purchasing this study guide for your SHRM-CP exam. We hope that we exceeded your expectations.

Our goal in creating this study guide was to cover all of the topics that you will see on the test. We also strove to make our practice questions as similar as possible to what you will encounter on test day. With that being said, if you found something that you feel was not up to your standards, please send us an email and let us know.

We would also like to let you know about another book in our catalog that may interest you.

PHR Exam

This can be found on Amazon: amazon.com/dp/1637757514

We have study guides in a wide variety of fields. If the one you are looking for isn't listed above, then try searching for it on Amazon or send us an email.

Thanks Again and Happy Testing!
Product Development Team
info@studyguideteam.com

FREE Test Taking Tips Video/DVD Offer

To better serve you, we created videos covering test taking tips that we want to give you for FREE. **These videos cover world-class tips that will help you succeed on your test.**

We just ask that you send us feedback about this product. Please let us know what you thought about it—whether good, bad, or indifferent.

To get your **FREE videos**, you can use the QR code below or email freevideos@studyguideteam.com with "Free Videos" in the subject line and the following information in the body of the email:

    a. The title of your product

    b. Your product rating on a scale of 1-5, with 5 being the highest

    c. Your feedback about the product

If you have any questions or concerns, please don't hesitate to contact us at info@studyguideteam.com.

Thank you!

Made in the USA
Monee, IL
27 March 2023

30621890R00155